The Cambridge Companio

Byron's life and work have fascinated readers around the world for two hundred years, but it is the complex i

beliefs and sexuality that has attra
In three parts devoted to the histori
life and times, these specially comm
scholars provide a compelling pict
essays cover topics such as Byron's
publishing world, his attitudes to ge
century literature, and his fit in a p

vides an invaluable resource for students and scholars, including a chronology and a guide to further reading.

THE CAMBRIDGE COMPANION TO BYRON

EDITED BY

DRUMMOND BONE

PUBLISHED BY THE PRESS SYNDICATE OF THE UNIVERSITY OF CAMBRIDGE
The Pitt Building, Trumpington Street, Cambridge, United Kingdom

CAMBRIDGE UNIVERSITY PRESS
The Edinburgh Building, Cambridge, CB2 2RU, UK
40 West 20th Street, New York, NY 10011–4211, USA
477 Williamstown Road, Port Melbourne, VIC 3207, Australia
Ruiz de Alarcón 13, 28014 Madrid, Spain
Dock House, The Waterfront, Cape Town 8001, South Africa

http://www.cambridge.org

First published 2004

Printed in the United Kingdom at the University Press, Cambridge

Typeface Sabon 10/13 pt. *System* LaTeX 2ε [TB]

A catalogue record for this book is available from the British Library

Library of Congress Cataloguing in Publication data
The Cambridge Companion to Byron / edited by Drummond Bone.
p. cm. – (Cambridge companions to literature)
Includes bibliographical references and index.
ISBN 0 521 78146 9 – ISBN 0 521 78676 2 (pb.)
1. Byron, George Gordon Byron, Baron, 1788–1824 – Criticism and
interpretation – Handbooks, manuals, etc. 2. Poets, English – Biography – History and
criticism – Handbooks, manuals, etc. I. Title: Companion to Byron. II. Bone, Drummond.
III. Series.
PR4381.C3423 2004
821′.7 – dc22 2004045102
[B]

ISBN 0 521 78146 9 hardback
ISBN 0 521 78676 2 paperback

CONTENTS

ACKNOWLEDGEMENTS

My main debts are to Josie Dixon, who set this project sailing, and to David Leyland, here at the University of Liverpool, without whose help it would not have reached port. Many thanks too are due for the patience of contributors and of Linda Bree at Cambridge University Press. All those in this volume would also like to thank Bernard Beatty, who retires as it is published, for his career-long contribution to Byron studies. And thanks is not quite the right word for all that I owe V. for understanding beyond understanding, and C. for her ever cheerful support.

CONTRIBUTORS

PAUL DOUGLASS is Professor of English at San Jose State University. He has published on American Literature, Modernism and Byron. His books include *Bergson, Eliot, and American Literature* (1986) and *A Selection of Hebrew Melodies, Ancient and Modern* (1988).

PETER W. GRAHAM is Clifford Cutchins Professor of English at Virginia Polytechnic Institute and State University. His special interest is nineteenth-century British literature and culture and he is the author of studies of Byron including *Byron's Bulldog: Letters to Lord Byron* (1986), *Don Juan and Regency England* (1992), *Articulating the Elephant Man* (with Fritz Oehlschlaeger) (1992), *The Portable Darwin* (with Duncan M. Porter) (1993), and *Lord Byron* (1998).

MALCOLM KELSALL is Professor at the University of Cardiff. His publications include *Byron's Politics* (1987), *The Great Good Place: The Country House and English Literature* (1993), and *Jefferson and the Iconography of Romanticism* (1999).

ANDREW ELFENBEIN is Professor at the Department of English, University of Minnesota. His publications include *Byron and the Victorians* (1995) and *Romantic Genius: The Prehistory of a Homosexual Role* (1999).

PHILIP W. MARTIN was formerly Director of the English Subject Centre at Royal Holloway University of London and is currently Dean of the Faculty of Humanities at De Montfort University. His major publications include *Byron: A Poet Before his Public* (1982), *Mad Women in Romantic Writing* (1987), and *Reviewing Romanticism* (with Robin Jarvis, 1992). He is currently working on the history of handwriting during the Romantic period, and on an edition of the writings of Henry Kirke White.

NIGEL LEASK is Regius Professor of English Literature at the University of Glasgow. In addition to editing Coleridge's *Biographia Literaria* for

Everyman, he has published *The Politics of Imagination in Coleridge's Critical Thought* (1988), *British Romantic Writers and the East* (1992), and *Curiosity and the Aesthetics of Travel-Writing 1770–1840* (2002).

ALAN RAWES lectures at Canterbury Christ Church University College where his research interests are mainly in the poetry of the Romantic period. His publications include *Byron's Poetic Experimentation* (2000), *English Romanticism and The Celtic World* (2003) and *Romantic Biography* (2003). He is the current editor of the *British Association for Romantic Studies Bulletin and Review.*

ALAN RICHARDSON is Professor of English at Boston College. He is author of: *A Mental Theater: Poetic Drama and Consciousness in the Romantic Age* (1988) and *Literature, Education, and Romanticism: Reading as Social Practice, 1780–1832* (1994). He is co-editor (with Sonia Hofkosh) of *Romanticism, Race, and Imperial Culture 1780–1834* (1996). His most recent publication is *British Romanticism and the Science of the Mind* (2001). He has also published numerous essays on Romantic-era literature and culture, particularly in relation to gender, colonialism, and the social construction of childhood.

DRUMMOND BONE is Vice-Chancellor of the University of Liverpool. Formerly Principal of Royal Holloway University of London and Professor of English at the Universities of Glasgow and London, he has been academic editor of *The Byron Journal* and is currently a co-editor of *Romanticism.* He has written the Byron volume in the British Council's 'Writers and their Work' series.

SUSAN J. WOLFSON is Professor of English at Princeton University. Her books include *Formal Charges: The Shaping of Poetry in British Romanticism* (1996), *The Questioning Presence: Wordsworth, Keats, and the Interrogative Mode in Romantic Poetry* (1986), and *Lord Byron: Selected Poems*, co-edited with Peter Manning (1996). She has published numerous essays and articles on such subjects as 'Romanticism and Gender Criticism' and on specific issues of gender in the Romantic era.

ANDREW NICHOLSON is the editor of *Lord Byron: The Complete Miscellaneous Prose* (1991) and of various facsimile editions of *Don Juan*, *Beppo* and other poems in *The Manuscripts of the Younger Romantics* series published by Garland. He co-edited with Donald Mitchell *The Mahler Companion* (1999; rev. edn 2002) and is at present editing the letters of John Murray to Byron.

JEROME McGANN is the editor of the standard edition of *Byron's Poetical Works*, and his many books include *Fiery Dust* (1968), *The Beauty of Inflections* (1985), and *Radiant Textuality* (2004). He has lectured widely in the United States, Canada and the United Kingdom, and is presently John Stewart Bryan Professor of Nineteenth and Twentieth Century History and Theory of Texts at the University of Virginia.

ANNE BARTON is a Fellow of Trinity College, Cambridge. She is the author of numerous studies of both Byron and Shakespeare including *Byron's* Don Juan (1992) and *Essays, Mainly Shakespearean* (1994).

BERNARD BEATTY teaches at the University of Liverpool and has edited *The Byron Journal* since 1988. Amongst his published works he has written two books on Byron and has edited collections of Byron essays including, with Charles Robinson, *Liberty and Poetic Licence: New Essays on Byron* (2004).

PETER COCHRAN has written many articles on Byron, edited Byron for Garland and others, edits the *Newstead Abbey Byron Society Review* and is Research Fellow of the School of English of Liverpool University. He is currently working on an edition of Michael Rees's translation of Teresa Guiccioli's *Lord Byron's Life in Italy.*

JANE STABLER is Reader in English at the University of St Andrews. She writes on Romantic period poetry and prose, Byron, Shelley, Keats, Wordsworth, Coleridge, Jane Austen, Barbauld, and Romantic-period women travellers in Italy. Her publications include *Burke to Byron, Barbauld to Baillie, 1790–1830* (2002) and *Byron, Poetics and History* (2002).

CHRONOLOGY

Year	Byron's life	Historical and literary events
1778	John Byron elopes with Amelia D'Arcy, Marchioness Carmarthen.	William Hazlitt b.; Voltaire d.; Rousseau d.
1779	John Byron marries Marchioness Carmarthen.	Thomas Moore b.; John Galt b.; David Garrick d.
1780		Gordon Riots.
1781		British surrender at Yorktown; Schiller's *Die Räuber*; Kant's *Kritik der reinen Vernunft* (Critique of Pure Reason).
1782		Laclos, *Liaisons Dangereuses*; James Watt patents his double-acting steam engine.
1783	Birth of Augusta Byron, daughter of John Byron and Amelia D'Arcy.	Peace of Versailles; The Paris Peace Treaty; Britain recognises United States of America; Stendhal b.; Crabbe's *The Village*; Montgolfier brothers' hot-air balloon flights in Paris.
1784	Lady Carmarthen dies.	Leigh Hunt b.; Samuel Johnson d.; Diderot d.; Wesley establishes Methodism.

John Byron marries Catherine Gordon (13 May).	1785	Thomas de Quincey b.; Thomas Love Peacock b.; Lady Caroline Lamb b.
	1786	John Cam Hobhouse b.; Robert Burns, *Poems Chiefly in the Scottish Dialect*; Mozart's *The Marriage of Figaro*.
	1787	Signing of the American Constitution; Schiller's *Don Carlos*; Mozart's *Don Giovanni*.
George Gordon Byron, son of John Byron and Catherine Gordon, born on 22 January, at 16 Holles Street, Cavendish Square, London. Christened, 29 February, in Marylebone parish church.	1788	Kant's *Kritik der praktischen Venunft* (Critique of Practical Reason); *The Times* first published.
	1789	First colony established in Australia; Fall of the Bastille, 14 July; the beginning of the French Revolution; George Washington becomes first President of United States; Edmund Kean b.; Jeremy Bentham's *Introduction to the Principles of Morals and Legislation*.
	1790	Edmund Burke, *Reflections on the Revolution in France*; Adam Smith, author of *Wealth of Nations* (1776), d.
Death of Byron's father, John Byron.	1791	Mozart d.

1792

Percy Shelley b.; Samuel Rogers' *Pleasures of Memory, with Other Poems*; Wollstonecraft's *Vindication of the Rights of Women*; Tom Paine escapes to France whilst British government prepares for his treason trial.

1793

Louis XVI executed; John Clare b.; Blake's *The Marriage of Heaven and Hell*.

1794

Death of William Byron makes George Gordon heir to title and estates. Enters Aberdeen Grammar School.

Edward Gibbon d.; Gifford's *Baviad*; Godwin's *Caleb Williams*; Southey's *Fall of Robespierre*; Radcliffe's *Mysteries of Udolpho*.

1795

John Keats b.; Thomas Carlyle b.; James Boswell d.; William Blake's *Book of Los*; *Book of Ahania* and *Song of Los*; Southey's *Joan of Arc*; John Murray, Byron's future publisher, succeeds to his father's business.

1796

Robert Burns d.; Coleridge's *Poems on Various Subjects*.

1797

Franz Schubert b.; Mary Wollstonecraft Godwin (Shelley) b.; Mary Wollstonecraft d.; Horace Walpole d.

1798

Inherits title, Lord Byron of Newstead and Rochdale and moves to Newstead Abbey, Nottinghamshire.

Lyrical Ballads published anonymously; Malthus's *Essay on the Principle of Population*; the Irish rebellion.

Year	Life	Events
1799	Byron travels to London. His club foot is examined by Dr Baillie and Dr Laurie. Byron enters Dr Glennie's school in Dulwich.	Thomas Jefferson becomes second President of the United States; *coup d'etat* in France sees Napoleon seize power.
1800		Second edition of *Lyrical Ballads* published with Wordsworth's preface; Haydn's *The Seasons*; Alessandro Volta describes the voltaic 'pile' to Sir Joseph Banks, President of the Royal Society.
1801	Byron enters Harrow.	Peace of Amiens; William Pitt resigns as Prime Minister; the Act of Union with Ireland receives royal assent; invention of the steam-powered locomotive.
1802		War between Britain and France ends.
1803	Byron's mother moves into Burgage Manor, Southwell. In October, Byron begins his unrequited idealised love for his cousin, Mary Chaworth.	After Napoleon breaks peace treaty, Britain declares war on France; US pays $15 million to France for the Louisiana Territory.
1804	In Southwell, meets Elizabeth Pigot; returns to Harrow and takes part in the Speech Day.	Sir Walter Scott, *Lay of the Last Minstrel*; Schiller's *Wilhelm Tell*.
1805	Byron takes part in Harrow's Speech Day. In Harrow cricket team for their match in London, 2 August. Byron arrives at Trinity College, Cambridge.	Napoleon proclaimed king of Italy. Vice-Admiral Lord Nelson dies at Trafalgar; Beethoven's Eroica symphony first performed; Joseph Turner's *The Shipwreck*.

1806

Fugitive Pieces published.

John Stuart Mill b.; publication of Bowles's edition of Pope.

1807

Poems on Various Occasions published, January. Keeps tame bear at Cambridge; joins Cambridge Whig club; returns to London, July; Byron's review of Wordsworth's *Poems* in *Monthly Literary Recreations*; *Hours of Idleness* published.

William Pitt d.; The Abolition Bill is passed, outlawing the slave trade; Crabb's *The Parish Register*; Thomas Moore's *Irish Melodies*; Mme De Staël's *Corinne*; first gas-lights in streets of London.

1808

Received his MA from Cambridge; receives scathing criticism from the *Edinburgh Review*.

Start of the Peninsular War; the United States bans the import of slaves; Convention of Cintra signed; Leigh Hunt founds *The Examiner*; Goethe's *Faust* (Pt. I); Goya's *Execution of the Citizens of Madrid*.

1809

Takes seat in House of Lords; anonymous publication of *English Bards and Scotch Reviewers;* Byron leaves Falmouth on the *Princess Elizabeth* to begin his first tour of Portugal, Spain, Malta, Albania and Greece. Reception by Ali Pasha. Byron finishes the first canto of *Childe Harold*

Charles Darwin b.; Alfred Tennyson b.; Thomas Paine d.

1810

Completes *Childe Harold* Canto II. On 16 April, Byron attempts to swim across the Hellespont but fails because of cold weather and strong currents. Successfully swims the Hellespont, 3 May.

Baillie's *Family Legend*; Hogg's *Forest Minstrel*, Goethe's *Pandora*; H. von Kleist's *Käthchen von Heilbronn*.

1811

Moved by hearing of the death of John Edleston, Byron writes poems addressed to 'Thyzra'. Hears Coleridge lecture. Death, on 1 August, of Byron's mother, Catherine Gordon. He writes 'Hints from Horace' and *The Curse of Minerva*.

Shelley expelled from Oxford, marries Harriet Westbrook; the Prince of Wales becomes Regent; Austen's *Sense and Sensibility*; Luddite riots.

1812

Maiden speech in the House of Lords. *Childe Harold's Pilgrimage*, Cantos I and II published. In March, he meets Lady Caroline Lamb with whom he begins a three-month affair. On 12 March, writes letter to Walter Scott apologising for *English Bards*. Writes *The Waltz*. '*Parenthetical Address*, by Dr. Plagiary' printed in the *Morning Chronicle*.

Robert Browning b.; Charles Dickens b.; Prime Minister, Spencer Perceval, assassinated in the lobby of the House of Commons. US declares war on Great Britain; Beethoven meets Goethe; Napoleon invades Russia

1813

Lionised by London society; politically active in Whig cause; Byron attends dinner at Lady Jersey's and meets Madame de Staël; speaks in the House of Lords; possible affair with half-sister, Augusta; publications of *The Giaour*, and *The Bride of Abydos*.

Hobhouse's *A Journey Through Albania and Other Provinces of Turkey in Europe and Asia to Constantinople*; Austen's *Pride and Prejudice*; Robert Southey becomes poet laureate; Leigh Hunt imprisoned.

1814

Publication of *The Corsair* and *Lara*. 10,000 copies of *The Corsair* sold in a day. Byron admires Edmund Kean's performance in *Richard III*.

Napoleon abdicates; Scott's *Waverley*.

1815

Byron marries Annabella Milbanke on 2 January. Birth, 10 December, of daughter, Ada. Publication of *Hebrew Melodies*, containing many of Byron's best-known lyrics.

Riots in London against the Corn Law; restored Bourbon monarchy in France under Louis XVIII; Napoleon escapes Elba; British victory at Waterloo.

1816

Separation of Byron and Annabella. Publication of *The Prisonar of Chillan, The Siege of Corinth* and *Parisina*. Byron's books are sold in a public auction for a total of £723 12*s* 6*d*. Byron leaves England for last time. Visits the fields of Waterloo. Byron and Shelley sail around the northern shore of Lake Geneva. Spends the summer with the Shelleys in Switzerland. Views Voltaire's château with 'Monk' Lewis. Moves in October to Milan and meets Italian revolutionary circle. Moves in November to Venice. Completes Canto III of *Childe Harold*'s *Pilgrimage*. *Childe Harold* Canto III published.

Richard Sheridan d.; marriage of Shelley and Mary Godwin; Shelley's *Alastor*; anonymous publication of Lady Caroline Lamb's *Glenarvon*; Southey's *Poet's Pilgrimage to Waterloo*; Leigh Hunt's *The Story of Rimini*; Jane Austen's *Emma*; Walter Scott's *Old Mortality*; Goethe's *Italienische Reise*; Schubert's Symphonies nos. 4–5.

1817

Claire Claremont (Mary Shelley's half-sister) gives birth to Byron's illegitimate daughter, Allegra; publication of *Manfred;* Newstead Abbey sold to Thomas Wildman for £94,500; visits Rome and *Childe Harold* Canto IV written.

Jane Austen d.; Keats' *Poems*; the 21-year-old Princess Charlotte dies in childbirth; Coleridge's *Biographia Literaria*; Heman's *Modern Greece*; Scott's *Rob Roy*; Monroe becomes President of USA; *Blackwood's Magazine* founded.

1818	Mainly in or near Venice. Sends Murray manuscript of *Beppo*. *Beppo* is published. First meets Teresa Guiccioli. Lady Melbourne dies. *Childe Harold* Canto IV published. Byron wins swimming contest against Mengaldo. Begins *Don Juan*.	Mary Shelley's *Frankenstein*; Percy Shelley's *Ozymandias* and *Revolt of Islam*; Thomas Love Peacock's *Nightmare Abbey*; Hazlitt's *Lectures on the English Poets*; Keats's *Endymion*; Caspar David Friedrich's *Wanderer above the Sea of Fog*; attack on Keats in *Quarterly Review*.
1819	Begins affair with Countess Teresa Guiccioli. Writes the *Prophecy of Dante*; leaves Venice for Ravenna; arrives in Ravenna; *Mazeppa* is published with the *Ode on Venice*. *Don Juan* Cantos I and II published anonymously by John Murray. Accompanies Thomas Moore to Venice. Gives Moore his memoirs.	Wordsworth's *Peter Bell* and *The Waggoner*; Shelley's *Masque of Anarchy*; the Peterloo massacre in which 11 are killed and over 500 injured; US purchases Florida from Spain.
1820	Moves to Ravenna; Teresa Guiccioli separates from her husband; Byron sends Murray Cantos III and IV of *Don Juan*; Pope grants Teresa Guiccioli separation; Byron begins Canto V of *Don Juan*.	George III dies; George IV proclaimed king; Shelley's *The Cenci*; Keats's *Lamia*, *Isabella*, and *Hyperion*; Shelley's *Prometheus Unbound* published; Scott's *Ivanhoe*; Venus de Milo discovered on Greek island of Melos.

1821

Byron follows Teresa Guiccioli's exiled family to Pisa; Byron begins his 'Ravenna Journal'; *Marino Faliero* published 21 April; writes *Sardanapalus*, *The Two Foscari*, and *Cain*, all of which are published in a single volume on 19 December; writes *The Blues;* writes *The Vision of Judgment*; begins *Heaven and Earth*.	Napoleon d.; Keats d. (aged 25); Queen Caroline d.; Baillie's *Metrical Legends*; Hazlitt's *Table Talk*; Southey's *A Vision of Judgement*; Michael Faraday demonstrates electro-magnetic rotation; Greek War of Independence begins.

1822

September, Byron moves with the Gambas to Genoa; daughter, Allegra, dies in convent at Bagnacavallo; Byron begins Canto XI of *Don Juan*; *Vision of Judgment* and *Werner* published; begins to write *Age of Bronze*.	Shelley publishes *Hellas*; Shelley drowns off the coast of Viareggio, Italy; Robert Stewart, Viscount Castlereagh, commits suicide; Heine's *Gedichte*.

1823

Byron sails for Greece, July; arrives in Cephalonia on 3 August; *Heaven and Earth*, *Age of Bronze*, and *The Island* published.	Ann Radcliffe d.; Carlyle's *Life of Schiller*; Lamartine, *Nouvelles Méditations*; Hazlitt's *Liber Amoris* and *Characteristics*; Beethoven's Symphony No. 9.

1824

Byron arrives in Missolonghi, Greece on 5 January; develops fever; dies, aged 36, on 19 April; public attend Byron's lying in state, 10 and 11 July; buried at Hucknall Church, England, 16 July.	James Hogg's *Confessions of a Justified Sinner*; Thomas Medwin's *Journal of Conversations with Lord Byron*; Scott's *Redgauntlet*; Southey's *Book of the Church*.

1825

	Dallas's *Correspondence of Lord Byron*; Moore's *Life of Sheridan* and *Evenings in Greece*; Hazlitt's *Spirit of the Age*; John Quincy Adams becomes President of the USA; opening of the Stockton and Darlington railway in England.

ABBREVIATIONS

The following short titles have been used throughout this volume:

BLJ: *Byron's Letters and Journals*, ed. by Leslie A. Marchand, 13 vols. (London: John Murray, 1973–94);

CMP: *Lord Byron: The Complete Miscellaneous Prose*, ed. Andrew Nicholson (Oxford: Clarendon Press, 1991);

CPW: *Lord Byron: The Complete Poetical Works*, ed. Jerome J. McGann, 7 vols. (Oxford: Clarendon Press, 1980–93);

HVSV: *His Very Self and Voice: Collected Conversations of Lord Byron*, ed. Ernest J. Lovell Jnr (New York: Macmillan, 1954).

Introduction

Byron hated an author who was 'all author' and he himself was anything but that. He has been a public figure whose private life has been the subject of intense interest since the publication of *Childe Harold* Cantos I and II made him 'famous overnight'. He continues to be the subject not only of scholarly biographical interest but of popular films and television documentaries. To politicians, his political views remain of intense interest, while his sexual mores not only continue to be analysed but have been appropriated by various interest groups to serve their own ends. He is a cultural villain, an anti-hero, and a hero pure and simple. He has the status of a national hero in Greece because of his participation in the Greek War of Independence, and he is also a cultural hero in places as far apart as Russia and Japan. So we have sought in this *Companion* to place him first of all in the context of the narratives surrounding his own life, and then in the particular circumstances of that life, picking out three obvious areas of particular interest – his relationship to the world of books, to politics, and to sexuality. Only then have we attempted a closer focus on some of Byron's major works. In an output as large as that of Byron his poetical works alone fill some seven volumes. We do not attempt to be comprehensive in this section, but many texts not picked up here are referred to in the other two sections of the volume. Once some familiarity with the issues of the works, including Byron's very considerable contribution to English prose, has been achieved, we have moved on to broader literary and cultural contexts and focused there on Byron's ambivalent relationship to Shakespeare, his massive impact on European literature, and the strange way in which he can be seen in the light either of his attachment to the socially centred poetry of the eighteenth century, or of his prefiguring of postmodernism.

Taken as a whole, the Companion should provide a good overview of what one can only call the Byron phenomenon, a phenomenon that has cultural importance not only in the United Kingdom but throughout the world. He is arguably still the most read English author after Shakespeare.

But as well as providing an overview, we have also tried to present the state of Byron studies as they are at the beginning of the twenty-first century, and to avoid mere introductory paraphrase of previous views. It is quite possible therefore to dip into the Companion and, we certainly hope, to find something interestingly new.

Thus in the first group of essays, Paul Douglass, in his chapter on Byron's biography, has dealt with the influence which Byron has had on biographical art, as well as simply the fact of the biographies and their changing view of Byron. We hope too that Peter Graham's chapter on how 'Byron's literary career was crucially shaped by the practical contingencies of publishing' reveals that for all his unwillingness to be seen as a professional writer Byron was more willing than most to invest his energies in the practical considerations of authorship. Malcolm Kelsall refocuses the work of his major study of Byron's politics looking at Byron's relationship to British party politics, not always what it might have seemed on the surface. Andrew Elfenbein provides a relatively surprising reaffirmation of how central the sexual agenda has always been to the Byronic image in which he argues that the most shocking aspect of Byron's gender agenda is that 'he dared to make sexuality banal'.

The second group of essays are, as we have said, more textually focused. Philip Martin argues that *Childe Harold* I and II is a profoundly public work written in a style designed to appeal to a new audience sympathetic to its coherent and anti-teleological explorations of history, politics, and contemporary affairs. Nigel Leask has a lot to say about *Childe Harold*'s Canto II as well, but angles his discussion specifically towards Greek nationalism and the uneasy question of the relationship between liberty and nationalism, concluding that 'Byron never allowed nationalist idealism to smother sceptical cosmopolitanism'. His first years of exile, 1816 and 1817, are crucial for Byron's development and Alan Rawes focuses closely on the third canto of *Childe Harold's Pilgrimage* and on *Manfred*, highlighting the shift away from Byron's 'Sturm und Drang' period towards a more socially centred individualism. This social and political dimension is taken up by Alan Richardson in his study of Byron's dramas which Richardson sees as 'resolutely engaged with political and social issues' of the time. I myself look at the further development of Byron's view of life as an individually generated narrative told in a social context by looking in close focus at *Childe Harold* Canto IV, *Don Juan*, and *Beppo*. Susan Wolfson tracks the same progress in a different way by emphasising that it is perhaps too easy to explain the experience of *The Vision of Judgment* in purely political terms. Particularly given its relationship to the public interest in his life, Byron's prose output might well have made his reputation even had there not been the poetry.

Andrew Nicholson reads Byron's character through the immense output of his letters and journals and introduces us to the 'generosity' of his prose.

The final section of the Companion tries various other strategies for 'explaining' the Byron phenomenon. Ann Barton focuses on the seriously ambiguous nature of Byron's relationship to Shakespeare whom he mined and in his protean manner in some way resembled, but whom he also pilloried. Bernard Beatty looks at the strange fact that it was when Byron was most obviously in debt to the eighteenth century that he was also most obviously creating textures for the twentieth and twenty-first. Professor McGann's essay on the lyric raises the context of the lyric idea, so important to the period, and to which Byron has a unique relationship. Peter Cochran creates for English readers the necessary sense of scale to appreciate Byron's influence and reputation overseas by looking at France, Germany, Italy, Russia and Poland. During the 1950s and 1960s in particular, it was often fashionable to see Byron as essentially an eighteenth-century poet. In the last essay in the volume, Jane Stabler's piece takes up some of the arguments of Susan Wolfson and myself on the *ottava rima* arguing that while Byron's poetry sometimes seems to flirt with denying 'the possibility of sincerity altogether' it actually invites its readers to 'invest imaginative energy' – an investment for which the poetry promises a profitable return.

Byron was a protean figure and also a protean poet. If this can be called a single theme then this is the theme which emerges from this collection. Significantly for the business of English studies, however, there are essays in this volume which could loosely be called historicist, new historicist, and in some manner or other formalist. It may be that the days of power struggles between conflicting critical ideologies are past, or it may be that Byron's multiple nature, while uncomfortable with any one view, is comfortable with all.

> Temperate I am – yet never had a temper;
> Modest I am – yet with some slight assurance;
> Changeable too – yet somehow '*Idem semper*':
> Patient – but not enamoured of endurance;
> Cheerful – but, sometimes, rather apt to whimper:
> Mild – but at times a sort of '*Hercules furens*':
> So that I almost think that the same skin
> For one without – has two or three within.
>
> (*Don Juan*, XVII.11)

I

HISTORICAL CONTEXTS

I

PAUL DOUGLASS

Byron's life and his biographers

Introduction

After the mid-nineteenth century, it became a stereotype that asylum inmates imagined themselves as the omnipotent Napoleon – but also the brilliant Byron.[1] Extreme as it seems, this desire for vicarious experience, this tendency to translate one's life into the idealization of another, is common – so common that it led Albert Camus to define biography itself as 'nostalgia for other people's lives'.[2] Camus notes that our fascination with the careers of the famous stems from our belief that such lives have strong plots, while our own seem fragmentary and directionless. However, since even the careers of celebrities are not as neatly plotted as we could wish, the production of that 'nostalgia' has required an unholy alliance between fiction and biography. Lord Byron knew this as well as perhaps anyone in history. In writing his own story and seeming to live what he wrote, he made it impossible to discuss his work apart from his life. The vignettes and anecdotes he relished and promulgated produced a tale unified around themes of sex, violence, genius, and adventure, or – in the case of hostile biographers – sex, violence, cruelty, and hypocrisy. But in either case, the indivisibility of the life and work explains much of the delight and frustration to be found in the immense canon of Byron Biography, everything from laurel wreaths to slash-and-burn character assassination, from factual accounts to encounters beyond the grave, such as Quevedo Redivivus's *A Spiritual Interview with Lord Byron* (1840) and Amanda Prantera's *Conversations with Lord Byron on Perversion, 163 Years after His Lordship's Death* (1987).

The deepest vein in Byronic portraits is the one that runs along the Gothic. The literary masks of transgressors like Childe Harold, Selim, Lara, Conrad, Manfred, Cain, and Don Juan have inspired scores of writers. Before he died, Byron had appeared as such a character in at least a dozen novels, most notably as the eponymous heroes of Lady Caroline Lamb's *Glenarvon* (1816) and *Ada Reis* (1823), and the self-dramatizing Mr Cypress in Thomas Love

Peacock's *Nightmare Abbey* (1818) – but also in hilariously serious works like Bridget Bluemantle's *The Baron of Falconberg; or, Childe Harolde in Prose* (1815); and *Prodigious!!! or Childe Paddie in London* (1818). Blake's *The Ghost of Abel* employs Byron's character, as does Goethe's *Faust* Part 2. Byron biography has frequently employed the devices of Gothic melodrama. That is not accidental, for Byron encouraged his readers to imagine him as a composite of the heroes of such novels as Horace Walpole's *The Castle of Otranto*, William Beckford's *Vathek*, and Ann Radcliffe's *The Italian*, all of which he read when he was young. He knew the character he must portray. As he wrote to his former friend at Cambridge, Francis Hodgson, 'the *hero* of tragedy and (I add meo periculo) a *tragic* poem must be *guilty*, to *excite* "terror and pity"'. And, he asked blithely, 'Who is the hero of "Paradise Lost"? Why Satan' (*BLJ*, VIII, 115). If Byron's biographers have been drawn to Gothic elements in his life, that is because Byron helped them along, portraying himself as a fallen angel who was able to dash off a brilliant poem in minutes but was haunted by a secret past.

That image was born in 1812 when, at the age of twenty-four, he published what everyone took to be a thinly disguised autobiography titled *Childe Harold's Pilgrimage*. His own hero had been Napoleon, whose bust he kept upon his desk at Harrow, and his goal was to establish himself as a conquering force in letters: *Harold* was his first major victory. Byron was strongly identified with the protagonist of his work, and the poem made him an object of personal fascination. The Gothic–Satanic elements of his story have proven to be perennially mesmerizing – his lame foot, imperious (and painfully crass) mother, prodigious swimming ability, sexual ambivalence, incestuous attraction to his half-sister, illegitimate children, widely publicized separation from his wife, exile from England, effortless writing talent, friendships with the famous, and death while promoting the Greek independence movement in 1824. This irresistible material has made a mountain of biographical writing, including over 200 substantial biographies, dozens of memoirs, countless pamphlets and biographical essays, and innumerable fictional treatments in novels, poems, plays, and operas.

Prodigious as it is, and prompt as it was to pursue Byron after his death in 1824, biography still arrived late. Byron had already been telling his own story for years, engaging others in a creative process of living through him and his fictional personae. At thirty-three, less than two-and-a-half years before his death in Greece, Byron ruminated on his own growing legend:

> I have seen myself compared personally or poetically – in English French German (as interpreted to me) Italian and Portuguese within these nine years – to Rousseau – Goethe – Young – Aretine – Timon of Athens – 'An Alabaster Vase

> lighted up within', Satan – Shakespeare – Buonaparte – Tiberius – Aeschylus – Sophocles – Euripides – Harlequin – The Clown – Sternhold and Hopkins – to the Phantasmagoria – to Henry the 8th, to Chenier – to Mirabeau – to young R[obert] Dallas (the Schoolboy) to Michael Angelo – to Raphael – to a petit maitre – to Diogenes, to Childe Harold – to Lara – to the Count in Beppo – to Milton – to Pope – to Dryden – to Burns – to Savage – to Chatterton – to 'oft have I heard of thee my Lord Biron' in Shakespeare [*Love's Labour's Lost*, V.2.921], to Churchill the poet – to Kean the Actor – to Alfieri &c. &c. &c.
>
> . . .
>
> The object of so many contradictory comparisons must probably be like something different from them all, – but what that is, is more than I know, or any body else. (*BLJ*, IX, 11)

Rankled by the comparison to Rousseau, he was intrigued by others, especially to Alexander Pope, whose wit and physical infirmity had stirred Byron's nascent imagination when he was merely a boy with a bad foot. Better to 'err with Pope' (*English Bards*, 102) than to shine with another choice. He was all too aware of becoming a legend – of the inevitability of those comparisons to Napoleon and Satan, for example – and yet he conveys a bemused sense of joining the spectators peering at this curious object. Indeed, Byron left a remarkable record of dispassionate self-evaluation that has generally been validated by his greatest biographer to date, Leslie Marchand, and corroborated in the hundreds of letters Marchand edited and published between 1973 and 1994. Thus, although Byron used the tools of fiction to create illusions about himself as an author and a man, he also recorded his life in fact, believing it would be important to posterity. He strongly felt he was creating a life to be read, now and in future years. It is in this sense that we may see Byron as attempting to write his own biography.

The life

Byron's childhood was not easy. He was born in London on 22 January 1788, to a first-time mother and a father who shortly abandoned child and wife. Captain John Byron, nicknamed 'Mad Jack', was the son of a vice-admiral, and he had been married before, to a woman with a lifetime guaranteed income of £4,000 per annum. When she died, leaving him to care for a daughter named Augusta, Jack looked for another heiress, and he found her in Catherine Gordon of Gight. She was an impetuous woman who had, by all accounts, few prepossessing characteristics beyond the income of her estate, which rapidly disappeared after marriage to the captain. Pursued by debtors and wounded emotionally by her son's deformed foot, she retreated to her ancestral Scotland where she and the child lived in Aberdeen. There Byron received a book education at the Grammar School and a sexual initiation at the hands of his nurse, May Gray, neither of which would ever fade from memory. His father died in 1791 – perhaps by his own hand – bequeathing nothing but debts.

In 1794, Byron became the heir to the barony held by his profligate great-uncle, to which he acceded as the sixth baron upon the Wicked Lord's death in 1798. Though the family seat, Newstead Abbey, still had to be rented out, Byron's prospects had improved, and his sense of entitlement increased astronomically. He moved to England and attended school at Dulwich and Harrow. During his Harrow years, he formed the first of his many 'attachments' to females, including Elizabeth Pigot, Margaret Parker (his cousin), and Mary Chaworth, the last of whom inspired pain and poetry. Harrow was unappealing to him at first, but toward the end of his time there he found his stride. He played cricket avidly and met the Earl of Clare, a friend for life. He also began corresponding with his half-sister, Augusta. At this time he had a shocking encounter with Lord Grey de Ruthyn, the leaseholder for Newstead Abbey. Most likely, de Ruthyn invited Byron to participate in his own homosexual initiation. The ruins at Newstead never looked the same to him. They came to symbolize only 'the wreck of the [family] line' ('Newstead Abbey', 24). At Cambridge, by virtue of his peerage, he suffered no examinations or other scholarly indignities. He became a legendary student from the privileged class, keeping a pet bear, drinking, betting on the horses and the fights. It was a wild life, memorialized in 'Hints from Horace' (1811):

> Fines, tutors, tasks, conventions threat in vain,
> Before hounds, hunters, and Newmarket plain.
> Rough with his elders, with his equals rash,
> Civil to sharpers, prodigal of cash,
> Constant to nought – save hazard and a whore,
> Yet cursing both, for both have made him sore.
>
> ('Hints from Horace', 229–34)

But in addition to excess there was abstemiousness. At one point, he appears to have dieted off fifty-one pounds over a period of five months. He formed several close relationships here, as well, including those with John Cam Hobhouse, Charles Matthews, and with a young chorister named John Edleston, who inspired several beautiful poems dedicated to a sexually ambiguous figure named 'Thyrza'. He wrote more earnestly than he studied, and published by private means four books of poetry: *Fugitive Pieces* (1806), *Poems on Various Occasions* (1807), *Hours of Idleness* (1807), and *Poems*

Original and Translated (1808). *Hours of Idleness* received a stinging dismissal in the *Edinburgh Review*, a quarterly which was the mouthpiece for Whig literary and political criticism. Two years later, Byron turned twenty-one and entered the House of Lords. He also finished at Cambridge and retorted to his critics with *English Bards and Scotch Reviewers* (1809). He looked forward now to crossing Europe with his friend Hobhouse, cavalierly ignoring the Napoleonic wars.

Travelling through Portugal and Spain to Greece, Albania and Turkey was a mind-expanding experience that brought many adventures, including the swimming of the Hellespont, an achievement of which Byron was rightly proud. He experimented with everything, including homo- and heterosexual partners, and visited the tyrannical ruler of Albania, Ali Pasha. He began to write *Childe Harold's Pilgrimage*, composing it in 'Spenserian stanzas', the nine-line stanza adapted by Edmund Spenser for his masterwork, *The Faerie Queene*.[3] After his return to England, he learned that his mother had died almost simultaneously with his arrival, and immediately thereafter he was informed of the deaths of his Cambridge friends, Matthews and Edleston. This sequence of events apparently made Byron feel his life was running away with him – that he was living at a faster rate than a normal human being.

The day after the publication of the two cantos of *Childe Harold's Pilgrimage* in March 1812, Byron 'awoke one morning and found himself famous' as he described it to Thomas Moore.[4] In *Childe Harold*, Byron had invented a special kind of hero, behind whose mask he easily slipped. Sought after by a growing public, he was perceived as having an infectious charisma that his future bride described as 'the Byromania'. Miss Anna Isabella (or 'Annabella') Milbanke observed the sycophancy of her female contemporaries and wrote: 'Reforming Byron with his magic sway / Compels all hearts to love him and obey.'[5] Byron was, in fact, the prototypical celebrity, and *Childe Harold's Pilgrimage* produced a fan base for Byron among female readers. Lady Caroline Lamb is the most famous of those who wrote to 'Harold' offering him solace for the murky sorrows and shadowy demons haunting his pallid features. They carried on an intense and very public affair over that summer, until finally her family was forced to send her to Ireland. She returned that autumn, gaunt and deranged, and never entirely got over the experience. But it was not just Byron's sexual power that had made such an impression; it was also his writing. Lady Caroline was inspired to write three novels and a number of poems as she tried to work out what had happened to her. In this regard, she was not atypical of Byron's female readership, who fantasized about becoming Byron as much as about possessing him.

In Childe Harold, Byron had invented a character who was an astonishing amalgam of the Aristotelian tragic hero and other heroic elements, as Peter Thorslev shows in his seminal study, *The Byronic Hero* (1962). But Harold was also a character he would outgrow. Like modern celebrities, Byron confronted the paradox that his audience loved him not for himself, but for what they imagined him to be. James Soderholm, who has detailed ways in which Byron's female interlocutors – whether lovers or friends – contributed to his work by enlightening him about their responses to him and his writing, cites this passage from the fifteenth canto of *Don Juan*:

> with women he was what
> They pleased to make or take him for; and their
> Imagination's quite enough for that:
> So that the outline's tolerably fair,
> They fill the canvas up – and '*Verbum sat*'.
> If once their phantasies be brought to bear
> Upon an object, whether sad or playful,
> They can transfigure brighter than a Raphael.
> (*Don Juan*, XV.16.1–8)

Byron knew that readers were meeting him half-way – and more.[6] Awareness of the power of the audience made him more anxious to present himself – in person, in portraits, and in print – as a man of action and not a foppish poet. He had himself painted in various military get-ups, and popularized a rugged, open-shirted look. Like celebrities of two centuries later, he was obsessed with his weight and carefully prepared for public appearances. He practised a special gloomy, smouldering glance he called his 'under-look' that simply devastated his public.

A student of stagecraft, he created characters who paralleled his personality and circumstances so closely that it is still impossible to avoid asking, in the words of Peter Cochran, 'Is this then verse, or documentation? Poetry, or journalism? Art, or life?'[7] In embracing this contradiction, Byron speaks to our time. Again and again, biography stumbles back to the cold truth that almost anything it may say of Byron he has already said of himself – in his jottings, poetry, or letters. He found himself protean; so do we. He found himself mad (and maddening), brilliant and perverse, magnanimous and competitive, egotistic and idealistic, homosexual and heterosexual, domineering and acquiescent, and a host of other contradictory things – and so do we. Byron described himself in language so memorable that all one can do is quote it: 'My muse admires digression' ('To the Earl of Clare', 72).

Among poets published and read in England, Byron is one of the most antagonistic to England. The decisive period of his life may have been the time that intervened between his marriage in 1815 and his departure in 1816. Having disentangled himself from Lady Caroline, more or less, and having had a lengthy affair with Lady Oxford, he pursued and eventually won the hand of Miss Milbanke, who happened to be the niece of Lady Caroline's mother-in-law, Lady Melbourne. Byron's motives for marrying were two. His financial problems had become more and more pressing, annoying, and finally maddening. He needed income while the sale of Newstead Abbey was concluded. His second reason, harder to fathom, was to be rescued from his own demons – to be made, in some sense, good and moral. This would turn out to be an impossible role for a spouse, as anyone could have imagined. The marriage started off badly, and Byron's 'attachment' to his half-sister Augusta became obtrusive. By the time he separated from his wife, he had a daughter by her, and probably also a daughter by Augusta. His money problems exacerbated his tendency to outbursts of temper and violent alterations of mood. His behaviour during his wife's pregnancy was apparently so terrifying that she longed to believe he was mad.

When Annabella made it clear that there would have to be a separation, Byron decided to leave England in order to avoid pursuit by creditors and those who might make public any information that might lead to charges of sodomy. He and his country now rejected and vilified each other. He had invented himself as a brooding and restless figure of sexual allure, haunted by transgressions of the past. Now he seemed to have become the Corsair he wrote about in the poem of that name: Conrad whose name was 'link'd with one virtue, and a thousand crimes' (3.696). When he left, stories circulated that he had abused his pregnant wife, that he had fathered a child by his half-sister, and that he had committed sodomy with boys. The last was an offence punishable by execution or the public pillory. As Lewis Crompton has argued, the public revulsion that inundated such transgressors was so heinous that many would have chosen the gallows over the pillory. Byron's permanent exile from England, and the stories and denials it occasioned, became an overwhelming force in the development of his biographical legacy.

It is therefore especially sad that we do not have Byron's own account of his marriage, contained in a special journal which he had entrusted to his friend, Thomas Moore. John Cam Hobhouse, along with Moore, the publisher John Murray, and others, burned the manuscript in an infamous act of loyalty just days after receiving news of Byron's death in May 1824. Doris Langley Moore has given us a compelling account of the loss of this important document in *The Late Lord Byron: Posthumous Dramas* (1961). Though we cannot absolve those who did the burning, neither should we fail to note Byron's ambivalence. He left his manuscript to an uncertain fate, just as he had put his illegitimate daughter, Allegra (born to Claire Clairmont, Mary Shelley's stepsister), in a convent where she would die of cold and neglect. In short, he miscalculated.

When John Cam Hobhouse learned Moore had the manuscript, he jealously impugned Moore's motives. Byron responded that Moore had only done as Byron wished:

> Do you really mean to say that I have not as good a right to leave such a M.S. after my death – as the thousands before me who have done the same? Is there no *reason* that I should? Will not my life (it is egotism but you know this is true of all men who have *had* a name even if they survive it) be given in a false and unfair point of view by others? – I mean *false* as to *praise* as well as *censure*?
>
> (*BLJ*, IX, 68)

Unsatisfied, Hobhouse accused Byron of 'purchasing a biographer under pretext of doing a generous action'. Byron retorted:

> I am willing to bear that imputation rather than have Moore or anyone else suppose that He is at all obliged to me. – I suppose however that like most men who have been talked about – I might have had – (if I did not outlive my reputation which however is not unlikely) a biographer without purchase – since most other scribblers have two or three gratis. Besides – I thought I had written my own. (*BLJ*, IX, 88)

Byron died believing the manuscript would survive. One of his acquaintances later reported that he said, 'Literary lives are compiled for the bibliopolists, as puffs to sell their wares; they are nothing. When I die you will see mine, written by myself.'[8] Not that he necessarily thought the facts would make him revered. Quite the opposite:

> All these are, certes, entertaining facts,
> Like Shakespeare's stealing deer, Lord Bacon's bribes;
> Like Titus' youth, and Caesar's earliest acts;
> Like Burns (whom Doctor Currie well describes);
> Like Cromwell's pranks; – but although truth exacts
> These amiable descriptions from the scribes,
> As most essential to their hero's story,
> They do not much contribute to his glory.
>
> (*Don Juan*, III.92)

He had underestimated the determination of his friends to protect him, and possibly themselves, from revelations of Byron's bad behaviour. The memoirs are almost certainly gone for good, although there are still those who nurse the hope that the manuscript was copied, or that it was never really burned. The burning of the memoirs is emblematic of the problems Byron's biographers have faced in gathering the literary and social remains of their subject. The record is always damaged. The surviving allies always 'spin' the story by silence if not publication. There are, even today, still proprietary interests that influence the writing of Byronic biography. The descendants of Byron and of his acquaintances and publishers control access to large archives of primary materials in London, Oxford and West Sussex, which biographers absolutely must consult if they wish to publish respectable work.[9]

And readers still tend to prefer Gothic drama to facts. Byron harnessed the power of his readers' imaginations, and what happened then, as he himself acknowledged, no one could predict or control. Many of the episodes of his life subsequent to the collapse of his marriage became raw material for poems, novels, plays and operas, and (lately) movies. His friendship with the Shelleys, for example, though it was fleeting, has been frequently recounted. Byron did not continue to cooperate with the creation of this myth of the doomed poets and their fatal passions. Indeed, in the years before he conceived the desire to aid in the Greek independence movement, he adopted a very different incarnation: the character of Don Juan, the sex-addict who, in Byron's retelling, seems more victim than victimizer. Though the poem is now considered a work of genius, to Byron's contemporaries it appeared he had settled for 'the literary lower Empire' (*Don Juan*, II.62.1). What had happened to the grandiosity of *Manfred* and *Cain*? When Byron died in Greece, it appeared they had been totally eclipsed by the chatty, catty, risqué narrator of *Don Juan*. Thus a quandary arose: must one sacrifice Don Juan to sanctify Manfred? Many have done so in order to preserve what they believed to be the Faustian quintessence of Byron.

As Byron's life neared its sudden end, he had already become the desire of covetous minds. Some, obviously, cared not at all to preserve his 'original' character. They only cared that his name brought in money. After 1813, many works were falsely attributed to him. Some were satirical send-ups, some straight forgeries. One famous example is *The Vampyre*, a very short story penned by his unstable and pretentious doctor-assistant John Polidori, who wrote it during the famous 'Frankenstein' summer of 1816. Polidori's publishers fudged the distinction between its being influenced by Byron and its being written by him in order to increase sales. Byron's protestations failed to squelch the canard of his authorship, and the rumour still occasionally reappears, like a vampire that cannot be finished off.

He was not merely the victim of such hoaxes, however. He chose to circulate some of his own works anonymously at first, just to see how they were received. For example, *The Waltz*, a condemnation of the dance fad, was published under the pen-name 'Horace Hornem' in 1813 because Byron feared to attack the German influence upon England through the Hanoverian kings (that is, the Georges, the fourth of whom adored waltzing). At the same time, he would also be able to take credit for the poem in liberal Whig circles. Thus, he took advantage of the pirated and forged work that appeared under his name to say things he would otherwise have been forced to keep private. Such are the complications the biographer faces in seeking the truth of Byron's relatively short life, which ended, so we are now convinced, because his ignorant doctors bled him promiscuously, despite his protests.[10]

The biographers

What *was* biography from the perspective of Byron's era? Its roots lie in hagiography, a term originating in the third division of the Jewish Scripture, referring to the stories of saints and venerated persons. The lives of the saints were intended to inspire readers, and, with few exceptions, hagiography was the principal mode of biography down through the reign of Elizabeth the First, as young Don Juan knew well: 'sermons he read, and lectures he endured, / And homilies, and lives of all the Saints' (1.47). Seventeenth-century biography had focused primarily upon the lives of religious men, most of whom were writers of sermons and tracts, and this had led to a greater interest in literary figures – Milton, for example. Byron was just three years old when Boswell's *The Life of Samuel Johnson* was published in 1791. By then, Benjamin Franklin had already laboured hard over his own *Autobiography*, which would not appear in any form until the 1820s. Boswell's work was a harbinger of the modern biographical mode, with its meticulous research and psychological sophistication. Unfortunately, it was ahead of its time. While it showed that literary men made excellent subjects, its example was honoured relentlessly in the breach. More importantly, perhaps, the artist had yet to emerge as a cultural force, another change in which Byron played a crucial role. The handful of English 'lives' of literary men published in the 1700s had afforded the reading public 'curiosity and amusement'. Byron's life was a different matter.

The first to publish was Thomas Medwin, whose *Conversations of Lord Byron* was rushed into print in October 1824, just six months after the poet's death. It was followed immediately by Robert Dallas's *Recollections of the Life of Lord Byron, from the Year 1808 to the end of 1814* (1824), Pietro Gamba's *A Narrative of Lord Byron's Last Journey to Greece* (1825), and William Parry's *The Last Days of Lord Byron* (1825). Each of these depictions of Byron incorporates conversation quoted from the author's notes.

Before any full-scale biography could be produced, the ranks of the memoirists swelled. In 1828, Leigh Hunt produced *Lord Byron and Some of His Contemporaries*, an account of the ill-fated plans of Byron, Hunt, and Shelley in 1822 to found a journal to be called *The Liberal*. Shelley had drowned, the journal project disintegrated, and so did Hunt's relations with Byron, on whom he vented his frustration in an act of character assassination that did serious damage to Byron's reputation. After the death of Lady Caroline Lamb in 1828, her friend and collaborator Isaac Nathan published *Fugitive Pieces and Reminiscences of Lord Byron: Containing an Entire New Edition of the Hebrew Melodies . . . also some Original Poetry, Letters, and Recollections of Lady Caroline Lamb* (1829). Nathan's praise of Byron and Lady Caroline (who was godmother to his children) was viewed sceptically by a readership that preferred not to believe a Jew had standing with either the Lady or the Lord.

Finally, after all this publishing of Byron's private conversations, Thomas Moore finished his *Letters and Journals of Lord Byron with Notices of His Life* (1830), sold by Byron's publisher, John Murray. Moore's work has stood up well, considering its closeness in time to Byron's death and the intense political pressures placed upon him by Byron's many powerful friends and enemies. Moore is also one of the few who had read Byron's memoirs before they were burned, and this has prompted careful rereading of the 1830 biography for clues to lost material. *Letters and Journals* is an edition of Byron's correspondence and other writings, with commentary and anecdotes contributed by Moore, who had known Byron many years.

However candid, Moore nonetheless drew the curtain over many aspects of Byron's life. Faced with the impossible task of describing (much less explaining) Byron's abominable behaviour toward his wife, Moore offered the bromide that great persons are ill-equipped to pursue domestic happiness. Yet Moore knew that readers wished to be told that famous people are as flawed as anyone, and he gave his audience what it wanted. Though he defended Byron stoutly and gave ample evidence of the poet's genial character in the letters, he also recounted such anecdotes, and quoted such letters, as would leave the reader in no doubt about Byron's gloomy temper and violent outbursts. Moore's was the party line: Byron's difficult nature must be acknowledged, but it was all part of his genius – and ultimately a strength of his remarkable character. If there were rumours of indiscretions, including incest and homosexuality, these were to be ignored. In time (so it was believed), such things would pass.

Moore was Byron's competitor as well as his biographer. Out of deference to those with whom he and Murray still maintained relationships, he omitted much troublesome detail – like Byron's affair with Lady Caroline Lamb and the very existence of Isaac Nathan, who had collaborated with Byron on the *Hebrew Melodies*. That collection had competed with Moore's own *Irish Melodies*, to Moore's annoyance. Equally annoying to Moore was John Galt's *The Life of Lord Byron* (1830), which cribbed two-thirds of its material from him and the other books published to that date. The remaining third of the book focused on Galt's short personal acquaintance with Byron in 1809–10, amounting to perhaps seven weeks of contact. Galt put on a show of trying to balance Moore's overly positive view of Byron, and he damaged Byron's reputation by impugning his motives for going to Greece and charging (falsely) that Byron was a plagiarist.

And still the memoirs spilled forth. An army doctor named James Kennedy had once tried to convert Byron; now he produced *Conversations on Religion with Lord Byron and Others* (1830). Julius Millingen, one of the physicians who had inadvertently hastened Byron's death, published *Memoirs of the Affairs of Greece* (1831). Another acquaintance of Byron's, the Countess Blessington, offered her own extensive volume of recollected *Conversations* (1834). Among the last accounts of Byron written by a contemporary was that of Edward John Trelawny titled *Recollections of Shelley and Byron* (1858). Twenty years later he revised and republished it as *Records of Shelley, Byron, and the Author* (1878). His is among the least reliable of the works discussed here, as might be guessed from the changes in his title. In the interim, Countess Teresa Guiccioli, Byron's 'last attachment', finally came out with her own memoir, a volume of hero-worship entitled *My Recollections of Lord Byron and Those of Eye-Witnesses of His Life* (Paris, 1868; translated 1869). It may have surprised any surviving objects of Byron's satirical pen to learn that 'To praise was almost a besetting sin in Lord Byron', and that he had been 'indulgent to mediocrity'.[11]

Tainted invariably by self-interest, these memoirs are still not without value – quite the opposite. Biographers have revisited them continuously for fresh insights. But each is limited by the problematic nature of the author's relationship to Byron. Each book has provided tantalizing and often misleading material for biographers, who must evaluate the testimony without benefit of cross-examination. Sometimes, as is especially true of Dallas, the memoirist has tried faithfully to present the poet in his own voice, but has failed to notice that Byron finds him funny. In all cases, the motives of the memoirist have to be taken into account. Dallas wanted money and had some personal grudges to settle with his late benefactor. Medwin sought to make himself appear Byron's equal and close friend, though he had known

Byron scarcely four months (Hobhouse was so offended by the exaggeration that he published an attack on Medwin in the *Westminster Review* detailing at least fifty errors of fact). Gamba was the brother of Byron's last love, Teresa Guiccioli, and an ardent supporter and admirer of Byron. Isaac Nathan clearly knew his collaboration with Byron on the *Hebrew Melodies* was the pinnacle of his career as a composer. He has often been ignored as a self-promoter, but his recollections of that collaboration have gained credence among recent biographers, just as some of the accounts canonized by earlier biographers, like that of Blessington's, have been subjected to more and more scrutiny. It has taken almost two centuries of research to separate the myths, apocrypha, legends, and flim-flam from the facts. And we have not finished yet.

Despite the plethora of memoirs and sketches of Byron in the three decades after his death, two key persons chose to remain mostly silent, namely Lady Byron and John Cam Hobhouse. Hobhouse may have regretted leaving a vacuum to be filled by the imaginations of sharply antagonistic camps who revered and reviled his friend. He, who knew so much, had forgone his chance to publish his own version when it could more effectively have countered the misstatements of Hunt, Medwin, Galt, and Dallas. Byron's reputation had eroded. Gradually, so had the public's general interest. When Hobhouse, now Baron Broughton de Gyfford, finally printed privately his own memoir, *Some Account of a Long Life* (1865), most of the actors in the drama were dead, including Lady Byron, who had passed away in 1860. The Victorian attitude to Byron is epitomized in Thomas Carlyle's phrase, 'Close thy Byron, open thy Goethe.' One read Byron only to comprehend Romantic excess. Still, one did read Byron. In the late 1860s, the wide dissemination of Byron's poems through pirated editions angered Harriet Beecher Stowe, one of Lady Byron's surviving friends. She grew further incensed in early 1869 when she read Teresa Guiccioli's *My Recollections of Lord Byron and Those of Eye-Witnesses of His Life*, which she thought gave too favourable a picture of Byron and slighted his wife. Mrs Stowe then inaugurated a campaign of fury against Byron by publishing a twenty-page article in the September 1869 editions of *Macmillan's Magazine* and the *Atlantic Monthly* titled 'The True Story of Lady Byron's Life'.

Mrs Stowe's defence of her friend consisted in an attempt to demonstrate that Byron had been guilty of incest with his half-sister, Augusta Leigh, and that Lady Byron had gone to her grave as a martyr to her estranged husband's egotism and perversity. Hobhouse attempted to counter this story. In response to Mrs Stowe's attack, he wrote *A Contemporary Account of the Separation of Lord and Lady Byron. Also of the Destruction of Lord Byron's Memoirs*, which was published after his death (1870). His work was drowned out as a new wave of memoirists and commentators weighed in. Hobhouse's contribution to the story of Byron's turbulent career would not be fully realized until Lady Dorchester edited and republished his *Recollections of a Long Life* in 1909. In the meantime, Mrs Stowe expanded her attack and published *Lady Byron Vindicated* (1870). Anyone who had met Byron and failed to publish now seized the opportunity to offer reminiscences, including Byron's school chum at Harrow, William Harness (*Personal Reminiscences*, 1875), and his friend at Cambridge, Francis Hodgson (*Memoir*, 1878).

The history of biography is filled with irony. One such is the fact that after Harriet Beecher Stowe's attack, Byron's reputation actually rose. For forty years, no one had seriously challenged Moore's biography. Over the course of the next twenty, full-length biographies were published by Karl Elze, J. C. Jeaffreson, Roden Noel, and John Nichol. As Clement Goode has noted, the issues raised by Mrs Stowe's attack passed rather quickly from the public eye, but the result was a massive re-evaluation of Byron and his work.[12] Many unpublished letters began to appear in print, and scholars began to buckle down to the tasks of bibliography and textual scholarship, relying heavily upon developments in the biographical realm. Nineteenth-century Byron scholarship was crowned by the appearance of Coleridge and Prothero's thirteen-volume *The Works of Lord Byron* (1898).

Mrs Stowe's inability to make the charge of incest stick would seem to have returned us to Moore's deflection of the issue. (Interestingly, Byron's sexual interest in boys was not even on Mrs Stowe's list of charges.) However, the increasing availability of Byron's correspondence inevitably led critics back to the incest question. Motivated apparently by recollections of his grandmother's outrage and sense of injustice, Lady Byron's grandson, Ralph, Earl of Lovelace, supported Mrs Stowe's argument against Byron in a privately printed book titled *Astarte* (1905). It was a pedantic, difficult work that failed to provide sufficient evidence to support its claims. But *Astarte* had been written by one of Byron's descendants, and it circulated widely. Its tone of certainty reignited the slumbering fires of Byronic controversy, prompting yet another round of publications, including *Lord Byron and His Detractors* (1906), which contained an essay by John Murray IV defending the publishing family's honour against the Earl of Lovelace's sometimes obscure imputations.

When *Astarte* was subsequently augmented and edited by the earl's wife for posthumous publication in 1921, some of Byron's correspondence, chiefly to Lady Melbourne, appeared. The letters tended to support the claims of the Earl of Lovelace and the redoubtable Mrs Stowe. This made it harder for Byron's defenders to refute the incest charges. The tide had turned in favour of admitting that Byron's behaviour toward his wife and half-sister was not all that might have been hoped from a gentleman. Richard Edgcumbe's *Byron: The Last Phase* (1909) wasted valuable ink defending Byron against charges upon which he would ultimately be convicted, but it also marks the first appearance of what became a series of objective and lively biographical treatments of restricted parts of Byron's life. To complete this intimate portrait, Ethel Colburn Mayne published her two-volume *Byron* in 1912, accepting the assertions of *Astarte* and in general supporting Lady Byron's perspective. Mayne abridged the book into one volume in 1924, updating and improving it. Scholarship was indeed doing its work. But Moore's version of Byron's life still had staying power. In 1932, John Murray brought out a centenary reprint of Moore's *Life, Letters and Journals of Lord Byron*, augmented by a cursory index and a sprinkling of commentary culled from the work of some of his contemporaries, like Walter Scott, Lord Broughton (Hobhouse), and Thomas Campbell.

Despite the reprinting of the Moore biography, there was no going back. As André Maurois wrote in his influential 1930 biography titled simply *Byron*, 'Willingly or unwillingly, every biographer of Byron must take sides on the incest question.' Maurois endorsed the views of Stowe, Lovelace, and Mayne, and declared the issue settled, though he observed that Byron and Augusta had not really known each other until adulthood, and he argued ingeniously that the charge of incest was more in the nature of 'an imaginary crime'.[13] Maurois's book assumes that there must now be index entries for Byron's affairs, for incest, and even for debauchery, but none for paedophilia, homosexuality, or sodomy, issues upon which a Byron biographer need not (apparently) take sides. For Maurois, it was enough to quote Byron's passionate description of his relationship with John Edleston and leave the rest to our imaginations.

At the midpoint of the twentieth century, a great period in Byron biography was inaugurated by the work of Leslie Marchand, whose exhaustive recounting of the poet's day-to-day existence, *Byron: A Biography*, was published in 1957. Marchand's research and his sympathetic but fair-minded approach set a high standard. Where others had been content to allude and to quote out of context, Marchand penetrated and documented, answering hundreds of questions himself, and opening the way to answering hundreds more about Byron's life. A shortened and updated one-volume edition of Marchand's biography appeared in 1971 under the title *Byron: A Portrait*. Marchand then crowned this achievement by adding a complete edition of Byron's letters. While he laboured at this task, Jerome McGann edited Byron's poetry in seven volumes, with extensive notes on the background and composition of each poem.

As one might have expected, however, Marchand's was not the last word on Byron. *Byron: A Biography* had scarcely appeared when an argument erupted in the pages of the *Times Literary Supplement* over the issue of Byron's sexual proclivities. Specifically, the question was debated whether Byron's attempt to engage in 'unnatural' intercourse with his wife rather than an incestuous relationship with his sister had driven Lady Byron to separate from her husband. G. Wilson Knight and Michael Joyce lined up for the affirmative. Malcolm Elwin and Doris Langley Moore took antagonistic views, sometimes with each other as well as with Knight and Joyce. Moore and Elwin had each had access to the papers of the 2nd Earl of Lovelace, and they tended to support the family's position that Augusta Leigh's relationship with Byron was the key to the break-up of their marriage, although both acknowledged Byron's abysmal behaviour toward his wife, without conceding that an overture toward anal intercourse could be assumed, much less proven. Agreeing on this point, Elwin nonetheless accused Moore of gross inaccuracies, and under his influence the 2nd Earl forbade her to quote further from the Lovelace papers.

Michael Joyce had first (in 1948) underscored the possibility that Byron had had 'unnatural' intercourse with his wife, or at least attempted it. Now, Knight called strongly for biography to confront the facts of Byron's queer life, asking that 'admission and a Greek name' be attached to the explanation for Byron's offence against his wife.[14] And yet Knight was not quite ready to insist on public acknowledgement that Byron was bisexual. It would be almost twenty-five years before Lewis Crompton extended Knight's charge, arguing that Marchand had consistently failed to explain and describe Byron's involvements with male lovers, like his page Robert Rushton and the Greek youths Nicolo Giraud and Loukas Chalandritsanos. Crompton's *Byron and Greek Love* (1985) exemplifies a type of biographical study that focuses Byron's life around a single issue, rather than attempting to create a larger view. Such studies prompt negative responses from those who feel the writer warps Byron to fit the theme, presenting a one-sided account. Nonetheless, Crompton makes a strong case that Byron's sense of doom and guilt for 'nameless crimes' stemmed from homosexual impulses and activities. The acknowledgement of Byron's bisexuality would seem to resolve disputes about his relationships with lovers like Edleston, Lady Caroline Lamb, Claire Clairmont, and his wife, Annabella Milbanke. That is not really the case, however, for despite the greater certainty about his sexual ambivalence, the exact nature of those relationships remains elusive.

Nonetheless, Crompton's work has had a significant impact upon later studies, particularly those apparently aimed at diminishing Byronic hero-worship. Two full-length traditional biographies published on Byron since the appearance of Crompton's book are marked by his approach: Phyllis Grosskurth's *Byron: The Flawed Angel* (1997) and Benita Eisler's *Byron: Child of Passion, Fool of Fame* (1999) have accepted Crompton's conclusions and employed them to create a much more sombre picture of Byron's character than that offered by Marchand. These two biographies are deeply indebted not only to Crompton but to Marchand, as well as to Doris Langley Moore and Malcolm Elwin. They nonetheless break new ground, exploring Byron's relationships more fully and openly. They have also added a significant and fresh perspective on certain episodes of Byron's life. For example, Eisler writes compellingly about Byron's marriage. Grosskurth writes with insight about his childhood. As is indicated by their subtitles, however, these books return us to the bad, dark, Gothic Byron. A more even-handed and better-researched biography has now been written by Fiona MacCarthy and published by the descendants of Byron's old friend, John Murray. *Byron: Life and Legend* is based on a great deal of original material that adds to our knowledge of Byron and his activities. It extends and deepens what others have done before and is well written. Less satisfactorily, MacCarthy takes the position that the poet was homosexual at the deepest level – an oversimplification of a riddle that will likely never be completely resolved. The most difficult thing in writing about Byron is to disentangle and then connect the poetry with the life. These biographies, though valuable, pay more attention to Byron's overt behaviour than his genius.

Conclusion

Biographers aim at historical truth, but they must create artistic illusion. Moreover, theirs is an illusion that threatens to become a delusion, for authorial empathy leads them, just as it leads novelists, to project themselves into their subjects. Moreover, the biographer is rarely able to work objectively. All life stories are written in a maelstrom, and all facts ferreted out over someone's objections. Even worse, the biographer always lacks essential information. As Freud said, 'Whoever undertakes to write a biography binds himself to lying, to concealment, to hypocrisy, to flummery, and even to hiding his own lack of understanding, since biographical material is not to be had and if it were it could not be used. Truth is not accessible.'[15] Or, to quote Byron and to put the case less charitably, biographers are like politicians who 'live by lies, yet dare not boldly lie' (*Don Juan*, II.36.5).

Byron played a crucial role in the development of the modern sense of biography. He rose to fame in a period when the individual strongly emerged. Along with Napoleon, he left his stamp upon subsequent portrayals of extraordinary people and all the theatre of celebrity. Also, Byron's life is well-documented and controversial.

But what seems most remarkable about Byron in this respect – and what makes him so interesting for students of the biographical genre – is that he fully understood the creative nature of truth. 'I really cannot know', he wrote to an admiring Isaac Disraeli in 1822, 'whether I am or am not the Genius you are pleased to call me, but I am very willing to put up with the mistake, if it be one' (*BLJ*, IX, 172). If human life is a sort of collaborative process of self-invention, then how can one represent it? To capture this protean subjectivity, the biographer must inevitably confront his or her own subjectivity and acknowledge ours. In biography we confront the mystery of personality, which was Byron's bailiwick, as Walter Scott recognized in the *Quarterly Review* in 1818 when he declared that the interest of Byron's works remains inseparable from his mind, wit, and (we might add) ironic detachment from his public image.[16]

Consistent with their subject's celebrity, biographies of Byron often seem haunted by the sense that they must be written not simply to establish facts but to render justice, either to Byron or to those who opposed him. A great deal of writing about him has been motivated by an apparent desire to vilify or exalt him, particularly in his behaviour toward his wife. Some support his wife and ex-lovers, on one hand, and others see him as he sometimes saw himself: persecuted by wrangling interlocutors – often women – who had it in for him. Nor has the issue fundamentally changed at the date of this writing, though the charges are different. Incest and bisexuality are generally viewed as Byron's guilty secrets, while his abusiveness is more hotly debated. Many critics (not all of them women) emphasize Byron's misogynist side, while others (not all of them men) come to Byron's defence.

Some believe that he was afflicted with manic-depressive illness. Some see him as a political radical: Byron's name has been invoked in Greece, Turkey, Russia, Czechoslovakia, Romania, the Republic of Georgia, and other places around the world as a rallying cry for revolution. After Shakespeare, he is undoubtedly the most influential English poet in the world, and he has been the subject of several biographically based studies exploring his political legacy. In the aftermath of the Romantic era, he was often viewed exclusively as an egotist and libertine, a bad father and husband, and (worst of all) a self-indulgent writer who squandered his God-given talents. At the beginning of the twentieth century, he was acquitted as a poet and elevated to the ranks of genius, yet convicted of incest. Latterly, he has been adopted into the evolving Gay Canon. The story of his life has changed as facts have emerged, but it has also changed with changes in culture and in practices of reading. With his ironic distance and scepticism, he appears more and more like our contemporary.

Is he really? Or are we labouring under our own illusions, responding to a portrait we have half-created? The slippage between life and art persists, even as the biographical facts have become more numerous and secure. Byron's life is the quintessential problem for biography, because it contains at its core that practice of fictionalization which is believed to 'taint' the genre. One does not just read about Byron, or read his works only, one enters into him, as the corpus of dream, a figure containing infinite possibilities. The term 'Byron' has become the site of artistic and intellectual speculations, and of repeated moral and ethical struggles.

Byron's apparent belief in the durability of an historical record and the authenticity of an authorial voice would seem to sit uneasily beside his knowledge that the imagination shapes reality. However, his belief in history and his embrace with imagination are not necessarily in conflict. Though there has been much said, much more will yet be written about why Byron was motivated to 'tell all the Truth, but tell slant'.[17] As a self-portraying artist, he understood the imaginative intensity created by saltatory jumps in narrative – the way the mind fills gaps and supplies continuity. His own personae rehearse such stuttering steps, from Harold to Conrad to Juan; we, as readers, meet him at least half-way. Perhaps Byron's story is as much as anything the tale of the self responding to its own questioning, re-forming under the pressure of its own demands and those of its friends and enemies. In our era, biography itself has undergone such self-questioning and reinvention, although the general public seems to take little notice of its tricks and illusions. A prize-winning biographer of Thomas Jefferson has confessed that he falsely claimed he saw action during the Vietnam War. If he crossed the line in his personal life, did he also do it in his books? The question seems trivial in comparison to those raised by other experiments in biographical form over the last twenty years. A biography of another American president actually inserted a fictional character in the historical narrative.[18] Such experiments were preceded by books like Richard Holmes's *Footsteps* (2000), which attempted to 'cross-question' the nature of biographical authenticity in the very act of creating it. Though such experimentation may suggest that biographers have now transcended the perennial problems of the genre, we would do well to remember that all biographical studies are ephemeral, written to excite the interest of particular people at specific times. To trace the many biographies written of Byron is to trace the development of the contemporary biographical mode, with its meticulous research, its psychological sophistication, and its awareness that imagination (as much as fact) is required for understanding another human being. In this, it so often seems, Byron anticipated everything.

NOTES

1. Poet John Clare, while incarcerated for mental illness, imagined himself Byron and wrote his own *Don Juan* and *Child* [*sic*] *Harold*.
2. Albert Camus, *Carnets 1942–51*, trans. P. Thody, 2 vols. (London: Hamilton, 1966), I, 17.
3. Spenser's stanza generally consisted of eight pentameter lines followed by one hexameter line. Byron led the Romantic poets in reviving Spenserian stanzas, also used, for example, by John Keats in 'The Eve of St Agnes'.
4. Thomas Moore, *Letters and Journals of Lord Byron with Notices of His Life*, 2 vols. (New York: J.J. Harper, 1830), I, 255.
5. Quoted in Ethel Colburn Mayne, *The Life and Letters of Anne Isabella, Lady Byron* (New York: Scribner, 1929).
6. James Soderholm, *Fantasy, Forgery, and the Byron Legend* (Lexington: University Press of Kentucky, 1996), p. 7.
7. Peter Cochran, 'Byron in the Weird World of 1999', *Byron Journal*, 28 (2000), 49–55: 54.
8. Edward John Trelawney, *Records of Shelley, Byron, and the Author* (New York: New York Review of Books, 2000; first published in 1858 as *Recollections of Shelley and Byron*), p. 48.
9. The John Murray archive is now closed prior to its sale by the publisher.
10. Raymond Mills, 'The Last Illness of Lord Byron', *Byron Journal*, 28 (2000), 56–67.
11. Countess Teresa Guiccioli, *My Recollections of Lord Byron and Those of Eye-Witnesses of His Life* (New York: Harper & Brothers, 1869), p. 268.
12. Clement Tyson Goode, Jr, 'A Critical Review of Research', in Oscar Jose Santucho (ed.), *George Gordon, Lord Byron: A Comprehensive Bibliography of Secondary Materials in English, 1809–1979* (Metuchen, N.J.: Scarecrow Press, 1977), p. 35.
13. André Maurois, *Byron*, trans. Hamish Miles (New York: D. Appleton, 1930), p. vi.
14. G. Wilson Knight, 'Lord Byron's Wife', *Times Literary Supplement* (1962), 955.
15. Sigmund Freud, as quoted in Ernest Jones, *The Life and Work of Sigmund Freud*, 3 vols. (New York: Basic Books, 1957), III, 208.
16. *Quarterly Review* 19 (April 1818) reprinted in Donald Reiman (ed.), *The Romantics Reviewed: Part B*, v (p. 2054).
17. Emily Dickinson, poem no. 1129, *The Complete Poems of Emily Dickinson*, ed. Thomas H. Johnson (Boston: Little, Brown, 1960), p. 506.
18. Edmund Morris, *Dutch: A Memoir of Ronald Reagan* (New York: Random House, 1999).

2

PETER W. GRAHAM

Byron and the business of publishing

None of the other Romantics was as loftily dismissive of the business (or 'trade') of publishing as Byron could be. Nonetheless, Byron's literary career was crucially shaped by the practical contingencies of publishing. In turn, his status as literary lion had significant effects on the Regency publishing world – not least in helping to make the name and fortune of what would become one of the great London houses, John Murray of Albemarle Street. Byron's mobility – his protean capacity to be of many minds, strike many poses, hold in suspension apparently contradictory opinions – is nowhere more evident than in his attitudes toward the business side of his 'scribbling labours'. Now he's the nonchalant aristocrat who writes for his own pleasure, now the canny best-selling author who gloats over sales – and mocks his gloating as if to disavow it. Now he disdains the critics' notice, now their disdain provokes his savage indignation. The following pages will take up Byron's relations with the various publishers to whom he entrusted his works (notably the conservative John Murray and the radical John Hunt), his fate at the hands of the pirates who brought out cheap, unauthorized editions of his works, and the connections between details of book production and the evolving nature of Byron's readership.[1] First, however, a few words on how and why a young lord comes to publish at all.

Byron began writing poetry in his Harrow years; and, not surprisingly, his first attempts tended to be conventional effusions written without a particular sense of poetic vocation. Young and mature, Byron was reluctant to acknowledge pride in his poetic achievements. His well-known disclaimer that 'I by no means rank poetry or poets high in the scale of intellect . . . it is the lava of the imagination whose eruption prevents an earthquake' (*BLJ*, III, 179) crystallizes an attitude he expressed intermittently, aloud and on paper, in prose and in verse, throughout his life. Nonetheless, he was pleased enough to have his work admired by others. His first audience of admirers was the coterie of Southwell friends for whom, in aristocratic amateur fashion, he had his first volume, *Fugitive Pieces*, privately printed in 1806. It is worth paying close attention to the circumstances surrounding *Fugitive Pieces* and its transformation to Byron's first published work, *Hours of Idleness* (1807), for this debut accurately shows what Byron's lifelong habits in writing and circulating poetry would be. The lordly nonchalance that left prosaic details to others but could suddenly change to keen resentment at editorial interference, the professed disdain for critics whose hostility in fact easily penetrated Byron's thin authorial skin, the intermittent reliance on and resentment of advice from friends, the subtle but not always prudent ways of distinguishing material suited for publication from texts meant for private dissemination, and the pose-striking that invited readers to collaborate in creating 'Byron' are all evident in the composition, revision, circulation, and publication of these first poems.

Having consigned his manuscript to the printer John Ridge in the nearby town of Newark, Byron left Southwell and, while away, counted on friends, Elizabeth and John Pigot, to midwife the manuscript. The collection of lyrics displays what would later emerge as characteristically Byronic moods and gestures along with their equally characteristic antidotes: elegy, love-longing, melancholy, the backward glance and the inward gaze – but also humour, irony, common sense, dandiacally slippery figure-cutting, cant-defying eroticism. As would be the case on a larger stage in later days, the more fastidious in the Southwell coterie, particularly the Reverend J. T. Becher, cried out. Byron, as he sometimes would and sometimes would not in maturity, bowed to his friends' advice, suppressed the volume, issued a 'miraculously chaste', still private revision called *Poems on Various Occasions*, and vented his spleen at his censors in a series of satirical verses.

What was liveliest had been skimmed off; what was blandest remained for general circulation when the poet-peer made his bow to the reading public beyond Southwell. Titling his first published collection *Hours of Idleness*, offering a languid prefatory deprecation of the verses as 'fruits of the lighter hours of a young man, who has lately completed his nineteenth year', and announcing that poetry is not his 'primary vocation' (*CPW*, I, 32, 33), Byron displayed the double-minded attitude toward authorship and publication that would endure throughout his literary career. He claimed to toss off mere trifles; yet by having Ridge publish the verses under his name, he solicited attention from the general public of readers and book-buyers. As his letters to Elizabeth Pigot indicate, he cared both how large that book-buying public was and what its demographics were.

Byron also cared what the special subset of readers called reviewers thought about his work, though as would be his lifelong habit, he was reluctant to admit being concerned over the verdict of 'periodical censors'. *Hours of Idleness*, which sold well enough to warrant a second edition, received seventeen reviews, with the generally favourable far outnumbering the unfavourable. But two reviews were stingingly negative: Hewson Clark's in the *Satirist* and, far more wounding, Henry Brougham's anonymous assessment in the *Edinburgh Review*. Under the editorship of Francis Jeffrey (whom Byron erroneously suspected as the hostile reviewer of his poems), the *Edinburgh* was both the pre-eminent organ of the Whigs, Byron's own political party, and the era's most distinguished purveyor of literary criticism – the first quarterly whose well-paid contributors were not hacks but professional men of letters and whose reviews were not publishers' puffs but thoughtful appraisals of literary practice. It is not surprising that young Byron's simultaneous invocation and repudiation of youthful, aristocratic privilege in his preface and his poetic pose of literary dilettante would provoke the scorn of a high-minded bourgeois journal's reviewer. Sure enough, Brougham took the poet-peer up on his preface's avowal that he would rather 'incur the bitterest censure of anonymous criticism, than triumph in honour granted solely to a title' (*CPW*, I, 34).

As Byron would later do, Brougham adopts a commonsense tone and allows the adolescent author's own prefatory and poetic words to damn him. To do so is not an especially difficult task when the author has called his volume a 'first, and last attempt', it being 'highly improbable from my situation, and pursuits hereafter, that I should ever obtrude myself a second time on the Public' (*CPW*, I, 34). After subjecting the poems to cool scrutiny, the *Edinburgh* reviewer dismisses the poetical peer with a mocking bow: 'We are well off to have got so much from a man of this Lord's station, who does not live in a garret but "has the sway" of Newstead Abbey.'[2]

Byron was not the first or last young writer to be caught in the act of embarrassing self-revelation. He learned from his humiliation at the hands of reviewers, and his literary career changed accordingly. Brougham's review taught him to distinguish private poems, the occasional verses sent to friends or circulated in a coterie, from candidates for publication. More immediately, the work then in progress, his Horatian satire *British Bards*, took a tack toward the Juvenalian and became *English Bards and Scotch Reviewers*. As the pairing in the title suggests, the satire attacked not only the weaknesses of his fellow poets but also the tyranny of the *Edinburgh*'s critics. From first to last, Byron was inclined to oppose rather than support established power, and in *English Bards* he sets himself against the growing authority of Jeffrey and the *Edinburgh Review*, the 'Judge of Poesy' and his seat of judgement, the most influential of the literary reviews that in Byron's day were setting the standards and tastes for a rapidly growing reading public. The authority Byron invokes is not that of the aristocratic amateur whose name alone should inspire respect. He published anonymously (until public approbation encouraged him to put his name on the amplified second edition), and his nameless voice utters the savage indignation of a commonsensical everyman. *English Bards* forswears the amateur pose of *Hours of Idleness*. Lord Byron turns pro.

But much of his lordly loftiness remains, as it would throughout his publishing career. Byron delegated the task of locating and dealing with a publisher and handling the details of turning manuscript to book to an intermediary more prosaic than his poetical self, a fawning distant kinsman named Robert Charles Dallas, to whom he assigned the royalties. Having put his name to the unrepentantly vitriolic, vastly enlarged (from 696 lines to 1,050) second edition, Byron embarked on an extended tour to the East with his friend John Cam Hobhouse – and in light of his absence and the poem's continued popularity, his publisher James Cawthorn brought out unemended third and fourth editions. Back from his travels in 1811, Byron slightly revised the second edition for a forthcoming fifth, which he eventually decided to suppress at the wish of Lord Holland – a diplomatic move for a young man hoping to get on in Whig politics. Cawthorn, first of Byron's many would-be pirates, had to be restrained from continuing to issue copies. Byron eventually came to disavow many of the satire's jaundiced opinions, including its invective against Francis Jeffrey; but if suppressing the poem ingratiated Byron with Holland's Whigs, writing and publishing it had earned him the favour of Tory readers. Thus *English Bards* had the presumably uncalculated effect of perfectly paving the way for a partnership between the poet Byron and the publisher John Murray. This long-standing relationship was to be the most significant single determinant of Byron's publishing life.

The 1812 debut of *Childe Harold's Pilgrimage* was the most dramatic event in two publishing careers: Byron's and Murray's. On first view, one might be surprised by the symbiotic relation, begun with *Childe Harold* and continued for over a decade, between the liberal poet-peer who saw himself as 'born for opposition' and the conservative publisher whose non-Byronic offerings included the *Quarterly Review* (Tory counterpart and rival of the Whig *Edinburgh*) and the Admiralty's Navy List. There seems to be an element of serendipity in Murray's publication of *Childe Harold*'s first two cantos, which Byron's factotum Dallas offered him only after Longman and Company and William Miller had rejected them. Ironically, the profits from *Childe Harold* enabled Murray's purchase of Miller's copyrights, book stock, and fashionably located publishing house at 50 Albemarle Street. Here Murray established what would become one of the great London literary salons of the century – and thus gave Byron a base for enlarging his literary acquaintance outside the circles of Whig society. At 50 Albemarle Street, for instance,

Byron met and made peace with Walter Scott, mocked (despite being a Scots poet) in *English Bards*.

There may be an element of chance in *Childe Harold* ending up on the booklist of John Murray. Nonetheless, as Caroline Franklin argues, Byron had in several ways, whether deliberately or inadvertently, positioned himself to become a Murray author.[3] *English Bards and Scotch Reviewers*, with its central attack on Francis Jeffrey and the *Edinburgh Review* and its endorsement of the neoclassical standards of William Gifford, came out a mere month after the initial volume of the *Quarterly Review* edited by Gifford and published by Murray. Furthermore John Murray (second publisher to bear the name, which continues to this day) was, like Byron, eager to make a reputation. The evolving reputation of the house of Murray would be based in great part on travel literature. Byron's loco-descriptive poem was perfect for the firm that, among other things, had brought out Mungo Park's narrative of his African journey (1799) and that would publish Charles Darwin's account of the HMS *Beagle* voyage (1839).

Vividly recorded in both Byron's and Murray's correspondences and reminiscences, the decade-long relationship of poet and publisher was complicated, often gratifying, sometimes irritating, but ultimately reputation-enhancing for both parties. Murray's influence on Byron was practical, personal, financial, and editorial. If Byron more than any other author set the seal of fashion on Murray's booklist, Murray's shrewd yet generous way of dealing with Byron and his manuscripts was indispensable in making Byron his era's 'grand Napoleon of the realms of rhyme' – and the archetype of postmodern celebrity, a half-real hero crafted by the mediated interactions of artist and public. The publishing relationship of Byron and Murray ended up putting about £15,000 into the coffers of Byron or the designated beneficiaries of his copyrights. What the reading public gained from the partnership was *Childe Harold's Pilgrimage*, the Eastern tales, *The Prisoner of Chillon*, *Manfred*, *Beppo*, the first five cantos of *Don Juan*, most of the dramatic poems, and various shorter works.

During Byron's 'years of fame' (1812–16) and for some time beyond, Murray's diplomacy and pragmatism smoothed the way for the poet's triumphal chariot. Despite Byron's personal charisma, this way-smoothing was not a particularly easy task. In Byron, Murray took on an author who had spoken harshly against many of his fellow poets in *English Bards*, whose ambivalence about his own poetry-writing remained unresolved, and whose attitudes toward editorial advice and payment for publication were yet more perplexed. How to keep a poet with anti-commercial prejudices, 'tempestuous passions', and liberal Whig sentiments suitable for the list of a conservative publishing house and an elite readership? One brilliant strategy was to capitalize on the respect Byron (whose principles were Augustan even if his practice was Romantic) cherished for William Gifford.

As middleman between Byron and Gifford, Murray was able to pass on the old Tory satirist's reactions to Byron's drafts and suggestions for emending them in ways the poet, complain though he would, generally ended up finding acceptable. When he first learned that Murray had shown the manuscript of *Childe Harold* to Gifford, Byron was outraged by the possible appearance of trying to guarantee a good review in the *Quarterly*. He wrote in high dudgeon to Dallas:

> I *will* be *angry* with Murray, it was a bookselling, backshop, Paternoster Row, paltry proceeding, & if the experiment had turned out as it deserved, I would have raised all Fleetstreet and borrowed the Giant's staff from St. Dunstan's church, to immolate the betrayer of trust. – I have written to him, as he was never written to before by an author, I'll be sworn, & I hope you will amplify my wrath, until it has an effect upon him. (*BLJ*, II, 105)

Despite his assertion of independence (or perhaps because of having vented it), Byron was ultimately able to accept Gifford's suggestions. He even specified that Gifford be consulted about ensuing publications and that his advice should trump other editorial suggestions when differences of opinion arose. Gifford approved the publication of the subsequent cantos of *Childe Harold*. His editorial intervention can be discerned in *The Bride of Abydos*, *The Siege of Corinth*, *Manfred*, *Beppo*, *Marino Faliero*, and *Cain*. The sort of advice Byron would call 'absurd half and half prudery' when offered by Murray or others was acceptable when it came from Gifford, Byron's 'grand patron' even when the two disagreed over *Cain*: 'I know of no praise which would compensate me in my own mind for his censure' (*BLJ*, II, 218).

Byron continued to admire Gifford and respect his advice largely thanks to the tact of Murray, who transmitted (and filtered) both Gifford's opinions and Byron's reactions. In doing so, Murray sometimes served as lightning rod for Byron's authorial outrage. One such case involved the metaphysical drama *Manfred*. Byron, keeping faith with his Faustian sources, had written a third act full of anti-clericalism but agreed to a substantial rewrite on receiving Gifford's advice through Murray. After posting his revision under separate cover, Byron wrote to Murray on 5 May 1817, 'You will find I think some good poetry in this new act here & there – & if so print it – without sending me further proofs – *under Mr. G[iffor]d's correction* – if he will have the goodness to overlook it' (*BLJ*, V, 219). When the first printing appeared, Murray had, on Gifford's advice, omitted the dying Manfred's last speech: 'Old man! 'tis not so difficult to die' (*CPW*, VI, 102), a line reinforcing the contrarian nature of the hero as a dying man comforting a survivor, a younger man advising his elder, a sceptic instructing a priest on the ways of a good death. The omission infuriated Byron. 'You have destroyed the whole effect & moral of the poem by omitting the last line of Manfred's speaking, – & why this was done I know not' (*BLJ*, v, 257), he wrote to Murray on 12 August 1817.

Murray may well have felt aggrieved at the injustice of such a complaint. After all, he had only obeyed Byron's instructions to consult Gifford, follow his recommendations, and not bother the author with further proofs. But by enduring the unmerited if proverbial fate of messengers and mediators, the long-suffering publisher kept liberal Byron amenable to conservative advice, deferred the day when the poet's works would become unacceptable to decorous readers, and for a long time kept the *Quarterly*, which routinely pilloried other Whig writers, from turning against him. Thus Murray's 'bookselling, backshop, Paternoster Row' diplomacy accomplished precisely what Byron had suspected it would when Gifford's advice on *Childe Harold* was first solicited.

Murray's more direct interventions were just as important to the shape of Byron's literary career. He successfully encouraged Byron to tone down *Childe Harold*'s unorthodox religious statements and its antagonism to Wellington (for his role in the Peninsular campaign loathed by the Whigs), Elgin (for carrying off the Parthenon marbles now housed in the British Museum), and others, persuaded him to put his name on the poem, and by urging him to add the two promised cantos that would eventually complete the poem – 'It were cruel indeed not to perfect a work which contains so much that is excellent'[4] – Murray went on to shape Byron's choice of subjects through discreet suggestion. He published Byron's anonymous *Waltz* (1812) but did not like it – then pushed Byron back towards his proven strength, description of the East. The result: a rapidly composed sequence of tales – *The Giaour* and *The Bride of Abydos* in 1813, *The Corsair* and *Lara* in 1814, *The Siege of Corinth* and *Parisina* in 1816 – perfectly suited to capture the attention of an audience hungry for romantic narratives with exotic backdrops. Although Byron sometimes deprecated his Eastern tales as mere effusions and emphasized the artistic negligence of the works, he displayed a classically educated, gentlemanly concern for their matters of fact. Murray's opinion of the Eastern tales was higher, and having paid Byron's designee Dallas £600 for the copyright of *Childe Harold*'s first two cantos, he offered yet more for *The Giaour* and *The Bride*: 'I beg leave to offer you the sum of One Thousand Guineas; and I shall be happy if you perceive that my estimation of your talents in my character of a man of business is not much under my admiration of them as a man.'[5] Byron recorded the offer and his refusal of it with a blend of complacent pride and aristocratic deprecation: 'I won't – it is too much, though I am strongly tempted, merely for the *say* of it. No bad price for a fortnight's (a week each) what? – the gods know – it was intended to be called Poetry' (*BLJ*, III, 212). After refusing the funds, Byron asked that the payment go to Dallas, and when Murray took umbrage at such a transfer finally left the money with the publisher.

Byron succeeded in designating Dallas as the recipient of Murray's payment of 500 guineas for the copyright of *The Corsair*, a transaction on which the publisher did very well indeed. As he reported to Byron, 'I sold, on the day of publication, – a thing perfectly unprecedented – 10,000 copies.'[6] Eventually, however, Byron's 'pecuniary embarrassments' forced him to overcome his lordly reluctance to accept money for his poetry – but not before Murray demonstrated disinterested generosity in offering to buy the poet's library when it was up for sale in 1815 and to sell the copyrights he held and give Byron the resulting funds. Byron, though deeply moved, did not accept Murray's offer. In the same volatile vein, he declined as '*liberal* in the extreme . . . and much more than the two poems can possibly be worth' (*BLJ*, V, 13) the total of £1,000 Murray sent for the copyrights of *Siege of Corinth* and *Parisina* – then asked Murray to give £600 to William Godwin and to divide the remainder between Coleridge and Maturin. Murray protested that he would 'strain every nerve in your service, but it is actually heartbreaking to throw away my earnings on others'.[7]

In 1816, with his finances, marriage, and reputation in ruin and continental exile in the offing, Byron finally was obliged to accept Murray's £1,000 for his own use. Having taken the publisher's money, he never reverted to his old high-minded ways. On the contrary, as an expatriate Byron took pleasure in negotiating the terms of publication. Through his banker friend Douglas Kinnaird, he turned down the 1,500 guineas Murray offered for the third canto of *Childe Harold* and held out for 2,000. When Murray offered 1,500 for the fourth canto, Byron demanded 2,500, with *Beppo* thrown in 'to eke you out'. Byron gained 1,575 for the first two cantos of *Don Juan* plus the *Ode on Venice*, 1525 for cantos III–V of *Don Juan*, and 2,710 for *Cain*, *Sardanapalus*, and *The Two Foscari*.

Interestingly, Byron's increased keenness for moneymaking coincided with his long-delayed attainment of unencumbered prosperity. In 1817, Colonel Thomas Wildman at last had bought Newstead Abbey for 90,000 guineas – a sum that settled Byron's debts and left a residue that established a trust for Annabella and, invested in the 5 per cent funds, gave Byron an unearned £3,300 pounds per annum. Starting to care more about his writing income just when it became less necessary may seem perverse. But the sale of

Newstead that freed Byron of debt also stripped him of his status as landed lord, and a more professional attitude toward authorship may have arisen by default.

The expatriate Byron's changed relationship with Murray extended beyond taking more interest in payment for his poetry. No longer a charismatic physical presence in Whig society, Byron counted on cutting a long-distance dash in his old haunts by power of the pen. Writing from various Italian venues, Byron dispatched what Max Beerbohm plausibly called 'the best letters ever written – the fullest and most spontaneous'. Murray was the designated recipient of many of the most brilliant, detail-packed, verse-enriched letters because Byron was certain that the publisher would selectively circulate them. Impressed with Byron's epistolary travelogues, Murray asked for publishable prose and poetry in the same vein. 'Pray keep an exact Journal of all you see', he wrote, requesting 'faithful accounts of sights, curiosities, shows, and manners'.[8] Similarly, Murray asked for 'a poem – a good Venetian tale' – and evoked *Beppo*.[9] Requesting 'another lively tale like "Beppo"' or 'some prose in three volumes', Murray received, to his consternation, *Don Juan*.[10] Thus, with results that sometimes pleased Murray and sometimes distressed him, the old role of directing (or trying to direct) Byron's pen continued at long distance.

So did the job of correcting that pen's errors and turning manuscripts into books. In this matter Byron continued to be the high-maintenance author he had been from the outset, personally negligent in attending to petty details but peremptory in his demands for accuracy. Distance and the vagaries of the post aggravated the problem. Despite Murray's continued financial generosity, Byron's sustained productivity, and the mutual convenience of their epistolary relationship, poet and publisher quarrelled frequently between 1816 and 1822. Byron, who in this phase of life seems to have needed Murray more than Murray needed him, took the publisher to task for botching details of publication, delaying payments, and failing to reply to letters. Murray attributed his tardiness sometimes to constitutional indolence, sometimes to the pressures of his successful business: 'I am constantly harassed by shoals of MSS. poems – two, three, or four a day. I require a porter to carry, an author to read, and a secretary to answer them.'[11] But a deeper flaw was becoming evident in the relationship between Byron and Murray. Byron, who had always sailed too close to the wind for the prudent Murray's tastes, had moved ever farther out of the British mainstream. As Byron's liberalism, free-thinking, and cosmopolitan sophistication intensified, tastes back home had taken a moralistic turn. In reaction to radical insurgency, the Tory government had resorted to repressive measures aimed at curbing sedition, obscenity, and blasphemy, uttered or published. Thus it was not the best of times for a respectable London publisher to be associated with the expatriate leader of the so-called 'Satanic School of poetry'.

What were the material contingencies determining the publishing relationship of Byron and Murray? Briefly put, the Regency was an era of expensive books, expanding rights for those authors who could take advantage of copyright law, and increased activity of 'pirates', anti-establishment publishers who circumvented legal and commercial procedures to produce cheap editions for a mass market as hungry for books as were the ruling-class readers who bought costly quartos and the middle-class purchasers of the octavos and collected editions that would typically follow in the wake of the quartos. Looking at Byron's publications as material objects, produced and marketed by designated or undesignated publishers and purchased or borrowed by readers at various socio-economic levels, William St Clair has concluded that Byron's publications divide into two streams, with his scandalous 1816 marital separation and self-exile signalling the watershed.[12] An elite readership St Clair terms the 'romantic respectful' bought the relatively expensive editions of *Childe Harold* and the Eastern tales. This public admired Byron more as a poet of sentiment than as a champion of liberal ideas and politics. St Clair calls Byron's later readership the 'realistic subversive'. Drawn principally from the classes existing below the level of gentility, this readership valued Byron as a poet of freedom and purchased cheap, often illicit, editions of his works, with *Don Juan* being the runaway favourite. Not surprisingly, Murray's constant strategy was to steer Byron towards the discourse congenial to the first of these readerships and away from the discourse that would alienate them and appeal to the second reading public. Despite Murray's personal diplomacy and commercial prudence, though, his strategy proved increasingly unsuccessful after Byron turned his back on the homeland that had turned its back on him.

Several factors combined to make books relatively costly during Byron's publishing lifetime. Raw materials were expensive throughout the years when England was at war with Napoleonic France. The technological innovations of the Industrial Revolution were comparatively slow to influence book production. The 1814 Copyright Act, which lengthened the terms of copyright to twenty-eight years or the life of the author, whichever proved longer, kept prices high. Mainstream publishers like Murray produced and marketed books as luxury items for a relatively select audience. St Clair points out that at a time when a minimal gentleman's income was 100*s* a week and printers, the highest-paid skilled workers in Britain, received 36*s* a week, Murray's quarto of *Childe Harold* I and II was priced at 30*s* in wrappers, 50*s* bound.[13] *Childe Harold* in octavo form was 12*s* in wrappers, 25*s* bound. Individual octavos of *The Giaour*, *The Bride of Abydos*, and *The Corsair* were 5*s* 6*d* in wrappers. The collected tales in octavo were 22*s* in wrappers, 32*s* bound. During this period, the cost of bread (main indicator of the British cost of living) remained close to its 1812 peak of 1*s* 8*d*. Accordingly, Byron's latest poem would be an expensive luxury item even for people living at the lower levels of gentility. Nevertheless, up through 1816 the market penetration of Byron's works proved remarkable. Sales figures suggest that Byron's bestseller, *The Corsair*, ended up on the shelves of 8 per cent of the households who could only just afford it.

Murray's system of publishing Byron's poems worked well prior to 1816; but after the scandalous break-up had alienated a cant-ridden reading public, production and sales figures show that Byron's works seldom went beyond a first edition. Despite this general decline in Byron's sales and despite general reluctance to publish *Don Juan* at all, in 1819 Murray produced *Don Juan*'s first two cantos according it the luxury strategy used for *Childe Harold*. Murray's prices did not allow *Don Juan* to trickle down to the populace, where the choice was between bread and books. Furthermore, in a legally cautious gesture that seemed to designate *Don Juan* illegitimate at birth, Murray had brought out an anonymous first edition carrying only the printer Davison's imprint. The circumstances were perfect for piracy.

Illicit publication had been a problem for Byron before *Don Juan*'s debut. In 1816 'Fare Thee Well!' and 'A Sketch from Private Life', poems associated with his marital separation which Byron had chosen to have printed and circulated privately by Murray, found their way via Byron's old nemesis Brougham into the hands of John Scott, were published without Byron's consent in *The Champion*, and later appeared in unauthorized pamphlets brought out by Richard Edwards and William Hone. The latter had also issued an unauthorized prose redaction of *The Corsair* to help the cause of Jeremiah Brandreth, a radical on trial for seditious acts. But *Don Juan* was uniquely suited to make trouble for Byron and Murray in the publishing world, as Hobhouse and the other first readers of the manuscript immediately recognized.

Hobhouse, in a long and tactful letter of 5 January 1819 presenting the collective verdict arrived at by himself, Douglas Kinnaird, Scrope Davies, and John Hookham Frere, acknowledges that Byron may have found his 'real forte in this singular style' but argues against publication, 'particularly as the objectionable parts are in point of wit humour & poetry the very best beyond all doubt of the whole poem'.[14] Byron's advisors feared that the details patterned on his own domestic circumstances and marital break-up, especially the thinly veiled portrait of Annabella in the priggish hypocrite Donna Inez, would repulse public opinion, which had begun to shift in Byron's favour. The half-real rake of a hero would make credulous readers believe the exaggerated rumours of Byron's continental dissipations. The irreverent and blasphemous passages, such as the parody of the Ten Commandments, would undercut Byron's position as a liberal satirist. The attacks on Southey and the other Lake Poets – all of whom ranked far below Byron in terms of contemporary literary prestige – would seem wanton and pointless. But Byron stood firm; and Murray, though apprehensive, obliged him. The defensive measures Murray enacted to avoid prosecution – producing a lavish, expensive (31*s*) quarto conspicuously lacking both Byron's and Murray's names – made the poem more vulnerable to piracy.

Only days after Cantos I and II of *Don Juan* appeared, Hone published *'Don John'; or, Don Juan Unmasked*, a self-described 'key to the mystery' with a 'descriptive review' and extracts. Later in 1819, Hone brought out *Don Juan, Canto the Third*, a quasi-continuation in which Don Juan sets up as radical publisher of a London periodical, *The Devilled Biscuit*. Soon after Hone, the Radical publishers J. Onwhyn and William Sherwin produced cheap 'exact copy' piracies of the quarto edition. Later piracies included Sherwin's of Cantos III–V, William Benbow's 2*s* 6*d* duodecimo of all five cantos, and similar collections by Hodgson and Company in 1822, Peter Griffin in 1823, and G. Smeeton in 1826. Cheap pirated editions pre-empted the success of Murray's octavo reprints, even at 9*s* 6*d* (1819) or 5*s* (1822); but the damage was not confined to Murray's pocketbook. Hone's parodic imitation of *Don Juan* did to Murray the establishment publisher ('Drab John' in *Canto the Third*) exactly what Byron had done to Southey the establishment poet in *Don Juan*. Byron's *Don Juan* had appropriated the rhetoric of radicalism, but Hone's imitation recaptured that discourse. His parodic piracy had the democratic effect, as Kyle Grimes observes, of levelling peer and commoner, respectable publisher and radical press.[15] Similarly, it seemed to a *Quarterly* reviewer, the pirate publications drastically changed *Don Juan*'s moral impact by changing its circumstances of distribution. Legally published, the poem would reach an audience of readers 'who would have turned with disgust from its indecencies and remembered only its poetry and wit'. Pirated and sometimes augmented with 'obscene engravings', the poem would reach purchasers 'who would treasure up all its evil without comprehending what it contains of good. "Don Juan" in quarto and on hot-pressed paper would have been almost innocent – in a whity brown duodecimo it was one of the worst of the mischievous publications that have made the press a snare.'[16]

When it became evident that *Don Juan* was not selling well in large quarto, Byron offered to reimburse Murray for the copyright (an offer the publisher declined) but urged him not to seek an injunction against unauthorized publication. Byron feared that if the legal action went against them it would jeopardize his custodial rights over his daughter Ada. Despite Byron's fears, Murray took legal action; and as it turned out the Lord Chancellor found in his favour. Nonetheless, the chronic problems associated with *Don Juan* slowly killed the publishing relationship of Byron and Murray.

Faced with profit-reducing piracy and scurrilous mockery from the radicals and sanctimonious disapproval and looming threats of legal prosecution from the conservatives, Murray became increasingly reluctant to publish Byron manuscripts in which he detected potential controversy. He brought out the biblical mystery *Cain* only because Byron had refused to allow *The Two Foscari* and *Sardanapalus* to appear without it: 'I presume that the *three plays* are to be published together – ' Byron warned, 'because if not – I will not permit their *separate* publication' (*BLJ*, IX, 59). Just after this triple publication *Cain* was pirated by the radical Benbow. Murray applied for an injunction and eventually received it – but only after suffering the humiliation of Lord Eldon's initial decision against him, followed by Benbow's gloating formal announcement of his *Cain* piracy in the March 1822 *Rambler's Magazine*.

In light of his setbacks in the marketplace and the courts, Murray refused to publish both Byron's second mystery play *Heaven and Earth*, which he had ready in print, and *The Vision of Judgment*, a brilliant but potentially actionable satire demolishing *A Vision of Judgement*, Southey's hack apotheosis of George III. On receiving Cantos VI–VIII of *Don Juan*, Murray reacted with uncharacteristically blunt revulsion: 'I declare to you they were so outrageously shocking that I would not publish them if you were to give me your estate – Title and Genius.'[17] Eventually taking Murray at his word, Byron ended the publishing relationship that had done so much for them both. 'I shall withdraw from you as publisher, on every account, even on your own, and I wish you good luck elsewhere' (*BLJ*, X, 36). Murray was not quite through with Byron's manuscripts – contrary to the poet's instructions to hand over all unpublished works to John Hunt, he brought out the uncontroversial drama *Werner* in November 1822 – but his circumspection had at last driven Byron by default into the radical camp.

It is deeply ironic that Byron, who had repeatedly deprecated the publishing trade, should, like Murray, become proprietor of a journal – and that having so often professed to despise reformers while favouring Reform he should ally himself with the Radicals more closely than Hobhouse, whom he had teased and scolded for doing so, ever had. But that is just what happened. As publication of his controversial works became increasingly problematic, Byron began to think of starting his own newspaper, a potential collaboration he mentioned to Thomas Moore as early as 1820. When plans for a periodical took more definite shape in 1822, Byron was in close contact with the Shelley circle at Pisa. Largely due to Shelley's influence, the two poets invited Leigh Hunt and his family to join them in Italy, from whence the three would issue a quarterly to be called *The Liberal*. Byron admired Hunt as an anti-establishment poet and journalist who had suffered imprisonment for his political principles and had supported Byron throughout the separation scandal. But the two men were not closely acquainted, and when they had to live and work together their temperaments proved incompatible. The sophisticated aristocrat who had developed a good head for business could not coexist amicably with the Cockney Radical whose children were as ill-regulated as were his finances. To have collaborated smoothly on *The Liberal*, Byron and Hunt would have needed the mediation of Shelley. But Shelley's tragic fate was to drown on 8 July 1822, only days after Hunt and his family arrived to take up residence with Byron at Casa Lanfranchi. For personal reasons, then, *The Liberal* was crippled before its first issue was even planned. Hostile reviewers' attacks on the first number, friends' disapproval of his association with the Hunts, and financial problems caused when the second number failed to recoup its production costs deepened Byron's doubts of the venture and his own part in it.

Nonetheless, had it continued as it began, *The Liberal* might well have become a left-wing counterpart to the *Edinburgh* and the *Quarterly*. The first two of its four issues contained some of the strongest progressive writing to appear in the 1820s. Byron's own contributions to the first numbers included *The Vision of Judgment* and *Heaven and Earth*, both of which Byron had insisted that Murray hand over to Leigh Hunt's brother John, the Radical publisher charged with bringing out *The Liberal*. Having lost his star author to John Hunt, Murray exacted a passive–aggressive revenge by ignoring Byron's explicit instructions and giving Hunt the original manuscript rather than the revised and softened proofs, which included a preface intended to stave off prosecution by explaining the poem as an attack on the living laureate rather than the dead king. Byron became aware of Murray's omission only when *The Liberal* made its debut. On 24 October 1822, he angrily wrote charging Murray with either a breach of trust or an act of '*culpable* negligence' (*BLJ*, x, 17). On 3 November, Hunt's *Examiner* announced Murray's having 'contrived to evade sending the preface to the present publisher'. Byron's fears about the prefaceless poem turned out to be well founded: the Constitutional Association charged Hunt as publisher with libelling the late king. When finally tried in 1824, Hunt was found guilty, though his punishment (a £100 fine) was relatively light. The mere act of indictment, however, had cleared the way for publishing pirates to have their way with *The Vision*.

The Liberal turned out to be a failed attempt at progressive activism. It left Leigh Hunt embittered by the withdrawal of Byron's patronage and no richer than when he and his family had left England. It involved John Hunt in legal battles. It discouraged Byron, who believed that 'the two pieces of my contribution have precipitated that failure more than any other' (*BLJ*, x, 123). In terms of *Don Juan*, though, the new publishing connection with John Hunt proved beneficial. Byron offered the six completed but unpublished cantos of *Don Juan* to Hunt, who would receive a percentage of the profits, with Byron retaining the copyright and publishing at his own risk. The bargain thus struck was good for both the composition and the publication. Freed from his complicated relationship with the deferential but censorious Murray circle, Byron composed the last cantos rapidly, with little of the revising and expanding that had characterized earlier cantos. One reason for this increased fluency may be that, allying himself with a Radical publisher, Byron was able to shed any remaining ambivalence about the subversive nature of his poem.

Byron's single-mindedness appears in the prose preface to Cantos VI–VIII, a defiant avowal of pride in the title of blasphemer conferred by a cant-ridden literary and political establishment. And Canto IX's mocking invocation of Wellington ('Vilainton'), who quite apart from having defeated Napoleon had founded the Constitutional Association for prosecuting seditious publishers, offers a clear and confrontational announcement that Byron's poem is beginning anew with this, the first canto never submitted to Murray. Furthermore, the marketing strategy Byron had unsuccessfully urged on Murray was acceptable to Hunt, whose four-volume publication of Cantos VI–VIII (July 1823), IX–XI (August 1823), XII–XIV (December 1823), and XV–XVI (March 1824) appeared in three affordable versions aimed at a mass readership: demi-octavo at *9s 6d*, foolscap octavo at *7s*, and 'common edition' at *1s*. Even these prices failed to discourage piracies, but the change in circumstances of publication shows how far Byron had come since the Years of Fame when he had been 'a ball-room bard, a foolscap, hot-press darling' whose works were produced for and marketed to the elite and respectable.

After his death, however, Byron rejoined the John Murray catalogue of authors. Murray commissioned Thomas Moore to produce a life-and-letters, purchased Byron's remaining copyrights (apart from a portion of *Don Juan*), and brought out the first collected edition of his poetical works in 1830. Along with Hobhouse and other advisors, Murray also played a crucial role in the most important non-publication of Byron's posthumous career. The manuscript memoirs Byron had entrusted to Moore were, after heated discussion among Byron's relations and closest friends, burned in the fireplace of 50 Albemarle Street, the very address from which so many of Byron's written words, published and non-published alike, had issued forth into the world.

NOTES

1. Some of the material in this essay has previously appeared in Peter W. Graham, *Lord Byron* (New York: Twayne; London: Prentice Hall, 1998). Quotations from John Murray's correspondence come from Samuel Smiles, *A Publisher and His Friends: Memoir and Correspondence of the Late John Murray, with an Account of the Origin and Progress of the House, 1768–1843*, 2 vols. (London, 1891).
2. Henry Brougham, unsigned review, *Edinburgh Review*, 40 (January 1808), 285–9. Reprinted in Andrew Rutherford (ed.), *Byron: The Critical Heritage* (New York: Barnes and Noble, 1970), 28, 22.
3. Caroline Franklin, *Byron: A Literary Life* (London and New York: Macmillan and St Martin's Press, 2000), pp. 42–7.
4. Smiles, *Memoir and Correspondence*, p. 208.
5. *Ibid.*, p. 221.
6. *Ibid.*, p. 223.
7. *Ibid.*, p. 355.
8. *Ibid.*, p. 371.
9. *Ibid.*, p. 372.
10. *Ibid.*, p. 396.
11. *Ibid.*, p. 370.
12. William St Clair, 'The Impact of Byron's Writings: An Evaluative Approach', in Andrew Rutherford ed., *Byron: Augustan and Romantic*, (London: Macmillan, 1990).
13. Explaining the technical terms used in this recapitulation of William St Clair's argument would be obscure and interrupt the flow of ideas, so all such terms are defined here together. 'Quarto', 'octavo', and 'duodecimo' all refer to book size, which at the time was generally determined by how many times a sheet of paper was folded. Two folds in a sheet would produce a unit called a 'signature' with four 'leaves' and eight 'pages' and thus constitute a quarto. Three folds, resulting in a signature with eight leaves and sixteen pages, would make an octavo. A duodecimo would contain a signature of twelve leaves and twenty-four pages. Obviously, the larger formats tended to be the more expensive. Words such as 'foolscap' and 'demy' would further specify the size of the book. These terms refer to the size of a sheet of paper. 'Foolscap' sheets range from 12 in × 15 in to 13½ in × 17 in. 'Demy' or 'demi' sheets range from 15½ in × 20 in to 18 in × 23 in. Thus a 'demi octavo' book would be larger than a 'foolscap octavo'. The terms 'bound' versus 'wrappers' have to do with the book's cover. 'Bound' books would be in the publisher's binding, whereas those in 'wrappers' would be paperbacks, which buyers would typically have custom-bound, often in materials, colours, and styles uniform with other books in their collections.
14. John Cam Hobhouse, *Byron's Bulldog: The Letters of John Cam Hobhouse to Lord Byron*, ed. Peter W. Graham (Columbus: Ohio State University, 1984), pp. 256–62.

15. Kyle Grimes, 'William Hone, John Murray, and the Uses of Byron', in Stephen C. Behrendt (ed.), *Romanticism, Radicalism, and the Press* (Detroit: Wayne State University Press, 1997), p. 200.
16. Hugh J. Luke, 'The Publishing of Byron's *Don Juan*', *PMLA*, 80 (1965), 202.
17. Quoted in Leslie A. Marchand, *Byron: A Biography* (New York: Knopf, 1957), III, 1040.

3

MALCOLM KELSALL

Byron's politics

'Ambition was my idol', Byron wrote, looking back to his 'hot youth – when George the Third was King' (*Don Juan*, I.212.8). That ambition had been political. As an hereditary legislator of the British Empire, he had hoped to sway the destiny of nations by the power of oratory. His classical education offered the examples of men like Demosthenes in Greece and Cicero in Rome. Among his elder contemporaries were figures such as Henry Grattan, a founding father of the Irish 'patriot' parliament, and Byron's friends, Richard Brinsley Sheridan, the eloquent manager of the impeachment of Warren Hastings, and Thomas Erskine, the famous advocate of freedom of speech. A greater ambition yet might move a young man called by the duty of rank to public service. The statesman might also be a war leader and a maker of nations. The pre-eminent example for the age was George Washington and, for a European aristocrat, the example of Washington's ally, the Marquis de la Fayette, was close behind. More dangerously dazzling was the career of the disastrous comet, Napoleon Bonaparte and the meteoric disaster of the Irish revolutionary, Lord Edward Fitzgerald.

Byron's political affiliations were to the Whig party in opposition and began at Cambridge where he was a member of a small and intimate political circle including the Duke of Devonshire, Lord Tavistock, John Cam Hobhouse (the future Lord Broughton), and Douglas Kinnaird. In London he was recruited by the Holland House circle where he was indoctrinated in the hagiography of the great dead Whig leader, Charles James Fox, Lord Holland's uncle and mentor. It was Lord Holland who was instrumental in promoting Byron's inaugural speech in the House of Lords. In the circle of Lady Oxford, he moved towards the more radical wing of the party represented by Sir Francis Burdett and John Horne Tooke (who had been tried for high treason and acquitted, 1794). That radicalism was demonstrated by his symbolic action in visiting Leigh Hunt in jail (imprisoned for libelling the Prince Regent). Hunt was to be his future collaborator on the political journal *The Liberal* (in which *The Vision of Judgment* was first published).

Byron's association with the Whigs provided him with both an ideology and a discourse of 'liberty'. His political position was rooted in the mythology of the 'Glorious Revolution' of 1688/9. As a political party, the Whigs had originated in opposition to what was described as Stuart 'tyranny'. They drew upon a teleological view of history in which the forces of liberty (enshrined in the 'ancient constitution' of the free Saxon peoples) were locked in a long struggle with the powers of oppression (now represented by those adherents of 'passive obedience' to the Crown nominated as 'Tories'). Certain great historical landmarks had recorded the advance of the principles of liberty, witness the acceptance by King John of Magna Carta, or John Hampden's refusal to pay the tax of ship money to Charles I on the emergent principle of 'no taxation without representation'. The revolution of 1688/9 had guaranteed the rule of law as sanctioned by parliament (with the monarch as the chief 'magistrate' in a 'balanced' constitution of King, Lords, and Commons). A Bill of Rights guaranteed the life, liberty, and the property of the subject. Among such essential 'rights' (it was claimed) were freedom of speech, the freedom of the subject to petition for redress of grievances, freedom from arbitrary arrest (habeas corpus) and trial by jury. In practice many of these rights were to prove extremely fragile (Roman Catholics, for instance, were excluded from the body politic) but the foundational principles of 'resistance' to the arbitrary power of the Crown and of the 'rights' of the subject continued to shape the Whig thinking during the eighteenth century. The classic formulation of party principle was John Dunning's motion passed in the House of Commons (1780): 'The power of the Crown has increased, is increasing, and ought to be diminished.' Famous among Byron's older contemporaries had been the case of the Whig hero, John Wilkes, imprisoned for criticising the Crown as 'prostitute' (*The North Briton*, 45, 23 April 1763) and the attacks on the abuses of power by George III and his ministers in the 'Junius' *Letters* (1769–72).

Whig principles were internationalised by the revolt of the British colonists in North America. The men of property who led the revolution (great plantation owners like Washington) used (and applied) the by then well-established discourse of Whig opposition. They drew their examples from the classic authorities of the Glorious Revolution (figures like Hampden and Algernon Sydney) but radically linked with more obviously republican figures such as John Milton and John Harrington. Thomas Jefferson's vitriolic abuse of the tyranny of George III in the Declaration of Independence is directly in the tradition of Whig polemic, as was his declaration, inscribed in his Memorial in Washington, DC: 'I have sworn upon the altar of God eternal hostility against every form of tyranny over the mind of man.' The first ten amendments to the American Constitution derive from the Whig Bill of Rights and, historically, led to the Declaration of the Rights of Man and of the Citizen of the French Revolution.

It was the impact upon the Whig party of the revolution in France which provided the last great moments of heroic opposition (of which Byron was the late heir) and which broke the Whigs as a political force. The rise of Jacobinism in France, and the consequent 'radicalisation' of British politics, fundamentally changed the signification of Whig opposition to 'the Crown'. There was a substantial gap between the claim of great Whig lords to act as 'the friends of the people' (and the defenders of property) and, in France, the execution of the monarch and the aristocracy, the confiscation of property and the proclamation of universal republican war. Meantime, in Britain, the political establishment was challenged by a developing working-class movement, philosophically based on Thomas Paine's *The Rights of Man*, and, in practical terms, demanding a 'democracy' based on universal male suffrage and the delegation of members to annual parliaments. This threatened the established constitution with what the 'Tories' called 'anarchy'.

The dilemma for the Whigs was that the ideology and discourse of the party was potentially republican in its application (as the North American revolution had shown), but, in practice, their power and property was intrinsically interwoven with the maintenance of the so-called 'balanced' constitution between King, Lords, and Commons. They were caught, therefore, between the upper and nether millstones of 'Tory' reactionism and the Jacobinical 'radicals' (the political use of the word originates about this time). In keeping with the 'principles' of 1688/9 the party leader, Charles James Fox, welcomed both the American and the French revolutions. Accordingly, the Foxite wing of the Whigs opposed war with France. Sir James Mackintosh's defence of the revolution, *Vindiciae Gallicae* (1791) and Erskine's criticism of British war policy, *On the Causes and Consequences of the War with France* (1797), were to become key texts underpinning Byron's subsequent support for Napoleon. But this theoretical position became increasingly difficult to sustain. The threat from France (militarily and ideologically) caused the overwhelming majority of the Whig opposition to adopt the 'Tory' position. Eventually, the rump of the Foxite Whigs in 1797 seceded in despair from parliament. Apart from a brief spell in coalition after the death of the great war leader, William Pitt, the Whigs no longer existed as a force.

This was the party which Byron joined in 1812. It seemed an opportune moment. The establishment of the Regency because of the insanity of George III appeared to open a window of opportunity for the Whigs, for the Prince Regent had numerous friends among the opposition. Byron himself had assiduously prepared himself for a political career. Before embarking on his Grand Tour in 1809, he had already attended the House of Lords seven times, and his list of essential reading had included the parliamentary debates from the heartland of the Whig/Tory struggles of 1688 to 1745. On his return to Britain he attended all the major debates between January and July 1812 and also some of the minor work of committees. His maiden speech was on 27 February 1812, when he was chosen to lead a debate for the opposition on industrial unrest in his home county of Nottinghamshire. Unemployment among the stocking-knitters had provoked major civil disorder (the 'Luddite' riots) and the government was in process of introducing a Bill to make the breaking of the new manufacturing machinery a capital offence. The Whig position, as 'friends of the people', was that conciliation of grievances would be more effective than hanging workers. They proposed instead a committee of enquiry.

Byron spoke again on two other classic Whig issues. On 21 April 1812, in conjunction with his party, he advocated the removal of the residual constitutional disabilities from Roman Catholic subjects of the United Kingdom (Byron concentrated upon the position of the Catholic majority in Ireland). Finally, on 1 June 1813, he briefly presented a plea for freedom to petition on behalf of the veteran campaigner for parliamentary reform, Major John Cartwright. Cartwright claimed to have been harassed by the authorities during one of his campaigns. Consideration of his petition might have led to debate on the perennial Whig topic of reform of parliament (by a moderate extension of the franchise among men of property). Thereafter Byron's most significant action was to vote with the forty-four peers, led by Lord Grey, who on 23 May 1815 opposed renewal of war against Napoleon after the emperor's escape from Elba (the 'Hundred Days' which culminated in the battle of Waterloo).

The two major speeches (on the 'Luddites' and on the position of Roman Catholics in Ireland) are characterised by deep compassion for the sufferings of the common people and by an eloquent invective against the tyranny of the government. In context of the normal manner of proceeding of the House, however, they are out of kilter. The established mode of the Lords was formal and proceeded by 'mutual politeness' (to adopt Byron's own description in *The Vision of Judgment*, line 280). It was not the custom of the House, for instance, to liken Lord Liverpool to 'that Athenian lawgiver [Draco] whose edicts were said to be written . . . in blood' (in the Luddite debate), nor to warn the government (in the Catholic debate) that they were traitors to the people whose heads might end up on 'the greedy niches' of Temple Bar. This kind of invective in the House was supported by a series of poetical squibs, some anonymous or not written *in propria persona*. Of the latter kind, the 'Song for the Luddites' (1816) is the most violent:

> As the Liberty lads o'er the sea
> Bought their freedom, and cheaply, with blood,
> So we, boys, we
> Will die fighting, or live free,
> And down with all kings but King Ludd!

This was way off the scale of acceptable Whig polemic and unpublishable. It flirts dangerously with 'Jacobinism'. The argument, ultimately, is that the 'anarchy' which the government seeks to repress was, in fact, justly provoked by the very tyranny of the government.

How seriously did Byron subscribe to the revolutionary tendency of what he said? Thomas Moore, in his *Life* of Byron, tells how the poet came to see him 'in a state of the most humorous exaltation' after delivering the Cartwright petition.

> 'I told them', he said, 'that it was a most flagrant violation of the Constitution – that, if such things were permitted, there was an end of English freedom, and that – ' – 'but what was this dreadful grievance?' I asked . . . 'the grievance?' he repeated, pausing as if to consider – 'Oh, *that* I forget'.
>
> (Moore, *Life*, 1832, II, 207)

Such flippancy is hard to reconcile with the passion of the parliamentary rhetoric. It suggests that Byron saw his invective as a kind of superheated discourse of 'English freedom' easily turned on or off. Alternatively, the self-subversion suggests that by the summer of 1813 Byron was already disenchanted with what he called the 'mummeries' of parliamentary government.

There was reason for the disenchantment. Whig reliance on the patronage of the Prince Regent proved unfounded. He continued with his father's administration. Meantime, Byron had been unsuccessful on every major issue on which he had spoken. Machine-breaking had been made a capital offence; Catholic emancipation was rejected (and not fully achieved until after Byron's death); Cartwright's petition was rejected. In the Luddite debate, Byron was studiously insulted by the administration, which did not deign even to respond to his speech; in the affair of the Cartwright petition, even members of his own party spoke against him. Perhaps most symptomatic of the gap between rhetoric and reality were the results of his one partial success. The Whig proposal for enquiry into the Luddite disturbances was accepted. Consequentially, 'A Bill for Preventing Fraud and Abuses in the Frame-work Knitting Manufacture, and in the Payment of Persons Employed Therein' was introduced in the summer of 1812. It was totally emasculated. One of the leading opponents of this 'mistaken and mischievous' Bill was Lord Holland, Byron's mentor who had put him up to lead for the Whigs in February. Embarrassing the administration was one thing; interference in the conditions of trade was something quiet alien to the aristocrats at Holland House. Byron himself did not speak in the debate. He relieved his feelings in a poem to Lady Melbourne, 21 September 1813:

> 'Tis said – *Indifference* marks the present time,
> Then hear the reason – though 'tis told in rhyme –
> A King who *can't* – a Prince of Wales who *don't* –
> Patriots who *shan't* – and Ministers who *won't* –
> What matters who are *in* or *out* of place
> The *Mad* – the *Bad* – the *Useless* – or the *Base*?
>
> (*BLJ*, III, 117)

But the nadir of Byron's political career was marked by his paralysis during the Napoleonic Hundred Days. Although he voted with the rump of forty-four Whigs against renewal of the war, he remained silent in the House of Lords. How might one explain that silence? He had always admired the French emperor from the time when he had fought for his bust of Napoleon while a schoolboy at Harrow. Moreover, it is with great issues of European politics that Byron's name is associated both as a poet and a man of action. In addition, there was substantial pressure exerted on the poet to go public in support of Napoleon. Byron's friend, Hobhouse, was in Paris during the Hundred Days and in correspondence with the poet and parliamentarian. Hobhouse's letters were classically Whig. The events of 1688/9 were being repeated in France. The Bourbons, held in power by the bayonets of the monarchical powers of Europe, were like the tyrannical Stuarts of old. Napoleon was a liberator like William III, called to govern by the mandate of the people. As a great European statesman, now become a Constitutional ruler, he represented the best hope for the establishment of liberal policies in his country. It was unacceptable for Britain to interfere in the internal affairs of France. Hobhouse's letters were written to move Byron and public opinion and were subsequently collected (and revised) as *The Substance of Some Letters Written by an Englishman Resident at Paris during the Last Reign of the Emperor Napoleon* (1816). The second edition (1817) eventually revealed Byron's name as the principal recipient. But during the entire crisis of the Napoleonic restoration, Byron did no more than leak some of the correspondence anonymously to Leigh Hunt's opposition journal *The Examiner*. He voted against renewal of the war but otherwise kept his head down. In verse, nothing appeared until after Waterloo, and then in squibs published anonymously in *The Examiner* and *The Morning Chronicle* (the standard Whig newspaper). He only went public in the *Poems* of 1816 and *in propria persona* in the famous Waterloo stanzas of *Childe Harold* III.

The reasons for Byron's paralysis in 1815 are complex (not least the sexual and financial mess of his personal life). As far as party politics are concerned, however, the Hundred Days provide the clearest of indications of the impasse to which the Whig opposition had been brought. Hobhouse's historical Whig paradigm was irrelevant. The simple fact was that restoration of Napoleon meant war. If the emperor were defeated, the *ancien régime* would be restored. That had always been the war aim of the Allies. If Napoleon won, then, in Lord Holland's words, 'we must have twenty years more war'. It was, on the European scene, the same aporia between 'tyranny' or 'anarchy' which paralysed Whig attempts on the domestic front. It is a reasonable guess that Byron, after three years in politics, was sufficiently astute to perceive the cause of the paralysis. There was nothing he could say. But there is another possibility for his silence. He did not have the guts to get up in the House of Lords and speak out.

Byron's political career, therefore, is a record of failure ending in inarticulateness. There are a couple of exciting 'burns' of humanitarian rhetoric and indignant invective in the Luddite and Catholic debates, but they resemble a kind of hot-air ballooning. He was not fit for the long haul. In part this was the result of circumstance. The Whigs could offer nothing more than a rhetoric of opposition; and there were elements in the party who preferred it that way. But there is also an element of wilful nihilism in Byron's political career, as if the external impasse found a correspondent psychological response. His journal for 16 January 1814 provides a typical example:

> I have simplified my politics into an utter detestation of all existing governments; and, as it is the shortest and most agreeable and summary feeling imaginable, the first moment of an universal republic would convert me into an advocate for single and uncontradicted despotism. The fact is, riches are power, and poverty is slavery all over the earth, and one sort of establishment is no better, nor worse, for a *people* than another.

Even more nihilistic is his explosion of tragic rage of 19 April 1814:

> the Bourbons are restored!!! – 'Hang up philosophy'. To be sure, I have long despised myself and man, but I never spat in the face of my species before – 'O fool! I shall go mad'.

The tragic role he would assume here is that of the dispossessed and powerless monarch, King Lear (a fantastic and gross exaggeration of his role as a statesman). More provocative, and utterly self-destructive in relation to domestic politics, was his pretence of being the British equivalent of Napoleon Bonaparte. His post-Waterloo departure into 'exile' (provoked in fact by debts and sexual scandal) was marked by his commissioning of a replica of Napoleon's own coach in which Byron embarked on Childe Harold's second European tour (of necessity avoiding France). It was an analogy he was to develop later by signing his letters N[oel] B[yron] and by his claim to be the 'grand Napoleon of the realms of rhyme' (*Don Juan*, XI.55.8). This myth-building suggests a form of self-fashioning developed as a compensation for the utter failure, in the real world, of the 'idol' of his own political 'ambition'.

Although Byron's role in British party politics was insignificant, yet, as part of the education of a poet's mind his experiences were fundamental. They provided a schooling in scepticism about idealistic rhetoric and a bitter experience of failure. This experience might be readily generalised as paradigmatic of the age itself. This was a time which Shelley called in the Preface to *The Revolt of Islam* (1818) the 'age of despair', and Shelley, in *Julian and Maddalo* (written 1818, published 1824), dramatised Byron as the voice of that despair. Byron himself in a late, bitter political satire nominated the epoch, *The Age of Bronze* (1823). There had been a giant race before the flood, and he names as heroes the American Whigs Patrick Henry ('give me liberty, or give me death'), Benjamin Franklin, and George Washington. He associated these men with the Continental Congress of the American founding fathers. The American republic was now parodied by the reactionary Congress of the monarchical powers of Europe. Meantime, in Britain, the one preoccupation of the governing caste (the landed self-interest) was the preservation of their rents. Reform was a dead letter. The poem contains a long disquisition on the fall of Napoleon:

> A single step into the right had made
> This man the Washington of worlds betrayed;
> A single step into the wrong has given
> His name a doubt to all the winds of heaven.
>
> (*The Age of Bronze*, 233–6)

In a 'betrayed' Britain and Europe, it is little wonder that Byron's *Don Juan* begins with the demand 'I want a hero'.

Byron's personal attempt to reconstitute his own heroic status is associated with his commitment to direct-action anti-colonial politics in Italy and then in Greece. It is commonplace to describe Byron as a Foxite Whig at home (which is a party affiliation) and a constitutional nationalist abroad (to which the name 'Liberal' was given). The obvious attraction of direct-action politics in Europe was that they were freed (for Byron) from the class and party complexities of Britain. Single-issue demonstrations – Austrians 'out'; Turks 'out' – are much easier than, for instance, finding a *modus vivendi* for competing Catholic and Protestant interests in Ireland. But much of Byron's political verse remained more concerned with British political affairs (home thoughts from abroad) than the simplified, heart-on-sleeve, militant nationalism for which he is famous.

His writing after his 'exile' repeatedly revisits the topics and the problems of his years in the House of Lords either to rewrite the record as he would wish it to have been, or to come to terms with issues which still deeply perplexed him. As soon as he was abroad Byron relieved himself of some of the feelings suppressed during the Hundred Days. His account of the battle of Waterloo in *Childe Harold* III (1816) laments the fall of the flawed tragic hero, Napoleon, and declines to lend support to the triumphalist celebrations of the Duke of Wellington, represented, for instance, by Walter Scott's *The Field of Waterloo*, Robert Southey's *The Poet's Pilgrimage to Waterloo*, or William Wordsworth's *Ode* (1815). The poem, accordingly, might be read as a complaint by an anti-war Whig faced with a Tory victory. In Canto IV (1818), Hobhouse's notes radicalised the historical generalities of Byron's seemingly remote historical reflections on the fall of the Venetian and Roman republics. Britain's collusion with the reactionary continental imperial powers, it is claimed, had betrayed the cause of national revival in Italy (as elsewhere in Europe).

Subsequently, the Venetian plays, *Marino Faliero* and *The Two Foscari* (1821), were directly applied to British affairs. Byron's portrayal of the clash between a corrupt Senate and a disaffected populace was seized upon during the anti-monarchical turmoil generated by George IV's divorce proceedings against Queen Caroline. Domestic politics, and Whig party preoccupations, therefore, remained pervasive. Even the European cantos of *Don Juan* (1819–23) might be interpreted as loosely veiled allegories of what the original epigraph called in transparent Latin *domestica facta*. The domestic scene emerges directly in the derisive satire of the subsequent English cantos. These are concerned with the fundamental basis of establishment power, for Lord Henry Amundeville's country-house gathering (the central subject of the cantos) is not just a 'party' but is party political. The great landowner and placeman consolidates his electoral support by entertaining men of influence from London and in the locality. Equally essential is the 'marriage market' which operates at Norman Abbey, Lord Henry's home (ironically modelled on Byron's former estate at Newstead Abbey). It is upon dynastic relationships among the ruling caste that the political power of both Tories and

Whigs depends, and Lord Henry claims that he nicely hits the mean between 'place' (support for the Tories) and 'patriotism' (the rhetoric of Whig opposition). As an astute politician he speaks for 'middle' England (and, in fact, pursues his selfish interests in the name of the public weal).

In many respects, therefore, Byron's verse after his 'exile' is a continuation of the original adversarial stance he had taken in the House of Lords. He even characterised himself in *Don Juan* as a man 'born for opposition' (*Don Juan*, XIV.22.8). He had not deserted his earlier principles by leaving the country, so his apologetic claimed. It was apostate Britain which had left those principles of liberty enunciated by the successive revolutions of 1688/9, 1776 and 1789. On one side stood the hypocritical Lord Henrys of the age, against them are the working words of the spokesman of freedom. The great declarations of Byron's commitment to the historic Whig principle of 'liberty' were to become the most potent political elements in his writing. Moreover, in poetic utterance, the principle itself becomes liberated from the specifics of time and place, acquiring in Byron's provocative utterance a numinous and transhistorical resonance. Witness the sonnet on *The Prisoner of Chillon* (1816):

> Eternal Spirit of the chainless mind!
> Brightest in dungeons, Liberty! thou art,
> For there thy habitation is the heart –

These words are not specific merely to the case of one political prisoner, but apply to all the oppressed of the earth. It is essential, if Byron's politics are to be understood, that the power of poetry to free the spirit be recognised. He wrote that he warred with words because all other courses of action were closed to him (*Don Juan*, IX.24.1). Wherever 'Tyrants' or their 'Sycophants' exist, Byron's verse opposes the abuses of power. He is, in that respect, Jeffersonian in his 'eternal hostility against every form of tyranny over the mind of man'.

That concept of 'liberty', however, requires always something to oppose. Underlying the great utterances about the flag of 'Freedom' streaming like the thunderstorm against the wind (*CHP*, IV.98.2) there is a philosophy of history which depends upon the polarisation of events to extremes. (George III must be always nothing less than a tyrant, his laureate Southey always a sycophant.) These extremes, philosophically considered, always exist. The party political words 'Tory' and 'Whig', accordingly, acquire a universal signification in which they are bonded by mutual, transhistorical necessity. The Whig theorist, Thomas Jefferson, summarised the essential interrelationship between 'Tory' and 'Whig' in a letter to John Adams, 27 June 1813:

> Men have differed in opinion, and been divided into parties by these opinions, from the first origin of societies; and in all governments where they have been permitted freely to think and to speak. The same political parties . . . have existed thro' all time. Whether the power of the people, or that of the *aristoi* should prevail, were questions which kept the states of Greece and Rome in eternal convulsions: as they now schismatize every people whose minds and mouths are not shut up by the gag of a despot. And in fact the terms of whig and tory belong to natural, as well as to civil history.

This is an heroic (and convulsive) philosophy of history which functions by polarities, and, as Jefferson describes it, is necessary because it is intrinsic in the human psyche and, thus, in all human societies. It is, accordingly, a profoundly ironic philosophy because the liberationist ethic requires the hegemonic tendency to justify its opposition. You cannot have one without the other.

Hence the importance of the Satanic figure in Byron's verse, for Satan in rebellion against the power of God was the first 'Whig' and also, in Goethe's characterisation, eternally 'der Geist der stets verneint' ('the spirit that always denies', *Faust*, Part 1, 'Studierzimmer'). Whatever is must always be opposed. This Satanic irony structures Byron's profoundest political satire, *The Vision of Judgment* (1822). Here, George III is made to stand as the type of tyranny and the case against him is put by Satan with Jeffersonian fervour: 'The new world shook him off; the old yet groans / Beneath what he and his prepared' (*The Vision of Judgment*, 369–70). Yet it remains essential that Satanic rebellion does not succeed universally, for that would be to substitute the tyranny of the revolutionary ruler of hell for the tyranny of the status quo. Byron's poem, accordingly, creates a 'neutral space' (*The Vision of Judgment*, 257) between heaven and hell in which the forces of Tory and Whig remain perpetually suspended in unresolvable and necessary opposition.

Hence the irony of Byron's gloss in *Don Juan* on his existential dilemma as a man 'born for opposition':

> But then 'tis mostly on the weaker side:
> So that I verily believe if they
> Who now are basking in their full-blown pride,
> Were shaken down, and 'dogs had had their day',
> Though at the first I might perchance deride
> Their tumble, I should turn the other way,
> And wax an Ultra-royalist in loyalty,
> Because I hate even democratic royalty.
>
> (*Don Juan*, XV.23)

The price of liberty is eternal denial of all forms of hegemonic power whether of government or opposition. The aphorism 'Power tends to corrupt and absolute power corrupts absolutely' applies to Whig as much as to Tory. Ultimately it is not merely a philosophical theory but an existential imperative for the poet:

> I wish men to be free
> As much from mobs as kings, from you as me.
>
> (*Don Juan*, IX.25.7–8)

These lines seem proleptic of John Stuart Mill *On Liberty* (1859). But that is a history of liberalism which Byron did not live to see.

4

ANDREW ELFENBEIN

Byron: gender and sexuality

In 1997, when a friend of Andrew Cunanan wanted to defend the gay serial-killer's posthumous reputation, Byron helped him to make his case:

> I know people do not want to hear about [Cunanan's] good qualities, but I feel that if I don't say anything, no one will . . . The quality I most admired in him was his sensitivity. One of my most treasured possessions is a beautiful book of the poems of Lord Byron that he gave me on my 21st birthday.[1]

For this writer, invoking Byron raised Cunanan from the sordid world of drugs, violence, and queer sex with which the media surrounded him. Byron appears in his letter as an icon of high culture, a canonical British poet whose works appear in 'beautiful' books and are appreciated by sensitive men. While it would certainly be possible to read a gay subtext into this letter, in which giving a young man Byron's poems on his coming of age introduces a gay cultural past, the writer says nothing about sexuality, either his, Cunanan's, or Byron's. Instead, the gift of Byron's poems simply proves Cunanan's good character; a man who could like Byron and encourage others in that admiration could not be all bad.

Virtually no one in Byron's lifetime would have agreed. Especially after the publication of *Don Juan* and *Cain*, reading Byron's poetry seemed a sure path to damnation. About *Don Juan*, Cantos I and II, one reviewer wrote in 1819 that 'the deliberate purpose of the Author is to corrupt by inflaming the mind, to seduce to the love of evil'. According to him, Byron lured the reader to care about him, then immediately undercut the sympathy with 'the defiance of laughter'. In so doing, Byron let the reader 'know that all the Poet's pathos is but the sentimentalism of the drunkard between his cups, or the relenting softness of the courtesan, who the next moment resumes the bad boldness of her degraded character'.[2] The reviewer's metaphors reveal part of what made Byron so disturbing: his behaviour as a poet violated appropriate sex/gender roles. First, Byron appears as a sentimental drunkard, a man who has failed in his masculinity because he has succumbed to excess both in drinking and in his emotions. Second, Byron loses his masculinity to become a deceptive courtesan, who alternates between 'softness' and 'bad boldness'. For this reviewer, Byron's poetry was not merely immoral: it was unmanly.

Why did Byron's poetry create such gender panic? A complete answer would examine historical contexts (social, legal, religious, medical, political); Byron's biography, including his letters, journals, and the accounts of him by others; and his exceptionally varied *oeuvre*. Two valuable works from which I have learned much are Lewis Crompton's *Byron and Greek Love*, which describes the background of sodomy prosecution in Georgian England, Byron's affairs with other males, usually younger boys, and the relevance of 'Greek love' to his poetry; and Caroline Franklin's *Byron's Heroines*, which reads Byron's major female characters in relation to Regency cultural norms.[3] I will build on their work by discussing Byron and masculinity, especially his radical anti-didacticism and his insistence on masculine theatricality; I will then examine his representations of sexuality in terms of his transparent sexual coding. When describing taboo sexuality, Byron avoids direct naming but leaves little room for doubt in his reader's mind. In a characteristically Byronic way, he invites an interpretive struggle between knowledge and ignorance: the voyeuristic lure of discovering hidden sexual secrets versus the power that comes from not having to know what one knows about sex.[4]

In literary criticism, studying gender, as opposed to sex, means understanding how culture rather than biology defines masculine and feminine roles. In the English context, questions about gender arise in such areas as education (how have boys and girls been schooled?), religion (what has the Bible or the church said about good behaviour?), social mores (what have social leaders regarded as proper for men and proper for women?), legal prohibitions (what legal rights are available to men and not to women?), and social tradition (is the past a model for, or a warning about, men and women?). While most literary critics studying gender have concentrated on images of women, more recent criticism has begun to explore masculinity also. Byron's gift to masculinity is the notorious Byronic hero, the gloomy, brooding figure who scowls his way through his early poems. While the literary ancestors of the Byronic hero, such as Milton's Satan, are familiar, the Byronic hero's rebellion against standards of early nineteenth-century masculine behaviour deserves more attention.

Christian manliness dominated ideals of middle-class masculinity in the early nineteenth century. It set out to vanquish earlier models, such as the hard-living, rakish aristocrat (Samuel Richardson's Lovelace in *Clarissa* (1747–8)), the effeminate fop (Captain Whiffle in Tobias Smollett's *Roderick*

Random (1748)), or the hyper-emotional man of feeling (Henry Mackenzie's Harley in *The Man of Feeling* (1771) or Jane Austen's Willoughby in *Sense and Sensibility* (1811)). Its weapons were moral earnestness, sincerity, patriotic love of England as the haven of Protestant Christianity, and dedication to hard work and the family. Hannah More's wildly popular novel *Coelebs in Search of a Wife* (1809) modelled this new figure both in her hero and in Mr Stanley, the heroine's father. Coelebs notes about Mr Stanley:

> What chiefly struck me in his manner of conversing was, that without ever pressing religion unseasonably into the service, he had the talent of making the most ordinary topics subservient to instruction, and of extracting some profitable hint, or striking out some important light, from subjects, which in ordinary hands would have been unproductive of improvement. It was evident that piety was the predominating principle of his mind, and that he was consulting its interests as carefully when prudence made him forbear to press it, as when propriety allowed him to introduce it.[5]

Mr Stanley is an exemplary Christian gentleman: serious and instructive, yet never ungraciously fanatical. At least according to More, he knows how to teach those around him without becoming a crashing bore.

As Leonore Davidoff and Catherine Hall note about the Christian middle-class man,

> Many of the values associated with evangelical Christianity – the stress on moral earnestness, the belief in the power of love and a sensitivity to the weak and the helpless – ran counter to the worldly assumptions and pursuits of the gentry. Masculine nature, in gentry terms, was based on sport and codes of honour derived from military prowess, finding expression in hunting, riding, drinking and 'wenching'. Since many of the early Evangelicals came from gentry backgrounds they had to consciously establish novel patterns of manhood.[6]

This ideal of Christian manliness was not confined to the middle classes. In *Personal Nobility* (1793), Vicesimus Knox had stressed to the nobility that they had better become moral leaders or face grim consequences: 'All I contend is, that it [the aristocracy] cannot subsist long in any free country like our own, (especially since the example of France), when unsupported by personal merit.'[7] His point was not subtle: the aristocracy could either clean up its act or sign its death warrant, as it had in France. At least in appearance, many of England's politicians took Knox's message seriously. Whereas earlier men like Walpole and Newcastle had derived 'respect from display' and been 'uninhibited in . . . conduct', newer figures like Pitt, Peel, the Duke of Wellington, and Prince Leopold (the Regent's son-in-law) were 'discreet in manner, unpretentious in appearance, reserved if not cold, keeping [their] warmth for [their] home and hearth . . . devoted to public duties'. 'Propriety, decency, and modesty' had become watchwords for men in the public eye.[8]

The resulting model of masculinity paired stern moral duty with personal reserve and absence of theatricality. As the *Edinburgh Review* noted in 1815, a new fashion had made 'smart talking and pretensions to wit and vivacity rather vulgar accomplishments' and restored the 'original English taste for honest, manly good sense, and something of a cold and contemptuous severity of judgment'.[9] It soon became a commonplace among visitors to note the taciturn reserve of Englishmen.[10] The English were no longer competing with the perceived liveliness of the Continental (especially French and Italian) character, but had developed their own contrasting model of respectable masculine behaviour.

The more widespread this model of masculinity, the more spectacular the departures from it appeared. Top prize for un-Christian un-manliness went to the Prince Regent: overweight, alcoholic, showy, inconsistent, and unreliable. More interesting was the challenge offered by Beau Brummel, leader of the dandies. While the stereotypical image of the dandy is a splashily overdressed young man, Brummel was actually restrained in his appearance. Instead of striving for display, his simple, perfectly clean dress aimed for 'an anti-style, a denial of ostentation and self-congratulation'.[11] He took a characteristic of Christian manliness, the absence of display, and turned it into a paradoxical form of display: in his hands, reserve was unmasked as a pose like any other.

Byron admired Brummel, and his more serious and thoughtful criticism of Christian manliness shares aspects of Brummel's strategies. Like Brummel, Byron jolted his audience by cutting off masculinity from morality. Simple as this sounds, it was a dramatic innovation in a world of Mr Stanleys. In the eighteenth-century novel, the hero's success or failure at attaining manly character, however defined, was a touchstone of his moral success or failure. This convention shaped plots: a hero who demonstrated manliness was rewarded, usually with the heroine; the hero who failed in his manliness was punished. Literal or metaphoric violence typically established a clear distinction between good and bad characters. Flagrantly evil heroes, such as Zeluco in John Moore's novel of the same name (1786) and Ambrosio in M. G. Lewis's *The Monk* (1796), had unmistakable, elaborate downfalls. Unlike such conventional figures, Byron's heroes had neither the sincere earnestness nor the melodramatic wickedness that readers had come to expect. As Francis Jeffrey noted, Byron's works presented 'no very enlightened or equitable principles of morality', and Henry Crabb Robinson thought his poetry lacked 'the recommendation of teaching any moral truth'.[12] For readers used to moral instruction, Byron's heroes were a puzzle.

By freeing his heroes from moral exemplarity, Byron gave them more complicated minds and ambiguous personalities than most other male characters of the day. Outside of Byron, male heroes of the early nineteenth century were a colourless lot. The heroes of Sir Walter Scott's novels are notorious for their passivity and blandness, while Jane Austen's leading men rarely live up to the vividness of her heroines. Byron rescued masculinity for literature by transforming the masculine character, which elsewhere was a clue to moral worth, into an enigma, as his representation of Lara demonstrates:

> In him inexplicably mix'd appear'd
> Much to be loved and hated, sought and fear'd;
> Opinion varying o'er his hidden lot,
> In praise or railing ne'er his name forgot:
> His silence form'd a theme for others' prate
> They guess'd – they gazed – they fain would know his fate.
> What had he been? what was he, thus unknown,
> Who walk'd their world, his lineage only known?
> A hater of his kind? Yet some would say,
> With them he could seem gay amidst the gay;
> But own'd that smile, if oft observed and near,
> Waned in its mirth, and wither'd to a sneer;
> That smile might reach his lip, but pass'd not by,
> None e'er could trace its laughter to his eye
>
> (*Lara*, 1.289–302)

In Byron's hands, the masculine character is hidden, rendered permanently ambiguous by an unspeakable past whose traces are nevertheless present to the viewer. Rather than a straightforward description of Lara, Byron offers conjectures, none of which is ever answered. Shattered by experience, Lara's character shuttles between embittered presents; promising, ambitious pasts; and a mysterious history that has wrought drastic, painful change.

Other writers of the period, of course, create ambiguous men: Wollstonecraft and Austen, for example, highlight men who do not live up to their promising first impressions. Yet Byron's plots, unlike those of Wollstonecraft and Austen, never resolve the ambiguities of his hero. No moment of ultimate judgement arrives, and Byron neither unmasks him as truly evil nor lets him grow into an ideal. *Lara* is packed with violence, but it increases rather than resolves unanswerable questions about the hero because any information that might allow us to judge him is withheld: where he has been; what exactly his relation to Kaled might be; whether or not he killed Ezzelin; why Ezzelin accuses him in the first place.[13]

Byron replaces moral judgement with the exposition of Lara's baffling interiority. Instead of what the *Edinburgh Review* called 'honest, manly good sense', intensity of feeling, especially when veiled with indifference, defines masculinity. Byron's narrative stimulates curiosity and fascination about this intense feeling rather than offering a moral judgement on it. The effect is a perpetual deferral of closure about the hero, even after his death. We are never sure just what to make of him. Such deferral encouraged the repeated appearance of this hero in narrative after narrative. It would have made no sense for writers using older conventions to reproduce their heroes: at the end of their narratives, a judgement had been given, one way or another, and the hero's quasi-allegorical role had been divulged. In Byron, however, no such moment of enlightenment ever appears, leaving the narratives feeling always unfinished.

Instead of being objects for judgement, the Byronic heroes are spectacles for wonder. They gain their power through a quasi-magical ability to attract and retain attention, even though they do nothing to solicit it. Others insist on treating them as actors in a drama, even though they hold themselves aloof from conscious theatrical display. In foregrounding the unconscious power of their theatricality, Byron, like Brummel, was both adapting and criticizing the convention whereby reserve, above all, had come to signal English masculinity. In respectable society, reserve signalled indifference to display and a focus on simplicity and directness. Yet in his Turkish Tales, Byron questions whether reserve is as anti-theatrical as it is supposed to be. Far from being a sober, steady English quality, reserve in Byron is a mysteriously threatening, eerie magnet for attention. Whereas heroes like Coelebs proved their masculinity through their sterling moral character, Byron's heroes increase their masculinity by attaining talismanic powers of drawing out sympathy.

For example, Lara's renunciation of theatricality rivets attention on him:

> With all that chilling mystery of mien,
> And seeming gladness to remain unseen,
> He had (if 'twere not nature's boon) an art
> Of fixing memory on another's heart . . .
> You could not penetrate his soul, but found,
> Despite your wonder, to your own he wound;
> His presence haunted still; and from the breast
> He forced an all unwilling interest.
>
> (*Lara*, I.361–4, 377–80)

Masculine reserve, rather than effacing the self, empowers it. Byron hesitates over how much conscious control Lara has over his fascination for others: is it an 'art' or 'nature's boon'? His hesitation underscores that if this is an art, it is an almost unconscious one. In spite of himself, Lara gains power over others; with an almost magical force, like Geraldine in *Christabel*, he mesmerizes onlookers. Byron's phrase 'unwilling interest' in this context has two meanings: 'an interest that is not voluntary' and 'an interest that is not desired'. The ambiguity lends a negative cast to Lara's fascination: being attracted by the Byronic hero is not a happy experience, but a compelled fascination. Byron furthers the sense of the hero's unpleasant power with his verb 'wound', which makes Lara weirdly spidery, as if the viewer were an insect trapped in his lethal web.

Whether or not a given reader finds Lara as interesting as the poem does, Byron's contemporaries eagerly assumed the role of enthralled audience for such unfathomable heroes. His popularity proves that his audience enjoyed his criticism of masculine models, whether or not they chose to imitate it. Their enjoyment depended on a significant change in the relation between art and morality during the Romantic period. From being a consolidator of commonly held values, as Alexander Pope claimed in his *Essay on Criticism* (1711), art was becoming a privileged but contained space for values that ran against the norm. No conduct-book characters, Byron's heroes encouraged readers to think of literature not as a site for teaching proper behaviour but as a refuge from it. He split the masculinity of daily life from the masculinity of art, so that the second could make up for the perceived shortcomings or limitations of the first. Byron's early poems show both his challenge to conventional masculinity and his containment of that challenge: radical as his heroes are, for example, he makes sure that their radicalism takes place in exotic settings far from contemporary England. If he had set his poems closer to home, it is questionable whether or not his audience would have been quite so enthusiastic.

In his later works, Byron returns to these images of manliness and subjects them to critical scrutiny and demystification. *Sardanapalus*, arguably his best closet drama (a term for a play that is not meant to be performed), has much in common with *Lara*: both works feature a hero who keeps out of the public eye and who, despite his efforts at benevolent leadership, is dragged into war. Yet *Sardanapalus* strips away the Byronic hero's compelling aura of mystery to reveal a beleaguered, even comical figure. Whereas Lara keeps to himself, Sardanapalus luxuriates in pleasure and flagrantly ignores masculine standards of behaviour, as his first entrance reveals: '*Enter SARDANAPALUS effeminately dressed, his Head crowned with Flowers and his Robe negligently flowing, attended by a Train of Women and young Slaves*' (I.ii. opening stage direction). His flowers and flowing robe are an anti-costume, a refusal of the masculine discipline that earned Lara unwilling respect. Rather than making him fascinating, his effeminacy exposes him to contempt and encourages civil war from those who believe him to be weak.

Sardanapalus hides himself because he knows that to be visible as a ruler demands being a soldier. In his eyes, manly men are little better than bloodthirsty murderers. For much of the play, he struggles against attempts by other characters to persuade him to fight. His favourite slave Myrrha emphasizes that, whatever his personal philosophy may be, effective leadership depends on aggressive masculinity:

> SARDANAPALUS: Why, child, I loathe all war, and warriors;
> I live in peace and pleasure; what can man
> Do more?
> MYRRHA: Alas! My lord, with common men
> There needs too oft the show of war to keep
> The substance of sweet peace; and, for a king,
> 'Tis sometimes better to be fear'd than loved.
> SARDANAPALUS: And I have never sought but for the last.
> MYRRHA: And now art neither.
> SARDANAPALUS: Does thou say so, Myrrha?
> MYRRHA: I speak of civic popular love, self-love,
> Which means that men are kept in awe and law,
> Yet not oppress'd – at least they must not think so;
> Or if they think so, deem it necessary
> To ward off worse oppression, their own passions.
> (*Sardanapalus*, I.ii.529–41)

According to Myrrha, kingly power needs theatre and deception. Her phrase 'the show of war' is a telling one: it means both 'the visible appearance of a war' and 'a war put on for the sake of appearances'. If successfully manipulated, violence can repress popular passions and earn respect for the government without creating the impression of a tyranny. According to Myrrha, masculinity may be a charade, but one necessary for peace.

In treating masculinity as a charade, Byron highlights the illusoriness of male autonomy. Whereas in *Lara*, Lara involuntarily attracted attention and felt little responsibility to the many who wondered about him, Sardanapalus knows that to play the king is to enslave himself to popular perception. As Myrrha suggests, the true, albeit unwitting, rulers are the people, who want a king to fear, not to love. Sardanapalus's effeminacy is an attempt to live by his own principles, even though Byron invites us to see them as somewhat self-indulgent. He eventually gives in to others and assumes the masculine theatricality that has been thrust on him. Having done so, he fails miserably. While for a few moments, his spectacular appearance in battle rallies his troops, Byron treats the saving power of masculine aggression as a fraud. Flushed with confidence, Sardanapalus ventures into battle without sufficient reinforcements, and his troops are butchered. In the end, he joins Myrrha on a funeral pyre with the recognition that he has failed both in peace and in war: 'Adieu, Assyria! . . . I sated thee with peace and joys; and this / Is my reward! and now I owe thee nothing' (v.i.492–6). Neither refusing nor assuming masculinity provides Sardanapalus with a satisfactory model for leadership.

Although in *Lara*, Byron avoided linking masculinity to morality, in *Sardanapalus* he has a more overtly polemical point: conventional masculinity is death. Yet refusing it, at least for a leader like Sardanapalus, is also impossible, because, as Myrrha suggests, the people demand a military show and ignoring them foments rebellion. The play presents masculinity as an impasse that both empowers and disempowers by making men both masters and slaves of their audience.

As such, Byron demystifies the fantasy in his earlier works like *Lara* that masculinity could be entirely autonomous, not subject even to the conventions of moral analysis. Yet what remains constant throughout his career is a rejection of his contemporaries' idealization of masculinity as an unproblematic, transparent category of sincerity, moral earnestness, and adherence to duty. Byron instead foregrounds the frictions within this masculinity by underscoring, for example, the paradoxical theatricality of reserve or the death-trap of masculine leadership.

When we shift the focus from Byron and gender to Byron and sexuality, he presents a notorious embarrassment of riches. His sexual conquests were many and have given biographers, film-makers, and even opera composers plenty of material. Yet, as with my treatment of gender, I care less about the juicy details of Byron's bed than about understanding his work as a response to early nineteenth-century developments in sexual mores. In current usage, sexuality splits into two large, opposed categories: the homosexual and the heterosexual. Defending these categories as identities that need legal and political protection constitutes an ongoing struggle in contemporary life. But sexuality in Byron's day looked rather different. First, it was not a distinct area of human behaviour that could be sifted out from class, gender, education, religion, and other markers of identity. Moreover, the most important aspect of sexuality was not necessarily a sexual partner's biological maleness or femaleness. At least in Byron's case, other kinds of distinctions (old/young, active/passive, upper-class/lower-class, voluntary/coerced, married/unmarried, unpaid/paid) were just as important. As a result, while it is certainly true that Byron had sex with males and females, trying to fit him into the categories like 'homosexual', 'heterosexual', or 'bisexual' is frustratingly clunky.

I prefer to locate Byron and sexuality within two sets of what Mary Poovey calls 'uneven developments' in British culture. By uneven developments,

Poovey means historical changes that do not take the form of tidy transitions but that involve the messy coexistence of older and newer patterns of behaviour.[14] In the early nineteenth century, one set of such developments included sexual propriety. Changes in masculinity that elevated Christian manliness to respectability had powerful repercussions for what counted as appropriate sexual behaviour. The high society that Byron enjoyed during his heyday in England was most striking for adhering to older, looser codes. In such society, adultery was commonplace and unremarkable so long as it was conducted with a proper degree of discretion. Many of the great Whig ladies of London society had chequered pasts and were known to have had numerous out-of-wedlock affairs. Byron's adulterous flings with such women become a biographical blur because they succeeded each other so quickly. As for working-class women, men of Byron's class traditionally had assumed that such women were sexually available, and Byron seems to have treated them essentially as prostitutes.

Byron's most notorious affair, his love for his half-sister, Augusta Leigh, was partly an extension of this aristocratic sexual ethos. Aristocratic privilege depended on intermarriage: aristocrats defined themselves by drastically limiting the pool of prospective marriage partners to those of recognized bloodlines, and marriages between cousins were quite common. Scandalous as Byron's incest may seem, it should be thought of less as a practice completely out of the mainstream than as an exaggerated, pressured version of the sex between relations that was typical of aristocrats.

This adulterous, incestuous high society countered the strict, middle-class mores that demanded marital fidelity and serious devotion to domesticity. Yet by the early nineteenth century, such mores had made significant inroads even among the aristocracy, though not necessarily in Byron's circle. As Linda Colley notes, 'By 1800, the fashion among politicians in office at home . . . was for ostentatious uxoriousness. Spencer Perceval, Lord Liverpool, George Canning, Lord Sidmouth, Lord Castlereagh and Robert Peel all wallowed in domesticity.'[15] As for women, Hannah More addressed conduct books to young women of the upper classes, reproving them for their levity and exhorting them to a life of Christian seriousness and fidelity to their husbands. Increasingly, such ideals were taken seriously. Although Queen Caroline was no model of proper sexual behaviour, she was praised as such in the notorious fracas that occurred when George IV threatened to divorce her. Women who transgressed too obviously against respectable norms, such as Caroline Lamb or Lady Blessington, had no chance in respectable society. Even Byron felt the effect of such ideals insofar as he was persuaded to marry Annabella Milbanke. Milbanke was less a prude, as she is often characterized, than a woman who followed what were increasingly becoming admired ideals for female behaviour: she took her marriage to Byron seriously and expected him to behave like a decent husband. Byron's appalling violence against her and his complete inability to cope with his marriage signalled his collapse in the face of the clash between an older, relaxed, aristocratic sexual ethos and a newer, stricter bourgeois one, which he resolved only by leaving England.

With regard to same-sex love, the uneven developments of the early nineteenth century were even more complicated. Previous scholars, especially Lewis Crompton, have painted a picture of a repressive society that violently condemned sodomy. In it, Byron supposedly masked his same-sex affairs and used his poetry to express his sense of shame and guilt. Byron, in other words, was the arch-inhabitant of the homosexual closet. While this image is powerful, Byron would not have recognized it. On the face of it, he seems to have cared little about sexual secrecy, especially in his youth: he bragged in his letters describing his foreign travels about how many times he had had homosexual intercourse; he hired a young boy as a page, travelled with him, and even had his picture painted with him; and he assiduously courted a beautiful choirboy, John Edleston, while he was at Cambridge. Admittedly, Byron was most open in his attachments to adolescents when he was overseas, but the overall image he presents is not that of a man trembling at the possibility of detection. My point is not that Byron did not acknowledge the taboos of his day, but that they seem to have influenced his behaviour less than we might expect.

Paedophilia, or at least sex between older and much younger men, had a long aristocratic pedigree, much like marriage between relations. In the seventeenth century, James I surrounded himself with handsome young favourites; in Byron's day, the Duke of Cumberland, the Regent's younger brother, was rumoured to have murdered a valet who threatened to expose his affair with a male servant. Aristocratic schooling reinforced this pedigree. Elite public schools as well as Oxford and Cambridge were all-male institutions, and sex between boys was commonplace. At Cambridge, Byron's university, there seems to have been a long tradition of college students patronizing younger boys, especially those, like John Edleston, who sang in the famed college choirs. Such students, including Byron, formed an informal club, complete with its own slang and tone of snobbish connoisseurship.[16] Nor were such informal clubs limited to the universities. William Henry 'Master' Betty, an extraordinarily popular actor, attracted a 'large influential, and primarily male aristocratic following', who enjoyed watching his father 'rubbing down his naked body from the perspiration after the exertion in performing his part on the stage'.[17]

While same-sex love between women did not have the same socially validated spaces, high society nevertheless included several examples of women who did not conform to heterosexual expectations. With enough money and privilege, they could sustain lesbian relationships in ways that would have been quite difficult for middle-class women. Lady Melbourne, Byron's confidante, was a close friend of Anne Damer, a sculptor famous for her affairs with other women; Byron knew her well enough to be invited to meet her at dinner.[18] In Wales, Lady Eleanor Butler and Sarah Ponsonby, known as the Ladies of Llangollen, had become so familiar as a model of a same-sex couple that Byron boasted that his love for Edleston would outdo theirs.[19] Byron's shared sense of aristocratic privilege undergirded his comparison of love between men to love between women.

Complicating this image of cosy aristocratic privilege, however, were prominent men who had suffered public humiliation because of their paedophilia. The most famous was William Beckford, ostracized from society after he was discovered having sex with a young aristocrat, William Courtenay. Beckford's immense wealth cushioned him from the devastation that such humiliation could cause, and he consoled himself by walling himself up in an elaborate, extravagant estate, Fonthill Abbey. Although Beckford married and had daughters, he never erased in the public mind the association between himself and forbidden love. Byron knew a great deal about Beckford, whom he discusses in Canto I of *Childe Harold's Pilgrimage*; in his manuscript version of the poem, he even included a stanza specifically condemning Beckford for his paedophilia.

The darkest part of this picture involves the dangers facing men of less privileged backgrounds. Convicted sodomites were killed in Georgian England. While there was a flourishing underground network of coteries for sex between men, usually members of the lower classes, they were subject to brutal raids and exposure. Contemporary accounts of the public degradation and murder of these men make chilling reading even today.[20] These executions need to be kept in mind as the flip side of the aristocratic protection enjoyed by men like Byron. A possible edge of danger lurked in the same-sex liaisons of even the most protected man: society had to agree to look the other way, as it did for the Duke of Cumberland. For some, at least, this danger may have added to the allure of behaviour that could be either protected or punished, often with baffling arbitrariness.

What such uneven developments meant for Byron, as well as for anyone else during the Regency, was that sexual relations were risky. With attitudes and practices in such a state of flux, no one could be sure of a safe course of action. As Annabella Milbanke found out to her cost, even the most sanctioned sexual relation, a heterosexual marriage, was no guarantee of smooth sailing. Many early nineteenth-century authors responded to the quicksands of changing contemporary attitudes with a hyper-idealization of faithful heterosexual love. Writers from all sectors of the political spectrum agreed that love between man and woman was the highest form of happiness. Virtually alone among early nineteenth-century writers, Byron loudly disputes his contemporaries' consensus. In his work, love is a dangerous, taboo mode of behaviour, one that was irresistible but also inherently dangerous. Far from guaranteeing happiness, it tears apart the social fabric, usually because lovers violate norms held by others. Byron offers a dark, turbulent counter-current to the almost religious faith with which writers as different as William Wordsworth and Percy Bysshe Shelley, in their very different ways, surrounded heterosexual love.

In and of itself, Byron's link between desire and danger was nothing new; it is as old as literature. What is striking about Byron is the way he positions his reader in relation to sexuality. He invites his reader to become complicit with illicit desire by leaving significant gaps in his poems, which the reader is encouraged to complete. In the face of changing sexual mores, he suggests that any desire outside of sanctioned heterosexual love has lost an adequate language. The more forbidden the desire, the less explicit it becomes, so that the reader must become more active to complete what the text does not say. Although only sodomy was legally codified as the desire that could not be named between Christians ('inter christianos non nominandum'), Byron expands this definition to include virtually all desire worth writing about.[21]

In *Manfred*, for example, Byron focuses on what the nineteenth-century middle class would have found to be one of the most charged modes of taboo desire: incest. Francis Jeffrey, writing for the *Edinburgh Review*, was so upset by Byron's portrayal that he wrote that 'incest . . . is not a thing to be at all brought before the imagination'.[22] As usual, Jeffrey's wording is remarkably precise: Byron brings incest before the imagination but not actually before the eyes, because the word itself never appears. Although Manfred spends most of the first two acts brooding about his love for his sister Astarte, the play's language cloaks her identity. The word 'sister' is steadily, even ostentatiously, avoided, as in this speech from Manfred's servant Manuel in Act III:

MANUEL: Count Manfred was, as now, within his tower, –
How occupied, we knew not, but with him
The sole companion of his wanderings
And watchings – her, whom of all earthly things

That lived, the only thing he seem'd to love, –
As he, indeed, by blood was bound to do,
The lady Astarte, his –
Hush! who comes here?

(*Manfred*, III.iii.41–7)

Just as Manuel is about to say the word 'sister', he is conveniently cut off by the Abbot's entrance. In such moments, Byron is playing with his audience, bowing to conventions of propriety by not naming the relationship between Manfred and Astarte, yet doing so in a way that nevertheless renders it unmistakable. The reader has to fill in the gaps by admitting knowledge of the forbidden desires that the play points to but stops just short of articulating. The result blends ignorance and knowledge. The lack of specificity lets the reader retreat from facing taboo sexuality too plainly, yet also intensifies the confrontation because Byron implies that any reader can fill in the blanks competently. In the shifting tides of Regency attitudes about sexuality, Byron generates a pseudo-ignorance that undercuts any pretensions to sexual innocence.

Having fostered this pseudo-ignorance, Byron takes his masking of sexuality one step further. Alongside this veiled language that can easily be penetrated, he produces more genuine bafflement, not about Manfred's love for Astarte but about its effects:

MANFRED: Her faults were mine – her virtues were her own –
I loved her, and destroy'd her!
WITCH: With thy hand?
MANFRED: Not with my hand, but heart – which broke her heart –
It gazed on mine, and wither'd. I have shed
Blood, but not hers – and yet her blood was shed –
I saw – and could not staunch it.

(*Manfred*, II.ii.100–21)

After having set his reader up for a sophisticated, insider knowledge of sexuality, Byron here upsets the reader's interpretive mastery. No coherent narrative emerges from Manfred's broken clauses. He claims agency and denies it; admits to violence, but not in the case of Astarte's death; and moves from describing her death in terms of organic decay ('wither'd') to violence ('her blood was shed'). Their love sets in motion chains of events that are beyond the control of those involved and that produce fatal but indescribable effects. The fragmentation of Manfred's language becomes a metaphor for the violence that he describes and the breaking of Astarte's heart.

Manfred's account yokes sexuality and violence together in a way characteristic of much of Byron's poetry. Sexuality becomes a catalyst for events that break apart both established social ties and narrative itself. In the face of the comfortable Regency idealization of love, Byron forces his readers to confront forms of sexuality that they had rather not admit. Doing so challenges both the hegemony of conventional heterosexual love and the pretence that no other form of love is possible. What Byron offers instead is desire that thrives on the forbidden and that violently overturns social norms.

In his later poetry, especially in *Don Juan*, Byron both continues and revises the masking of illicit desire in his earlier work. *Don Juan* pokes fun at the censorship that Regency sexual mores encouraged. Speaking of his college education, the narrator notes,

> For there one learns – 'tis not for me to boast,
> Though I acquired – but I pass over that,
> As well as all the Greek I since have lost:
> I say that there's the place – but '*Verbum sat*',
> I think I pick'd up too, as well as most,
> Knowledge of matters – but no matter *what* –
> I never married – but, I think, I know
> That sons should not be educated so.
>
> (*Don Juan*, I.53)

The dashes jokingly encourage the reader to conjure up a variety of unmentionable experiences, from visiting brothels to contracting venereal disease. In particular, Byron's narrator plants loud clues in the reader's mind that the love he describes was homoerotic: he has 'never married', so he has never settled down with a woman, and he emphasizes that college was where he learned Greek, a code word for 'Greek love', or paedophilia. As in *Manfred*, the ellipses are really no ellipses, since the blanks can easily be filled in. A word to the wise will do, and – if one is wise enough – one does not need even the full quotation from the Latin, especially if an abbreviated version will help a demanding rhyme scheme. Yet whereas the gaps in *Manfred* created an atmosphere of sublime unspeakability, the narrator of *Don Juan* mocks the conventions that silence him. Everyone already knows what he is talking about, so further information is superfluous: he is shocking and banal at the same time.

As in *Manfred*, sex in *Don Juan* often has dire consequences, yet, as the quotation above suggests, they are singularly unbaffling. For example, Byron describes the many catastrophes that force Juan to leave the women he loves. While he claims that Juan 'never left' his lovers 'while they had charms', Juan is the slave of circumstance: 'Unless compelled by fate, or wave, or wind / Or near relations, who are much the same' (VIII.53–4). In *Don Juan*, such compelling forces often ruin women, while Juan remains blithely unscathed.

The terrible consequences of desire that torture Manfred matter little to Juan, who undergoes no experience so painful that it cannot be forgotten by the next canto. If sexuality is the ultimate tragedy for Manfred, it is the ultimate banality in *Don Juan*. Under such circumstances, the play of ignorance and knowledge that made the investigation of desire so tantalizing in *Manfred* dissipates because the stakes are so low.

Byron's one refuge from the over-valorisation of love in works like *Manfred* and its under-valorisation in *Don Juan* is a quiet but pervasive fantasy of love that is released from the pressures of adulthood. Often, this fantasy involves an element of regression to a childlike, utopian state, as in *The Island* or the Haidée idyll in *Don Juan*. At times, it can even acquire a slightly death-like quality because Byron is captivated by moments in which the beloved is asleep or in some way withheld from consciousness. One of the most beautiful passages in *Don Juan* describes the joy of watching a sleeping lover:

> For there it lies so tranquil, so beloved,
>   All that it hath of life with us is living;
> So gentle, stirless, helpless, and unmoved,
>   And all unconscious of the joy 'tis giving;
> All it hath felt, inflicted, pass'd, and proved,
>   Hush'd into depths beyond the watcher's diving;
> There lies the thing we love with all its errors
> And all its charms, like death without its terrors.
>
> (*Don Juan*, II.197)

Interestingly, this passage arises not from a man describing a sleeping woman but from Haidee's watch over the sleeping Juan. Seeing a beloved asleep releases the lover who is awake from too rigid an adherence to conventional gender roles. While it might seem that the polarity of a waking versus a sleeping lover would automatically fit into an active, masculine role and a passive, feminine one, Byron's language suggests not masculine dominance but maternal, protective care. Viewing the sleeper is a privileged stance, but not one of triumph or conquest.

Such a moment revisits the compelling allure of a figure like Lara. To see him was to look past a callous, indifferent surface to a cauldron of seething emotions barely held in check. A sleeping beloved also offers an alluring contrast between the placid surface, 'gentle, stirless, helpless, and unmoved', and the darker emotions known to be present but temporarily suspended, 'all it hath felt, inflicted, pass'd, and proved'. The rhyme on 'unmoved' and 'proved' drives home the difference between sleeping and waking, in which sleep presents a transient image of a soul purified of its passions. As such, the beloved holds out a dream of simplicity, as if all that love involved was protecting and needing protection. Byron's fantasy has a utopian drive underneath it, a longing for a purer form of desire than he knows is possible in a world as relentlessly unpredictable as the one of *Don Juan*.

What might sum up Byron's contribution to the history of gender and sexuality is that he shocked contemporary audiences less by what he did than by what he did not do: he did not condemn his heroes for their misdeeds; he did not prevent heroes from becoming spectacles; he did not allow sexual desire to fit easily into language; he dared to make sexuality banal in *Don Juan*; and he did not let 'healthiness' taint his image of sexuality. It is all too easy to forget or ignore the disquieting aspects of sex/gender representation in his poetry. Within the confines of biography, he can be neatly explained and pigeonholed, turned into an icon who can be evaluated as an interesting historical figure. His work, in contrast, provides far darker, more disturbing images of sex/gender roles, as his contemporaries recognized. In Byron, sexuality guarantees that no one gets to live happily ever after.

NOTES

1. Donald E. Buchwalter, Letter to the Editor, *Star Tribune* (Sunday, 3 August 1997), A22.
2. Anonymous, review of *Mazeppa* in the *Eclectic Review* for August 1819, quoted in Andrew Rutherford (ed.), *Byron: The Critical Heritage* (London: Routledge, 1970), p. 258.
3. See Lewis Crompton, *Byron and Greek Love: Homophobia in 19th-Century England* (Berkeley: University of California Press, 1995) and Caroline Franklin, *Byron's Heroines* (Oxford: Clarendon Press, 1992).
4. I have been helped in my thinking about this topic by Eve Kosofsky Sedgwick, *Tendencies* (Durham, NC: Duke University Press, 1993), esp. pp. 23–5.
5. Hannah More, *Coelebs in Search of a Wife Comprehending Observations on Domestic Habits, and Manners, Religion, and Morals*, 2 vols. (London: Cadell & Davies, 1809), I, 170.
6. Leonore Davidoff and Catherine Hall, *Family Fortunes: Men and Women of the English Middle Class 1780–1850* (London: Hutchinson, 1987), p. 110.
7. Vicesimus Knox, *Personal Nobility, Or, Letters to a Nobleman on the Conduct of his Studies, and the Dignity of the Peerage* (1793) (New York: Garland, 1970), p. 288; this edition is a facsimile.
8. Paul Langford, 'Politics and Manners from Sir Robert Walpole to Sir Robert Peel', *Proceedings of the British Academy*, 94 (1996): 103–25: 118, 119.
9. Anonymous, *Edinburgh Review*, 24 (1815), 397, quoted in Maurice J. Quinlan, *Victorian Prelude: A History of English Manners, 1700–1830* (1941; rpr. Hamden: Archon, 1965), pp. 264–5.
10. Paul Langford, *Englishness Identified: Manners and Character, 1650–1850* (Oxford University Press, 2000), pp. 219–66.

11. Carolly Erickson, *Our Tempestuous Day: A History of Regency England* (New York: William Morrow, 1986), p. 239.
12. Jeffrey and Crabb Robinson quoted in Rutherford (ed.), *Byron: The Critical Heritage*. p. 68.
13. For a brilliant exploration of Lara's mysteriousness, see Leslie Brisman, *Romantic Origins* (Ithaca: Cornell University Press, 1978), pp. 114–31.
14. Mary Poovey, *Uneven Developments: The Ideological Work of Gender in Mid-Victorian England* (University of Chicago Press, 1988), pp. 3–4.
15. Linda Colley, *Britons: Forging the Nation, 1707–1837* (New Haven, Conn.: Yale University Press, 1992), p. 189.
16. For details, see Crompton, *Byron and Greek Love*, ch. 2.
17. Marilyn Gaull, *English Romanticism: The Human Context* (New York: W. W. Norton, 1988), p. 96.
18. On Damer, see my *Romantic Genius: The Prehistory of a Homosexual Role* (New York: Columbia University. Press, 1999), ch. 3; for Byron's knowledge of Damer, see *BLJ*, IV, 112, 229.
19. See Crompton, *Byron and Greek Love*, pp. 102–3.
20. For details, see ibid., ch. 1.
21. William Blackstone, *Commentaries*, quoted in Crompton, *Byron and Greek Love*, p. 25n.
22. Jeffrey, quoted in Rutherford (ed.), *Byron: The Critical Heritage*, p. 117.

2

TEXTUAL CONTEXTS

5

PHILIP W. MARTIN

Heroism and history: *Childe Harold* I and II and the Tales

For generations of readers, the experience of *Childe Harold's Pilgrimage* has been caught up with a reading of Byron's psychology, for the poem has commonly been seen as the expression of an incompletely repressed *alter ego* to be read in parallel with Byron's own life and expressed opinions. It therefore finds itself firmly placed within the bounds of an interpretative frame whose constant reference point is the concept of a flawed and melancholic psyche. Within this, approving critics may note the perspicuity of the poem's dark opinions, or the fascination of its psychology, while disapproving critics might censure the indulgence of high Romantic self-expression or dramatisation. These approaches, and their approving or disapproving reflexes are not misreadings. In many ways, they constitute a meta-narrative which is historically continuous, amply echoing the response of Byron's contemporary audience, which enjoyed the poem precisely because it seemingly alluded to the authentic experience of its author. But in general, such a view is likely to eclipse other of the poem's achievements, for it tends to reinforce the Romantic cult of introversion wherein the isolation of the private poet is seen as a necessary condition of a gifted perception. I will argue here for an understanding of *Childe Harold's Pilgrimage* I and II as a profoundly public work written in a style designed to appeal to a new audience sympathetic to its coherent and anti-teleological explorations of history, politics and contemporary affairs. It is an ambitious poem which constructs a world-view for the modern – that is to say 'Romantic' – post-revolutionary intellectual, a view which in turn produces the psychology of the Byronic hero as a dramatisation of its effects. Significantly, its perspective is European, discarding orthodox or nationalistic understandings of history and empire, in favour of an all-embracing scepticism, which interrogates ideals of civilisation's progress and nationhood through a series of meditations around posterity's judgements on heroism, fame and achievement. I will argue that the verse tales that followed the first two cantos of *Childe Harold's Pilgrimage* may be read in continuity with it, but that the nature of this continuum constitutes displacements, in which the significance of history is at best vestigial. The reading offered here is not radically disruptive of established views, but it does require the reader to look again at *Childe Harold*'s most familiar characteristics – its scepticism, and its vision of a devastated Europe – and regard them darkly, as if they were being seen for the first time.

The publication of the first two cantos of *Childe Harold's Pilgrimage* in 1812 marks a defining moment in literary history. It is the point at which, effectively, second-generation Romanticism took root in the culture of the age, and it is the moment at which the best-seller poem gave notice that it had emphatically arrived. The poem inaugurated a fresh rage for poetry which exceeded even that of Scott's highly popular romantic narratives. Byron capitalised on his popularity in the rapid publication of the poems commonly known as the Turkish Tales (1812–16) and his fame in these years was such that it led to the streets being blocked because of the multitude's eagerness to catch a glimpse of him, and to his publisher, so flushed with the success of *Childe Harold*, offering him 1,000 guineas for a sequel.[1] This period was an era which saw the commodification of literature increase at an unprecedented rate, one in which literature came to be regarded as a profession, and in which success, fame and regard were attributed not by literary coteries, but by the combination of sales, marketing and the influence of the powerful reviewing journals. *Childe Harold's Pilgrimage* successfully negotiated this complex of influences to become an outstandingly popular poem on account of its novelty, and its innovations were both influential and important in their establishment of poetry's civic function.

Byron's poem gave a distinctly new turn to the movement that we now know as Romanticism and, simultaneously, it interrupted the modes of the popular poetry of the day. First, its style and location were markedly unusual. Above all else, *Childe Harold* is a rhetorical *tour de force*, in which the artistry of declamation assumes primacy. While the poem develops a meditative dimension, its style of thinking is a long way from the ruminative introversion of Wordsworth and Coleridge. Byron's interest in contemplation is not that it might lead to some inner wisdom, vision or higher morality greater than those inhabiting the common frames of thought: it is vitally concerned with the position of the individual in the world ('the world' at that time meaning largely, but not exclusively, Western Europe). Where the early Romantics' poetry constructed for itself a domestic landscape, in which the home figured large, Byron's poem announced an utterly different location and stimulation for the poet's ideas, in which the settled traditions of domesticity figured not at all. This is a poem of unconventional travel and exile, a poem whose scenery is that of Europe, and more particularly a Europe defined by two distinct features: its history, and its boundaries. The first two cantos of *Childe Harold* construct a world riven by political and military strife that is bounded by regions of wilderness and exotic barbarism. This is a new world for the Romantic poet, or indeed the popular poet of the opening decade of the nineteenth century, and it was one that Byron made his own, and in a way, never left. Indeed, his rejection of Romantic metaphysics is announced here no less forcefully than in *Don Juan*, even if that announcement is implicit rather than declared in *Childe Harold*'s modern, first-decade assumption that to be in the world is primarily a political and not an ontological matter.

The poets that are commonly placed alongside Byron as second-generation Romantics, Shelley and Keats, owe more to this defining moment than is commonly acknowledged. Neither of these authors wrote anything like *Childe Harold's Pilgrimage*, but their poems have important genealogical roots here. For Shelley is a poet whose identity is more European than English, and his position as an exile whose perspective on the norms of British society is sceptical, atheistic and informed by theories of history, owes much to the political and civic precedents created by Byron's poem. In another region entirely, Byron's creation of a poetic voice that is strongly inflected by what was seen at the time as a form of sickness or morbidity and simultaneously able to acknowledge the sensual regions of human experience may be very different in tone to anything found in Keats, but its emotional or affective structures are replicated there. In so many of his poems, Keats depends heavily on the interchange between satiety and the incapacity to feel on the one hand and the stimulation of dream, sexuality and excess on the other. That dynamic has its foundation in the emotional spectrum of *Childe Harold*, and even more significantly perhaps, *Childe Harold*'s fostering of the public's taste for liberal, yet polite (as opposed to 'vulgar' or radical) poetry.

It is as well to acknowledge that *Childe Harold's Pilgrimage* I and II is a difficult poem, particularly for the modern reader. This difficulty inheres not so much in the devious archiving of hidden meanings, as in its surface, and it is compounded by a current (and late twentieth-century) interpretative habit which has a strong preference for the discovery or creation of subtexts. The poem's originality, and its political and historical relevance, are ironically too readily obscured by its allusive, topical difficulties on the one hand, and the distractions offered by the emerging figure of the Byronic hero on the other. In addition, the poem's complex movements back and forth through time, place and mode initially militate against the clarity of its abiding concerns. Frequently seen as a medley (or 'a hodgepodge', as a recent critic has put it),[2] it is, in fact, as I will argue, a consistent engagement with a series of connected themes and ideas revolving around a fascination with the making of history: war, empire, tradition, loyalty, heroism and, perhaps above all, the judgements of posterity. These topics are not simply convenient romantic themes for a young poet; they are the subjects which this poem is reviewing and re-evaluating in the political chaos of Europe at the end of the nineteenth century's first decade. It is the extent of that political chaos, and its devastating consequence for the significance of history, that presents the appearance of a medley or formlessness, for it distends the poem, wrenching it away from the stable structure of a travelogue into something less neat, more ambitious and more distorted, an irregular procession of declamations which deny the ordinance of reasoned argument, but present together a disillusioned evacuation of history's significance, the status of heroism and the historical agency of great men. At the same time, these declamations effectively dramatise the disappointment that attends such a loss.

When Byron left England to travel to the Peninsula and the Levant in 1809, Europe was in a state of turmoil. 'The Continent is in a fine state!' he wrote to his mother shortly before leaving Falmouth, 'an insurrection has broken out at Paris, and the Austrians are beating Buonaparte, the Tyrolese have risen' (*BLJ*, I, 206). His journey through Spain and Portugal was to take him to countries which perhaps exemplified more than any other the chaotic state of European international affairs. The recent history of both nations was strewn with broken treaties and internal and external treacheries. Some understanding of this is necessary if we are to appreciate the nature and tone of much of the political commentary that the poem embodies.

Since 1792, when the French Assembly required Spain either to form a close alliance with France or to enter into open hostilities, Spain's position had been strongly compromised by the political intrigues of its monarchy and Prime Minister, Manuel de Godoy.[3] Charles IV of Spain was a conservative Bourbon king, who had staunchly supported Louis XVI and had gone to war with France in 1793 after Louis's execution. After significant defeats and the ascent of Godoy to a position of greater influence (he was also the Queen's lover), Spain had signed the Treaty of Ildefonso in 1796, effectively an offensive alliance with France against England. The succeeding years were disastrous for Spain and the country's relations with Portugal. Napoleon ruthlessly exploited Godoy's compliance, and Spain suffered continuous defeats in the war with England, while being constantly under threat of French invasion. Godoy attempted to create a principality for himself in southern Portugal, paying Napoleon 24 million francs for the privilege, before realising that he was being played along, at which point he tried to form an alliance with England. This was rebuffed, and incurred Napoleon's displeasure. When Portugal refused to declare war on England in 1807 to reinforce the continental blockade at Napoleon's behest, the French took the opportunity to agree with Godoy that they could march across the Pyrenees through Spain into Portugal. Having installed a brutal and exploitative government of generals in Portugal, Napoleon's troops then invaded Spain, and the ensuing struggle resulted finally, after Charles IV's farcical abdication and reclamation of the throne, in Napoleon's capturing of the crown for his brother, Joseph Bonaparte. On 2 May 1808, the day after the monarchy departed for safe havens in France, the Madrid populace rose in revolt, a rising that not only proved to be a turning point in the history of Spain, but also led eventually to Napoleon's downfall. Portugal and Spain united against the French invaders, bringing the British generals Wellesley (shortly to become the Duke of Wellington after the victory at Talevera) and Moore into the Peninsula. After a series of terrible battles and the controversy over the Convention of Cintra (in which Britain's agreement with Napoleon sacrificed the Spanish popular cause), France was driven out of Portugal, and Wellington advanced up through Spain, taking Madrid in 1812, and then marching on to France. Within fifteen days of the last French defeat in Spain, Napoleon abdicated to Elba in April 1814.

Byron left England on 2 July 1809, arriving in Lisbon four days later. He was in Portugal and Spain for no more than a month, leaving Lisbon in mid-July, and riding horseback quickly to Cadiz, and then by boat to Gibraltar. His presence in the Peninsula followed the popular risings, and coincided with Napoleon's successes at Saragossa and Corunna. By the spring of 1810, Cadiz was besieged. It is hard to imagine a more politically volatile location for Byron's travels, and the poem that granted him fame, than Portugal and Spain in 1809, and Byron's journey was a long way from the conventional Grand Tour commonly undertaken by the aristocratic gentlemen of the eighteenth century upon coming of age. His original plan, to travel to Constantinople via Malta was thwarted by his having missed the boat to Malta from Falmouth, and he and his travelling companion, John Cam Hobhouse, took the alternative route to Lisbon, travelling thereafter overland through Portugal and Spain to Gibraltar, and then on to Malta, Albania, Greece and Turkey. Reading Byron's letters from this brief period (he was in Spain and Portugal for around five weeks) provides only a partial view of his reactions to his journey. Political and military affairs are given relatively scant attention ('This country is in a state of great disorder, but beautiful in itself, the army is in Spain, and a battle is daily expected' (*BLJ*, I, 214–15) he writes casually from Lisbon to his solicitor, John Hanson, in July 1809); more prevalent are remarks on manners, personalities and the appearance of Spanish women (*BLJ*, I, 216–19). Yet almost the whole of the first canto of *Childe Harold* is given over to a retrospective meditation on Spain, in which, alongside the descriptions of the landscape and the people, the current condition of the country is related to its history, and to the common condition of a Europe ravaged by war. Spain may have been an unexpected detour for Byron's travelling schedule, and he may have lost no time in passing through it, but this projection into the unstable and bloody theatre of European warfare forces the poet to confront the momentous subject of national histories, and develop forms of poetic utterance equal to the challenge of historical commentary. There is no doubt that when Byron came to write the first canto between October and December 1809, he recognised Spain as the *locus* of European chaos ('the land of war and crimes' (*BLJ*, II, 16)) in which a recent history of continuous betrayal, imperial ambition and popular resentment provided the context for a revision of international affairs to be rendered on behalf of – in the terms of the poem's epigraph – a citizen of the world, whose extensive, sceptical views are not constrained by national boundaries or patriotic affiliation.

In accordance with this wider view, one of the strongest features of this poetry is its consistent attempt to insert the consequences of present and past times into a context governed by the judgements of posterity. These judgements are offered as hypotheses (since posterity is always in a state of impending arrival) and, simultaneously, as verdicts filtered by historical perspectives informed by distance and better understanding. Thus, the Childe ruminates on the Convention of Cintra and expostulates, 'How will posterity the deed proclaim! / Will not our own and fellow-nations sneer', and throughout both cantos there is a sustained concern with the gaining and status of fame and notoriety, ranging from that of the ancient heroes and writers to the degenerate infamy earned by such as Lord Elgin, whose deeds make Europe 'blush' (*CHP*, II.13.2). Byron uses the spectre of posterity as a means of censoring the degraded politics and actions of the present day, but the device is more than a satirical trick, for the vision of *Childe Harold* is one concerned to situate the modern liberal mind contemplating the imperial ambitions of France and other nations in an historical perspective. Posterity is Byron's rhetorical means of imagining the future judgements of history. It is also realised as the active agent in contemporary revisions of previous actions and ideologies.

This poem has a ubiquitous concern with a re-reading of the historical landscape through which its wanderer proceeds. The crosses by the roadside (I.xxi.2) are not 'devotion's offering' but marks of the continuous violence in a land where 'law secures not life'. The Catholic Church at Mafra, which Byron describes as 'superb' in his notes to the poem, is interpreted as an emblem of Catholicism's bloody history:

> But here the Babylonian whore hath built
> A dome where flaunts she in such glorious sheen,
> That men forget the blood which she hath spilt
> And bow the knee to Pomp that loves to varnish guilt.
>
> (*CHP*, I.29.6–9)

The better view of posterity is rendered more conventionally in the re-reading of another edifice in the landscape in the apostrophe to William Beckford (*CHP*, I.22–3), in which Beckford's wrecked hopes of 'paradise' are to be recognised in the deserted halls of his one-time residence, now the classic image of mutability with its overgrown passages and 'gaping portals'. At the simplest and most orthodox level, *Childe Harold* deconstructs the illusory permanence of architectural ambition through the readily available motif of decay, and advances, similarly, the view that Time ('accursed time' (*CHP*, I.66.1)) rules over all things. The poem moves a long way beyond this, however, in its attempt to apply historical perspectives to the overwhelming events of contemporary Spain.

The sceptical interrogation of grandeur is repeated, with more weight and immediate topical reference in Canto I, stanzas 40 to 44, in which the great battles of Talavera and Albuera are invoked. Here, famously, Byron casts the renown of victory in the longer perspective provided by the history of imperial ambition's folly, acknowledging the honour attending the dead ('Yes, Honour decks the turf that wraps their clay') but simultaneously reading this as a 'vain sophistry' through which the dead may be recognised as 'ambition's honour'd fools'. The battles of Talavera and Albuera were indeed successes for the British, but they incurred massive, unprecedented casualties on both sides. The losses at Albuera, together with the tactical failures of the Spanish after Talavera, made both battles pyrrhic victories, even while they remained landmarks in the liberation of the Peninsula and the eventual defeat of Napoleon. In its representation of these battles, *Childe Harold* evolves a polyphonic register capable of simultaneously evoking the heroic and the satiric:

> By Heaven! it is a splendid sight to see
> (For one who hath no friend, no brother there)
> Their rival scarfs of mix'd embroidery,
> Their various arms that glitter in the air!
> What gallant war-hounds rouse them from their lair,
> And gnash their fangs, loud yelling for the prey!
> All join the chase, but few the triumph share;
> The Grave shall bear the chiefest prize away
> And Havoc scarce for joy can number their array.

> Three hosts combine to offer sacrifice;
> Three tongues prefer strange orisons on high;
> Three gaudy standards flout the pale blue skies;
> The shouts are France, Spain, Albion, Victory!
> The foe, the victim, and the fond ally
> That fights for all, but ever fights in vain,
> Are met – as if at home they could not die –
> To feed the crow on Talavera's plain,
> And fertilize the field that each pretends to gain.
>
> (*CHP*, I.40–41)

There is a lot of movement here, as Byron mobilises a vocabulary which can invoke the pageant of warfare as well as its patriotism, while steadily working the stanza towards a withdrawal of the values it seemingly endorses, in a manner that predicates *Don Juan*'s mastery of the technique. But like that later poem, the poetry is not concerned simply to undermine itself through such qualifying ironies. While there are moments which effectively cancel out the heroic statements, *Childe Harold* also operates in an oxymoronic frame of reference, to hold opposites in suspension, as in the phrase 'Oh, Albuera! glorious field of grief!' (*CHP*, I.43.1), or indeed, in its broad historical vision, which recognises the competing claim of the immediate and the contemporary within the great span of time and the judgements of the future.

So deeply suffused is the long view of posterity that even poetry is vulnerable to its penetrating scrutiny:

> Childe Harold was he hight: – but whence his name
> And lineage long, it suits me not to say;
> Suffice it, that perchance they were of fame,
> And had been glorious in another day:
> But one sad losel soils a name for aye,
> However mighty in the olden time;
> Nor all that herald rake from coffin'd clay,
> Nor florid prose, nor honied lies of rhyme
> Can blazon evil deeds, or consecrate a crime.
>
> (*CHP*, I.3)

Rhetoric is given a very uncertain status here. Its capacity to deceive, Byron suggests, is countered by the more lasting effects of criminality, which cannot be erased. *Childe Harold* may be a poem that invests heavily in its own declamations, but it is also a poem consistently informed by its own suspicion of rhetorical propagandas and the metaphors of fame and reputation. There is a sense, therefore, in which the poem is founded upon a conflict between its medium and its message but, for the most part, such a conflict is avoided by way of a consistently articulated scepticism which requires its readers to look beyond the facades of grandeur or patriotic rhetoric to the wider view.

The first canto of the poem ends in an extravagant development of Spain's allegorical significance which, taken together with the opening of the second canto, offers the widest view of all, in the form of the history of civilisation as Byron knew it. Not only is Spain the epitome of contemporary political chaos, in which 'They fight for freedom who were never free, / A Kingless people for a nerveless state' (*CHP*, I.86.2–3), it also defines the very condition of imperial warfare and struggle in its incorporation of all previous histories of violent struggle (*CHP*, I.87.1–4).

Even more startling perhaps is the poem's vision of Spain as an Armageddon. Its 'reeking plain' and 'bleach'd bones, and blood's unbleaching stain, / Long mark the battle-field with hideous awe' (*CHP*, I.88.7–8) and yet are, in a sense, only the beginning, as Napoleon's campaign took the sheer numbers of men engaged in European battle to unprecedented heights:

> Nor yet, alas! the dreadful work is done,
> Fresh legions pour adown the Pyrenees;
> It deepens still, the work is scarce begun
> No mortal eye the distant end foresees.
> (*CHP*, I.89.1–4)

Byron has brought his readers to the borderlands of contemporary civilisation, here mapped as the dire conflation of imperial expansion, political intrigue and barbarism. It is no coincidence therefore, that the opening of the second canto traces this rhetoric on to the history of Greece to redefine classical civilisation within a history of barbarism before crossing the borders to enter the undiscovered regions outside the Europe which defines modern experience. What is found there is identical, but – in a way – it assembles itself the other way round.

The pilgrimage of the poem, it turns out, is to the Parthenon at Athens, the origin of civilisation which, in the conventional Whig accounts of the eighteenth century, spread through an imperial expansion justified by an enlightened understanding of civic freedom. Athena, apostrophised here as the origin of all things in the scriptural phrase 'The Ancient of days' (*CHP*, II.2.1) and also as Homer's 'blue-eyed maid of heaven' (*CHP*, II.1.1), stands as the emblem of human potential that, in the context of *Childe Harold*'s new history, is now unrealisable. The goddess of wisdom has inspired, in this retrospective view, no mortal songs (*CHP*, II.2.2), and her temple bears the marks of 'war and wasting fire'. Worst of all, it stands now in the Ottoman Empire ('men who never felt the sacred glow'), its ruined grandeur ironically enclosed by an imperial power whose ideology is diametrically opposed to that attributed to the Greek Republic. At the centre of these two cantos, the irony of the poem's title is most deeply marked. Here is a poem which announces itself as an indulgent and sacred journey into the arcane and quaint, a poem which will perhaps withdraw into the past, but, of course, the opposite proves to be the case. The 'pilgrimage' forces a radical revision of the liberal historical view. Greece is not the beginning of a gradual and progressive spread of freedom, but only a false dawn, a 'wonder of an hour' in a longer, continuous history of tyrannies. The opening stanzas of the second canto condemn the conventional understanding of Greece's afterlife as fully as the subsequent stanzas deny Christian immortality. *Childe Harold* has come to the beginning of things only to find the end: the apocalypse of Spain is succeeded by the 'sepulchre' (*CHP*, II.3.3) of Greece. He stands at the edge of Europe, and the end of history, with nowhere to go but across the border.

The poem's entry into Albania leaves its reader in no doubt about the liminal nature of this experience.[4] The landscape itself denotes a region of wilderness bereft of familiar sights, customs and values:

> Morn dawns; and with it stern Albania's hills,
> Dark Suli's rocks, and Pindus' inland peak,
> Rob'd half in mist, bedew'd with snowy rills,
> Array'd in many a dun and purple streak,
> Arise; and, as the clouds along them break,
> Disclose the dwelling of the mountaineer:
> Here roams the wolf, the eagle whets his beak,
> Birds, beasts of prey, and wilder men appear,
> And gathering storms around convulse the closing year.
>
> Now Harold felt himself at length alone,
> And bade to Christian tongues a long adieu;
> Now he adventur'd on a shore unknown,
> Which all admire, but many dread to view:
> His breast was arm'd 'gainst fate, his wants were few;
> Peril he sought not, but ne'er shrank to meet,
> The scene was savage, but the scene was new;
> This made the ceaseless toil of travel sweet,
> Beat back keen winter's blast, and welcom'd summer's heat.
>
> (*CHP*, II.42–43)

These two stanzas announce a number of symbolic transitions. A new morning finds a dark, obscure and largely dehumanised landscape in which predatory nature and an even wilder form of human life are revealed. A closing year, marked out by storms, accompanies a new condition of isolation, and a frontier whose novelty is welcomed alongside the anticipation of seasonal change. This, then, is a very different place from the Europe which defined Harold's modernity within its history. For here, momentarily at least, the weight of history is lifted (Harold passes through 'lands scarce noticed in historic tales' (*CHP*, II.46.4)) and the cosmopolitan environment of the citizen of the world is equally remote ('Ne city's towers pollute the lovely view' (*CHP*, II.52.1)). The Childe's travels have brought him to a kind of no man's land. Byron's editor rightly remarks that the poet's apostrophe to the river of Hades ('behold black Acheron!' (*CHP*, II.51.6)) indicates an intention to place this section of his poem in parallel with the epic descent to the underworld.[5] At the same time, this is a place of excessive delight ('pure pleasure' (*CHP*, II.1.6)), and hence the odd reversal:

> Pluto! If this be hell I look upon,
> Close sham'd Elysium's gates, my shade shall seek for none!
>
> (*CHP*, II.51.8–9)

And it is in this landscape, this strange ahistorical place of otherness, that Byron presents to his readers the Court of Ali Pasha, whose exotic inhabitants are of no fixed country or place. The poem makes much of what it describes as the 'strange groups' gathered here:

> Some high-capp'd Tartar spurr'd his steed away:
> The Turk, the Greek, the Albanian, and the Moor,
> Here mingled in their many-hued array,
> While the deep war-drum's sound announc'd the close of day.
>
> The wild Albanian kirtled to his knee,
> With shawl-girt head and ornamented gun,
> And gold-embroider'd garments, fair to see;
> The crimson-scarfed men of Macedon;
> The Delhi with his cap of terror on,
> And crooked glaive; the lively, supple Greek;
> And swarthy Nubia's mutilated son;
> The bearded Turk that rarely deigns to speak,
> Master of all around, too potent to be meek.
>
> Are mix'd conspicuous . . .
>
> (*CHP*, II.57.6–59.1)

This passage accomplishes a number of effects. It is clearly a fetishising of the exotic and, as such, it belongs to the commodification of the East, a major effect in Byron's poetry. At the same time, it belongs to the literature of encounter, in which the orthodox view (here that of the reader) is confronted with a scene of marvellous unfamiliarity which has the effect of disturbing and perplexing orthodox assumptions. Here those assumptions are those of nation and nationhood, religion and culture, gathered together in a 'conspicuous mixture'. Along with the rich novelty of this section of the poem – the 'many things most new to ear and eye' and the luxury of 'Wealth and Wantonness' – it is tempting to read the Kingdom of Ali Pasha as serving the function of a conventional eighteenth-century satiric utopia, wherein all the follies of the European nations might be exposed by way of the more civilised mores of an ostensibly barbaric culture, and, indeed, Childe Harold's symbolic passage across the frontier into this new world would give precedent to such a reading. But of course this is not the case. Byron is using the symbolic crossing of frontier ironically, for all that is discovered here is, in a way, a mirror image of that left behind. Thus, the virtues of Albanian loyalty, courage and friendship are extolled, and, famously, Ali Pasha himself is marked as a man of violence and bloodshed with 'a tyger's tooth'.

Although the poem's depiction of the Suliotes exploits the trope of the noble savage, it does so without idealism. Childe Harold notes that the hospitality and generous protection offered him by Ali Pasha is in contrast to that which might be offered by 'less barbarians' or 'fellow-countrymen . . . aloof' (*CHP*, II.66.8), but such kindness blinds neither him nor the narrator to the carnage which is an integral part of Ali's life and history. In Albania, as in Europe, courageous deeds and heroic actions may be found, but they are actions and deeds without cause or principle. It is no coincidence, therefore, that the Childe's benign regard for the spectacle of the Albanian warrior dance is succeeded by the famous meditation on Greece, which moves beyond its opening lament ('Fair Greece! Sad relic of departed worth!' (*CHP*, II.73.1)), and its romantic questing for great men ('Who now shall lead thy scatter'd children forth' (*CHP*, II.73.3)) to confront without delusion the baleful facts of recent imperial history. Thus, while the struggle for power may bring down the Ottoman Empire in Greece, this will not be a liberation ('not for you will freedom's altars flame' (*CHP*, II.76.6)), but only one more chapter in the continuous cycle of repressive regimes. Childe Harold's experience in Albania has returned him to the ruination of empires, and the double defacing, by history, and by pillagers such as Elgin, of the Greek landscape where the vestiges of its glory still remain. In the light of the broad sceptical history that *Childe Harold* develops, there is no prospect of an improved future, and no heroes or great men to bring it forward.

Childe Harold's discovery of the border of Europe and its history may be regarded as a precedent for Byron's turn to narrative in the Turkish Tales.

The change of location represented in the Tales is another border-crossing: a move into a geographical and historical paradigm, which, as will be seen, resists incorporation into Western models. This intractable otherness limits the possibilities of reading the Tales as allegories, yet this will, in a strongly modified way, be part of my intention in the argument that follows. First, it is necessary to provide a description of the Tales, noting their distinction from *Childe Harold*, so that we can better understand the metamorphoses they effect in Byron's representations of history and heroism.

In some ways, the Turkish Tales are discontinuous with the poetry of *Childe Harold's Pilgrimage*. Where *Childe Harold* is a thoroughly modern poem with intellectual ambitions, the Tales are novel, but not original, and without pretension for the most part. They demonstrate Byron's understanding of popular taste in their oriental setting and in their exploitation of heroic stereotypes, and they also tell us something about his developing interest in, and experiments with, narrative verse. Up until this time, Byron had been a writer of lyrics and satire. *Childe Harold* might be seen as a poetic structure combining these genres while touching on narrative in its travelogue. But the Tales are completely different, being primarily narratives. And while they all tell much the same tragic, swashbuckling story, they do it in different ways: in *The Giaour* we discover a narrative constructed through fragmentary points of view in octosyllabic verse; *The Bride of Abydos* is a paragraphed third-person narrative with an irregular oscillation between iambic pentameter and octosyllabics; *The Corsair* and *Lara* are rendered in more regular heroic iambics with a proliferation of dramatised speech; *The Siege of Corinth* and *Parisina* return to the octosyllabic line. Although the tales are to some extent formulaic, and while they undoubtedly pander to the public taste through such repetition, they also show Byron's expert facility as a teller of stories, as a poet determined to move beyond his proven success in lyric and satire, the genre of his previous publications as well as the genealogical source of the idiom of *Childe Harold*. Like Shelley, Byron's early career demonstrates a determination to develop a series of different forms and modes; and in parallel again, these encounters produce not virtuoso performances, but certainly remarkable facility in the production of poetry. Yet there is something more here too, for in such experimentation, we might detect the precedents for the extraordinary narrative of *Don Juan*, not only in the developing technique of telling stories, but also in the consciousness of the overbearing presence of a consuming public. Of course, there is little evidence of the self-conscious irony that produces and protects the comic vision of Byron's masterpiece.

A form made popular by Walter Scott and Robert Southey, the verse-tale commonly sustained a lengthy narrative of exotic adventure, and while Byron was always careful never to make large claims for his own tales, the mode bears something of an epic ambition about it. These are all poems about heroes. There have been attempts to read them as allegories, or as works with a profound philosophical undercurrent but, in the first instance, it is more profitable to read their surface rather than their imagined depths, for here we can realise more of their historical significance, the nature of their allegorising, and understand better the culture that fostered heroic exotica. These aspects are not discrete: what we are concerned with here is the new environment of the 'modern' poet, an environment that is commercially sophisticated in its marketing and consumption of cultural commodity; one that is concerned with the importation of exotic stories as part of an expanding horizon of such cultural (and colonising) expansion; and one that is historically ripe for a redefinition of the poetic constructions of modern heroism.

With the exception of one or two lyric interludes, asides or oblique commentaries, these poems do not aspire to the political or historical sonority of *Childe Harold*, neither do they overtly embrace its modernity, its sense of being of the European moment. They are, as it were, written from the 'other side' of *Childe Harold*'s border, where the fantasy of the end of history may be temporarily indulged in the strangeness of the other place. And, until the last decade or so, they were rarely seen as poems of political content or relevance, and were read largely within the critical story of the Byronic hero, as thematic revisions of Gothic or Shakespearean themes, or dismissed, perhaps, as bad poems, evidence of Byron's equivocal exploitation of an audience.

In recent years, there have been allegorical reclamations of the Tales that are rather more subtle. The interventions of historicist critics have argued against reading the Tales with political innocence, demonstrating their politically disruptive treatment of gender, for example, or their deeply engaged intertextual relations which place them centrally in the cultural discourse of imperialism. My argument here will, to some extent, concede to these readings (the most important of which are summarised below), but with a qualified regard for the notions of allegory they implicitly propose, and in a modified theoretical frame. For, in the context of the reading of *Childe Harold* I have offered, there is no rationale for the implied political unconscious that such radical, allegorical readings propose. While it is clearly the case that any writing may be considered to bear (in some encoded way) the politics of the period, there are specific questions which arise in Byron's case. The most obvious, and urgent, is this: why, given the political extroversion of *Childe Harold*, and its highly conscious engagement with history and politics, should these preoccupations suddenly be driven underground in the

Tales? What is the instrument or apparatus of repression that intervenes at this point, to produce either a subversive Byron who consciously encodes his stories in these ways, or a remarkably unconscious Byron who fails to recognise the political relevance of his own work?

Part of the answer may be seen to lie in the nature of *Childe Harold*'s success. Received by the public as an autobiographical poem with a developed psychological dimension, its historical dimension was effectively sidelined. The reviewers compounded this effect by their relatively gentle admonition of the poem's political and religious heterodoxies alongside a broad endorsement of its topological descriptions and its 'manly' strength and impetuosity, which Jeffrey, for one, read as stern medicine for what he regarded as the sickly affectations of the day.[6] The poem's centre (its discourse of history and politics) was thus displaced to its margin, but in the name of a certain masculine authenticity, located in the immediacy of the poem's present tense, its rhetorical power, and in its sense of place. *Childe Harold* represented itself, and was duly read, as the poetry of experience and, more, it offered to the reader a vicarious appeal in its engagements with the exotic. This emphasis on experience is one that is entirely consistent with Byron's ambitions and his aesthetics. As is well known, he set much store by his poetry's accuracy, and by its veracity grounded in the first-hand experience of a travelled man of the world. The Tales offered him the further opportunity of experimentation in the limits of fiction bounded by the voice of experience, through which he was to become the symbolic cultural representation of occidental and oriental relations. His poetry was that which encountered the other place, the strange region of unfamiliar mores, and it did so not through the transports of the imagination, but with the authenticity of ethnographic experience.

The new arguments about the Tales begin from the well-founded proposition that the broad frames of reference in which the poems are situated – those of empire, tyranny, despotism, struggle, revolution, freedom and so on – were of particular volatility in the period 1812–1816. Marilyn Butler and Caroline Franklin after her have both noted that 1813, the year of *The Giaour*'s publication, was the year in which attitudes to the conduct of the British Empire in India changed by way of a legitimation of proselytising Christianity.[7] This, in turn, was sanctioned by a refutation of the indigenous status of Hinduism, now recast as an historical and oppressive imposition to be contested by a liberating Christianity. Butler argues convincingly that such proselytising had substantial literary endorsement in Southey's popular poem, *The Curse of Kehama*, wherein the culture of the East is represented as a form of barbarism in need of the better knowledge of Christianity. She reads *The Giaour* as an emphatic *riposte* to the assumptions of Southey's poem and its style of Orientalism, noting that Byron's poem, far from setting up one religion as more enlightened than another, condemns the oppressive tyrannies of Christianity and Islam. In common with other historicist critics such as Kelsall, Butler has revealed that the ideology of empire in the period is shot through with a series of complex relations, and, in particular, the relations between notions of empire and ideas of liberty were of a vexed kind. Following the Whig version of the history of British liberty, to which I have referred above, Britain was viewed by many as the most recent incarnation of political formations whose constitution and practice exemplified the progressive spread of freedom, standing in a line of inheritance moving from Greece, through Rome to Venice. Its imperial ambitions were thus also viewed, in such a perspective, as embodying the potential for liberty's further expansion. Yet, in the sphere of international affairs, Napoleon's campaigns were seen as testimony to a tyranny endemic in imperial systems, and such a view was ratified by the Turkish Empire's subjugation of Greece, a tyranny easily represented (as in Byron's work) with all the resonances of a symbolic history. Historiography also contributed to such thinking: both Gibbon and Volney had given strong intellectual endorsement, in their different ways, to a sceptical regard for imperialism. Thus, while the British Empire in India was beginning to relocate its ideological justifications, the whole question of empire and its relation to the principle of liberty was being questioned (and not least, in the first two cantos of *Childe Harold's Pilgrimage*). In such an unstable matrix, it is not possible to model Byron's Tales as the cultural embodiment of a particular political view. They cannot be read, for example, simply as the cultural equivalent to a form of political colonisation, any more than they can be seen as championing native liberties over Ottoman oppression.[8]

The Tales draw on a semiology of the Orient that resonates powerfully with the discourse of despotism, but unlike *Childe Harold*, they do not participate directly in political commentary, neither is there much room here for overt political commentary. For the Tales' engagement with the East is of an anthropological kind: their setting is so overtly another place that connections with European history seem irrelevant. This anthropological neutrality or innocence has been read by Saree Makdisi as the effective construction of a discursive space that is agnostic to contemporary British assumptions. Makdisi understands Byron as remote from the dominant tradition of British imperial philosophy. Arguing with specific reference to the early *Childe Harold*, he reads the journey to the East as a refutation of a modernist tendency to homogenise histories into a Western diachronic model, and a recognition of the East's altereity: 'indeed, he [Byron] could conceive of the

Orient as a spatial alternative to Europe precisely because he sees European and Oriental histories as distinct – as synchronic *histories*, rather than one diachronic *History* narrated and controlled by Europe'. This altereity places Occident and Orient in parallel relations, not hierarchies, and is therefore entirely compatible with the anthropological caution found in Byron's letters, or indeed, in the Notes to *Childe Harold*. For Makdisi, Byron's notions of imperialism are riven and complex, but the poetry offers to preserve the East as non-Western, anti-Modern, and a place therefore, of 'liberatory possibilities for the critique of . . . Western concepts'.[9] Such a reading is consonant with that of Caroline Franklin, who achieved the first thoroughgoing re-reading of the Tales in her study of Byron's heroines. Franklin interprets the Tales as powerful revisions of gender politics working in a number of different directions. Thus they may offer women as passive victims of heroic romance, but they also make vigorous claims for female sexual autonomy. They may demonstrate the barbarism of Eastern tyrannies and inequalities, but they also disrupt Western patriarchal assumptions through implicit critiques of the verse romance structure, as well as through active heroines who serve as antidotes to the feudalism of Scott, or the imperialism of Southey.[10]

If we are to take Byron at his word, he placed a higher premium on his anthropological veracity than his poetry in his representations of the East. Writing to the distinguished Eastern traveller, Professor E. D. Clarke, who had complimented him on his accuracy, he remarked:

> Your very kind letter is the more agreeable because – setting aside talents – judgement – & ye. 'laudari a laudato' &c. *you* have been on ye spot – *you* have seen and described more of the East than any of your predecessors – I need not say how ably and successfully – and (excuse the *Bathos*) *you* are one of ye very few who can pronounce how far my *costume* (to use an affected but expressive word) is correct. – As to poesy – *that* is – as 'Men Gods and Columns' please to decide upon it – but I am sure that I am anxious to have an observer's – particularly a *famous* observer's testimony on ye. fidelity of my *manners & dresses*. (*BLJ*, III, 199)

Where 'poesy' is subject to critical fashion and the shifting tastes of posterity, the 'fidelity of . . . manners & dresses' can only be authenticated by the experienced traveller's eye, and especially when (as here) such experience is underpinned with scholarly expertise. It is clear that Byron set great store by such accuracy, which served as a constant touchstone for his judgement of self and others. Further, his understanding of this 'fidelity' extends to a refusal to assume, or incorporate, the Other into Western stereotypes or better knowledge. He would have interpreted such a reflex as an amateur response. We may see Byron's pride in this aspect of his poetry as something which sits comfortably alongside these new political readings of the Tales by recognising in them those qualities of anthropological narrative which James Clifford has argued are 'inescapably allegorical'. For Clifford, all ethnographic texts tell at least two stories: that of the surface or intended description, and that which is inherent in the act of narration itself, which necessarily embodies structures of meaning that make sense of difference by way of the familiar.[11] He regards the quality of allegory as a deep structure in the narrative; it consists of the familiarity in the act of telling. This does not transfer directly into the mode of the Turkish Tales, but it has a partial, and an important purchase there. Going back to the surface of the tales with which I began, and casting them again as representations of heroic exotica for an historically specific reading public, we can recognise Byron's act of telling as one that is primed by his audience's familiarity with such texts as the *Arabian Nights* on the one hand, and tales of epic heroism on the other. These mediations intervene strongly, I suggest: they do not permit us to ignore the form in which those concerns with history or heroism are concealed. The quality of allegory here, then, is not so much a deep structure, but a shimmering presence in the narrative. It can be seen in the peripheral vision, but it disappears when subjected to full scrutiny.

To render this more specific, we can assert that Byron's narratives are politically encoded at least in part by way of the allegorical structure which drags the otherness of the East back to revisions of epic heroism. The extent to which this happens in the Tales is different in each case. In a Tale such as *Lara*, which Byron claimed was set 'on the moon', the revision of heroism has no real purchase in the contemporary debate. The poem is, like Keats's 'The Eve of St Agnes', deliberately ahistorical: the vague references to baronial history have the effect of unmapping and dehistoricising human and political relations, so that the narrative is played out on the level of psychology, sexuality and desire. Here the redefinition of heroism has a dual aspect, comprising Kaled's loyalty (through which is asserted the greater value of woman's love (*Lara*, II.1158)), and Lara's heroic championship of the oppressed. A crude allegory pertaining to contemporary political events could, of course, be made of this, but the stronger allegorical axis is to be located in the disruption of conventional gender roles in heroic romance. But in *The Giaour*, *The Bride of Abydos* or *The Siege of Corinth*, that concern with the redescription of heroism is immediately inserted into the unstable chemistry of Occident and Orient or, indeed, the reading of historical events, and it is this far more allusive context which provides the precedent for political interpretation.[12]

The Tales address a similar problematic to that realised in the troubled scepticism of *Childe Harold*: how, in recent and contemporary history, are we to regard the place of agency, and in particular that apogee of agency – the making of history by great men? How, in the confused ethics of a post-revolutionary, Enlightenment Europe, are we to see the conventional virtues of epic heroism operating in relation to the affairs of the world? In these Tales, the question is displaced out of contemporary history into a more abstract, cross-cultural context, but one that is not so remote as to occlude references or parallels.[13] In *The Giaour* and *The Bride of Abydos*, the answer is tied into the romance plot, so that each hero, and heroine, is admired for his or her loyalty to his or her own nature, or what he or she sees as his or her own ineluctable task. Thus, famously, the Giaour admits within his confession that he stands outside morality, understanding Hassan's execution of his lover as a necessity – 'Faithless to him – he gave the blow; / But true to me – I laid him low' (*The Giaour*, 1064–5), and the poem seemingly celebrates this integrity. In *The Bride of Abydos*, Selim reveals his true nature, and his enduring love, and dies in a manner that testifies to both: glancing round at Zuleika in battle, he is fatally wounded. Yet despite this consistency, found equally starkly in *The Corsair* and *Lara*, the Tales also incorporate equivocal representations of heroism in their use of the device of disguise or masks. These heroes and heroines are never quite who we think they are and, what is more, they seemingly operate in an anarchic universe of their own making, eschewing connections with states, nations, ethics or family.

The Siege of Corinth, however, presents a break with the predominant pattern, while also developing this sense of anarchism. Here Alp's loyalty to his own creed is based on a 'deep, interminable pride' (*Corinth*, 609); his hatred of the Venetian state originates in the defiling of his name rather than some deeper principle. Similarly, Minotti's denial of him might be read as a form of religious intolerance, and the ghost of Francesca's pleading, as a further instrument of such intolerance.[14] The poem incorporates all the features of heroic romance (courage, loyalty, undying love) but it seemingly denies their value or effect in its apocalypse. Indeed, the conflagration with which the poem ends symbolically represents the destruction of political freedom itself. The poem is set in 1715, when Venetian control of Corinth was lost to the Turks; it was written in 1815, after Venice had been incorporated into the Napoleonic Empire. With the exception of the Ottoman Empire, each of the regimes and nations here had strong symbolic associations with liberty (Greece, Venice, post-revolutionary France) and, tellingly, the poem is haunted by the ghost of Francesca, whose figuring clearly alludes to the Goddess of Liberty.[15] The narrative seems set on denuding these states of their ancient virtues:

From Venice – once a race of worth
His gentle Sires – he drew his birth;
But late an exile from her shore,
Against his countrymen he bore
The arms they taught to bear; and now
The turban girt his shaven brow.
Though many a change had Corinth passed
With Greece to Venice' rule at last;
And here, before her walls, with those
To Greece and Venice equal foes,
He stood a foe, with all the zeal
Which young and fiery converts feel,
Within whose heated bosom throngs
The memory of a thousand wrongs.
To him had Venice ceased to be
Her ancient civic boast – 'the Free';
(*Corinth*, 70–85)

Alp's condition seems designed precisely to deconstruct the conventional political allusions in the symbolism of Greece and Venice, and the centre of the poem is occupied by his wandering and musing, within sight of Delphi's eternal shroud, upon the 'mighty times' (*Corinth*, 345) of Greek freedom and heroism, and the 'glorious dead / Who there in better cause had bled' (*Corinth*, 349–50). His journey takes him only to the dogs of war tearing the corpses apart under Corinth's walls, and the graphic descriptions of their mauling shocked Byron's contemporary readers (Gifford, for example, struck the lines out).[16] But this is an important part of the poem. It charts the journey of the course of freedom from its mythological beginnings to the chaotic carnage of modern imperial warfare, and in this poem, eventually, to the apocalypse of Minotti's blowing up of Corinth itself, a monument, perhaps, to the combined histories of Greece and Venice. *The Siege of Corinth* fights shy of attributing heroic virtues to its actions, and ends with an apocalyptic conflagration of republican freedom.

It might be thought that the opening words of *Don Juan*'s first canto ('I want a hero: an uncommon want, / When every year and month sends forth a new one') announce a new turn in Byron's poetry, a reversal into a quizzical and sceptical mode. But there is no doubt that, from the beginning, Byron had questioned the notion of the heroic in his verse, and *Childe Harold* is the prime example of this interrogation, which commences with the sceptical accounts of the carnage of modern warfare, and proceeds from there to repudiate teleological, imperial accounts of the progress of liberty, and to doubt the future possibility of histories made by great men. It is thus a post-revolutionary poem impelled not by the disillusion which leads to conservatism, but by a late-Enlightenment scepticism that is liberal, cosmopolitan and representative of a new freedom of thought. The Childe, or the Byronic hero, so uncertainly sketched by Byron in the poem, is perhaps best read as the psychological consequence of this alienation from the meaningful progress of history, a piece of self-fashioning which, however equivocal and awkward, represents a detached and wounded psychology that Byron understands as appropriate to the modern condition of historical and political bafflement. The Tales offer a further displacement of this condition, projecting it into exotic, unmapped and partially ahistorical locations where heroes and heroines contest extreme forms of prejudice and tyranny, their great acts remaining, for the most part, outside history, emptied of direct contemporary political reference, yet defiantly full of *potentia*, and generously suggestive of broad allegorical allusion. Taken together, *Childe Harold* I and II and the Tales may be seen as Byron's great engagement with the intellectual and historical crisis of his time. The pilgrimage represents the will to discover history's consequence and the manner of its continuous defeat in the face of a devastated Europe; the Tales represent the precarious afterlife of this desire in heroic acts evacuated of historical significance. In this period of Byron's writing there are no structural possibilities for history, and heroic acts are rendered ever more remote from the goal of civilisation's improvement.

NOTES

1. Samuel Smiles, *A Publisher and his Friends: Memoir and Correspondence of the Late John Murray*, 2 vols. (London, 1891), I, 215.
2. Jerome Christensen, *Lord Byron's Strength: Romantic Writing and Commercial Society* (Baltimore and London: Johns Hopkins University Press, 1993), p. 76.
3. See Byron's reference at *BLJ*, I, 508.
4. For an interesting discussion of this border and its significance in *Childe Harold*, see Saree Makdisi, *Romantic Imperialism: Universal Empire and the Culture of Modernity* (Cambridge University Press, 1998), pp. 124–8.
5. Jerome J. McGann, *CPW*, I, 288.
6. Francis Jeffrey praised the poem for exhibiting a 'plain manliness and strength of manner, which is infinitely refreshing after the sickly affectations of so many modern writers', *Edinburgh Review* (February 1812), 19, 466–77, in Andrew Rutherford, *Byron: The Critical Heritage* (London: Routledge, 1970; New York: Barnes and Noble, 1970), p. 39.
7. Marilyn Butler, 'Byron and the Empire in the East', in Andrew Rutherford (ed.), *Byron: Augustan and Romantic* (Basingstoke: Macmillan, 1990), pp. 70–1. Caroline Franklin, '"Some samples of the finest Orientalism": Byronic Philhellenism and Proto-Zionism at the Time of the Congress of Vienna', in Tim Fulford and Peter J. Kitson (eds.), *Romanticism and Colonialism: Writing and Empire, 1780–1830* (Cambridge University Press, 1998), pp. 222–4.

6

NIGEL LEASK

Byron and the Eastern Mediterranean: *Childe Harold* II and the 'polemic of Ottoman Greece'

> Slow sinks, more lovely ere his race be run,
> Along Morea's hills the setting sun;
> Not, as in Northern climes, obscurely bright,
> But one unclouded blaze of yellow light! . . .
> On old Aegina's rock and Idra's isle,
> The god of gladness sheds his parting smile;
> O'er his own regions lingering, loves to shine,
> Though there his altars are no more divine.
>
> (*The Corsair*, III.1–4, 7–10)

In these opening lines of the third canto of *The Corsair* (1814), Byron sets the mood for his narrative of the tragic death of Conrad's faithful wife Medora, by means of a sunset evocation of Greece, as the radiant sun of antiquity sinks over a land no longer consecrated to the antique spirit. The fact that Byron 'borrowed' the bravura sunset passage in its entirety (1–54) from his 'unpublished (though printed) poem' (*CPW*, III, 448), *The Curse of Minerva*, suggests that he was particularly wedded to the sublimity of sunset as a melancholy symbol of modern Greece. In the latter poem, the same lines introduce another betrayed female, the battered and insulted goddess Minerva, who curses Lord Elgin for despoiling her temple, as the shades of evening lengthen over the plundered ruins of the Parthenon. Byron's recycling of his lines suggests a conscious connection between the values of Conrad's apolitical love for the 'housewifely' Medora, and the philhellenic ideology flagged by Minerva.

The sunset melancholy of philhellenism also permeates the second canto of *Childe Harold's Pilgrimage*, best exemplified in stanza 73's lines: 'Fair Greece! Sad relic of departed worth! / Immortal, though no more; though fallen great!' (in political terms, this adds up to the resignation of stanza 76; 'But ne'er will freedom seek this fated soil, / But slave succeed to slave through years of endless toil') (*CHP*, II.76.8–9). Even in Byron's most militant statement of philhellenism, the anthem 'The Isles of Greece' sung in *Don Juan* Canto III (albeit one heavily ironised by the fact that the verses are sung by the 'trimmer poet'), he returns to the sunset metaphor in evoking a Hellenic glory now noticeably absent from the islands; 'Eternal summer gilds them yet, / But all, except their sun, is set' (*Don Juan*, III.86–7). Like Hegel's more famous owl, Byron's Minervan muse seems to take flight at dusk.

In this chapter, however, I want to suggest that the romantic image of sunset is far from exhausting Byron's poetical account of the Eastern Mediterranean. In the lines I've quoted from *The Corsair*, the shadows which lengthen over the tombs of Greek heroes, metonymically evoking the death of Medora, also symbolise the death of Conrad's chivalric idealism, the 'one virtue' which mitigates his 'thousand crimes' (*The Corsair*, III.696). In the symbolic economy of Byron's poems, as Caroline Franklin has indicated, the shift from 'passive' to 'active' heroine figures a transformation of the whole Byronic value system.[1] As *The Corsair* relates, Medora's death is symbolically instigated by Gulnare, the Turkish concubine whom Conrad rescues from the blazing Harem, and who in her turn saves the captive from the Ottoman Pasha Seyd's bloody vengeance. In return the 'unsexed' Gulnare exhorts from the pirate leader one single, over-determined kiss, at once the agent and exponent of his betrayal of Medora, and by extension of the ethical values supposedly distinguishing Hellenic/European civilisation from its Oriental 'other'. Whereas the efficacy of Conrad's action against the Pasha is compromised by his adherence to an aristocratic code of chivalry, Gulnare's 'oriental' assassination of her sleeping master is at once all too effective as an act of revolutionary liberation, and at the same time, transgressive of Conrad's 'occidental' system of values.

My point in dilating upon the allegorical function of Byron's heroines in these Levantine poems is to suggest two rival perspectives underpinning Byron's writings which (in deference to the allegorical importance of Byron's heroines) I characterise as the 'Medoran' and the 'Gulnarean' respectively. Whilst the abject, sepulchral Medora in *The Corsair* ('the only pang my bosom dare not brave, / Must be to find forgetfulness in thine', *The Corsair*, I, 357–58) personifies sentimental philhellenism, the orientalised 'regicide' of Gulnare aptly represents Byron's experiential insight into the contemporary culture and politics of the region which he encountered during his 'Levantine Tour' of 1809–11. While the 'Medoran' perspective was undoubtedly a major selling point of *Childe Harold's Pilgrimage*, I argue that the 'Gulnarean' view actually shaped Byron's critique of conventional ideology. Although quite uncharacteristic of Romantic Hellenism in general, 'Gulnarean' discourse also paradoxically empowered Byron's later involvement in the Greek War of Independence.

Ottoman Greeks and European philhellenes

The extraordinary story of the philhellenic intervention in the Greek War of Independence which provides the background to Byron's death has been well treated by scholars. Less has been said about Byron's fashionable 'grand tour' to the Eastern Mediterranean (my deliberate geographical vagueness here avoids the necessity of denominating the contested region 'Turkey' or 'Greece') in the company of his friend John Cam Hobhouse. Their travels between September 1809 and July 1810 through Epirus, Albania, Acarnania, the Morea, Attica, on to Smyrna in Asia Minor, culminating on the shores of the Hellespont and the Ottoman capital Istanbul, were minutely described in Hobhouse's massive, 1,154-page travel account, *A Journey through Albania, and Other Provinces of Turkey in Europe and Asia* (1813). Byron remained in Greece (Athens and the Peloponnese) for a further year after Hobhouse's departure: his travels provided material for the first and second cantos of *Childe Harold's Pilgrimage* (1812) begun during the tour, as well as the spate of 'Turkish Tales' which sprang from his pen during the years of fame.

As *The Giaour*, *The Corsair*, and *The Siege of Corinth* make clear, the region through which Byron and Hobhouse travelled was the front line between Islamic Turkey and Christian Europe. Ottoman victory in the late-sixteenth century had brought much of the region under the control of the Sublime Porte, although its inhabitants remained – then as now – a collection of different ethnic and religious groups. Ottoman Greeks, who traced their cultural roots back to Byzantium, the old Eastern Roman Empire, rather than to Hellenic antiquity, described themselves as 'Romaioi' (Romans) rather than Hellenes, at least those three million (out of a total of thirteen million-odd Orthodox Christians in the Empire), who spoke Romaic or modern Greek rather than Turkish, Albanian, Serbian, Bulgarian, or Macedonian.[2] Hence the justice of Hobhouse's claim that 'the Greeks, taken collectively, cannot, in fact, be so properly called an individual people, as a religious sect dissenting from the established church of the Ottoman Empire'.[3] Although Christians were more heavily taxed than Muslims and were forced to parade their ethnic and religious difference, the Sultans patronised the Greek Orthodox church, and its Patriarch (inheritor of the Byzantine emperors) was 'ethnarch' of thirteen million Christians, roughly a quarter of the population of the entire Ottoman empire. Moreover, by the early nineteenth century, the Greek merchant marine (based on islands like Idra, Spetsas and Psara), benefiting from the decline of Venetian power and increased European trade with the Levant, had established a commercial empire in the Mediterranean and the Black Sea, so that 'Greeks as traders, just as the Greeks as Christians, formed a kind of state within the Turkish state.'[4]

Costly military defeats of the Ottoman armies by expansionist Russia, and the increasing 'balkanisation' of the empire in the eighteenth century (witness the rise of regional magnates like Ali Pasha – of whom more below – in Epirus and Albania), as well as competing European interests in the eastern Mediterranean in the revolutionary and Napoleonic wars, provided a stimulus and opportunity for Greek independence. Despite the opposition of the 'Fanalite' Greek aristocracy which had for generations materially benefited from service to the Ottoman empire, after 1780 an increasingly nationalistic Greek identity began to emerge, especially amongst the diasporic Greek intelligentsia based in Russia or Western Europe, associated with figures like Adamantios Korais, Lambros Katsonis, and the 'jacobinical' patriot Rhigas Velestino. In these decades the Greeks turned successively to Russia, Napoleonic France, and Britain for help against their Ottoman masters, even making common cause with the refractory Ali Pasha, scourge of the local Greek *kleftes* (bandits). At least after 1814, it became clear that British foreign policy, dictated by a triumphalist Tory government, would be dedicated to shoring up Ottoman power and containing Russian influence in the region, turning a blind eye to the plight of the Greeks themselves. But official intransigence was qualified by 'philhellenic' enthusiasm in Britain, especially amongst liberals and philosophical radicals, consolidated by the formation of the London Greek Committee in 1818 and the outbreak of the Greek War of Independence in 1821. The fact that the Greek Committee's representative 'in the field' died of marsh fever in Missolonghi in April 1824 meant little in itself; the fact that he was none other than the celebrated Lord Byron did much to galvanise British and European support for the Greek cause.

The Levantine tour

Byron's poetical representations of the region are in many ways inseparable from the cultural practice and discourse of the Levantine tour, and even the generic form of *Childe Harold* embodies a particular critique of, and engagement with, the enormously popular contemporary discourse of travel about the Eastern Mediterranean. Conversely, the tour played a crucial role in the formation of the 'Byron phenomenon': the poet's early biographers insisted that 'travel conduced . . . to the formation of his poetical character' (Tom Moore)[5] and that 'the best of all Byron's works, the most racy and original, are undoubtedly those which relate to Greece' (John Galt).[6]

Although travel to Ottoman Greece had been hazardous in the seventeenth and eighteenth centuries, the dawning sense that Greece was the mother of Roman art and civilisation nevertheless attracted the more intrepid antiquarian travellers. George Wheler and Jacob Spon visited and described the ancient sites in 1676, Richard Pococke followed in the 1730s, and, perhaps most significant of all, James Stuart and Nicholas Revett were commissioned to draw the antiquities of Athens by the Society of Dilettanti in 1751–3. Oxford Don Richard Chandler (a major authority for Byron and Hobhouse) had revisited the classical sites in the following decade, publishing his *Travels in Asia Minor* in 1775. It was Cambridge University which was particularly well represented in the region between 1790 and 1810, however, and Cambridge graduates Byron and Hobhouse were conscious of following in the footsteps of earlier 'Cambridge Hellenists' like John Morritt, James Dallaway, John Tweddell, Edward Daniel Clarke, William Wilkins, Edward Dodwell, and William Gell.[7]

The dominant concern of all these travellers was with classical topography, the practice of identifying the modern locations of ancient sites, and describing and measuring the ruins of classical antiquity. Each traveller attempted to correct the errors of his predecessors, from classical geographers like Strabo and Pausanius to more recent seventeenth- and eighteenth-century antiquarians; in other words, they 'temporalised' Ottoman Greece – that is to say, viewed the modern reality through the spectacles of the classical past, more or less oblivious to the contemporary state of the country. Whilst most castigated the Turks as barbarous tyrants oblivious to the splendours of the Hellenic classical heritage, Byron's notes to *Childe Harold* lamented the antipathy to modern Greeks which was commonplace amongst European residents and tourists. In this respect they resembled the British public school boys who, Byron complained, wore themselves out studying 'the language and . . . the harangues of the Athenian demagogues in favour of freedom, [whilst] the real or supposed descendants of these sturdy republicans are left to the actual tyranny of their masters' (*CPW*, II, 202).

This sort of 'temporalisation' – the prototype of Byron's 'Medoran' perspective – was cognate with the common eighteenth-century trope of the 'ruins of empire', pioneered in the Whig account of the *translatio libertatis* – the translation of liberty – from Italy to Britain in works such as James Thomson's *Liberty* (1735–6).[8] As Byron wrote (on the eve of his departure) in *English Bards and Scotch Reviewers*, 'doubly blest is he whose heart expands / With hallow'd feelings for those classic lands; / Who rends the veil of ages long gone by, / And views their remnants with a poet's eye!' (*English Bards*, lines 873–6). 'Temporalisation' of Italy and Greece was initially committed to representing the irrecoverable nature of the classical past, precisely because liberty was thought to have migrated westwards to Whig Britain or republican America, depending on one's political persuasion. Applied to the case of Ottoman Greece this sentimental, 'Medoran' perspective might be described as 'weak philhellenism', because it held out no prospect for the revival of the classical values of the past.

With the rise of the Greek movement for independence during the global crisis precipitated by the Napoleonic wars, however, 'temporalisation' increasingly came to serve as a template for a restored Greek state, or 'strong philhellenism'. William St Clair has described how European philhellenes sought to 'regenerate' modern Greece by purging its oriental elements and 'restoring' a Hellenic state that was itself largely a construction of European classical scholarship, rather than a reflection of the actual cultural identity of modern Greeks.[9] In his controversial study *Black Athena*, Martin Bernal describes the early-nineteenth century replacement of an 'ancient model' of Greek civilisation deriving from Phoenician or Egyptian roots, by an 'Aryan hypothesis' whereby the Dorians were identified with northern, Teutonic tribes.[10] Percy Shelley's pronouncement in the notes to his lyrical drama *Hellas* (1821) that 'we are all Greeks', and his establishment of classical Greece as a transcendent ideal for contemporary republicanism is often taken to exemplify 'strong philhellenism' in this sense.

French occupation of Italy meant that the traditional 'beaten track' of the Grand Tour was off limits to Britons, but travel in the Levant (for those who could afford it) was facilitated after 1799 by Britain's political alliance with Ottoman Turkey in the wake of the French invasion of Egypt. Hence the justice of Byron's claim that 'the difficulties of travelling in Turkey have been much exaggerated, or rather have considerably diminished, in recent years' (*CPW*, II, 209). For elite British and French travellers, the pursuit of classical topography and removable antiquities also normally went hand in hand with diplomacy and *de facto* intelligence-gathering in a period of European war. Even the unpatriotic Byron's visit to the court of Ali Pasha at Tepalene (to which I return below), as well as his presentation to the Waiwode of Athens and the Ottoman Sultan himself, was not without its political motives given the contemporary importance of British influence in the region.

The gradual replacement of Augustan neoclassicism by a more 'primitivistic' Hellenism in eighteenth-century British culture (partly the result of the researches of the aforementioned travellers and antiquarians, together with the influential writings of German antiquarian Johann Winckelmann) had given a new kudos to the classical remains of Greece and Asia Minor. Lord Elgin's removal of the Parthenon marbles to London in 1807 can be seen as the act of a patriotic British virtuoso to establish London as the modern Athens, replete with objects of 'pure' Hellenic, rather than the derivative Romano–Grecian taste on display in the Napoleonic Louvre. As British ambassador to the Ottoman Porte, Elgin had acquired a firman from the Sultan at a time when the Ottoman authorities were anxious to encourage their British allies: his detractors, with some justice, accused him of abusing his public office in 'acquiring' the Parthenon frieze and other classical monuments. Athens became the site of heated competition between Elgin's agent Lusieri and the French Consul Fauvel for the best marbles, a rather sordid aesthetic reprise of the global war currently raging between British and French armies.

The Parthenon marbles were undoubtedly just as controversial in Byron's day as they are now, as the savage lampoons on Lord Elgin in *The Curse of Minerva*, and stanzas 11–15 of *Childe Harold* II remind us. Byron was by no means alone in attacking his luckless compatriot for despoiling the ruins of Athens (*CHP*, II, 11–15). However, as William St Clair points out, most of the Levantine tourists who attacked Elgin in the travelogues they published upon returning home were not averse to helping themselves to some choice fragments whenever they could lay their hands on them.[11] For example, Byron's friend Edward Daniel Clarke, future Professor of Mineralogy at Cambridge, described in his bulky *Travels in Various Countries of Europe, Asia and Africa* (1810–23) how he had witnessed Elgin's agents destroying part of the wall of the Acropolis whilst removing a metope – part of a Doric frieze – as the local Disdar shed impotent tears.[12] Yet elsewhere Clarke described how he had himself overcome strenuous local resistance to remove a beautiful statue of Ceres from Eleusis, which he deposited in the Cambridge University Museum: this in the very same volume which contained Clarke's condemnation of Elgin's 'lamentable operations'.[13]

Byron announced in a letter to Dr Valpy that 'my researches, such as they were, when in the East, were more directed to the language & the inhabitants than to the Antiquities' (*BLJ*, I, 134). In an August 1811 review of William Gell's *Geography and Antiquities of Ithaca* (1807), and *Itinerary of Greece* (1810), Byron's Cambridge friend Francis Hodgson (apparently with Byron's assistance) complained of the illusory 'transparency' of classical topography which pedantically described modern 'Mainotes' as 'Eleuthero-Lacones', and preferred giving ancient rather than modern names for the region.[14] 'Though there have been tourists and strangers in other countries, who have kindly permitted their readers to learn rather too much of their sweet selves [a veiled allusion to the unpublished *Childe Harold*], yet it is possible to carry delicacy, or cautious silence, or whatever it may be called, to an opposite extreme.' 'We like to know', Hodgson continued, perhaps in vindication of his noble friend, 'that there is a being still living who describes the scenes to which he introduces us; and that it is not a mere translation from Strabo or

Pausanius that we are reading.'[15] Hodgson's critique of Gell is fully in accord with Byron's own satire (in *English Bards*) on Lords Aberdeen and Elgin's 'misshapen monuments and maim'd antiques', and his summary resolution 'Of Dardan tours let dilettanti tell, / I leave topography to rapid Gell' (*English Bards*, 1030, 1033–4). The egotism of Byron's *Childe Harold* should be seen, therefore, as a 'modernist' break with the antiquarian tradition, whilst the notes to his poem poured scorn on the rapacity of topographical travellers.

The polemic of Ottoman Greece

Byron's wide reading in the orientalist archive of Knolles, Cantemir, D'Herbelot, Rycaut, and De Tott has been well documented by scholars, but most have overlooked the fact that his understanding of the region was also informed by a contemporary *logomachia* – a literary dispute – which I will denominate 'the polemic of Ottoman Greece'. Although numerous European 'authorities', including luminaries like Voltaire and Gibbon, had contributed to the polemic which an exasperated Byron later dismissed as 'paradox on one side, prejudice on the other' (*CPW*, II, 203), the most significant adversaries were the relatively unknown figures of William Eton and Thomas Thornton.

In his 1798 *A Survey of the Turkish Empire*, Eton, a former British consul in Turkey, showed his 'strong philhellenism' in lauding the modern Greeks, whilst violently attacking Ottoman 'despotism'. Eton 'temporalised' the Greeks by insisting (against the available evidence) that 'their ancient empire is fresh in their memory; it is the subject of their popular songs, and they speak of it in common conversation as a recent event'.[16] In conformity with his violently anti-Jacobin political sentiments, Eton advocated Russian intervention to liberate the Greeks and expel from Europe the Turks, whose empire he vilified as 'sui generis, a heteroclite monster among the various species of despotism'.[17] Eton had no doubt that the modern Greeks were thoroughly *occidental*, not oriental: 'an European feels himself as it were at home with them, and amongst creatures of his own species, for with Mahommetans there is a distance, a non-assimilation, a total difference of ideas'.[18]

Eton was answered in 1807 by a British Levantine merchant called Thomas Thornton, whose influential book, *The Present State of Turkey*, was based on fifteen years' residence at Pera, the European mercantile quarter of Istanbul. Thornton's only point of agreement with Eton concerned the unreliability of travellers as regional experts, for 'in his eagerness for information [the traveller] cannot expect to penetrate beyond the surface: the folds of the human heart cannot be distinguished by a transient glance'.[19] But Thornton was an unabashed partisan of the Ottoman Empire, distinguishing Ottoman rule as both rational and legitimate, a modified feudal polity rather than an 'oriental despotism', and citing Sir William Jones's 'Dissertation on Oriental Poetry' in praise of the rich literary and cultural legacy of modern Turks.[20] (Contrary to Edward Said's influential argument, this shows that European opinion could be pro-Ottoman and anti-Greek as well as philhellenic and 'orientalist' in Said's specialised sense of that word.)[21] Making hay with Eton's Turkophobia, Thornton demolished his rival's orientalist stereotypes by describing the Turkish character as a 'composition of contradictory qualities' 'brave and pusillanimous, gentle and ferocious; resolute and inconstant; active and indolent . . . delicate and coarse; fastidiously abstemious and indiscriminately indulgent'.[22]

Thornton was not, however, without his own prejudices, and made it clear that he had little time for modern Greeks whom he dismissed as 'a low, plodding, persecuted and miserable race'.[23] He denied any genealogical connection between them and 'the families which have immortalised Attica and Laconia',[24] 'blushing' over Eton's panegyric on the 'pirate' Lambros Katsonis, celebrated for having taken up arms against Turkish shipping in the wake of the Russo–Turkish war of 1788. For Thornton this was merely 'the devastation of banditti, and wholly undeserving the notice of history'.[25] In the notes to *Childe Harold*, Byron protested that it was 'very cruel' of Thornton to deny the persecuted Greeks 'possession of all that time has left them; viz. their pedigree' and suggested that his residence at Pera had given him no more insight into modern Greece than 'as many years spent at Wapping into that of the Western Highlands' (*CPW*, II, 203). (Byron tactfully avoided mentioning Hobhouse here, who described the modern Greeks as 'light, inconstant, and treacherous . . . remarkable for a total ignorance of the propriety of adhering to the truth'.)[26]

More significant for my present argument about Byron's shift from a 'Medoran' to an orientalised, 'Gulnarean', view of the region, however, is the fact that Thornton struck at the heart of philhellenic ideology by a form of 'counter-temporalisation' which argued that 'the nations of antiquity [i.e. Greece and Rome], if compared with modern Europe, will be found to possess many of those peculiarities which we have chosen to consider as exclusively characteristic of the Asiatics'.[27] In ethical terms, this correlation between ancient Greeks and modern Turks turned out to be highly equivocal in its focus on ideologies of gender. Following Scottish enlightenment philosophers like William Robertson and John Millar, Thornton regarded the condition of women as an index of the progress of any civilisation, insisting (conventionally) that the principal cultural distinction between modern Europeans and Orientals lay precisely in their attitude to women; for 'where the women are degraded from their rank in society, the European sinks into the Turk'.[28] For Thornton, the marker of European social progress was chivalry, the invention of the Gothic middle ages, absent both in the classical world and the modern orient. But Thornton went on to problematise his argument by suggesting that European men had paid a high price for the civilising manners of chivalry; 'we triumph in our acknowledged superiority over the Asiatics, but we must, in justice, lay down our laurels, like the heroes of chivalry, at the feet of our mistresses'.[29] The consequence of chivalry, he complained, was 'petticoat rule', also a recurrent complaint in Byron's peevish remarks on the cultural influence of Bluestockings from *The Blues* to *Don Juan*.

In his chapter entitled, 'Women and Domestic Economy', Thornton cited the authority of Lady Mary Wortley Montagu in arguing that women in the 'unchivalric' Ottoman world in fact enjoyed a certain agency, such as the possession of private property and the social anonymity of the veil, which supposedly more 'progressive' European women lacked.[30] Although Byron was as critical of Thornton's prejudice against the Greeks as he was of Eton's against the Turks (*CPW*, II, 201), he warmly praised his account of Turkish manners (*CPW*, II, 210). Hobhouse also accepted Thornton's defence of Ottoman political institutions,[31] and was particularly interested in his equation of modern Turkish attitudes to women with those of ancient Athens and Rome, on the grounds that chivalry, derived by Europeans from 'our German ancestors', was 'entirely unknown to the great nations of antiquity'.[32] We will see below that Byron in 'Gulnarean' mood, notwithstanding his sympathy for the modern Greeks, was evidently also influenced by Thornton's remarks on chivalry and the hypocrisy of Western 'sexual orientalism'.

Childe Harold II and 'weak philhellenism'

As a handsome quarto volume, beautifully printed on heavy paper, at thirty shillings on the expensive side, *Childe Harold* certainly did not look too different from the average prose travelogue when it was published in March 1812, inevitably inviting comparison with Hobhouse's *Journey* when it issued from the press the following year. Although written 'on the spot', one major difference between Byron's poem and Hobhouse's travelogue, however, was his employment of 'a fictitious character . . . for the sake of giving some connexion to the piece . . . Harold is the child of imagination' (*CPW*, II, 4). Byron's experiment involved the adoption of a 'narrator' and the fictionalised 'Harold', both of whom, despite autobiographical connections with their author, were not simply reducible to any stable 'Byronic' voice. Moreover, its series of lengthy prose notes often qualified the poem itself, especially salient in the notes on Levantine culture appended to the second canto, which were sometimes at odds with the poetic text they purportedly glossed. Byron's innovative grafting of poetical romance onto the conventions of travel narrative had the paradoxical effect of making his poem more rather than less powerful as an intervention in public debate about the regions which it treated. Francis Jeffrey captured this achievement in his 1818 review of *Childe Harold* IV when he wrote, 'All the scenes through which he has travelled, were, at the moment, of strong interest to the public mind, and the interest still hangs over them. His travels were not . . . the self-impelled act of a mind severing itself in lonely roaming from all participation with the society to which it belonged, but rather obeying the general motion of the mind of that society.'[33]

Canto II opens with the familiar 'sunset' apostrophe to Minerva; 'Ancient of days! august Athena! where, / Where are thy men of might? thy grand in soul? / Gone – glimmering through the dream of things that were' (*CHP*, II.2.1–3). The narrator's gloomy misanthropy in these opening stanzas, however, endorses the political critique of British antiquaries which follows:

> But worse than steel, and flame, and ages slow,
> Is the dread sceptre and dominion dire
> Of men who never felt the sacred glow
> That thoughts of thee and thine on polish'd breasts bestow
> (*CHP*, II.1.6–9)

Byron's footnote to the last line facetiously undercuts the melancholy of the verse in stating 'we can all feel, or imagine, the regret with which the ruins of cities, once the capitals of empire, are beheld: the reflections suggested by such objects are too trite to require recapitulation' (*CPW*, II, 189). Nevertheless, the hackneyed comparison of ancient and contemporary Athens is lent a new pathos in the light of the depredations of rapacious antiquaries. By the phrase 'men who never felt the sacred glow', Byron does not mean the Ottoman rulers of modern Greece, but rather men like the 'dull spoiler' Elgin who 'rive[s] what Goth, and Turk, and Time hath spar'd' (*CHP*, II.12.2). Harsh as Ottoman rule might have been, the Greeks had not really known the full 'weight of Despot's chains' (*CHP*, II.12.9) until the arrival of British antiquaries. For Byron (unlike Hobhouse, who expressed qualified support for the removal of the marbles to London),[34] the ruins of antiquity were part of the 'poetry' of the Greek landscape, which could never be recovered in a metropolitan museum.[35] In contrast to Elgin's rapacity, Byron's poetic persona indulges in a Yorick-like contemplation of a skull wrested from an ancient sarcophagus, 'Look on its broken arch, its ruin'd wall, / Its chambers desolate, and portals foul' (*CHP*, II.6.1–2). Notably, whilst Hobhouse brought back the customary marble fragments as souvenirs of his tour, Byron was content with (amongst various live animals and trinkets) '"Four ancient Athenian Skulls["] dug out of Sarcophagi' (*BLJ*, II, 59).

Perhaps the most notable instance of ironic interplay between Byron's poetic philhellenism and his polemical critique of such a sentimental 'Medoran' view is contained in the three long footnotes which gloss the stanzas beginning 'Fair Greece! Sad relic of departed worth!' (*CHP*, II.73.1). Byron's third note in particular suggests a climate of cultural renewal, centred on his defence of the modern Greek scholar Adamantios Korais's translation of Strabo against the recent strictures of the *Edinburgh Review*.[36] Byron dilates on the linguistic revival of modern Greek, the foundation of modern schools and the existence of a substantial body of modern poetry, which is discussed in considerable detail. Modern Greeks are given agency and voice in their ability to represent their own plight and forge an identity not based on classical texts, and their position within the Ottoman empire is subversively compared to the plight of Britain's Catholic Irish subjects. As an appendix to this note, Byron subjoined a long list of Romaic authors, a translation from a 'satire in dialogue', and a contemporary Greek translation of part of a drama by the Venetian dramatist Goldoni (*CPW*, II, 211–17). In a way Byron's defence of modern Greek language and literature foreshadows the later debate in independent Greece between the partisans of *katharevousa* (classical purists) and *dimotiki* (supporters of the vernacular as it was spoken). In the twentieth century, demotic became the 'official language' of the Greek Communist Party, and later, in 1970 after the fall of the Colonels' regime, of the country itself.[37]

A journey through Albania

Hobhouse's *Journey through Albania* and *Childe Harold* II share a common emphasis on Albania as an exotic, uncharted land, with a fresh romantic appeal not easily elicited by the latter-day tourist from the 'beaten track' of classical Greece. The short title of Hobhouse's book and over 200 pages of the text are dedicated to the Albanian itinerary, with digressions (in the conventional travelogue manner) to provide historical, geographical, and political information about the region. Stanzas 36–72 of *Childe Harold* II, in some respects the canto's dramatic and picturesque core, describe Harold's progress from Previsa, the main port of Epirus, overland to the capital Yanina, onwards to Ali Pasha's court at Tepalene, southwards via Acarnania to the Peloponnese, and thence to Attica. Both travellers cited Gibbon's opinion that Albania was less familiar to Europeans than the backwoods of America, elevating their status from tourists to travellers breaking new ground. In fact (as their critics pointed out) both were to some extent dependent upon information gleaned by the French resident Francois Pouqueville, who had in 1805 published an influential travelogue entitled *Voyage en Moree, a Constantinople, en Albanie . . . 1798–1801.*

The importance of Ali Pasha's Albania for both Byron and Hobhouse represents another break with the tradition of classical topography, and an attempt to establish an alternative framework for viewing the vexed politics of the region. In stanza 46 Byron represents Albania as a scene of nature rather than culture, its picturesque beauties offering a relief from the heavily associative topography of Greece: Childe Harold 'pass'd o'er many a mount sublime, / Through lands scarce noted in historic tales: / Yet in fam'd Attica such lovely dales / Are rarely seen' (*CPW*, II, 58). The climax of this passage is the description of the travellers' entry into Ali's stronghold, which, according to Byron's letter home of 12 November 1809, evoked 'Scott's description of Bransome Castle in his lay [of the last Minstrel], & the feudal system' (*BLJ*, I, 227). As if to capitalise on the literary fashion for Scott's feudal Highlanders, Byron's note proclaimed that 'The Arnouts, or Albanese, struck me forcibly by their resemblance to the Highlanders of Scotland, in dress, figure, and manner of living' (*CPW*, II, 192–3). But the comparison with Scott's dashing clansmen (upon whose warlike virtues and chivalric nobility the 'wizard of the north' was currently constructing Britain's ideological crusade against Napoleonic France) is arrested by Byron's claim that 'the Greeks hardly regard [the Albanians] as Christians, or the Turks as Moslems; and in fact they are a mixture of both, and sometimes neither' (*CPW*, II, 193). The hybrid Albanian, in other words, short-circuits the cut-and-dried cultural difference which fuelled the polemic of Ottoman Greece, offering a more reliable picture of the complex, multi-ethnic society of the modern Levant. In this respect Albania takes central place in Byron's 'Gulnarean' critique of weak philhellenism.

Byron's picture of Albanian manners also dilates upon the key question of homosexuality. In a June 1809 letter to Drury in which he had mocked Hobhouse's 'woundy preparations' for his travel account, Byron facetiously declared that he would contribute only a single chapter to the book, on 'the state of morals and a further treatise on the same to be entitled "Sodomy simplified or Paederasty proved to be praiseworthy from ancient authors and modern practice"' (*BLJ*, I, 208). Although Byron's 'chapter' never materialised, remarks in his correspondence from the Levant often read like a series of 'queer' footnotes to Hobhouse's travelogue, in which the celebrated predilection for homosexuality amongst Albanians, Greeks, and Turks is tersely glossed over during a discussion of Albanian misogyny. Despite the fact that Byron waited until the disapproving Hobhouse left for England before cultivating his boy lovers, Eustathios Georgiou and Nicolo Giraud, his interest in Levantine homosexuality was not just the *frisson* of the sexual tourist, but an integral part of his interest in comparing Eastern and Western manners. After all, in the 'Addition to the Preface' of the second edition of *Childe Harold*, Byron defended Harold's 'unknightly'(for which read 'effeminate' in its ambiguous contemporary sense) behaviour, as an integral part of his attack on Burkean chivalry as the ascendant ideology of counter-revolutionary Tory Britain.[38] The homosexual orientalism which the travellers sought out in Ali Pasha's court, and elsewhere in the Levant, represented a 'Gulnarean' antithesis to 'Medoran' chivalry, with its dedication to heterosexuality, matrimony, and the idealisation of women.

If Ali's masculinist feudal polity is described as being inimical to women (st. 61), it does provide a haven of homosexual gratification, as Byron hints in the (suppressed) lines following stanza 61:

> For boyish minions of unhallowed love
> The shameless torch of wild desire is lit
> Caressed, preferred even to woman's self above,
> Whose forms far Nature's gentler errors fit
> All frailties mote excuse save that which they command.
> (*CPW*, II, p. 63)

The absence of women permits Byron himself to adopt a feminised role, as in his letters home describing his flirtatious relationship with the Pasha, and noting Ali's admiration of his 'small ears, curling hair, & little white hands' (*BLJ*, I, 227). Homosexuality is another feature of oriental culture which maps onto 'Greek love', the homosexual strain of the classic Hellenic tradition, in stark contrast to European heterosexual chivalry. The bisexual Byron thus paradoxically finds himself closer to the spirit of ancient Greece in 'oriental' Albania, than all the philhellenes and antiquarians, with their sentimental idealism concerning the 'glory that was Greece'.

Byron's note to stanza 74 admits the difficulty of venturing opinions on the Turks 'since it is possible to live amongst them twenty years without acquiring information, at least from themselves' (*CPW*, II, 210): most of his positive examples of Turkish manners were in fact derived from his encounters with Albanians like the sixty-year-old Ali Pasha, his son, Veli, and his precocious grandson, Mouctar. Byron's description of Ali's court at Tepalene (more significant as a source of personal experience of Ottoman culture than his later sojourn in Asia Minor or Istanbul) supports Thornton's case for regarding Turkish rule as feudal rather than despotic; 'there does not exist a more honourable, friendly, and high-spirited character than the true Turkish provincial Aga, or Moslem country gentleman'. In establishing a positive image of the provincial Ottoman ruling class in terms of the gentlemanly ideal of Whig political discourse, Byron dispels the stereotype of oriental despotism and theocratic central government from Istanbul. Moreover, as the recent revolution against Sultan Selim II attests, Ottoman political culture enshrines the venerable Whig political principle of the 'right of resistance': '[The Turks] are faithful to their sultan till he becomes unfit to govern, and devout to their God without an inquisition.'

If Ali can be seen to serve as a synecdoche for some of the 'Gulnarean' values which attracted both Byron and Hobhouse, this was because he was in his own right a figure of considerable political importance for the whole region, a fact which quite possibly prompted the travellers' visit to Tepalene in November 1809, in the first place. In the years after 1800, the conspiracy of the Greek *eteria* or secret fraternities had in fact become closely linked with the intrigues of Ali Pasha, who played off French and British interests in his bid to sustain the autonomy of the Pashalik which he had carved out for himself from the Ottoman Porte.[39] Major William Leake, as British resident at Yanina, had managed to persuade Ali to sign an alliance with Britain, whose invasion of Zante in October 1809, and subsequent annexation of the other Ionian islands (with the exception of Corfu) from France in 1809–10 altered the balance of power in the region in favour of Britain. Peter Cochran has plausibly argued that, underlying Byron and Hobhouse's 'touristic' motives for visiting Albania, was a diplomatic imperative to 'sweeten' Ali Pasha in the wake of Britain's annexation of the Ionian islands – islands which Leake had promised to Ali as a reward for supporting British interests against Napoleon.[40] Looking forward a few years, Ali's declaration of war against Sultan Mahmoud in 1820 was encouraged by the British mission of Col. Charles Napier as part of a programme of Greek liberty, which promised to make him 'independent sovereign, not only of Albania, but all Greece, from Morea to Macedonia'.[41] In the event, Greek distrust of Ali's plotting and the pasha's own double-dealing prevented this happening, but the Greek insurgents used Ali's revolt against the Porte as a smoke-screen to strike the first blow for freedom. Whatever his intentions, Ali Pasha was a crucial player in the politics of the region on the eve of the Greek War of Independence.

Byron commented on the 'gentleness' of Ali Pasha's 'aged venerable face' which dissimulated 'the deeds that lurk beneath, and stain him with disgrace' (*CHP*, II.62.9), establishing a paradigm for Byronic hero/villains like the Giaour, Conrad, Seyd, and Alp. The fact that Byron held out some hopes for Ali (whom he described admiringly as 'the Mahometan Buonaparte', *BLJ*, I, 228) as a possible harbinger of independence for the oppressed Ottoman Greeks, as well as their Albanian neighbours, is suggested in his redaction of the 'palikar's war-song' 'Tambourgi!' heard by the travellers at Utraikee on their return journey, which closes the Albanian section of *Childe Harold* II. Hobhouse's narrative made much of the picturesque, gothic effect of the dancing Suliote warriors which 'would have made a fine picture in the hands of the author of the Mysteries of Udolpho'.[42] But for Hobhouse the Suliotes were clearly banditti and not freedom fighters, and the song they sing ('Tambourgi! Tambourgi!) is punctuated by the chorus 'Robbers all at Parga!'; 'all their songs were relations of some robbing exploit', he emphasised.[43] By contrast, in Byron's version the Suliotes celebrate the military prowess of 'A Chief ever glorious like Ali Pashaw' and his victories against the French at Previsa in 1799, and of his son Mouctar against the Russians on the Danube (*CPW*, II, 66–8). The song in Byron's redaction has political rather than merely picturesque content: the image of Ali Pasha as an effective, albeit 'Gulnarean', protector of the Greeks against foreign adventurism militates against the romantic visions of European philhellenism in its 'strong' form.

Ali's rugged mountain fiefdom, and cruelly unscrupulous policy, might seem a far cry from the philhellenic ideal of republican liberty for Greece, but as Byron wrote in his Journal in November 1813, 'the Asiatics are not qualified to be republicans, but they have the liberty of demolishing despots, which is the next thing to it' (*BLJ*, III, 218). As the ideologically compromised politics of the heroes of Byron's Tales suggest, to Byron at least the 'despotism of a republic' under the sway of Ali Pasha seemed more attractive than the solution recommended by William Eton, namely the exchange of Turkish for Russian empire and the consolidation of Byzantine religious legitimacy.

Conclusion

This chapter has argued that the contemporary 'polemic of Ottoman Greece' played an important role in determining Byron's understanding of the cultural and gender politics of the Eastern Mediterranean. Byron in 'renegado' mood embraced Thornton's oblique critique of chivalry as the marker of Western superiority over 'orientals', a fact which strongly inflected his attitude to the question of Greece. As in his hopes for Ali Pasha's instrumentality in liberating the Greeks, effective resistance to tyranny is rather achieved by 'active heroines' like Gulnare and the transvestite page Kaled working upon 'orientalised' Western heroes – Conrad or Lara – who have resigned their stakes in the cultural economy of chivalry. Caroline Franklin has argued that Byron's critique of chivalry in the Tales and *Don Juan* is at once 'anti-feminist' (as a libertine 'voice of opposition to [the] bourgeois, protestant ideology of [British] femininity')[44] and emancipatory inasmuch as it is critical of celibacy, the idealisation of women, and the sexual double standard characteristic of Christian chivalry. She persuasively argues that in *Don Juan*, Byron returned to his earlier attack on the 'sexual orientalism' of the West as a form of cultural hypocrisy, albeit in an anti-sentimental idiom.[45] As Byron expressed the matter in a later note defending his stance in *Don Juan*: 'Women all over the world always retain their freemasonry – and as that consists in the illusion of sentiment – which constitutes their sole empire – (all owing to Chivalry and the Goths – the Greeks knew better) all works which refer to the comedy of the passions – and laugh at sentimentalism – of course are proscribed by the whole Sect' (*BLJ*, VIII, 148).

Byron's decision to embark for Greece in 1823 and fight for Greek independence, and his death the following year at Missolonghi, rightly enshrined his name in the heroic pantheon of Greek nationalism.[46] Yet despite his willingness to sacrifice his life for the Greek cause, Byron never allowed nationalist idealism to smother sceptical cosmopolitanism. His coadjutant Col. Charles Napier paid him the ultimate tribute when he wrote,

> I never knew one, except Lord Byron and Mr Gordon, that seemed to have justly estimated [the Greeks'] character. All came expecting to find the Peloponnese filled with Plutarch's men, and all returned thinking the inhabitants of Newgate more moral. Lord Byron judged them fairly: he knew that half-civilised men are full of vices, and that great allowance must be made for emancipated slaves.[47]

To the modern reader there is sometimes a sense of noblesse oblige in Byron's attitude to the Greeks, even allowing for his understandable frustration at their incessant internal feuding and the treacherous desertion of his Suliote troops before the attack on Lepanto. Perhaps a more lasting tribute to his ethical pragmatism is Byron's letter from Missolonghi to the Turkish commandant Yussuff Pasha of 23 January 1824, accompanying four released Turkish prisoners, desiring that the bitterness of inter-ethnic warfare might be somewhat mitigated by a civilised system for exchanging rather than butchering prisoners.[48]

NOTES

1. Caroline Franklin, *Byron's Heroines* (Oxford: Clarendon Press, 1992), chs. 2 and 3.
2. Douglas Dakin, *The Greek Struggle for Independence* (London: B.T. Batsford, 1973), p. 9.

3. John Cam Hobhouse, *A Journey through Albania, and other Provinces of Turkey in Europe and Asia, to Constantinople, during the years 1809 and 1810*, 2nd edn (London: James Cawthorn, 1813), p. 596; henceforth *Journey*.
4. Dakin, *The Greek Struggle for Independence*, p. 22.
5. Thomas Moore, *Life, Letters, and Journals of Lord Byron* (London: John Murray, 1892), p. 119.
6. John Galt, *The Life of Lord Byron*, 3rd edn. (London, 1830), p. 124.
7. Brian Dolan, *Exploring European Frontiers: British Travellers in the Age of Enlightenment* (London: Macmillan, 2000), pp. 139–41. See also Nora Liassis, 'Travellers versus Factors' in *Lord Byron: A Multidisciplinary Forum*, ed. Terese Tessier (Paris 1999). My thanks to Peter Cochran for drawing my attention to this article.
8. Malcolm Kelsall, *Byron's Politics* (Brighton: Harvester Press, 1988), pp. 253–78.
9. William St Clair, *That Greece Might Still Be Free: The Philhellenes in the War of Independence* (London, New York and Toronto: Oxford University Press, 1972), pp. 13–22. See also Jennifer Wallace, '"We are all Greeks"?: National Identity and the Greek War of Independence', in *Byron Journal*, 23 (1995), 36–49.
10. Martin Bernal, *Black Athena: The Afroasiatic Roots of Classical Civilisation*, vol. I (London: Free Association Books, 1987).
11. William St Clair, *Lord Elgin and the Marbles: The Controversial History of the Parthenon Sculptures*, 3rd rev. edn (Oxford University Press, 1998), pp. 180–200.
12. E. D. Clarke, *Travels in Various Countries*; 4 vols. (1810–1819; 2nd edn 1811–1823), IV, pp. 223–4.
13. Clarke, *Travels*, III, Part II, section 2, p. 465. His account of the Eleusinian Ceres is on pp. 772–90.
14. *Monthly Review* (August, 1811), in Moore, *Life, Letters, and Journals*, pp. 670–5.
15. Moore, *Life*, p. 678.
16. William Eton, *A Survey of the Turkish Empire, in which are considered 1. Its Government, 2. The State of the Provinces, 3. The Causes of the Decline of Turkey, 4. The British Commerce with Turkey and the Necessity of Abolishing the Levant Company* (London: Cadell & Davies, 1798), p. 342.
17. *Ibid.*, p. 17.
18. *Ibid.*, p. 340.
19. Thomas Thornton, *The Present State of Turkey; or a description of the political, civil, and religious, constitution, government and laws of the Ottoman Empire* (1807), 2 vols., 2nd edn, corrected with additions (London, 1809) I, p. x.
20. Cited in Thornton, *The Present State of Turkey*, I, p. 30.
21. Edward Said, *Orientalism* (London: Routledge and Kegan Paul, 1978).
22. Thomton, *Present State*, I, p. 3.
23. *Ibid.*, II, p. 82.
24. *Ibid.*, II, p. 69.
25. *Ibid.*, II, p. 77.
26. Hobhouse, *Journey*, p. 598.
27. Thomton, *Present State*, II, p. 189.
28. *Ibid.*, II, p. 195.
29. *Ibid.*, II, p. 196.

30. *Ibid.*, II, pp. 229–67.
31. Hobhouse, *Journey*, p. 919.
32. *Ibid.*, p. 844.
33. *Edinburgh Review*, 30, 59 (June, 1818).
34. Hobhouse, *Journey*, p. 347.
35. 'Letter to John Murray Esq', in *CMP*, p. 133.
36. *Edinburgh Review*, 16 (1810), 55–62.
37. Roderick Beaton, 'Romanticism in Greece' in Roy Porter and Mikulas Teich (eds.), *Romanticism in National Context* (Cambridge University Press, 1988), pp. 97–9.
38. 'Effeminate' could refer either to a form of masculinity enervated by an obsessive desire for women, or to a womanly man. See Lewis Crompton, *Byron and Greek Love: Homophobia in 19th Century England* (London: Faber & Faber, 1985).
39. Dakin, *The Greek Struggle for Independence*, p. 30.
40. Cochran, 'Nature's Gentler Errors', *The Byron Journal* 23 (1995), pp. 22–35.
41. *Ibid.*, p.50. 'On Ali Pasha, see K. E. Fleming, *The Muslim Bonaparte: Diplomacy and Orientalism in Ali Pasha's Greece* (Princeton, NJ: Princeton University Press, 1999).
42. Hobhouse, *Journey*, p. 196.
43. *Ibid.*, p. 196.
44. Franklin, *Byron's Heroines*, p. 119.
45. *Ibid.*, pp. 128–56.
46. E. G. Protopsaltos, 'Byron and Greece', in P. Graham Trueblood (ed.), *Byron's Political and Cultural Influence in Nineteenth-Century Europe* (London: Palgrave Macmillan, 1981).
47. Moore, *Life*, p. 607.
48. *Ibid.*, p. 618.

7

ALAN RAWES

1816–17: *Childe Harold* III and *Manfred*

The years 1816–17 saw a major shift in the direction of Byron's poetry. This began in *Childe Harold* III, where Byron turned away from the vision of extreme human suffering that had dominated his poetry since 1812 to explore other areas of human experience and consciousness. Here began the movement towards *Don Juan*, as Byron set his sights not on a future of painful memory but on the redemptive possibilities opened up by the human capacity to forget.

A glance back at the Tales will help to situate *Childe Harold* III in its immediate literary context. In the Tales, the heroes are emotionally blasted by some devastating event. They are temporarily sustained by thoughts of revenge, but once this is accomplished they find themselves in a 'dreary' emotional 'void' (*Giaour*, 958) where the capacity to feel is crushed, the mind is a 'leafless desart' (*Giaour*, 959) and the future is a stretch of 'journeying years . . . where not a flower appears' (*CHP*, III.3.8–9). But the Tales are studies of the power of painful memory to simultaneously devastate and, in a sense, redeem. The heroes find in their ability, indeed compulsion, to remember the pain that devastated them the capacity to still feel and the vacant bosom discovers a 'pang' (*Giaour*, 940) that makes it less vacant. Yet in remembering what devastated him, the hero subjects himself once again to its devastating power, locking himself in a tortured life of 'sleepless nights and heavy days' (*Parisina*, 547). Emotional death is escaped only through intense, indeed potentially fatal, pain. *Childe Harold* III turns away from this Pyrrhic victory.

A second context powerfully informs *Childe Harold* III. Begun in May 1816, it is Byron's 'expressed attempt to come to terms with the collapse of his marriage and the public response to that event in England'.[1] In the poem we watch Byron exploring possible futures he himself might move towards. And while he is haunted by, or tempted by, the idea of himself as a Byronic hero, he is not one. His 'heart' has 'perchance . . . lost a string' (*CHP*, III.4.2), but he is not at the final extremity experienced by his tragic heroes.

This offers Byron a poetic opportunity: to explore the means of recovery from pain, and movement forward from and beyond it, that are available to him.

A third context, however, gives *Childe Harold* III much wider significance. 'The momentous crisis' of Byron's 'private life had coincided with that of Europe itself' following the French Revolution and Napoleonic Wars.[2] Byron was fully aware of this and in *Childe Harold* III we see a 'grand Byronic identification of psyche and world historical moment'.[3] Byron makes it clear that, for him, his sufferings 'mirror those of war-torn Europe',[4] and that his poem is written not just with himself in mind, but a whole continent. Imagining the 'kind and kindred' of those 'thousands' who had died in the recent wars, Byron states that it would be 'mercy' to 'teach' them 'forgetfulness' (*CHP*, IV.31.3–4). His quest is not just for a way forward out of the memory of his own personal pain, then, but an attempt to pioneer a way forward out of the memory of the 'triumph and subsequent defeat of the French republic in the sickening revolution of the great wheel of history' and of the wars generated by Napoleon's imperialistic designs on much of Europe.[5]

Byron steps forward at the beginning of the canto, as a pioneer and example, to explore his own capacity for forgetfulness. He does this by experimenting with his own ability to distract himself from memory, to become completely absorbed in two kinds of activity: imaginative creativity and the sort of attentiveness to the natural world that Wordsworth's poetry claims can, even in its recollection, create a 'blessed mood, / In which the burthen of the mystery, / In which the heavy and the weary weight / Of all this unintelligible world, / Is lightened' ('Lines Written a Few Miles Above Tintern Abbey', 38–42).

Imaginative creativity is undertaken in the hope that 'earth-born jars, / And human frailties' might be 'forgotten quite' (*CHP*, III.14.3–4). The 'wonder-works of God and Nature's hand' (*CHP*, III.10.9) are contemplated in the hope that 'I live not in myself, but . . . become / Portion of that around me' (*CHP*, III.72.1–2). What is looked for here is not a kind of Keatsian death of self, but an escape from 'the weary dream / Of selfish grief or gladness' (*CHP*, III.4.7–8) and from the 'whirling gulf of phantasy and flame' (*CHP*, III.7.4) which is produced by painful memories and produces the wild and dark thoughts of guilt, remorse, bitterness, and revenge that the tragic narratives of 1812–15 explore again and again.

In *Childe Harold* III, Byron sets his sights on achieving forgetfulness as early as the fourth stanza. Yet he quickly reveals that forgetfulness is not the ultimate goal of *Childe Harold* III. Forgetfulness, in itself, offers only a kind of death and this was not very likely to appeal to a poet who claimed that the 'great object of life is Sensation – to feel that we exist – even though in pain'.[6] In fact, 'the whole text of *Childe Harold* is in a simple way an "energetic denial of the power of death"'.[7] At the beginning of the third canto, Byron depicts himself 'plunged into a kind of death-in-life in which he can find neither love, nor hope, nor meaning' but his 'immediate desire for forgetfulness is allied to his more fundamental need to recover . . . a sense of his own vitality'.[8]

Forgetfulness is sought so that sources of renewed life, of new vitality, which might exist on the other side of forgetting pain, can be discovered and explored. Imagining, for example, might 'fling forgetfulness around' the imagining self, but it also offers the prospect of much more than forgetfulness:

> 'Tis to create, and in creating live
> A being more intense, that we endow
> With form our fancy, gaining as we give
> The life we image, even as I do now.
> What am I? Nothing; but not so art thou,
> Soul of my thought! with whom I traverse earth,
> Invisible but gazing, as I glow
> Mix'd with thy spirit, blended with thy birth,
> And feeling still with thee in my crush'd feelings' dearth.
> (*CHP*, III.6)

To imagine is to 'gain' a 'life' that is not our own. To 'create' is to be animated by – 'blended' with – the 'life' of a 'soul' or 'spirit' that is not the self. And to be blended with the 'birth' of that spirit – to be revitalised in that blending and to find oneself 'feeling still' despite the 'dearth' of 'crush'd feelings' – is what Byron is looking for. Imaginative creativity, Byron claims, offers both forgetfulness and revitalisation.

Similarly, nature does not simply offer a distraction from memory, but also, Byron suggests, a source of new vitality. Describing a transformed Childe Harold at the beginning of the canto, Byron states that:

> Where rose the mountains, there to him were friends;
> Where roll'd the ocean, thereon was his home;
> Where a blue sky, and glowing clime, extends,
> He had the passion and the power to roam;
> The desert, forest, cavern, breaker's foam,
> Were unto him companionship. (*CHP*, III.13.1–6)

In the 'companionship' offered by nature, the Harold of *Childe Harold* III discovers a source of 'passion' and 'power' denied the Harold of *Childe Harold* I and II. Past pain is forgotten, but forgetfulness opens the self to influences that refresh and revitalise. *Childe Harold* III's quest for forgetfulness – literary, personal, and historical – is the first stage of a larger quest after new sources of vitality.

This quest progresses by means of series of engagements with European landscape and culture. Structurally, the canto follows Byron's journey, after he left England on 23 April 1816, to the field of Waterloo, along the Rhine and into Switzerland. It gives a lyrical account of the poet's responses to these 'scenes which fleet along' (*CHP*, III.112.3). In these responses we see the imagination responding to events such as the Battle of Waterloo, figures such as Napoleon, Rousseau, Voltaire and Gibbon, and landscapes such as the Rhine valley, Lake Leman, and Clarens. These responses do not move smoothly and easily forward to forgetfulness and the discovery of new vitality. The poem runs into frustrations and failures. The exercise of the imagination repeatedly reveals, for example, how easily creativity can become another form of remembering. This is what happens when Byron attempts to imaginatively recreate the internal lives of Napoleon and Rousseau: Byron's portraits of these figures are 'doublings of himself'.[9] Rousseau, for example, as a 'self-torturing . . . apostle of affliction' (*CHP*, III.77.1–2) suffering 'a fever at the core' (*CHP*, III.42.8) and living 'one long war with self-sought foes' (*CHP*, III.80.1), is clearly a version, if a 'distorted version',[10] of the Byron who suffers his own 'gulf of phantasy and flame'. Byron's imagination does not offer forgetfulness here but conjures up a reminder. Imaginative recreation mutates into a form of recollection.

The poem encounters a number of such twists of consciousness but at the very beginning of its famous storm sequence (*CHP*, III.17–96) it does dramatise the discovery of both forgetfulness and 'a being more intense' in imaginative activity:

> The sky is changed! – and such a change! Oh night,
> And storm, and darkness, ye are wondrous strong,
> Yet lovely in your strength, as is the light
> Of a dark eye in woman! Far along,
> From peak to peak, the rattling crags among
> Leaps the live thunder! Not from one lone cloud,
> But every mountain now hath found a tongue,
> And Jura answers, through her misty shroud,
> Back to the joyous Alps, who call to her aloud!
>
> (*CHP*, III.92)

'Earth-born jars, / And human frailties' are 'forgotten quite' as the creative imagination distracts the self from memory, peopling the landscape by giving the mountains voices and having them converse. A joyous sense of universal community is projected into all. And as the creative imagination projects joy into the landscape, the imagining self discovers that a capacity to feel joy is 'blended with' the birth of that projection – the speaker feels a 'glow' that is born of the idea of such massive joy and 'mix'd with' the 'spirit' of the 'thought' that recreates the storm. We might note a further vitality, too, in the idea of 'the light / Of a dark eye in woman'. Imagining darkness, 'strength' of being, reciprocity, the speaker seems to discover a renewed sexual vitality in his 'crush'd feelings' dearth'.

Similarly, the quest into possibilities for forgetfulness and vitality offered by a more Wordsworthian idea of communing with nature discovers repeated failure before it discovers success. The mind is again and again pulled back from nature's influence to memory by, for example, the 'shattered wall' of Ehrenbreitstein (*CHP*, III.58.1) or 'a small and simple pyramid' near Coblenz beneath which lie the 'ashes' of 'heroes' (*CHP*, III.56.2–4). Physical reminders of Europe's violent history litter the European landscape, interposing reminders of that history between self and nature. Personal memory is not easily escaped either. Byron's 1816 'Alpine Journal', 'a coda to and commentary on' *Childe Harold* III,[11] and containing 'the germs' of *Manfred*,[12] offers a striking example of personal memory intervening between self and nature: 'Passed *whole woods of withered pines – all withered* – trunks stripped & barkless – branches lifeless – done by a single winter – their appearance reminded me of me & my family.'[13] Painful memory here acts like a prism that transforms landscape into an image of itself. The poem, too, dramatises the power of personal memory to reclaim the self even while it is in the midst of attending to otherness:

> Clear, placid Leman! thy contrasted lake,
> With the wild world I dwelt in, is a thing
> Which warns me, with its stillness, to forsake
> Earth's troubled waters for a purer spring.
> This quiet sail is as a noiseless wing
> To waft me from distraction; once I loved
> Torn ocean's roar, but thy soft murmuring
> Sounds sweet as if a sister's voice reproved,
> That I with stern delights should e'er have been so moved.
>
> (*CHP*, III.85)

Byron seems on the verge of being able to 'forsake', forget, 'troubled waters' – of following Harold and filling his 'cup' (*CHP*, III.8.9) from 'a purer fount' (*CHP*, III.9.3) than the 'poisoned' 'springs' (*CHP*, III.7.6) of memory on the 'holier ground' (*CHP*, III.9.3) of nature. He is already being distracted from 'distraction' (here meaning 'disorder or confusion caused by internal dissension' or 'mental derangement, craziness, insanity' (*OED*)). Yet without warning memory intervenes – 'once I loved' – and with it comes the recollection of separation: the mention of a 'sister's voice' brings both Augusta and Byron's separation from her to mind. Deliberate forgetting is clearly a finely balanced mental activity always under threat of being overwhelmed by the return of memory.

Yet forgetfulness is found in the contemplation of nature, and with it another discovery of 'life intense':

> All heaven and earth are still – though not in sleep,
> But breathless, as we grow when feeling most;
> And silent, as we stand in thoughts too deep: –
> All heaven and earth are still: From the high host
> Of stars, to the lull'd lake and mountain-coast,
> All is concentered in a life intense,
> Where not a beam, nor air, nor leaf is lost,
> But hath a part of being, and a sense
> Of that which is of all Creator and defence.
>
> (*CHP*, III.89)

In this moment of absolute attentiveness to 'all heaven and earth', 'feelings' dearth' has become 'feeling most'; the image of the 'leafless desart' of the blasted Byronic hero's mind is replaced by the image of a mind standing 'in thoughts too deep' for words. This transformation is born of forgetfulness: not only is there no hint of painful memory here but also absolutely no reference to self. The self is distracted from the self, the mind from memory, and both discover that they are part of 'a life intense' that is 'concentered' in something other than self.

This is the climax of the poem's quest for forgetfulness and for sources of new vitality in a 'Wordsworthian' communion with 'the wonder-works of God and Nature's hand'. In this climax, 'absorption in nature' appears to be 'nothing less than a personal salvation'.[14] Yet the canto also discovers limits to its success. Forgetfulness and replenishment are available, but access to either cannot be sustained indefinitely. The mind can be distracted and revitalised but

> this clay will sink
> Its spark immortal, envying it the light
> To which it mounts as if to break the link
> That keeps us from yon heaven which woos us to its brink.
>
> (*CHP*, III.14.6–9)

Forgetfulness and intensity can only temporarily be found in either imaginative creativity or contemplating nature and participating in its 'life intense'. Both activities are shown to inevitably mutate into recollection. Within seven stanzas of discovering 'a life intense' in the landscape, and four stanzas after Byron's joyful imaginative transformation of the storm, comes the following stanza:

> Sky, mountains, river, winds, lake, lightnings! ye!
> With night, and clouds, and thunder, and a soul
> To make these felt and feeling, well may be
> Things that have made me feel watchful; the far roll
> Of your departing voices, is the knoll
> Of what in me is sleepless, – if I rest.
> But where of ye, oh tempests! is the goal?
> Are ye like those within the human breast?
> Or do ye find, at length, like eagles, some high rest?
>
> (*CHP*, III.96)

Imaginative projections of voices, conversations, and community have become self-projection and recollection. Byron is pulled back down from his imaginative 'flight' by the self-conscious thought of his own watchfulness. His watchfulness reminds him of the reasons for it – the desire for forgetfulness and the pain he wishes to forget ('what in me is sleepless') – and the poem finds itself back where it began, at the painful recollection of separation bereft of natural or imaginative distractions, as the storm passes away. The end of the canto repeats this return to painful memory by returning to the canto's starting point, Byron's daughter and his separation from her: 'My daughter! with thy name this song begun – / My daughter! with thy name thus much shall end' (*CHP*, III.115.1–2). Creativity and nature, the poem insists, offer only a temporary escape from painful memory. They might 'beguile' the 'breast', but only 'for a while' (*CHP*, III.112.5). In the end, Byron's account of his own experience confirms another image of Harold offered at the beginning of the canto:

> His had been quaff'd too quickly, and he found
> The dregs were wormwood; but he fill'd again,
> And from a purer fount, on holier ground,
> And deem'd its spring perpetual; but in vain!
> Still round him clung invisibly a chain
> Which gall'd for ever, fettering though unseen,
> And heavy though it clank'd not; worn with pain,
> Which pined although it spoke not, and grew keen,
> Entering with every step, he took, through many a scene.
>
> (*CHP*, III.9)

Byron, like Harold, finds himself chained to his past, and discovers what he feared at the outset: that painful memory cannot finally be shaken off.

The literary, personal, and historical implications of this failure to sustain forgetfulness are clear: the Byronic hero must remain chained to his galling past, Byron must accept the fact that the separation will continue to cause him intense pain, Europe must continue to weep for its dead.

Nevertheless we should hold in mind the fact that *Childe Harold* III does not offer only failure. There are still moments described in the poem when forgetfulness and new vitality are discovered. And, before closing, Byron presents himself as about to embark on more 'testing' of the 'redemptive possibilities' these moments open up to him:[15]

> But let me quit man's work, again to read
> His maker's
> . . .
> The clouds above me to the white Alps tend,
> And I must pierce them, and survey whate'er
> May be permitted. (*CHP*, III.109.1–2; 5–7)

Childe Harold III's conclusions – that forgetfulness of the past and a renewed connection with the present are available, but only fleetingly – are, finally, provisional, and Byron continued to explore the territory opened up in this canto in the works that followed it. In *Manfred*, he redramatised the unavailability of sustained forgetting but went on to consider what 'redemptive possibilities' might be uncovered despite this. In *Childe Harold* IV, Byron built on *Childe Harold* III's vision of creativity to offer celebrations of the personally, historically, and culturally redemptive capacities of creative thought, and of thought more generally. *Beppo* and *Don Juan* build on all these works to create a comic vision in many ways diametrically opposed to the tragic vision of the Tales.

Manfred, begun in August or September 1816 and completed in April 1817, is informed by and addressed to many of the same personal, literary, and historical contexts as *Childe Harold* III. In the figure of Manfred, Byron is returning to and reconsidering the Byronic hero in the light of *Childe Harold* III. He is also continuing to grapple emotionally with the 'public disaster of his failed marriage and his enforced departure from England amidst rumours of incest with Augusta and ill-treatment of Lady Byron'.[16] But Byron 'rarely lost sight of the larger contexts . . . of his particular situation', often responding 'to personal pressures by seeing his life in historical terms', and *Manfred* is 'about complex struggles and conflicts defining the entire Romantic Age' across Europe.[17] Like *Childe Harold* III, *Manfred* also explores the human capacity to forget and discover renewed vitality after devastation and is, then, 'in certain ways a clear reprise on the third canto of *Childe Harold*'.[18] But *Manfred* also advances beyond the insights and conclusions of *Childe Harold* III – even though, at the outset, it seems to take a step back.

Manfred begins the play on a quest after 'forgetfulness' (I.i.136). He claims to have 'loved' but 'destroy'd' (II.ii.117) the 'lady Astarte' (III.iii.47) and it is the memory of this he wants to escape. Unlike the speaker of *Childe Harold* III, however, Manfred is not looking for revitalisation. He is seeking 'Oblivion, self-oblivion' (I.i.144) and escape from the tortures of memory is his only aim. He quests after this 'self-oblivion' by summoning supernatural aid, attempting to commit suicide, and communing with the natural world as personified by the Witch of the Alps. In each case, he is denied. Finally, he looks for it in a confrontation with the dead Astarte. This he achieves through the supernatural aid of Arimanes ('the Evil principle')[19] and Nemesis. His aim here is to find some relief from his own guilt in Astarte's forgiveness.[20] He is again denied. In response to Manfred's 'am I forgiven?' (II.iii.153), Astarte, having already told him that he will die the next day (II.iii.152), offers only 'Farewell' and his own name (II.iii.154, 156). At the end of Act II, Manfred's quest concludes in failure.

In Act III, however, things change in surprising ways. The Act opens with a moment of calm in which Manfred is suddenly free from both painful memory and the obsession with finding forgetfulness:

> There is a calm upon me –
> Inexplicable stillness! which till now
> Did not belong to what I knew of life.
> If that I did not know philosophy
> To be of all our vanities the motliest,
> The merest word that ever fool'd the ear
> From out the schoolman's jargon, I should deem
> The golden secret, the sought 'Kalon', found,
> And seated in my soul. It will not last,
> But it is well to have known it, though but once:
> It hath enlarged my thoughts with a new sense,
> And I within my tablets would note down
> That there is such a feeling. (*Manfred*, III.i.6–18)

Manfred responds to this 'inexplicable stillness' with the suspicion that it is a foolish delusion and the assumption that 'it will not last'. Yet he acknowledges that he is strangely untortured by memory – that he is experiencing the kind of relief and peace that he had 'sought' in 'self-oblivion'. And Manfred's scepticism begins to give way to a new kind of interest as the speech progresses. Whether it is a transitory delusion or not, what his determined quest failed to find nevertheless appears to be 'seated in' his own 'soul'. His thoughts are 'enlarged' by the 'sense' – by the intimation, intuition, 'feeling' – that, while he could not make the universe give him relief from painful memory, his own being might itself have the capacity to supply his needs. And it is not with scepticism that the speech ends, but with the idea that he would have liked to learn more about this 'feeling'. He 'would note down' that it exists and think on it further.

He knows he is going to die and so does not have time for this. Yet in the time left to him we see a radical change in Manfred and this opening speech 'sets the dynamics for the whole' of Act III and the change it dramatises.[21] Manfred's speech inaugurates a new attentiveness to and appreciation of his own being and what it makes available that will grow rapidly during the final Act and climax in a surprising commitment to that being, and what it opens up to him, at the moment Manfred dies. Manfred is particularly intrigued by a memory that presents itself as he recalls standing 'within the Colosseum's wall' (III.iv.9–10):

> And thou didst shine, thou rolling moon, upon
> All this, and cast a wide and tender light,
> Which soften'd down the hoar austerity
> Of rugged desolation, and fill'd up,
> As 'twere, anew, the gaps of centuries;
> Leaving that beautiful which still was so,
> And making that which was not.
>
> (*Manfred*, III.iv.31–7)

Manfred is attending to his own mental activity in a way we have not seen him do before and the result is that memory lifts his mood and lightens, for a moment, the 'heavy and the weary weight / Of all this unintelligible world'. It is here that the exploration of resources for recovery available to suffering humanity that runs through *Childe Harold* III and *Manfred* finally breaks clear of the absolute limits of the Tales. There, as in *Childe Harold* III, the self is limited by, finally contained by, inescapable, painful memory. At this point in *Manfred*, however, painful memory is located within a larger *variety* of memories thrown at Manfred. Manfred begins to recognise that memory is not only capable of imposing intensely painful recollections on him, but also capable of offering him consoling, comforting, and revitalising memories like this one. Obsessed with finding an escape from one kind of memory he has sought escape from all. Forced to give up his obsession, he re-encounters his own mind's ability to recollect pleasure – and begins to recognise the value of that ability. In it, there is an unlooked-for vitality: his 'thought' is taking 'wildest flight' (III.iv.43). It is a vitality that asserts its power unexpectedly – a spontaneity that is unprompted, unpredictable, and very different from the pain brought by torturing memory – and Manfred yields to it and enjoys it. Memory, as well as having the power to crush, now begins to reveal its redemptive potential to Manfred, and he is attentive and open to its influence.

Other positive capacities of his own being suddenly come into sharp focus for Manfred in Act III. There is, for example, his ability to 'stand upon' his own 'strength' (III.iv.119–20) and bear suffering. Manfred celebrates the power of his will, but the sudden moment of calm that opens Act III also suggests the idea that what seemed to be an inescapable devastation imposed by painful memory may, in fact, have been imposed, in part at least, by that will. Manfred's moment of calm follows immediately after, as if caused by, the dropping of the determined will to find forgetfulness; as if all along the determination to forget had been imposing memory upon him and making escape from it impossible. To obsessively seek escape, we might say, is to insist on one's prison.

The idea that Manfred has been imposing suffering on himself in this way combines with a recognition of the self-destructive power of his own sense of guilt to produce his insistence that he was his 'own destroyer' (III.iv.139). Manfred does not dismiss the will, but reassesses its value and usefulness, redirecting it into a defiant rejection of the religious doctrines of the Abbot and the Faustian claims of the spirits that come to claim his soul in payment for their help in conjuring Astarte. In this defiance we see Manfred refusing 'to acknowledge the power of any agency outside' the 'self' and wilfully assuming 'responsibility for his life'.[22] But Manfred does not assume wilful control over his life: he willingly relinquishes such control. Over the course of Act III he has come to recognise, and increasingly value, the surprising vitality and variousness of his own being and what is made available to him through it. His final moments show him simultaneously fighting to clear a space for his being in all its variety and giving himself over to that being on its own terms. His dying words, ''tis not so difficult to die' (III.iv.151), which resist explication but which Byron claimed contained 'the whole effect & moral of the poem',[23] suggest a final acquiescence in his own being, a 'repose' in the flow of his existence,[24] and an openness to whatever his being presents him with – even, paradoxically, death.[25]

Manfred does not play out the implications of this new attitude, or offer it as a sustainable way forward for the Byronic hero, Byron, or post-Waterloo Europe. But Byron is glimpsing the beginning of a way forward and he is offering it as a beginning. It is a beginning that rejects transcendental answers to human problems, but looks instead to resources to be found within human existence. Here we can see Byron 'symbolically' working 'his way through to the mental sanity' and renewed vitality glimpsed but finally overwhelmed by memory in *Childe Harold* III.[26] We can also see the Byronic hero moving out from beneath the shadow of crushing memory and towards 'the psychological perspective that made *Don Juan* possible'[27] with the discovery that various vitalities, not just a single dominant and destructive vitality, exist within his own being. But *Manfred* is also looking for an answer to Europe's sense of living under the weight of a long and violent past *and* in a diminished, withered present, and it is glimpsing a possible answer in a Prometheanesque resistance to the transcendental solutions offered by religious traditions combined with a yielding to human vitality in all its spontaneity, unpredictability, and variety.

Manfred only offers the beginning of such an answer. A range of later works extend and develop Byron's thinking in *Manfred*, however. *Mazeppa* and *Childe Harold* IV are important examples here. But most important are Byron's comic narratives, *Beppo* and *Don Juan*, which build on the explorations and insights of both *Manfred* and *Childe Harold* III.

Forgetfulness and submission to the vitalities of being and the flow of existence, for example, are fundamental to Byron's comic vision. In *Beppo*, for instance, masculine energies that push the narrative towards violence are distracted by the feminine (83–98), and male anger and vengefulness are momentarily forgotten at precisely the moment they might begin to push events towards tragedy. This temporary forgetting helps to ensure a comic ending of reconciliation. Such narrative forgetfulness is itself made possible by another kind of forgetting – vital to Byronic comedy – that also has its origins in *Childe Harold* III. The narrator of *Beppo* is a 'broken Dandy' (52) but passes over his own brokenness.

This ability to detach writing from suffering is rooted in a lesson first 'taught' to Byron during the writing of *Childe Harold* III: 'to conceal . . . the tyrant spirit of our thought, / Is a stern task of soul: – No matter, – it is taught' (*CHP*, III.111.8–9). The 'task' here, 'taught' by the recognition that to fully 'embody and unbosom . . . / That which is most within me' (*CHP*, III.97.1–2) is not possible, is to relinquish the hope of therapeutically 'unbosoming' what is painful and to resolve to 'live and die unheard / With a most voiceless thought, sheathing it as a sword' (*CHP*, III.97.8–9), wilfully divorcing the act of writing from the suffering of pain. And such self-discipline paid very real poetic dividends in Byron's poetry by creating space for kinds of writing other than self-expression, self-therapy, and the scrutiny of the effects of painful recollection. In terms of *Childe Harold* III it created space for the celebration of Clarens as the 'birth-place of deep Love' (99); in terms of Byron's career as a whole it created space for comic poetry.

Like *Beppo*, *Don Juan* often moves forward past disaster and devastation by means of moments of forgetfulness. The relationship between Juan and Haidee is possible, for example, because Juan can forget Julia. But in *Don*

Juan, moments of forgetfulness are repeatedly linked to an often unavoidable submission to immediate vitality. In an attempt to explain Juan's forgetting Julia, and perhaps recalling Manfred's beautifying moon, the narrator of *Don Juan* offers:

> . . . no doubt, the moon
> Does these things for us, and whenever newly a
> Strong palpitation rises, 'tis her boon,
> Else how the devil is it that fresh features
> Have such a charm for us poor human creatures?
> (*Don Juan*, II.208.4–8)

The narrator can only speculate about the moon's influence, but he makes it very clear that, for whatever reason and under whatever benevolent cosmic influence, Juan is 'charmed' out of memory by 'fresh features' – that a 'strong palpitation rises' in him and carries him out of recollection. A very different example comes when Juan is distracted from the pain of the separation by seasickness (II.19–21). Of course, Juan does not escape memory entirely – the memory of Haidee is very present when he is being seduced by the Sultana (V.117, 124), for instance – but he can be distracted from memory by a sudden sympathy for the tearful Sultana (V.140–3) and by sexual desire – see, for example, Juan 'ogling all' the 'charms' of the women in the Harem (VI.29).

This is clearly some way from the wilful and deeply self-conscious quest after forgetfulness and renewal of *Childe Harold* III, and different from the deliberate acquiescence of Manfred's final moments. Juan is seemingly subjected to moments of arousal and forgetfulness whether he wants them or not. Indeed, in *Don Juan* devastating recollection is as difficult to sustain, at times, as forgetting. Forgetfulness is recognised as being as much a part of human life as memory, and the power and value of a variety of contrary human impulses is a principal theme of *Don Juan*. It is here we see *Don Juan* building on and extending *Manfred*'s location of painful memory within a larger variousness of memory, and can begin to see the importance of *Manfred* in the genesis of *Don Juan*. Equally, Byron's exploration of forgetfulness, its availability and value, which reaches its fullest and finest expression in *Don Juan*, begins in 1816 with *Childe Harold* III. And in *Don Juan* it is still sustained by the kind of separation of poetic articulation from suffering that Byron claimed to have been first 'taught' in 1816. The poem's progress from Julia to Haidee, for example, is partly made possible by the narrator's wilful narrative 'shelving' of Julia: 'But let me change this theme, which grows too sad, / And lay this sheet of sorrows on the shelf' (IV.74.1–2).

The poems of 1816–17 paved the way for Byron's greatest poetry in other ways too and they represent one of the most important transitional phases in Byron's career as poet. Pushing away from the tragic vision of the Tales and moving forward in new directions, exploring new areas of human consciousness and developing a vision of humanity as 'antithetically mixt' (*CHP*, III.36.2) – capable of forgetting and of pleasurable recollection as well as tortured by crushing memories, capable of imaginative creativity as well as violent destruction, in touch with powerful sources of vitality as well as subject to death, capable of yielding and submission as well as determination and defiant wilfulness – *Childe Harold* III and *Manfred* made Byron's masterpiece, *Don Juan*, possible.

NOTES

1. Jerome McGann, in McGann (ed.), *Lord Byron: The Complete Poetical Works*, 7 vols. (Oxford: Clarendon Press, 1980–93) I, 300.
2. Caroline Franklin, *Byron: A Literary Life* (Basingstoke: Macmillan, 2000), p. 91.
3. Jerome Christensen, *Lord Byron's Strength: Romantic Writing and Commercial Society* (Baltimore: Johns Hopkins University Press, 1993), p. 156.
4. Franklin, *Byron: A Literary Life*, p. 91.
5. *Ibid.*, p. 92.
6. Letter to Annabella Milbanke, 6 September 1813, in *BLJ*, III, 109.
7. Vincent Newey, quoting Otto Rank, 'Authoring the Self: *Childe Harold* III and IV', in *Centring the Self: Subjectivity, Society and Reading from Thomas Gray to Thomas Hardy* (Aldershot: Scolar Press, 1995), pp. 178–210: p. 185.
8. Jerome McGann, *Fiery Dust* (Chicago and London: University of Chicago Press, 1968), p. 114.
9. Newey, 'Authoring the Self', p. 185.
10. Michael O'Neill, '"A Being More Intense": Byron', in *Romanticism and the Self Conscious Poem* (Oxford: Clarendon Press, 1997), p. 109.
11. Jerome McGann, 'Byron and Wordsworth', in James Soderholm (ed.), *Byron and Romanticism* (Cambridge University Press, 2002), p. 177.
12. Letter to John Murray, 17 September 1817, in *BLJ*, V, 268.
13. 'Alpine Journal', in *BLJ*, V, 96–105; 102.
14. Newey, 'Authoring the Self', p. 187.
15. *Ibid.*, p. 188.
16. Jane Stabler, *Burke to Byron, Barbauld to Baillie, 1790–1830* (Basingstoke: Palgrave, 2002), p. 65.
17. Daniel P. Watkins, 'The Dramas of Lord Byron: *Manfred* and *Marino Faliero*', in Jane Stabler (ed.), *Byron* (London: Longman, 1998), pp. 52–65: pp. 53, 54.
18. McGann, 'Byron and Wordsworth', p. 181.
19. Letter to John Murray, 15 February 1817, in *BLJ*, V, 170.
20. If 'his treatment of Astarte . . . can be forgiven, then the torture' of his 'interminable despair will at least be moderated' (Martyn Corbett, *Byron and Tragedy* (Basingstoke: Macmillan, 1988), p. 40).
21. Corbett, *Byron and Tragedy*, p. 41.
22. Drummond Bone, *Byron* (Tavistock: Northcote House, 2000), pp. 44, 45.
23. Letter to John Murray, 12 August 1817, in *BLJ*, V, 257.

8

ALAN RICHARDSON

Byron and the theatre

Byron's considerable body of dramatic poetry poses special challenges for literary criticism, and studies of Byron have often had little to say about the plays as plays. In part, this neglect reflects a larger failure to bring the verse drama of the Romantic poets comfortably within the standard categories of literary history. All of the canonical Romantics – Coleridge, Wordsworth, Byron, Shelley, and Keats – wrote at least one verse play, but until the last dozen years or so these have tended to be dismissed as misguided attempts at 'closet drama': plays meant to be read but not performed. The counter-impulse to read at least some works of Romantic verse drama as 'mental theatre' (Byron's term) – innovative and iconoclastic poetic forms rather than stage plays *manqués* – can work well enough for a 'dramatic poem' like *Manfred* or an intellectual drama like *Cain*.[1] It tends, though, to lose sight of the productive tension between the dramatic works of the Romantic poets and the lively and politically fraught theatrical culture of their time.[2] Byron not only produced a larger and more varied canon of verse drama – eight works, if one counts *Manfred* and the fragmentary *Deformed Transformed* – than any of the other canonical poets, but he also stands out as the only one with extensive, practical experience of the stage. This overview of Byron's poetic drama, then, opens with a look at his relation to the contemporary theatre.

To begin with, Byron was a gifted and enthusiastic amateur actor, dating from his schooldays at Harrow, where he recited Lear and other roles to gratifying applause. As late as 1822, Byron attempted to get up an amateur production of *Othello* while living in exile at Pisa. Though the plan fell through, Byron's interpretation of Iago inspired Thomas Medwin to remark that 'perhaps Lord Byron would have made the finest actor in the world'.[3] Medwin was also impressed with Byron's ability to recall and convincingly mimic the actors he had heard on the London stage years before. In a note added to the preface to *Marino Faliero*, Byron professes his admiration for the great actors of the Romantic-era stage: John Philip Kemble, G. F. Cooke,

Edmund Kean, Sarah Siddons, and (in comic parts) Robert William Elliston. The 'long complaints of the actual state of the drama arise', he stresses, 'from no fault of the performers' (*CPW*, IV, 563).

Nevertheless, the 'state of the drama' was indeed a favourite subject for adverse criticism at the time, and Byron's most extensive experience with the contemporary stage, his association with the Drury Lane theatre, came about as a direct result of such 'complaints'.

Drury Lane, along with its rival theatre at Covent Garden, held a monopoly on London productions of all 'legitimate' drama during the regular season: that is, on tragedy and what Byron called 'gentleman's comedy' (*CPW*, IV, 563). Despite the efforts of great, even legendary, actors, however, both Drury Lane and Covent Garden were widely viewed as failing in their mission to guarantee the health of what was variously called 'legitimate', 'regular', or 'national' drama. One problem inhered in the design of the theatres themselves: in an effort to increase profits, theatre managers had insisted on an absurdly enlarged house, and many spectators simply could not hear the actors' spoken lines as a result. Gesture, attitude, and declamation were relied on to convey action and emotion, resulting in what was widely seen as a loss of nuance and a constant temptation toward 'ranting' and other forms of overacting. Meanwhile, the unlicensed, 'illegitimate' stage – including pantomime, burlesque, puppet shows, melodrama, spectacle, and extravaganza – had entered an especially lively and inventive era and began drawing audiences away from the two patent theatres. The attempts of beleaguered theatre managers to borrow such innovations for the licensed stage – most notoriously including 'quadruped drama', the incorporation of horses, dogs, camels, and even elephants into the action – only served to deepen the perceived crisis of 'legitimate' theatre.[4] Drury Lane and Covent Garden were constantly running up losses, and various rescue plans were broached to revivify the licensed theatres, or at least to keep them solvent.

One such plan, led by the brewer and Whig politician Samuel Whitbread, came to involve the establishment of an amateur board of directors for the recently rebuilt Drury Lane, with a subcommittee empowered to run the theatre as a renewed centre for 'national' culture. As a titled aristocrat aligned with the liberal Whigs and as an acclaimed poet, Byron was seen as an ideal choice for the subcommittee: his talent, reputation, and social status would help restore confidence in Whitbread's stewardship. Byron duly became a member in June 1815, and his addition was initially seen as a coup for those wishing to restore the 'regular' drama. The arrangement did not work out, however, and by the time Byron had begun his period of exile in April 1816, there was little to regret so far as abandoning the Drury Lane project was concerned. The theatre continued to lose money, and control was eventually given over to a professional, the actor-manager Elliston, who brought back the 'illegitimate' conventions and effects he had mastered in the unlicensed playhouses.[5] The experience, however, gave Byron a full season of active experience behind the scenes of a working stage, a stint that left him both more knowing in the ways of the theatre and more cynical regarding the immediate prospects for serious poetic drama in London.

Byron's special duty – a dreary enough one – involved working through Drury Lane's massive stockpile of unsolicited scripts looking for decent plays, in addition to soliciting new works from noted writers. The 'number of plays upon the shelves were about five hundred', he later recalled; 'I do not think that of those which I saw – there was one which could be conscientiously tolerated' (*BLJ*, IX, 35). Invitations to Coleridge and Scott led nowhere, though Byron did successfully promote the production of Charles Maturin's *Bertram*, which enjoyed a good run some weeks after Byron himself had left England for good. Given the dearth of material suitable to the theatre's renewed 'national' mission, why did Byron not contribute a play himself? He did make a start on one – *Werner* – which he left behind him with only the first act partially finished, eventually writing it over from scratch six years later. (After Byron's death, *Werner* became his one popular stage success.) His published verse plays, however, Byron repeatedly insisted 'were not composed with the most remote view to the stage' (*CPW*, VI, 16). The poet who (in *Hours of Idleness*) had urged Richard Brinsley Sheridan to produce 'One classic drama, and reform the stage' (*Hours of Idleness*, 585) seemed curiously averse to doing so himself.

Byron's disavowal of any wish for theatrical production, in the face of his active interest in a reformed stage, has struck many critics as problematic. David V. Erdman's 1939 essay 'Byron's Stage Fright' is still cited as the definitive statement of the issue, despite serious flaws in its argument. For one, Erdman relies on a crudely applied Adlerian psychology, a (now dated) school of psychoanalysis that stresses adult overcompensation for childhood traumas. In this spirit, Erdman argues that Byron's inordinate sensitivity to public exposure (with dual origins in his lameness and in inadequate mothering) led him to crave popular success in the theatre while dreading the potential humiliation should his plays fail. Any psychopathological explanation for Byron's ambivalence, however, must occlude the larger cultural issues that help account for the similar resistance to stage representation evinced by a number of Romantic-era poets and critics alike.[6] More troubling, perhaps, is Erdman's extensive reliance on carefully selected and sometimes misleadingly pruned quotations from Byron, 'lifted out of context and assembled to support a predetermined theory'.[7] If the 'stage fright' thesis needs rethinking, however, Erdman unquestionably established Byron's intense and long-term interest in acting, theatricals, and the London stage.

Byron's claim that his own dramatic works were written 'without regard to the Stage' but for the 'mental theatre of the reader' (*BLJ*, VIII, 210) is entirely compatible with a wish for their eventual representation on a more suitable stage of the future. Byron's resistance concerns a specific theatrical climate that, as he well knew from his Drury Lane days, would have all but guaranteed failure for the 'regular English drama' (*BLJ*, VIII, 187) he attempted to create with his historical tragedies, *Marino Faliero*, *Sardanapalus*, and *The Two Foscari*. As Margaret Howell demonstrates in amusing detail throughout her study, Byron's verse plays needed major cutting, reworking, and livening up even to imperfectly meet the expectations of nineteenth-century London audiences. Early productions of *Sardanapalus*, for example, were enlivened by musical interludes like the catchy 'Assyrian Cymbal Dance' and most admired for the spectacular fire effects that all but literally brought down the house in the final scene. Yet Byron remained open to the potential revival of his plays on a reformed stage of the future: 'the Stage is not my object – and even interferes with it – as long as it is in it's [*sic*] present state' (*BLJ*, VIII, 210).[8] Writing immediately for 'a mental theatre', however, allowed Byron not only to envision a new era of 'regular' drama, but to write dramatic works of a much greater length, and touching on more sensitive political, ideological, and religious issues than would have been allowed on the licensed stage of the time.

The question of Byron's ambivalence toward stage representation does not have a single answer in any case. As Erdman himself concedes, Byron seems not to have intended what he called his 'metaphysical' dramas – *Manfred*, *Cain*, and *Heaven and Earth* – for production on any stage, present or future.[9] Rather, these works are more usefully understood as experiments in poetic form, combining lyric, dialogic, and choric elements and drawing eclectically for inspiration on Aeschylean drama, descriptions of medieval plays, and Gothic melodrama, as well as on contemporary experimental works like Goethe's *Faust* and Shelley's *Prometheus Unbound*. Their relation to the nineteenth-century stage is an axiomatically oblique one. The three historical tragedies, on the other hand, are presented in direct reaction to the crisis of the legitimate London theatre that Byron had experienced first hand, models of what a restored 'regular' drama might look like. These are neoclassical in form: 'It has been my object to be as simple and severe as Alfieri' (*BLJ*, VIII, 152), the Italian neoclassical dramatist whose works Byron greatly admired. *Werner*, in its completed version, has often been seen as Byron's attempt (ironical or not) to craft a play that would succeed on the stage of the time, 'calculated' as Erdman dourly puts it 'to suit the degraded tastes of the contemporary audience'.[10] Byron's final play, *The Deformed Transformed*, which he left as a fragment, draws again on *Faust*, but in a manner of its own. For all their differences in form, style, and stage-worthiness, however, the dramatic works share a number of recurring themes, character types, and plot elements that lend a measure of continuity – if nothing like unity – to Byron's experiments in dramatic writing considered as a group.

Byron subtitled *Manfred* (1816) a 'Dramatic Poem' and described it as a 'sort of metaphysical drama', the 'very Antipodes of the stage and is meant to be so' (*BLJ*, v, 194). If *Manfred* was designed to be unstageable, however, it still borrowed motifs, effects, and even 'mental' scenery from the Gothic melodramas then popular in the London theatres. More than one critic has seen *Manfred* as approaching burlesque in its relation to the witch plays and Gothic shockers of the day. But contemporary reviewers like John Wilson found *Manfred* an 'extraordinary' if flawed work of dramatic poetry; a 'very powerful and most poetical production' in the words of Francis Jeffrey, one of Byron's most astute critics. Jeffrey noted the formal and stylistic daring of the piece, including its incorporation of choric elements and lyrical songs, reminiscent of early Greek drama: *Manfred* 'reminds us much more of the Prometheus of Aeschylus, than of any more modern performance',[11] not least in the character of the title figure, tormented, sleepless, rebellious, larger than life.

Jeffrey also began a long tradition of viewing *Manfred* as a static monodrama: 'It has no action; no plot – and no characters; Manfred merely muses and suffers from beginning to end.'[12] It is true that *Manfred* deals more with reaction than with action. Haunted by a crime committed in the past, recounted with deliberate obscurity but involving violence, incest, bloodshed, and the death of his beloved sister, Astarte, Manfred alternately seeks 'self-oblivion' and renewed contact with Astarte, or at least with her shade. Deploying a 'mixed mythology of [his] own', Byron confronts Manfred with a series of spirits, demons, witches, and deities, including the 'Evil principle' (*BLJ*, v, 195) of Manichaean tradition. These confrontations invariably leave Manfred in the same self-involved, self-tormented state as before. The foreshortening and deflation of one potential dramatic encounter after another is intentional, enacting the 'withering of social life' that ideological critics have located at the poem's thematic core.[13] Having felt 'no sympathy with breathing flesh' in his youth, Manfred finds no more kinship with spirits, however powerful. They inspire a competing show of Manfred's own power – he refuses to worship or to bargain with them – but each attenuated struggle ends in stalemate, and Manfred remains his own master but categorically alone.

The failure to break out of a profoundly isolated self-consciousness finds its ultimate expression in Manfred's memories and invocations of Astarte (a name Byron borrowed from a tale of incestuous siblings in Montesquieu's *Persian Letters*).[14] Astarte is evidently not only Manfred's sister but his twin:

> She was like to me in lineaments – her eyes,
> Her hair, her features, all, to the very tone
> Even of her voice, they said were like to mine
> (*Manfred*, II.ii.105–7)

The only being with whom Manfred could feel anything like sympathy is virtually a mirror image of Manfred himself. The potential for an idealized androgynous hero gives way to the absorption of a desired feminine counterpart into an aggressively incorporative masculine self: 'I loved her, and destroy'd her!' (II.ii.117). When he finally confronts her reticent shade, the 'Phantom of Astarte' speaks fragmentary lines, the first and last of which are merely 'Manfred!' (I.iv.150–5). If this is monodrama, it is a monodrama acutely aware of and self-consciously revealing its own formal limitations.

In seeking to restore a serious, 'national', poetic drama, the Romantic poets were constantly aware of the precedent of Shakespeare, who had become an icon both for tragedy at its highest pitch and for the staging of a British national identity. Although Byron held that Shakespeare was the '*worst* of models' (*BLJ*, VIII, 152) for a renewed drama and would turn to Alfieri and other neoclassicists for alternative examples of regular dramatic structure, the verbal texture of Byron's dramatic poetry is everywhere interwoven with Shakespearean echoes and allusions. *Macbeth*, with its own brooding, sleepless, criminal protagonist, hovers behind *Manfred*. Byron echoes the famous banquet scene (made much of in Romantic-era stagings of *Macbeth*) when Manfred, about to drink from a wine goblet, sees 'blood upon the brim' (II.i.21); the entry of the Destinies a bit later (II.iii) is modelled on the entry of the witches in *Macbeth* (I.iii). The final act of *Manfred*, however, makes repeated allusion not to Shakespearean tragedy but to Miltonic epic, borrowing the very terms of Manfred's enduring defiance from Milton's Satan. In lines that reverberate throughout Byron's dramatic writing, Satan had announced a rebellious yet dubious autonomy in the first book of *Paradise Lost* – 'the mind is its own place, and in itself / Can make a Heav'n of Hell, a Hell of Heav'n' (I.254–5); the corollary, as Satan discovers in Book IV, is: 'myself am Hell' (IV.75). Resisting the local Abbot's efforts at an eleventh-hour conversion, Manfred grounds his own claim to autonomy on

> The innate tortures of that deep despair,
> Which is remorse without the fear of hell
> But all in all sufficient of itself
> Would make a hell of heaven
>
> (*Manfred*, III.i.70–3)

'Back to thy hell!', Manfred commands the demon who arrives to claim his soul:

> The mind which is immortal makes itself
> Requital for its good or evil thoughts,
> Is its own origin of ill and end,
> And its own place and time
>
> (*Manfred*, III.iv.389–92)

The presence of quotation within these assertions of psychic independence and absolute self-identity discloses the emptiness of Manfred's radically autonomous pose. In *Manfred*, Byron models an asocial, isolated, heroic selfhood of titanic proportions only to underscore its limitations. The failure of dramatic action does not so much compromise as constitute the fragmented tragic trajectory followed by the work and its hero.

Marino Faliero (1821), published four years after *Manfred*, represents a remarkably different approach, more verse play than dramatic poem. It launches Byron's remarkable 'experiment', conducted over the next two years, to displace the 'wild old English drama' with a 'regular tragedy' (*BLJ*, VIII, 210) constructed along neoclassical lines. Like *The Two Foscari* (1821), also set in Venice, *Marino Faliero* reflects as well Byron's frustrations with a post-Waterloo political climate dominated by reactionary pragmatists like Castlereagh and Metternich. Although Byron did not write the Venetian tragedies as allegorical commentaries on the present, their concerns with political oppression, the corruptions of empire, the state's encroachment on private life, and the impoverishment of individual agency all speak to the social and political constraints of the post-Napoleonic moment. The 'claustrophobic' effect that critics have attributed to Byron's approach to the classical 'unities' of time and place, as well as the drama of 'tableaux and rhetorical gestures' displacing more energetic forms of stage action, might be read as formal responses to the same set of concerns.[15] More broadly, Byron's experiment with neoclassical tragedy fits with his defence of Pope and of a neoclassical aesthetic, while providing a formal alternative to the 'seductive but dangerous ghost of Shakespeare' and the 'irregular' English dramaturgy he represents.[16]

As a dramatic hero, Faliero inherits something of Manfred's fierce isolation, though he comes by it in a remarkably different manner. 'Unlike / To other spirits of his order' (II.i.14–15), Faliero has nevertheless striven to serve Venice as an exemplary citizen-soldier over a very long and dignified career. His dubious reward, however, is to be given the position of Doge, nominal head of state but in practical terms a 'slave' to the aristocratic oligarchy that rules behind Faliero's noble façade (I.ii.106). When the old Doge's young wife is libelled as an adulteress – in graffiti written on the Doge's very throne – and the affront goes virtually unpunished, Faliero's political impotence is exposed at the very moment that any illusion of a sacrosanct private life is blasted. Suffering the '*hell* within me and around' (III.ii.519) that, like Manfred, he inherits from Milton's Satan, Faliero emulates the 'first Rebel' in agreeing to lead a violent coup against the patrician overclass (*BLJ*, IX, 103). Envisioning the blood-bath that will overwhelm his kinsmen and former friends, Faliero takes on something of Macbeth as well, accepting 'hands incarnadine' (III.ii.509) as the price for revenge and political renewal.[17] His isolation from his own class becomes absolute as the Doge bids 'farewell' to 'all social memory' and steels himself to oversee the butchering of the entire oligarchy (III.ii.327).

Faliero's dilemma as an uneasy aristocrat who would break ranks to establish a 'fair free commonwealth' (III.ii.169), yet feels a distinct antipathy to the 'common ruffians' with whom he conspires (I.ii.582), finds resonance in Byron's own political statements of the period. In an appendix to *The Two Foscari*, Byron declares future 'convulsions' of the state 'inevitable', yet claims to be 'no revolutionist': 'I wish to see the English constitution restored and not destroyed.' 'Born an aristocrat', he continues, 'and naturally one by temperament . . . what have I to gain by a revolution?' (*CPW*, VI, 223). Faliero's internal struggles with a 'naturally' aristocratic temper, not to mention an aversion to slaughtering his former playmates and friends wholesale, impels the 'mental' drama of the unfolding tragedy as each successive burst of remorse yields to the Doge's bitter, angry, yet strangely idealistic resolve. His compromise political stance – 'Not rash equality but equal rights' (III.ii.170) – seems obviously impracticable in context, yet the corruption of the Venetian republic seems to demand resolute action. A maritime empire with its 'hundred isles' (III.ii.134), having 'open'd India's wealth / To Europe' (V.i.14–15), Venice follows classical Rome and precedes nineteenth-century Britain as a state facing the implosion of its republican institutions under the pressures of imperial extension and rule. At the same time, the Doge's ineffectual plotting for 'his people's freedom' (III.2.438) foreshadows Byron's own frustrations with the Carbonari, the rather feckless revolutionaries he aided in their campaign to throw off Austrian rule in Italy. Faliero's curse preceding his execution prophesies the end of the republic and Venice's enslavement first to a 'bastard Attila' – Napoleon – and then to the 'Hun' (V.iii.49, 59).

Although the internal struggles of the title character dominate the action of the play, *Marino Faliero* does not lack strong supporting roles. The plebeian conspirator, Israel Bertuccio, who provides the Doge with a coup in progress, acts to catalyse Faliero's latent energies, while the patrician senator Lioni convincingly embodies the stubborn vitality of the aristocracy, however corrupt. The characterization of the Doge's wife, Angiolina, can be initially offputting. Some critics have found her sexual naiveté unbelievable and her sexual apathy (she dedicates herself to subduing her 'baser passions' (II.i.98)) unpalatable. As Caroline Franklin points out, however, the awkward coupling of the 'octogenarian' Doge with his young and beautiful wife – all the more striking if witnessed, or at least visualized, on the stage – functions to underscore Faliero's role as 'sterile and impotent symbol of patrician rule'.[18] The slander on Angiolina festers in her husband's mind not because he is jealous – Byron did not want to compete with *Othello* – but because it exposes his double impotence as political figure-head and passionless husband. He has no interest in Angiolina's 'girlish beauty' (II.i.312), he tells her, and feels for her not 'romantic' but 'patriarchal' love (II.i.363). Patrician domination proves as problematic in the bedroom as in the council hall.

Marino Faliero was staged by Elliston at Drury Lane in 1821, against Byron's express wishes and despite the court injunction his publisher, Murray, had obtained at Byron's urging. It ran for seven nights and attracted neither full houses nor fulsome reviews. Its failure pained Byron but did not surprise him. 'Murray writes that they want to act the Tragedy of Marino Faliero', he wrote in his journal; 'more fools they, it was written for the closet' (*BLJ*, VIII, 22). Byron knew that it was much too long for the contemporary stage – Elliston had it cut by 1,462 lines – and that it was 'too regular', both in its neoclassical structure and its avoidance of the 'melodramatic – no surprises, no starts, nor trap-doors . . . and no love – the grand ingredient of a modern play' (*BLJ*, VIII, 23). *The Two Foscari*, his second Venetian tragedy, is even more austere. Whereas Faliero's indignities propel him inexorably toward fatal action, the Doge Foscari watches with excruciating passivity as his son is imprisoned, judicially tortured, banished, deprived of his children, and finally dies before he can return to exile. *The Two Foscari* shares not only its setting but a number of thematic concerns with *Marino Faliero*: the impotence of the Doge, the remorseless 'despotism' of oligarchic rule (I.i.267), the corroding effect of empire – Venice has become an 'ocean-Rome' (III.i.154) – on republican institutions. The condition exemplified by Faliero is now universalized to Venice itself: 'this is hell', Doge Foscari laments, and all are 'slaves, / The greatest as the meanest' (II.i.365, 357–8).

Yet Foscari in some ways proves the antithesis of his 'attainted predecessor' (V.i.232); he not only refuses to act, but refuses so much as to 'curse' at the drama's end (V.i.223). His son, Jacopo, also contrasts with Faliero, who (even in defeat) insists that certain men can 'make their own minds all in all' (IV.ii.278). Jacopo eschews the Satanic pose of Faliero – and Manfred – before him, conceding instead that the 'mind is much, but is not all' (III.i.87). The chastened passivity of both Foscaris makes for an uncomfortably (if intentionally) attenuated scope of action. With its emphasis on reaction rather than event, *The Two Foscari* seems more operatic than dramatic in structure, and Verdi transformed it into a successful opera, *I Due Foscari*, in 1844. The main relief from what Verdi himself diagnosed as the plot's 'too unvarying' (and potentially 'deadly') tone can be found in the characterization of Marina, Jacopo's outspoken and indomitable wife.[19] Her outbursts expose the 'contempt for female powerlessness' beneath the superficial 'reverencing' for women and the private sphere professed by the patricians, and her silencing underscores the ultimate irrelevance of 'individual subjective judgement', however passionately expressed.[20] *The Two Foscari* never gained popularity as a stage play, but the actress Adelaide Calvert made a warmly admired vehicle of the part of Marina.[21]

Between the two Venetian plays, Byron had written *Sardanapalus* (1821), generally regarded as the most successful of his regular tragedies. More a legendary than historical figure, amalgamated from several late Assyrian kings, Sardanapalus was described by Diodorus Siculus (Byron's source) as the last ruler of the Assyrian empire, with his capital at Nineveh. In the absence of the detailed histories he consulted for the Venetian tragedies, Byron created an original and in some ways startlingly modern figure from the semi-mythical account provided by Diodorus. With its thematic oppositions of power and pleasure, eros and empire, Sardanapalus is often seen as Byron's restaging of Shakespeare's *Antony and Cleopatra* (with an eye to Dryden's neoclassical version of the same story in *All for Love*). In the role of Sardanapalus, however, Antony and Cleopatra are collapsed together, the debauched man of (potential) action and the luxurious and exotic queen. Making his stage entrance '*effeminately dressed*', the 'she-king' Sardanapalus flirts throughout the drama with a campy, effeminate persona (II.i.48). Byron described Sardanapalus as 'almost a comic character' (*BLJ*, VIII, 155): his vacillations between hedonism and responsibility, blood-wrath and pacifism, sincerity and satire, gravity and pettishness lend a comic energy to the tragedy entirely lacking in the Venetian plays. The role-playing, costume changes, and sudden shifts in behaviour exemplified by its central character give *Sardanapalus* a high degree of theatricality, as well, that plays deftly off the structural constraints demanded by the neoclassical 'unities' of place and time (*CPW*, VI, 16). If too long to be stage-worthy in contemporary terms, *Sardanapalus* could still be called the stagiest of Byron's dramas.

Casting Assyria as the 'first / Of empires' (V.i.444–5), Byron returns to the critique of imperialism adumbrated in *Marino Faliero*. The Assyrian empire maintained its dominance through a programme of relentless expansion, ruthless conquest, and constant victory celebrations. The violence and institutionalized terrorism of imperial expansion and control are represented in the play by Sardanapalus's fierce ancestors, the god Baal, to whom the dynasty traces its divine origin, Nimrod, the 'mighty hunter' of the Bible, and Semiramis, the warrior empress fabled to have killed her husband and ruled in men's clothing, 'man-queen' to her grandson's woman-king. Sardanapalus poses his harmless pursuit of pleasure as a counterweight to the heritage of sanguinary conquest he wishes to disclaim. In this respect, the play anticipates the critique of war developed in Byron's portrayal of the Siege of Ismail in *Don Juan* VII–VIII (1823). Yet Sardanapalus has distanced himself from one Orientalist stereotype – the cruel and absolute tyrant – by taking on the lineaments of another, the effeminate and licentious harem-master (with its own connotations of Oriental tyranny). As he continues to flit from one persona and posture to another, Sardanapalus seems to pursue mobility among various possible identities (or theatrical roles) in order to avoid the limitations – and full responsibilities – of any one. Like Marino Faliero's premature and ambivalent egalitarianism, the policy of pacific and passive rule that Sardanapalus adopts is both untimely and self-contradictory in its fiction of benign absolutism. At the end of the drama, he offers not a prophecy but a 'problem' for future eras to contemplate (V.i.447).

The range of sexual personae available to Sardanapalus is limited in any case by his pronounced heterosexuality.[22] Unlike the sybaritic bisexual described by Diodorus, Byron's Sardanapalus, however 'effeminate' (I.i.9), seems attracted only to women and is currently in love with Myrrha, the favourite of his harem. As a Greek slave, Myrrha represents 'Western' values of freedom, autonomy, and a distinctly masculine sense of virtue; she presides over the movement toward Sardanapalus's remasculinization that critics have seen as a driving force in the play.[23] Myrrha remains aware of the irony of her own position, bringing out the oppressive structure of Sardanapalus's seemingly benign dominion, as a slave who loves her 'master' at the steep price of embracing her hated servility (I.ii.497). She also complicates Byron's 'plot of masculine emergence' by becoming warlike, implicitly manly, along with Sardanapalus himself, whose 'latent energies' (I.i.11) are unleashed by the inevitable rebellion against his velvet autocracy.[24] After

Sardanapalus exchanges his women's clothes for armour to lead the counter-attack and Myrrha, sword in hand, urges on the troops with 'floating hair and flashing eyes', Sardanapalus experiences a surge of revulsion captured in his disturbing nightmare of a bloody banquet with his forebears. (Again, the example of Macbeth hovers dimly but recognizably in the background.) Semiramis sits in the place of Myrrha, 'bloody-handed' and 'leering' with lust, locking Sardanapalus in an incestuous embrace (IV.i.105–8). The anxious identification of Myrrha with *se-mira*-mis – a telling play on names pointed out by Susan Wolfson[25] – is complicated, however, by the 'horrid kind / Of sympathy' that binds Sardanapalus himself to the ancestors he reviles (IV.i.124–5). For Sardanapalus, taking on a masculine role paradoxically entails becoming the double of a 'human monster' and transvestite queen (I.ii.181).

Sardanapalus does not follow a straight path to normative masculinity in any case. Repeatedly, his exertions of male 'energy' are undercut by moments of high camp that reanimate the opening image of Sardanapalus mincing onstage *en travestie*, his '*Robe negligently flowing*'. After he grabs a guard's sword to forcibly separate retainers fighting in his presence, he complains that the weapon is too heavy: 'the hilt, too, hurts my hand' (II.i.194). After arming himself and beginning to rush out to battle, he stops short calling out, 'bring the mirror', pausing to admire his new costume and discarding his helmet when he finds it spoils the effect (III.i.145). He goes on to fight 'like a king', a revalidation of his proper masculine role immediately undercut by mention of his 'silk tiara and his flowing hair' (III.i.200, 205). When his manly brother-in-law, Salamenes, congratulates him on the 'most glorious' hour of his life, Sardanapalus responds, 'And the most tiresome' (III.i.344). Not without cause does Sardanapalus continue to worry that, having 'remann'd' himself, events will again 'unman' him (IV.i.402–3; compare V.i.401). His final gesture, joint suicide with Myrrha atop the huge pyre meant to destroy his palace before it can be ransacked, presents a crowning, spectacular image of passivity as action. Assuring Sardanapalus of her resolve, Myrrha rhetorically asks whether a 'Greek girl dare not do for love, that which / An Indian widow braves for custom?' (V.i.466–7). If the final conflagration is a version of suttee, Sardanapalus, the oriental transvestite, assumes the position of 'Indian widow' no less than does Myrrha, choosing self-immolation over outliving the loss of his accustomed role and station in life. His sexually ambivalent and wavering character, like the contradiction of a benevolent empire, remains a 'problem' to the end.

The 1821 volume that presented *Sardanapalus* and *The Two Foscari* to Byron's readership concluded with a third and quite different poetic drama, *Cain, A Mystery*. In *Cain*, Byron returned to what he called his 'Manfred, metaphysical style' (*BLJ*, VIII, 215), complicating the work's otherwise tidy dramatic structure with a middle act set in alternate worlds – Hades and the '*Abyss of Space*' – and governed by an alternate temporality, in which 'hours' pass like 'years' (III.i.59). Early in the opening scene, Cain's challenge to Adam, who regrets plucking the 'tree of knowledge' – 'And wherefore pluck'd ye not the tree of life?' (I.i.32) – launches a thematic dialogue with *Manfred*, whose protagonist laments that the 'Tree of Knowledge is not that of Life' in its opening scene (I.i.12). In terms of verbal style as well, the 'cool, understated texture' of the tragedies gives way to something resembling the interplay of lyricism, dialogue, and declamation in Byron's 'dramatic poem'.[26] In contrast to *Manfred*, with its brief and abortive dramatic confrontations, however, *Cain* features an extended and charged interchange between two powerful figures, Cain and Lucifer. In part Cain's education, partly his temptation, and ultimately a struggle of titanic wills, the confrontation between the 'first Rebel' and the first human outlaw gives Byron's 'Mystery' a tense dramatic arc. It also gives Lucifer a number of good lines, calculated to further provoke contemporary readers and reviewers already eager to enlist Byron in a 'Satanic' school of rebellious and irreverent poets.

Byron's heterodox mythology in *Manfred* – placing pagan witches, Classical Greek deities, and the Zoroastrian evil principle (from the pre-Muslim Persian religion) on the same footing as the Abbot's Christian references – implies a cosmopolitan religious scepticism, as does Sardanapalus's comparative approach to religion ('Jove – ay, your Baal' (II.i.549)), intensified by his open dislike of priests. In *Cain*, Byron gives the devil himself the chance to put a caustically unorthodox spin on Christian doctrine. God is the 'Omnipotent tyrant' (I.i.138), Lucifer his great opposite, the other of the '*two Principles*!' (II.ii.404), willing to endure an 'independency of torture' in order to 'divide / *His*, and possess a kingdom which is not / His' (I.i.385, 552–4). As the intentionally awkward line-breaks suggest, Lucifer is obsessed with division, and relentlessly presses Cain toward a divided vision of the world and a split experience of the self.

> Think and endure, – and form an inner world
> In your own bosom – where the outward fails;
> So shall you nearer be the spiritual
> Nature, and war triumphant with your own.
>
> (*Cain*, II.ii.463–6)

Some reviewers were fairly confident as to Byron's purpose: 'it is a wicked and blasphemous performance', fulminated John Gibson Lockhart in *Blackwood's*.[27] But Lucifer's insistent rhetoric of division and its disastrous effect on Cain – who goes on to commit the first murder – suggest that, like the serpent before him, Lucifer is willing to 'betray . . . with truth' in order to enlarge his 'kingdom' (I.i.355). Byron may have created a seductively glib devil, but that does not automatically enlist Byron in the devil's party.

Anticipating reactions like Lockhart's, Byron drily remarks in the Preface to *Cain* that it was difficult to make Lucifer 'talk like a Clergyman' (CPW, VI, 229). Yet Lucifer's insistent dualism, with its ranking of the 'spiritual' over the human and material, at times lends him the accents of a puritan divine. Lucifer asks Cain to think of the body as a 'servile mass of matter', its desires 'foul and fulsome', sexual enjoyment a 'sweet degradation' (II.i.51,56); compared to the pre-Adamite beings he shows Cain in Hades, humans boast a 'pettier portion of the immortal part', the harsh alliteration again underscoring Lucifer's divisive rhetoric (II.ii.93). When Cain persists in finding the earth – and his sister-wife Adah – beautiful, Lucifer taunts him: 'I pity thee who lovest what must perish' (II.ii.337). Cain's response – 'And I thee who lov'st nothing' – indicates the distance between Lucifer's blatantly anti-humanistic rhetoric and any view that could be simply attributed to Byron. Yet Adah's language of empathy and love – 'what else can joy be but the spreading joy?' (I.i.481) – remains curiously inert, powerless to reconcile Cain with the 'politics of Paradise' that condemn him, and everyone, to exile from the Garden and to eventual death (*BLJ*, VIII, 216). The more ironic, then, that Cain himself, insidiously led by Lucifer ('It may be death leads to the *highest* knowledge' (II.ii.164)), brings death into the world. Cain ends by repeating the tragic career of Manfred: self-tormented, isolated, marked and haunted by his crime, and an apter disciple of Lucifer than he knows.

Later in 1821, Byron wrote a second 'Mystery' play, *Heaven and Earth*, which he initially hoped could be included in the same volume with *Cain* and the historical tragedies. Byron described *Heaven and Earth* as a 'lyrical drama' and a 'sort of Oratorio' – 'choral and mystical' (*BLJ*, IX, 58, 81). Like *Manfred*, but even more extensively, it alternates dramatic dialogue in verse with lyrical and choral passages, putting a number of different verse forms into play as had Shelley in *Prometheus Unbound* (1820). Like *Cain*, it presents a revisionary take on a scriptural narrative – here the Flood – with Milton's example in *Paradise Lost* constantly in view. Byron juxtaposes the onset of the Deluge with a plot concerning the illicit relation between two errant angels and the beautiful descendants of Cain, Anah and Aholibamah, whom they love. He elaborates their story from the biblical passage he quotes on the title page – the 'sons of God saw the daughters of men that they were fair; and they took them wives of all which they chose' (*CPW*, VI, 346) – which he interprets, in the best sceptical tradition, as a fragment from a rival, unorthodox account of biblical events, accidentally lodged in Genesis and underscoring the contingency and textual instability of divine scripture. The Flood is presented as morally unacceptable: if Lucifer's words reveal his contempt for humanity and the earthly creation in *Cain*, no less does God's catastrophic destruction of the world and all but an 'elect' handful of its inhabitants in *Heaven and Earth*. Anah and especially Aholibamah, her more rebellious and more 'stern' sister (III.406), take up the burden of their forefather Cain, refusing to passively accept the diminished possibilities of life after the Fall:

> Change us he may, but not o'erwhelm; we are
> Of as eternal essence, and must war
> With him if he will war with us.
>
> (*Heaven and Earth*, I.ii.120–22)

The sisters' fate is left tantalizingly open as they fly off with the disobedient angels, who refuse to forsake them, as the Earth becomes a 'universal tomb' (III.926).

If the 'lyrical & Greek' *Heaven and Earth* represents Byron's dramatic writing at its furthest remove from the contemporary theatre (*BLJ*, IX, 59), *Werner* (1822) seems expressly designed for the London stage. It is full of the 'surprises' and 'starts' that Byron associated with the popular melodrama of the time, featuring veiled identities, improbable reunions, mysterious strangers, prescient dreams, duels and asides, not to mention a ruined castle with a secret passageway. In the title character, Byron creates a weathered, played-out version of his earlier heroes, born (like Sardanapalus) to 'unmake an empire', but now 'Chasten'd, subdued, outworn', and taught by bitter experience to know himself (I.i.153–6). Taking advantage of the hidden passage to rob his enemy, arrived by chance at the same ruined hall, Werner endures a 'hell' of remorse for the uncharacteristic (and unByronic) baseness of the act (III.i.71). It is nothing, however, to what he feels when he discovers that his long-lost son, Ulric, also there by chance, has followed his father's example and made use of the same passage to murder their common foe. '*Who* proclaimed to me', Ulric challenges Werner, 'that *there were crimes* made venial by the occasion?' (V.ii.453). Whether or not Byron, as some critics have assumed, returned to *Werner* to prove that he could write a play suited to contemporary tastes, *Werner* did succeed on the nineteenth-century stage. The actor-producer William Charles Macready made the play into a popular repertory piece and the role of Werner into an acclaimed vehicle for his own emotional range, from deeply affecting paternal love to overpowering guilt and remorse. (In Macready's version, Werner dies on stage after forcing Ulric to confess to the murder.) Although the themes of crime, remorse, and a mental 'hell' within run through Byron's dramatic writing from *Manfred* onward, *Werner* stands well apart from Byron's other poetic dramas in its uncritical adoption of melodramatic conventions.

The Deformed Transformed (1824), left unfinished at Byron's death, also stands out from Byron's other dramatic works. It concerns a morose hunchback, Arnold, who is about to commit suicide when a Mephistophelean 'Stranger' appears and offers him the body of his choice. Arnold chooses a heroic Greek form and the Stranger takes Arnold's deformed and discarded body, taking also a new identity ('Caesar') in order to accompany Arnold on his adventures and provide a running satiric commentary. (Arnold calls him 'the everlasting Sneerer' (I.ii.117)). Partly inspired by Goethe's example in *Faust*, Byron seems to have planned anything but a regular tragedy, with the action jumping from Arnold's native forest, to the sack of Rome, to a castle in the Apennines. The scenes in Rome give Byron another opportunity to develop the darkly satirical side of his portrayal of war. Arnold's plot seems to be moving towards a critique of the dualism that prompts him to accept a new body in the first place, as a fitter housing for the 'gem' of his soul than the 'dunghill' he was born into (I.i.432). Because Arnold's deformity (which includes a 'cloven foot' (I.i.104)) and his mother's cruel taunts have obvious parallels in Byron's own life, critics have found the fragment intriguing for its autobiographical resonance as well as for its relation to *Faust*.

No one would place Byron next to Shakespeare, yet as a prolific and innovative dramatic poet he bears comparison with John Dryden in the seventeenth century and William Butler Yeats in the twentieth. His poetic plays and dramatic poems respond to the contemporary stage in remarkably different ways, some experimenting with a deliberately anti-theatrical format (whatever their debt to theatrical conventions), others providing a 'mental' drama in pointed contrast to what Byron (not alone) saw as the debased theatre of the time. Byron's plays invite the reader to imagine a renewed theatre of the future and ask for – and repay – the effort required for a 'staging' in the theatre of the mind. Although the plays, with the awkward exception of *Werner*, did not prove popular on the material stage of the nineteenth century – for which they were not written – recent academic revivals have shown that works as diverse in structure and intention as *Cain* and *Sardanapalus* can succeed with modern audiences. In their diversity, the dramatic works showcase Byron's experimentalism and formal range, in both his Romantic and neoclassical modes. As stagings of ideological debates and 'metaphysical' critiques, they significantly add to Byron's development of a poetry resolutely engaged with the political and social issues of his era. The plays did not 'reform' the drama, despite Byron's hopes, then or later (*BLJ*, VIII, 186). They represent, nevertheless, a significant facet of Byron's poetic achievement, one that underscores the dramatic and dialogic character of his later poetic style, and the performative aspect of a life conducted in and often for the public eye.

NOTES

1. Alan Richardson, *A Mental Theater: Poetic Drama and Consciousness in the Romantic Age* (University Park: Pennsylvania State University Press, 1988).
2. Julie A. Carlson's *In the Theatre of Romanticism: Coleridge, Nationalism, Women* (Cambridge University Press, 1994) makes this point most forcefully (esp. pp. 1–29).
3. Thomas Medwin, *Conversations of Lord Byron: Noted During a Residence with His Lordship at Pisa, in the Years 1821 and 1822* (London: Henry Colburn, 1824), pp. 99–100.
4. Jane Moody, *Illegitimate Theatre in London, 1770–1840* (Cambridge University Press, 2000), pp. 10–78.
5. *Ibid.*, p. 127.
6. Carlson, for example, argues that Byron and other male Romantics found the presence of women on the stage problematic for cultural and political reasons, virtually equating women with the theatre (*In the Theatre*, pp. 199–204).
7. Margaret Howell, *Byron Tonight: A Poet's Plays on the Nineteenth Century Stage* (Windlesham: Springwood Books, 1982).
8. Byron's position as a dramatic poet disenchanted with the theatre of his time may productively be compared to that of his admired contemporary Joanna Baillie, especially as Baillie's theory has been delineated by Catherine B. Burrough in *Closet Stages: Joanna Baillie and the Theater Theory of British Romantic Women Writers* (Philadelphia: University of Pennsylvania Press, 1997).
9. David V. Erdman, 'Byron's Stage Fright: The History of His Ambition and Fear of Writing for the Stage', *ELH*, 6 (1939), 219–43: 241.
10. *Ibid.*, p. 241
11. Jeffrey, in Andrew Rutherford (ed.), *Byron: The Critical Heritage* (London: Routledge, 1970; New York: Barnes and Noble, 1970), p. 118
12. *Ibid.*, p. 116.
13. Daniel Watkins, *A Materialist Critique of English Romantic Drama* (Gainesville: University Press of Florida, 1993), p. 151.
14. Alan Richardson, 'Astarté: Byron's *Manfred* and Montesquieu's *Lettres persanes*', *Keats-Shelley Journal*, 40 (Keats-Shelley Association of America, New York, 1991), 19–22.
15. Anne Barton, '"A Light to Lesson Ages": Byron's Political Plays', in John D. Jump (ed.), *Byron: A Symposium* (London: Macmillan, 1975), p. 152; Philip W. Martin, *Byron: a Poet Before His Public* (Cambridge University Press, 1982), p. 140.
16. *Ibid.*, p. 151.
17. Macbeth worries that the blood on his hands will the 'multitudinous seas incarnadine' rather than wash clean (II.2.59). Byron echoes the same passage from *Macbeth* again in the next act (IV.2.147).
18. Caroline Franklin, *Byron's Heroines* (Oxford: Clarendon Press, 1992), p. 185.
19. Verdi's comment is quoted in McGann and Weller's notes to *CPW* (VI, 630).
20. Franklin, *Byron's Heroines*, p. 204.

21. Howell, *Byron Tonight*, pp. 141–2.
22. As Susan J. Wolfson stresses in '"A Problem Few Dare Imitate": *Sardanapalus* and "Effeminate Character"', *ELH*, 58 (1991), 867–902.
23. See especially *ibid.*, and Franklin, *Byron's Heroines*, p. 207.
24. Wolfson, 'A Problem', p. 874.
25. *Ibid.*, p. 887.
26. Martyn Corbett, 'Lugging Byron out of the Library', *Studies in Romanticism*, 31 (1992), 364.
27. Cited in Rutherford, *Critical Heritage*, p. 217.

9

DRUMMOND BONE

Childe Harold's Pilgrimage IV, *Don Juan* and *Beppo*

Childe Harold's Pilgrimage Canto IV

Whereas *Childe Harold* I and II sought the goal of their pilgrimage in the classical world of Greece, at the boundary of civilization and Nature, and Canto III seeks its elusive goal in Nature beyond civilization, Canto IV concentrates on the high civilization of the Renaissance and of Rome. While obviously to some extent dictated by Byron's own whereabouts, the move also expresses a very significant shift in his world view. In *Manfred* (pp. 118) we have seen how the individual becomes responsible for the meaning of his or her own life. This is a secular view of meaning, seeing life as a construct of man's own mental activity. This mental activity is represented in and by civilization and culture.[1] Life made meaningful has the form of an artwork – it is a product of civilization and culture. This is the view that dominates Canto IV. The canto opens with the famous image of the Bridge of Sighs in Venice:

> I stood in Venice, on the Bridge of Sighs;
> A palace and a prison on each hand:
> I saw from out the wave her structures rise
> As from the stroke of the enchanter's wand:
> A thousand years their cloudy wings expand
> Around me, and a dying Glory smiles
> O'er the far times, when many a subject land
> Look'd to the winged Lion's marble piles,
> Where Venice sate in state, thron'd on her hundred isles!
>
> (*CHP*, IV.1)

The image of civilization's ambiguous structures (both beautiful and repressive) arising from the ocean, history spinning itself out of unknowable natural time, sets the key theme of the canto. The image will be picked up in the concluding stanzas (175–86), which form a sort of coda to the *Pilgrimage* as a whole, and I will look at this below. Though Venice was for Byron an archetype of the dual nature of civilization in its social structures – shaping but also oppressing, as is clear from two of his late dramas (p. 133) – it is here also physically an image both of continuity and of decay, the power and the limitations of human artefacts. Other cultural products are stronger than physical buildings or political structures:

> In Venice Tasso's echoes are no more,
> And silent rows the songless gondolier;
> Her palaces are crumbling to the shore,
> And music meets not always now the ear:
> Those days are gone – but Beauty still is here.
> States fall, arts fade – but Nature doth not die,
> Nor yet forget how Venice once was dear,
> The pleasant place of all festivity,
> The revel of the earth, the masque of Italy!
>
> But unto us she hath a spell beyond
> Her name in story, and her long array
> Of mighty shadows, whose dim forms despond
> Above the dogeless city's vanished sway;
> Ours is a trophy which will not decay
> With the Rialto; Shylock and the Moor,
> And Pierre, can not be swept or worn away –
> The keystones of the arch! though all were o'er,
> For us repeopled were the solitary shore.
>
> The beings of the mind are not of clay;
> Essentially immortal, they create
> And multiply in us a brighter ray
> And more beloved existence: that which Fate
> Prohibits to dull life, in this our state
> Of mortal bondage, by these spirits supplied
> First exiles, then replaces what we hate;
> Watering the heart whose early flowers have died,
> And with a fresher growth replenishing the void.
>
> (*CHP*, IV.3–5)

These stanzas are confusing. Possibly and indeed probably because Byron was himself confused, and using rhetoric from *Childe Harold* III which no longer fitted his purpose. In stanza 3 we are told that civilization fades but Nature 'doth not die' – a very Canto III locution. But in stanza 4 it is revealed that what has in fact remained is not Nature, but civilization – not in its political but its artistic realization – the works of Shakespeare and Otway. It is this idea that is taken up in stanza 5. Byron is still wrestling with the central doubt that his emerging view of life as human artefact provokes – can we lean on these creations, will they support our weight? What if there is indeed something 'more' real behind them. This is a doubt which never vanishes, but it can be incorporated into the activity of life-creation, inside its art, rather than as here standing outside it, dialogically, arguing in its own voice. The confusion that this gives rise to can be seen in stanzas 6 and 7:

> Such is the refuge of our youth and age,
> The first from Hope, the last from Vacancy;
> And this worn feeling peoples many a page,
> And, may be, that which grows beneath mine eye:
> Yet there are things whose strong reality
> Outshines our fairy-land; in shape and hues
> More beautiful than our fantastic sky,
> And the strange constellations which the Muse
> O'er her wild universe is skilful to diffuse:
>
> I saw or dreamed of such, – but let them go –
> They came like truth, and disappeared like dreams;
> And whatsoe'er they were – are now but so:
> I could replace them if I would, still teems
> My mind with many a form which aptly seems
> Such as I sought for, and at moments found;
> Let these too go – for waking Reason deems
> Such over-weening phantasies unsound,
> And other voices speak, and other sights surround.
>
> (*CHP*, IV.6–7)

The 'solid' world beyond art in stanza 6 crumbles in 7 into a 'dream' which can be 'replaced' (renewed) by the imagination – except that it can't be ('for waking Reason deems/Such over-weening phantasies unsound'), because the 'solid' world undercuts the reality of imaginative creation. This is confused and confusing, but the motivation of the thought is consistent with the path Byron has set out on in his post-*Manfred* life. Life is made meaningful only through civilization and art in particular; even with this knowledge there is a residual nostalgia for meaning 'more real', independent of the individual. Where this nostalgia is not recognized as itself a product of civilization, its emergence confuses the new stance. By the time we reach stanza 17 this confusion has receded – what is important in Venice is its culture and its cultural associations. This idea of the mind 'repeopling' the barrenness of life, the source of its own meaning even in pain is expanded through the following stanzas up to stanza 25, in phrases which remind us of *Manfred*:

> All suffering doth destroy, or is destroy'd,
> Even by the sufferer; and, in each event
> Ends: (*CHP*, IV.22.1–3)

> And how and why we know not, nor can trace
> Home to its cloud this lightning of the mind,
> But feel the shock renew'd, (*CHP*, IV.24.1–3)

And from the appearance of Rome 'the home/Of all Art yields, and Nature can decree' in stanza 26 it is Roman civilization rather than Attic nature which has the upper hand. The Canto is dominated by works of poetry (Boccaccio, Tasso, Dante, Petrarch); architecture and art (Florence's dome, Michelangelo's sculptures); and the great cities of Renaissance Italy and its great minds (Galileo, Machiavelli). From time to time this 'artificiality' is still seen as a perverse failure of the human condition:

> Of its own beauty is the mind diseased,
> And fevers into false creation: – where,
> Where are the forms the sculptor's soul hath seized?
> In him alone. Can Nature shew so fair?
> Where are the charms and virtues which we dare
> Conceive in boyhood and pursue as men,
> The unreach'd Paradise of our despair,
> Which o'er-informs the pencil and the pen,
> And overpowers the page where it would bloom again?
> (*CHP*, IV.122)

But it is, if a failure, an unavoidable one:

> Yet let us ponder boldly – 'tis a base
> Abandonment of reason to resign
> Our right of thought – our last and only place
> Of refuge; this, at least, shall still be mine:
> Though from our birth the faculty divine
> Is chain'd and tortured – cabin'd, cribb'd, confined,
> And bred in darkness, lest the truth should shine
> Too brightly on the unprepared mind,
> The beam pours in, for time and skill will couch the blind.
> (*CHP*, IV.127)[2]

The final goal of the *Pilgrimage*, following the descriptions of St Paul's and the Vatican is, arguably, a statue, the Apollo Belvedere (stanzas 161–3). A marble God of 'poesy', representing the acme of civilization. 'Arguably' because the canto has a three-stage coda, introduced in 164 by a valedictory reinvocation of Harold himself, which wanders meditatively, partly in nature, until stanza 175:

> But I forget. – My pilgrim's shrine is won,
> And he and I must part, – so let it be, –
> His task and mine alike are nearly done;
> Yet once more let us look upon the sea;
> The midland ocean breaks on him and me,
> And from the Alban Mount we now behold
> Our friend of youth, that ocean
>
> (*CHP*, IV.175–81)

This longest of the closing 'sections', returning us to the Ocean with which we began this canto and which we associate with the Childe setting sail in Canto I, seems in mood yet again a reprise of Canto III:

> I love not Man the less, but Nature more,
> From these our interviews, in which I steal
> From all I may be, or have been before,
> To mingle with the Universe, and feel
> What I can ne'er express, yet can not all conceal.
>
> (*CHP*, IV.178.5–9)

Nature and the Ocean are the truly real and permanent, beyond the mere transience of civilization. Is this a failure of nerve at the end of the poem? Or has an aesthetic sense, demanding a reprise to signal an ending, taken over from Byron's thematic sense? These possibilities are mutually reinforcing of course,[3] but the climax of this passage leaves us with a subtly different possibility:

> And I have loved thee, Ocean! and my joy
> Of youthful sports was on thy breast to be
> Borne, like thy bubbles, onward: from a boy
> I wantoned with thy breakers – they to me
> Were a delight; and if the freshening sea
> Made them a terror – 'twas a pleasing fear,
> For I was as it were a child of thee,
> And trusted to thy billows far and near,
> And laid my hand upon thy mane – as I do here.
>
> (*CHP*, IV.184)

This dramatic return to the personal (the first person has been totally abandoned since stanza 178), the introduction of a 'real' present tense ('as I do here' as opposed to the 'thou goest forth' of the last line of the previous stanza), and the action of the hand patting the mane, draw the Ocean into the domain of the human. Thus the infinite world beyond the human is suddenly perceived as domestic, it is as it were drawn in under the hand on its mane. In the long struggle of the poem to articulate the relationship of man and his environment, the gesture is finally more than reconciliatory, it is an act of companionship initiated by Man. This is a moment, however described, of intense feeling, and the poem then has only two stanzas of valediction before closing.

Canto IV of *Childe Harold* continues, more calmly, uncertainly but recognizably, the movement of Byron's thought most dramatically laid out in *Manfred*. But it does so in a form shaped for and conditioned by Byron's earlier more simply 'Romantic' views. A new art was necessary.

Don Juan and *Beppo*

Byron wrote three major poems in *ottava rima*, a complex Italian stanza he had first used significantly in 'Epistle to Augusta' in 1816. The rhyme scheme (abababcc) sounds exotic in English, and Byron uses many devices to increase this sense of unnaturalness.[4] The stanza almost always sounds contrived, and its artifice is rarely invisible. *Beppo* was begun and completed in 1818. *Don Juan* was also begun in 1818 but left unfinished when Byron left for Greece in the early summer of 1823, having been worked on every year in the interim except for 1821, the year in which the third *ottava rima* poem, *Vision of Judgment*, was written. All of the poems are comedies, and *Beppo* and *Don Juan* mix sexual and political interests – *Vision of Judgment* is more single-mindedly (though not entirely) political, and is treated in a separate chapter.

It is perhaps easiest to think of *Beppo* as a verse novel, and *Don Juan* as some form of epic or mock-epic. But although both poems are self-reflexive (discussing their own composition) only *Don Juan* is reflexively concerned with its genre:

> I feel this tediousness will never do –
> 'Tis being *too* epic, and I must cut down
> (In copying) this long canto into two;
> (*Don Juan*, III.III.1–3)

> Hail, Muse! *et cetera*. – We left Juan sleeping,
> Pillow'd upon a fair and happy breast,
> (*Don Juan*, III.1.1–2)

> My poem's epic, and is meant to be
> Divided in twelve books; each book containing,
> With love, and war, a heavy gale at sea,

> A list of ships, and captains, and kings reigning,
> New characters; the episodes are three:
> A panorama view of hell's in training,
> After the style of Virgil and of Homer,
> So that my name of Epic's no misnomer.
>
> (*Don Juan*, I.200)

On more than one occasion, Byron *in propria persona* referred to *Don Juan* as his epic, in doing so, not only marking it as his masterpiece (a view with which critics at least over the past forty-odd years have concurred), but underscoring its difference from previous epics – this was a secular epic, whose only 'spirits' were its author's:

> So you and Mr Foscolo etc. want me to undertake what you call a 'great work' an Epic poem I suppose or some such pyramid. – I'll try no such thing – I hate tasks – and then 'seven or eight years'! God send us all well this day three months – let alone years – if one's years can't be better employed than in sweating poesy – a man had better be a ditcher. – And works too! – is Childe Harold nothing? you have so many '*divine*' poems, is it nothing to have written a *Human* one? without any of your worn out machinery.[5]

Or again:

> Episodes it . . . will have out of number; and my spirits, good or bad, must serve for the machinery. If that be not epic . . . I don't know what an epic means.[6]

Byron is, of course, playing on two meanings of 'spirits' – immaterial beings and his own moods.

Beppo, by contrast, is domestic in feel and scope, and has an almost classical compression of action. Both poems are highly digressive, but *Beppo* is confined in location to Venice, and in time to one evening of Carnival, while *Don Juan* spans three years as we have it (and if we believe Byron – and there is little reason not to – would have spanned five when completed), and covers an enormous European and near-Asiatic sweep geographically. Moreover, although lacking the supernatural or religious dimension of historical epic, *Don Juan* does seem to take on the other epic task of cultural *Bildungsroman* – the anatomy of a culture – dissecting the approach to Revolution from the perspective of 1818, and dissecting the reactionary politics of 1818 from the point of view of the Revolution. But if *Don Juan* is Byron's 'great work', *Beppo* is the tuning of the lyre, and the voice of both poems is unmistakably the same.

The self-reflexive nature of *Don Juan* and its complex verse place artifice at the centre of the poem's world, enacting Byron's post-*Manfred* view of how things are, or rather how they come to mean:

No more – no more – Oh! never more on me
The freshness of the heart can fall like dew,
Which out of all the lovely things we see
Extracts emotions beautiful and new,
Hived in our bosoms like the bag o' the bee:
Think'st thou the honey with those objects grew?
Alas! 'twas not in them, but in thy power
To double even the sweetness of a flower.

(*Don Juan*, I.214)

This stanza is a good example of Byron's construction of opposites held together – of, as it were, bi-tonality. The freshness of the heart 'falls' like dew, but then 'extracts' emotions (the directions of the two actions of the 'freshness' seem opposite). Line 4 concentrates its alliteration in the beginning of the line ('extracts emotions') before releasing this constriction of sound into the sense of 'beautiful and new'; while the fifth line builds its alliteration into the second half, constricting the sound into the 'bag o' the bee'. The reader's sense of the couplet's form, typically the place where Byron reminds us, through highlighting the formal structure that meaning is produced by artifice, is blurred by the enjambement and by the broken rhythm of the last line, precisely when it is telling us 'meaning is produced by artifice'. For the reader accustomed to the shape of a *Don Juan* stanza (compare the highlighting of form in the concluding couplets of both the preceding and following two stanzas to go no further) this has the effect of relaxing the high-wire act of the human struggle for meaning, and in this relaxation underlining the nostalgia for a belief in the naturalness of meaning (the 'honey' in nature rather than produced by us). This nostalgia cracks the surface of the poem, and is an integral part of its patterning. Its digressive and picaresque nature enacts the contingency of things that swirl around, constraining and attacking the constructed, meaningful, civilised world.

I don't know that there may be much ability
Shown in this sort of desultory rhyme;
But there's a conversational facility,
Which may round off an hour upon a time.
Of this I'm sure at least, there's no servility
In mine irregularity of chime,
Which rings what's uppermost of new or hoary,
Just as I feel the 'Improvisatore'.

(*Don Juan*, XV.20)

The naïve reader, and, indeed, the very sophisticated reader, will almost certainly experience *Don Juan* as some kind of eddying stream (to adopt a Coleridgean phrase) with local episodes constantly emerging out of and flowing into an ever-changing contingent narrative ramble. But as well as the very local architecture of the formal *ottava rima* stanza, there are large architectural patterns which underpin the narrative. We can only speculate on whether these would have been more obvious, more part of the experience of the poem, had it been taken to a conclusion. As we have it they can at least help the student of the poem apprehend what can seem an alarmingly protean monster.

The key episodes of the picaresque plot are Juan's affair with Julia – a shipwreck and experience of cannibalism – his affair with Haidee – his attempted seduction by Gulbeyaz – the siege of Ismail – the rescue of Leila – his affair with Catherine the Great – the English cantos (involving Adeline, Aurora and the Duchess). If we start by picking out the first two love affairs and the two heroines of the English cantos, we can, however, discern an obvious symmetry which might help us grasp some sense of shape. Julia is worldly and self-conscious (if not at the start of her affair very self-aware), Haidee is unworldly and innocent. This contrast becomes a systole–diastole explicitly in the characters of Adeline and Aurora in the last cantos of the poem as we have it:

> She [Aurora] gazed upon a world she scarcely knew
> As seeking not to know it; silent, lone,
> As grows a flower, thus quietly she grew,
> And kept her heart serene within its zone.
> There was awe in the homage which she drew;
> Her spirit seem'd as seated on a throne
> Apart from the surrounding world, and strong
> In its own strength – most strange in one so young!
>
> (*Don Juan*, XV.47)

> But Adeline was far from that ripe age,
> Whose ripeness is but bitter at the best:
> 'Twas rather her experience made her sage,
> For she had seen the world, and stood its test,
> As I have said in – I forget what page;
> My Muse despises reference, as you have guess'd
> By this time; – but strike six from seven-and-twenty,
> And you will find her sum of years in plenty.
>
> (*Don Juan*, XIV.54)

In between, the meat in the sandwich, as it were, are two women with extreme political power, one of whom, Gulbeyaz, Juan refuses, and one of whom, Catherine the Great, he sleeps with. In turn, their episodes are separated (in time, though still linked thematically) by another investigation into the abuse of power, namely the description of the siege of Ismail. There are two other sexual escapades in the poem (with Dudù in the harem and with Fitzfulke in the English cantos) but they seem to act as simple physical affairs, subplots to the narrative hinges. Looking at the symmetry between the two pairs of heroines, Julia/Haidee and Adeline/Aurora the voices of innocence speak of the human nostalgia for or will towards external certainty, simplicity of motive, purity of meaning, the Other. Voices of experience speak of pragmatism, compromise, are sceptical but not cynical, and are prepared to shore up the human against the evidence of futility. Neither character is necessarily aware of these qualities, but these are the qualities which emerge through them, voiced by the narrator and the poem. In Julia's case her husband eventually discovers her affair. In Haidee's case, her father finds out. Haidee's innocent idyll, not for nothing on an island, is, as the reader knows virtually from the start, always going to end tragically. Julia's, as the reader can guess virtually from the start, is likely to end, not quite tragically, but messily:

> 'I [Julia] have no more to say, but linger still,
> And dare not set my seal upon this sheet,
> And yet I may as well the task fulfil,
> My misery can scarce be more complete:
> I had not lived till now, could sorrow kill;
> Death flies the wretch who fain the blow would meet,
> And I must even survive this last adieu,
> And bear with life, to love and pray for you!'
>
> (*Don Juan*, I.197)

In the reprise of this theme Byron puts the later two heroines together and is much more explicitly sophisticated in discussing what they represent:

> She [Adeline] also had a twilight tinge of '*Blue*,'
> Could write rhymes, and compose more than she wrote;
> Made epigrams occasionally too
> Upon her friends, as every body ought.
> But still from that sublimer azure hue,
> So much the present dye, she was remote,
> Was weak enough to deem Pope a great poet,
> And what was worse, was not ashamed to show it.
>
> Aurora – since we are touching upon taste,
> Which now-a-days is the thermometer
> By whose degrees all characters are classed –
> Was more Shakespearian, if I do not err.

The worlds beyond this world's perplexing waste
Had more of her existence, for in her
There was a depth of feeling to embrace
Thoughts, boundless, deep, but silent too as Space.
(*Don Juan*, XVI.47–8)

Like Adeline's 'mobility' discussed below (p. 163) this passage seems to identify her with Byron. She does not write everything she thinks of (Byron detested writers who did), she writes epigrams (so did he), and most importantly she admired Pope, whom Byron used as the archetype of the 'civilized' poet of art, as against the Romantic poets of Nature. Equally, Aurora's link to Shakespeare links her (from Byron's standpoint) to the Romantic 'natural' stance, where everything is either All or Nothing. The Romantic danger is that beyond human meaning there is only 'silence' – which may be everything, but may equally be nothing. Adeline may have a hint of affectation, 'a twilight tinge of "*Blue*"', but her feet are on the ground. Aurora is 'deep', but 'silent'.[7]

Adeline and Aurora 'reveal' the intellectual implications of the worldly/innocent dichotomy:[8]

Juan knew nought of such a character [Aurora] –
High, yet resembling not his lost Haidée;
Yet each was radiant in her proper sphere:
The Island girl, bred up by the lone sea,
More warm, as lovely, and not less sincere,
Was Nature's all: Aurora could not be
Nor would be thus; – the difference in them
Was such as lies between a flower and gem.
(*Don Juan*, XV.58)

So well she [Adeline] acted, all and every part
By turns – with that vivacious versatility,
Which many people take for want of heart.
They err – 'tis merely what is called mobility,
A thing of temperament and not of art,
Though seeming so, from its supposed facility;
And false – though true; for surely they're sincerest,
Who are strongly acted on by what is nearest.
(*Don Juan*, XVI.97)

But here, unlike the confusions of *Childe Harold* IV, the possibility of innocence (represented here by Aurora, immediately below by Haidee) is carried by a narrative voice which allows no other voice. Simply put, the artifice of the *ottava rima* is unignorable:

And down the cliff the island virgin came,
And near the cave her quick light footsteps drew,
While the sun smiled on her with his first flame,
And young Aurora kiss'd her lips with dew,
Taking her for a sister; just the same
Mistake you would have made on seeing the two,
Although the mortal, quite as fresh and fair,
Had all the advantage too of not being air.

(*Don Juan*, II.142)

Of Aurora:

But what was bad, she did not blush in turn,
Nor seem embarrassed – quite the contrary;
Her aspect was as usual, still – *not* stern –
And she withdrew, but cast not down, her eye,
Yet grew a little pale – with what? concern?
I know not; but her colour ne'er was high –
Though sometimes faintly flushed – and always clear,
As deep seas in a Sunny Atmosphere.

(*Don Juan*, XVI.94)

In the first stanza above Haidee's innocence (linked to 'Aurora' as the dawn) is oddly qualified by the reminder that she does have a body, and the epic simile is grounded in the last line with the literalness of the comparison. In the second stanza the jauntiness of the rhyme in the couplet covers the innocence with the knowing colours of the narrator – his voice suddenly dominates.

The possibility of natural innocence is a human 'possibility' – realisable only in the *ottava rima*. Beyond the *ottava rima*, beyond the art that is life, no one can 'know'.

But, more or less, the whole's a syncopé
Or a *singultus* – emblems of Emotion,
The grand Antithesis to great *Ennui*,
Wherewith we break our bubbles on the ocean,
That Watery Outline of Eternity,
Or miniature at least, as is my notion,
Which ministers unto the soul's delight,
In seeing matters which are out of sight.

(*Don Juan*, XV.2)

This does not mean that the meaning of innocence is compromised, but that innocence as meaning is inevitably 'artificial', since all meaning is artificial, and therefore, by the standards of innocence, compromised. The freedom of the narrative voice itself cannot escape the conventions of the *ottava rima*, but must use the *ottava rima* to enact its freedom. The secular consequences flowing from *Manfred* do not stop the dialogue with innocence or transcendence, but they do prevent that dialogue from being carried on in what to human ears is silence.

> Between two worlds life hovers like a star,
> 'Twixt night and morn, upon the horizon's verge:
> (*Don Juan*, XV.99.1–2)

Meaningful life exists only within time – that image of the narrower line (the 'verge') even within the line of the horizon encapsulates the moment of appearance and disappearance which is what alone can be known. Haidee's 'island out of time' is not 'out of time'[9], and Aurora's religious innocence is enacted inside an English country-house party. Yet both Haidee and Aurora are pure. This paradox Byron at one point terms 'mobility', in a note to Canto XVI, stanza 97, already quoted above, he adds:

> In French, 'mobilité'. I am not sure that mobility is English, but it is expressive of a quality which rather belongs to other climates, though it is sometimes seen to a great extent in our own. It may be defined as an excessive susceptibility of immediate impressions – at the same time without *losing* the past; and is, though sometimes apparently useful to the possessor, a most painful and unhappy attribute.[10]

Susceptibility to 'immediate impressions' is the curse of secular reality; the ability to retain past impressions is the sophisticated understanding that contingency and change do not destroy what has once been made to mean. Haidee and Aurora are subject to the world that is Julia's and Adeline's, and yet retain their own quality of being.

From a Romantic viewpoint this vision is tragic; from a secular viewpoint it is redemptive. This duality pervades most of the poem. The shipwreck reveals human nature as 'natural' in the sense of animal, and in the sense that it is subject to chance. And yet the world of Nature is also the world of Haidee. The awfulness of the siege of Ismail is the place where a good general can reveal his 'talent', but also where a child can be rescued. From a Romantic point of view this instability is equivalent to chaos. From Byron's viewpoint it is tractable material as long as the *ottava rima* can shape it – as long as there is civilized life to make the random mean. *Don Juan* is not so much a mock-epic as an epic-comedy, in the sense that Shakespeare's Romances are comedies. It is no wonder that the author of *Ulysses* was a devotee.

Beppo, as we have said, exists on a smaller scale metaphorically as well as literally. The plot, though mined by digression, is simple. Beppo goes off to sea, his wife Laura believing Beppo dead has an affair with the Count. Beppo returns and confronts the couple, the situation is defused by Laura's overwhelming verbosity, and the three live more or less happily ever after. Although there are hints of the larger world-view which is spun out in *Don Juan* – notably in *Beppo*'s last stanza but also elsewhere – the Romantic or tragic dimension is missing. The poem accepts that life is artifice if it is meaningful, and contingent if it is not artifice. Only if we read the poem in the context of Byron's earlier works can we really feel that there is a challenge to this sanely secular view of both narrator and, indeed, heroine. Nostalgia for a Romantic Reality rarely looks like overwhelming the poem's balance, and a tragic ending to the love affair is only the faintest possibility unless, to repeat, one reads intertextually the drama of the Turkish Tales. The poem transforms the trivial, and praises toleration based not on any ideology but on practical survival. It presents therefore an easier, more simply comic, version of Byron's post-*Manfred* stance.

It is set in Venice, during the Carnival:

> 'Tis known, at least it should be, that throughout
> All countries of the Catholic persuasion,
> Some weeks before Shrove Tuesday comes about,
> The people take their fill of recreation,
> And buy repentance, ere they grow devout,
> However high their rank, or low their station,
> With fiddling, feasting, dancing, drinking, masquing,
> And other things which may be had for asking.
>
> (*Beppo*, 1)

> This feast is named the Carnival, which being
> Interpreted, implies 'farewell to flesh:'
>
> (*Beppo*, 6.1–2)

Ironically, of course, the flesh is the last thing that is said farewell to by the plot's actors. The heroine's name, Laura, is an ironic reference to the unattainable Laura of Petrarch's sonnets – our Laura is all too obtainable. Venice is here again the archetype of the Italian super-civilized:

> But 'Cavalier Serventes' are quite common,
> And no one notices, nor cares a pin;
> And we may call this (not to say the worst)
> A *second* marriage which corrupts the *first*.
>
> (*Beppo*, 36.5–8)

> But 'Cavalier Servente' is the phrase
> Used in politest circles to express
> This supernumerary slave, who stays
> Close to the lady as a part of dress,
> Her word the only law which he obeys.
> His is no sinecure, as you may guess;
> Coach, servants, gondola, he goes to call,
> And carries fan, and tippet, gloves, and shawl.
>
> (*Beppo*, 40)

The narrator is himself a convinced Italo-phile:

> With all its sinful doings, I must say,
> That Italy's a pleasant place to me,
> Who love to see the Sun shine every day,
> And vines (not nail'd to walls) from tree to tree
> Festoon'd, much like the back scene of a play,
> Or melodrame, which people flock to see,
> When the first act is ended by a dance,
> In vineyards copied from the south of France.
>
> (*Beppo*, 41)

We can note here how the landscape is seen in 'artistic' terms, 'the back scene of a play'. The narrator frequently takes on the role of a cultural tourist guide to Venice, saturating the poem with both art and artificiality (as in stanzas 11 and 12), or here of Italian women:

> Eve of the land which still is Paradise!
> Italian beauty! didst thou not inspire
> Raphael, who died in thy embrace, and vies
> With all we know of Heaven, or can desire,
> In what he hath bequeath'd us? – in what guise,
> Though flashing from the fervour of the lyre,
> Would *words* describe thy past and present glow,
> While yet Canova can create below? (*Beppo*, 46)

If Raphael tells us of heaven, and if he is inspired by Italian woman, then Italian woman is divine – though the Eve reference could be double-edged. That words are less evocative than sculpture could be thought to be an anti-romantic trope in Byron's late 'materialist' manner (by and large for the Romantic the less material the art the better, with music the usual apogee), but it should also be compared with *Don Juan*, II.118.7–8: 'I've seen much finer women, ripe and real, / Than all the nonsense of their stone ideal.' This cleverly, if paradoxically, places the 'real' at the apogee of the aesthetic – see also the discussion of *Beppo* stanzas 12–14 below. And somewhat less flatteringly, but with the same 'artificial' point:

> Laura, when drest, was (as I sang before)
> A pretty woman as was ever seen,
> Fresh as the Angel o'er a new inn door,
> Or frontispiece of a new Magazine,
> With all the fashions which the last month wore,
> Coloured, and silver paper leav'd between
> That and the title-page, for fear the press
> Should soil with parts of speech the parts of dress.
>
> (*Beppo*, 57)

The self-reflexive artificializing is much more concentrated than in *Don Juan* – it is even harder to 'escape' the *ottava rima*:

> And so we'll call her Laura, if you please,
> Because it slips into my verse with ease.
>
> (*Beppo*, 21.7–8)

> Oh that I had the art of easy writing
> What should be easy reading! . . .
>
> (*Beppo*, 51.1–2)

> But I am but a nameless sort of person,
> (A broken Dandy lately on my travels)
> And take for rhyme, to hook my rambling verse on,
> The first that Walker's Lexicon unravels,
>
> (*Beppo*, 52.1–4)

> It was the Carnival, as I have said
> Some six and thirty stanzas back, and so
>
> (*Beppo*, 56.1–2)

The trivially material is also always fair game for the narrator:

> And therefore humbly I would recommend
> 'The curious in fish-sauce,' before they cross
> The sea, to bid their cook, or wife, or friend,
> Walk or ride to the Strand, and buy in gross
> (Or if set out beforehand, these may send
> By any means least liable to loss),
> Ketchup, Soy, Chili-vinegar, and Harvey,
> Or, by the Lord! a Lent will well nigh starve ye;
>
> (*Beppo*, 8)

Art can transform even the most trivial and the most mundane. It is not only the sublime which underpins culture, but the ability to make meaning out of the business of eating (cf *Don Juan*, XV). This transformation of the trivial into the texture of life reaches its climax in Laura's long outburst which attempts (successfully) to distract Beppo from the adulterous matter in hand:

> They entered, and for coffee called, – it came,
> A beverage for Turks and Christians both,
> Although the way they make it's not the same.
> Now Laura, much recovered, or less loth
> To speak, cries 'Beppo! what's your pagan name? . . .
>
> 'And are you *really*, *truly*, now a Turk?
> With any other women did you wive?
> Is't true they use their fingers for a fork?
> Well, that's the prettiest shawl – as I'm alive!
> You'll give it me? They say you eat no pork.
> And how so many years did you contrive
> To – Bless me! did I ever? No. I never
> Saw a man grown so yellow! How's your liver?
>
> 'Beppo! that beard of yours becomes you not;
> It shall be shaved before you're a day older;
> Why do you wear it? Oh! I had forgot –
> Pray don't you think the weather here is colder?
> How do I look? You shan't stir from this spot
> In that queer dress, for fear that some beholder
> Should find you out, and make the story known.
> How short your hair is! Lord! how grey it's grown!'
>
> (*Beppo*, 91–3)

At the beginning of this passage we note how the image of human brotherhood is carried in the mundane image of a shared taste for coffee. It is this explosion of triviality which averts a Romantic disaster in the shape of a 'showdown' duel. But in truth that possibility is always remote, so dominated is the poem by its temporal and material concerns. Only rarely, as we have said, does the poem flirt with Romantic nostalgia for the world beyond. One of the most arresting examples comes in another meditation on the relationship of art to life, this time a painting of Giorgione's:

> Whose tints are truth and beauty at their best;
> And when you to Manfrini's palace go,
> That picture (howsoever fine the rest)
> Is loveliest to my mind of all the show;
> It may perhaps be also to *your* zest,

And that's the cause I rhyme upon it so,
'Tis but a portrait of his son, and wife,
And self; but *such* a woman! love in life!

Love in full life and length, not love ideal,
No, nor ideal beauty, that fine name,
But something better still, so very real,
That the sweet model must have been the same;
A thing that you would purchase, beg, or steal,
Wer't not impossible, besides a shame:
The face recalls some face, as 'twere with pain,
You once have seen, but ne'er will see again;

One of those forms which flit by us, when we
Are young, and fix our eyes on every face;
And, oh! the loveliness at times we see
In momentary gliding, the soft grace,
The youth, the bloom, the beauty which agree,
In many a nameless being we retrace,
Whose course and home we knew not, nor shall know,
Like the lost Pleiad seen no more below.

(*Beppo*, 12–14)

The first move here is to see an artwork as real not ideal (12.7–8;13.1–5); the second is to see the real as inevitably transient and contingent (14.1–7); the third is to link this transience nostalgically to a lost 'higher' world (13.7–8;14.8). The first two moves are consistent with most of *Beppo* and the positive side of the later Byron stance; the last introduces the sense of loss which provides the tension in *Don Juan*, but is largely absent here. The poem ends, however, on another such example:

Whate'er his youth had suffered, his old age
With wealth and talking made him some amends;
Though Laura sometimes put him in rage,
I've heard the Count and he were always friends.
My pen is at the bottom of a page,
Which being finished, here the story ends;
'Tis to be wished it had been sooner done,
But stories somehow lengthen when begun.

(*Beppo*, 99)

The last two lines above, accepting the artificiality of life, which ends when contingency reasserts itself in silence or death, nevertheless have a shrug-of-the-shoulder weariness about the story-telling process of life, which threatens to leave the poem on an oddly elegiac note. But it does in fact end on the upswing (metrically apart from anything else) of the word 'begun', which reasserts, though not without some minor-key resonance, the major key of most of the poem. *Beppo* is a wonderful miniature, but there are parallels between its Venice and Haidee's island. One is an island of sophistication within which you could almost forget the meaningless roar of the ocean; the other an island of simplicity, with which for a time the ocean seems – but only seems – complicit.

The appropriate critical form for a discussion of both *Beppo* and *Don Juan* would eschew a conclusion, and contrive an accidental ending. I will end by quoting five lines drawn from the last two stanzas of *Don Juan* as they were left by Byron in the spring of 1823. They comically revalue the mundane (XVII.13.2), they self-reflexively refer to the poem's presumptive epic genre (XVII.13.3), they abandon any claim to absolute knowledge (XVII.13.1) – but they also hint that the loss of ghosts – replaced by the all-too physical 'frolic Grace' Fitzfulke – may be a loss indeed (XVII.14.1–2).

> I leave the thing a problem, like all things: –
> The morning came – and breakfast, tea and toast,
> Of which most men partake, but no one sings.
> (*Don Juan*, XVII.13.1–3)
>
> Which [were] best to encounter – Ghost, or none,
> 'Twere difficult to say – (*Don Juan*, XVII.14.1–2)

NOTES

1. Byron's position still has traces of Romantic egocentrism since it would seem to make civilization a consequence of culture, rather than vice versa. The social structure is necessary for the expression of the idea.
2. The syntax here is difficult – it demands to be parsed 'Though from our birth the faculty divine is chain'd, the beam pours in'. And though the reference is to Plato's cave, the mind (not divine reality) dominates the sense of the stanza.
3. Logically, that is. The experience of reading would distinguish them – the former perceived as confusion, the latter as climactic.
4. The most common of these is the weak or mis-stressed rhyme in the couplet. He also uses polysyllabic rhymes spread over two or even three words. These devices focus the reader's attention on the form, revealing the content as dependent rather than controlling.
5. *BLJ*, VI, 105.
6. Thomas Medwin, *Conversations of Lord Byron: Noted During a Residence with His Lordship at Pisa, in the Years 1821 and 1822* (London: Henry Colburn, 1824), pp. 164–5.

10

SUSAN J. WOLFSON

The Vision of Judgment and the visions of 'author'

When, in his last decade, Poet Laureate Robert Southey collected and edited his *Poetical Works*, he was willing to include in chronological sequence his sharply political playlet *Wat Tyler*, written in his republican youth in 1794, twenty years before a Tory conversion earned him his office at court, then published by his enemies in 1817 to embarrass him. But he set *A Vision of Judgement*, his epic ode on the occasion of George III's death, published April 1821, out of chronology, in the last of his ten volumes. Maybe he meant to give it capstone honours (as Wordsworth liked to use his Great Ode in his volumes). Or maybe he hoped to bury his praises, for the fame of his *Vision* proved not to be its beatification of King George, but its accidental inspiration for one of the most concise and hilarious satires in English letters, Byron's *The Vision of Judgment*. Despite the obvious political satire and literary parody, this visionary yoking is less heterogeneous than it might first seem, for Byron's high-spirited mockery contains within it an awareness of his own complicity in self-serving poetic performances. Southey is one of an array of authors, some embraced, some displaced, some disgraced. These involve the poet's pseudonymous visionary 'I'; St Peter; the diabolic chronicler of the monarchy, 'Sathan' (Byron thus distinguishes his adversary from Southey's); the hapless Laureate; and, most critically, the mysterious author-function 'Junius', a shadow that not only shames Southey but falls across Byron as well.

Byron's spur was Southey's pompous *Vision*.[1] Taking aim at the King's critics, Southey knocked himself out with a twelve-part ode of strenuous, proudly advertised hexameters. In part I, the visionary poet falls into a trance as he hears the funeral bells; part II conducts him to 'The Vault', whence he sees the King's spirit rise (III) to 'The Gate of Heaven' (IV), where his 'Accusers' (V), political opponents, John Wilkes and journalist 'Junius' (both appear in Byron's *Vision*) are so tongue-tied in shame that Satan in exasperation hurls them back to Hell. 'The Absolvers' (VI), including George Washington, affirm the honour of the king's principles. Parts VII and VIII tender 'The Beatification' and a parade of 'The Sovereigns'; in IX, the king is greeted by 'The Elder Worthies' (Chaucer, Spenser, Shakespeare, and even Milton, 'no longer . . . to Kings and Hierarchs hostile'). Then it's on to greetings from 'The Worthies of the Georgian Age' (X) and 'The Young Spirits' (XI), then the 'Meeting' (XII), where, amidst hosannas, the king is reunited with loved ones. Overjoyed, Southey 'press'd forward' to join them, but his 'feet . . . sunk, and [he] fell precipitate', to awake at home in the Lakes, with that funeral bell tolling 'thro' the silence of evening'.

Southey graced his vision with a dedicatory epistle to George IV and a long, preening Preface on his metrics, pausing to indulge in an attack on a Byron-stamped defilement of 'English poetry'.[2] Cherishing the 'moral purity, the effect, and in its turn, the cause of an improvement in national manners' that had 'distinguished' the last half century of 'English literature', Southey railed against 'those monstrous combinations of horrors and mockery, lewdness and impiety, with which English poetry has, in our days, first been polluted!'.[3] Warming to his subject, the Laureate exercised his first vision of judgement on its chief begetter:

> It is a sin, to the consequences of which no limits can be assigned, and those consequences no after repentance in the writer can counteract. Whatever remorse of conscience he may feel when his hour comes (and come it must!) will be of no avail. The poignancy of a death-bed repentance cannot cancel one copy of the thousands which are sent abroad; and as long as it continues to be read, so long is he the pandar of posterity, and so long is he heaping up guilt upon his soul in perpetual accumulation.[4]

This confidence notwithstanding, Southey itched for temporal judgement of these 'men of diseased hearts and depraved imaginations', insisting that 'moral and political evils are inseparably connected'. To help out, he indicated a memorable imaginary: 'The school which they have set up may properly be called the Satanic school', its productions 'characterized by a Satanic spirit of pride and audacious impiety'.[5] This School was the diabolical subverter of the institution honoured in his dedicatory epistle: the monarchy, an 'illustrious House' of Brunswick, to be congratulated for supervising 'the military renown of Great Britain . . . to the highest point of glory'; for 'mitigating the evils incident to our stage of society; for imbuing the rising race with those sound principles of religion on which the welfare of states has its only secure foundation'. Fluttering with gratitude, Southey closed with a prediction that the 'brightest portion of British history will be that which records the improvements, the works, and the achievements of the Georgian Age', secured 'under the favour of Divine Providence' and 'Your Majesty's protection'.[6]

At the time, Southey imagined himself as delivering a death-blow to the patron of the Satanic School. He was a David (so he put it) smiting 'Goliath in the forehead': 'I have fastened his name upon the gibbet for reproach and ignominy as long as it shall endure', he purred in self-congratulation, blind to how 'priggish, pompous, and presumptuous' he sounded.[7] Provoked 'to balance the incubus' of this 'impudent anticipation of the Apotheosis of George the Third', so Byron sputtered to a friend in October 1821, he decided 'to put the said George's Apotheosis in a Whig point of view, not forgetting the Poet Laureate for his preface and his other demerits'.[8] His Preface, in parody of Southey's, excoriated the Laureate's bald 'attempt to canonize a Monarch' who had warred against liberty at home and abroad, and then indicted the Laureate himself for 'gross flattery', 'dull impudence, and renegado intolerance and impious cant'.[9] 'Apotheosis' and 'canonize' point the real irritation: Southey's poetry was bad, but its arrogance was retailing partisan ideology: 'by many stories, / And true, we learn the angels all are Tories' as Byron put it in his own *Vision* (207–8). Southey, finding 'his denunciations or panegyrics are of little or no avail here' (Byron smirked to Shelley's cousin Medwin), 'indulges himself in a pleasant *vision* as to what will be their fate hereafter. The third Heaven is hardly good enough for a king, and Dante's worst birth in the "Inferno" hardly bad enough for me.'[10]

Having closed an appendix to *The Two Foscari*, published December 1821, with a sustained attack on Southey's various hypocrisies in the preface to his *Vision* and other authorial acts (see *CPW*, VI, 223–5), Byron was impatient to read Southey's letter to the *Courier*, 5 January 1822, where Southey unwisely challenged, 'When he attacks me again let it be in rhyme. For one who has so little command of himself, it will be a great advantage that his temper should be obliged to *keep tune*.' Byron was newly energized by the letter; 'as he glanced rapidly over the contents', reports Medwin,

> he looked perfectly awful: his colour changed almost prismatically – his lips were as pale as death. He said not a word. He read it a second time, and with more attention than his rage at first permitted, commenting on some of the passages as he went on. When he had finished, he threw down the paper, and asked me if I thought there was any thing of a personal nature in the reply that demanded satisfaction; as, if there was, he would instantly set off for England and call Southey to an account – muttering something about whips, and branding-irons, and gibbets, and wounding the heart of a woman – words of Mr. Southey's.[11]

Byron did call Southey to account (that is, challenged him to a duel of honour), but his friends prevented the communication; even so, the letter sharpened his resolve to publish his *Vision*.

He began immediately in spring 1821, but soon found that he was indeed of the devil's party when it came to the politics of publishing and reception, prior and prospective.[12] His long-time publisher John Murray, tied in with the temporal court, demurred and delayed. Other London publishers, even the radical press, backed off, and Byron finally gave the poem to John Hunt for the inaugural issue of *The Liberal*, October 1822, some six months after Southey's publication and nearly two years after George III's demise. Byron's *Vision* was further vexed by an accidentally absent Preface (Murray did not transmit it, and it didn't appear until the 2nd edition, January 1823). The loss not only lightened the attack on Southey, it also frustrated its anticipated resonance with Leigh Hunt's general Preface ('God defend us from the morality of slaves and turncoats') and other blasts by Byron himself: three epigrams on the suicide of reactionary Foreign Secretary Castlereagh, and a *Letter to My Grandmother's Review* ridiculing William Roberts, the credulous editor of the Tory *British Review* – in sum, a liberal macrotext.[13] Byron and the Hunts expected a partisan reception, with friends championing *The Vision*, radical and commercially opportunistic piracies, and heated Tory defences of the monarchy and indictments of Byron and the Hunts.

Even prefaceless, the 1822 title page displayed some key affiliations in its transparent pseudonym, full title, and a nasty epigraph. The pseudonym 'Quevedo Redivivus' ('Quevedo Reborn') declared the lineage of the seventeenth-century Spanish satirist whose 'Visions' (*Sueños*) took aim at the Spanish court, its first one (*The Vision of the Last Judgment*) especially germane. The full title, *The Vision of Judgment* / SUGGESTED BY THE COMPOSITION SO ENTITLED BY THE AUTHOR OF 'WAT TYLER', broadcast Southey's sorry apostasy. The epigraph collated two portentous lines from the climactic court scene in *The Merchant of Venice*:

> A Daniel come to judgment! yea, a Daniel!
> I thank thee, Jew, for teaching me that word.

The first (IV.222) is Shylock's gloat as a doctor of law (Portia disguised) refuses to set aside a legal decree, fearing precedent. The second (IV.340) is the gloat of a Shylock-hater as the law-doctor strips the 'Jew' of all rights, remedies, and human dignity. Byron's nonce couplet shapes a brief revenge drama, first parodying the Laureate's self-inflation to visionary judge, then heralding his deflation to despised abject in the court of Christian judgement he was so eager to enlist.

When Byron told a friend he was 'reversing Rogue Southey's' *Vision*[14] he meant both a reversal of the moral markers and a poetic re-versing. Southey devoted the bulk of his preface to his bold 'experiment' in unrhymed hexameters, an innovation he treats in his dedicatory epistle as only slightly less in 'importance' than the tribute to 'our late revered Sovereign'.[15] Byron mocks the metrics as a leaden Pegasus of 'spavin'd dactyls' and 'gouty feet' (719–26) – and trumped it with his signature *ottava rima*, patterned and pattered in briskly rhymed iambic pentameters. In parody of the little epic, Byron stages a kind of 'one-act play with unbroken unity of time, place, and action'[16] that answers Southey's sublime sycophancy with farce, foregrounding the epic machinery and refusing the epic judgement. 'I leave every man to his opinions' (822) is all Byron's visionary will say directly, and makes good on it by waving off the whole vision, in his last stanza, as a matter of 'optics' – a chance scanning with a dreamed 'telescope', rather than an authoritative revelation. The manuscript shows that Byron first wrote 'opinions' and then opted for 'optics'[17] to underscore point of view.

Byron's Heaven is as far from the Miltonic visionary sublime as it is from Southeyan pomp-sublime. It's a mundane front-office in decades of slow business; its sole site of activity is an overwhelmed 'recording angel's black bureau' of 'vice and woe' (20–2), especially in the world recently at war. These black records – the military victories that Southey trumpeted as the glory of the Georgian era – are not merely disqualification for heavenly admission; they constitute an inventory of 'disgust' (39) at the carnage of king-triumphant warfare. In this flood of corpses, George III's provides no 'great stir on earth' (65). His corpse is just the occasion for bad state theatre, its gilded 'pomp' (66) provoking Byron's ungentle but crafty review:

> Of all
> The fools who flock'd to swell or see the show,
> Who cared about the corpse? The funeral
> Made the attraction. (73–6)

This is a tacky affair of prescripted tears, commissioned elegies, and stage props: the 'profusion / Of velvet, gilding, brass', of 'torches, cloaks, and banners, / Heralds, and relics of old Gothic manners, // Form'd a sepulchral melo-drame' (66–68, 73).

This redressing of royal pomp prepares the stage for a burlesque of Southey's most portentous scenes: the ascent of the king's spirit to 'The Gates of Heaven' and the arraignment of 'The Accusers'. Gatekeeper St Peter ('Saint porter' (132) as one of the lower angels dubs him) has to be roused from slumber and convinced that a king is actually seeking 'heaven's good graces' (143). The next act of the celestial melodrama is the arrival of a stage villain, the namesake of the Satanic School, cast as a celebrity in the aesthetics of the sublime (rather than the theology of damnation), and the latest, lightly ironized, event of that famous prototype, 'the Byronic hero':

> But bringing up the rear of this bright host
> A spirit of a different aspect waved
> His wings, like thunder-clouds above some coast
> Whose barren beach with frequent wrecks is paved;
> His brow was like the deep when tempest-tost;
> Fierce and unfathomable thoughts engraved
> Eternal wrath on his immortal face,
> And *where* he gazed a gloom pervaded space. (185–92)

Byron's Sathan drolly trumps Southey's 'Prince of Darkness' (IV), a morality-play cartoon of false language and dangerous ideas:

> Many-headed and monstrous the Fiend; with numberless faces,
> Numberless bestial ears erect to all rumours, and restless,
> And with numberless mouths which were fill'd with lies as with arrows.
> Clamours arose as he came, a confusion of turbulent voices,
> Maledictions, and blatant tongues, and viperous hisses;
> And in the hubbub of senseless sounds the watchwords of faction,
> Freedom, Invaded Rights, Corruption, and War, and Oppression
> (*A Vision of Judgement*, V)

Southey's characters were stamped out with allegorical simplicity (evil Whigs; good Tories; and reformed revolutionaries). Byron rehabilitates Satan as a Byronic Whig – wry, satirical, and with more than a plausible claim on the monarch's soul for hell.

The ensuing parliamentary proceeding features, with Byronic flare, style as much as substance, but Byron does not forgo substantive arguments. His Sathan produces a bill of indictment against the Monarch:

> He ever warr'd with freedom and the free:
> Nations as men, home subjects, foreign foes,
> So that they utter'd the word 'Liberty!'
> Found George the Third their first opponent.
> Whose History was ever stain'd as his will be
> With national and individual woes? (353–8)

Nothing if not tactical, Sathan alternates the moral indictment with savvy appeals to St Peter's vanity: 'Five millions of the primitive, who hold / The faith which makes ye great on earth', he says of Roman Catholics ('primitive' meaning 'historically prior'), implored

> Freedom to worship – not alone your Lord,
> Michael, but you, and you, Saint Peter! Cold
> Must be your souls, if you have not abhorr'd

The foe to Catholic participation
    In all the license of a Christian nation.

True! he allow'd them to pray God; but as
    A consequence of prayer, refused the law
Which would have placed them upon the same base
    With those who did not hold the saints in awe.
(380–8)

Byron himself advocated Catholic civil rights, but he does not wage the case so much as set it in play as fodder for Sathan's political and rhetorical skills. So successfully does Sathan massage religious partisanship ('here Saint Peter started') that the saint ('himself an author' (744)) swears he'll go to hell before he accommodates this antagonist to his fame, 'this royal Bedlam bigot' (395). Archangel Michael intervenes, not as moral monitor, but as conduct master:

Here Michael interposed: 'Good saint! and devil!
    Pray, not so fast; you both out-run discretion.
Saint Peter! you were wont to be more civil!
    Sathan! excuse this warmth of his expression,
And condescension to the vulgar's level:
    Even saints sometimes forget themselves in session.
(401–6)

'Good' embraces both saint and devil; it is a social reproach. Peter's sin of incivility must beg pardon from the devil no less. Byron submits matters of eternal disposition to a mundane parliamentary session, replete with politicking, posturing, formal courtesies, and self-interested manoeuvring, with even political principle suspended in a plea for social grace.

Archfiend and Archangel meet not as fell and mighty moral opposites, but rather as spectacular contrasts, in a tableau of princely urbanity:

He and the sombre silent Spirit met –
    They knew each other both for good and ill;
Such was their power, that neither could forget
    His former friend and future foe; but still
There was a high, immortal, proud regret
    In either's eye, as if 'twere less their will
Than destiny to make the eternal years
Their date of war (249–56)

. . . Michael and the other wore
    A civil aspect: though they did not kiss,
Yet still between his Darkness and his Brightness
    There passed a mutual glance of great politeness.

The Archangel bowed, not like a modern beau,
    But with a graceful Oriental bend,
Pressing one radiant arm just where below
    The heart in good men is supposed to tend.
He turned as to an equal, not too low,
    But kindly; Sathan met his ancient friend
With more hauteur, as might an old Castilian
Poor noble meet a mushroom rich civilian.

He merely bent his diabolic brow
An instant (277–90)

In this bristling over status, Michael shows a kind of courtly style that Byron himself had admired in the Orient (he is Byronic in this way), and treats his erstwhile compeer, now fallen, with liberal kindness. Sathan, proud of his rank and lineage (he is Byronic in this way), condescends to Michael as *arriviste* (he's new to the office Sathan had, as Lucifer, held for ages).

If the Poet Laureate shaped politics into moral binaries, Byron reverses this, too: his adversaries, spirits of honour after all, express 'personal' respect, their differences merely partisan. In an exquisite parody of Southey's having the historical antagonists George III and George Washington embrace in Heaven (VI.14–50), Michael coos to Sathan:

    My good old friend, for such I deem you, though
Our different parties make us fight so shy,
    I ne'er mistake you for a *personal* foe;
Our difference is *political*, and I
    Trust that, whatever may occur below,
You know my great respect for you. (490–5)

Soon he is 'my dear Lucifer' (497), with Sathan sighing in kind that he is making 'his / Late Majesty of Britain's case' merely 'Upon a point of form', already having 'kings enough below' (509–12). This is 'no longer a lost Archangel', remarks Andrew Rutherford, but the leader of 'His Celestial Majesty's Opposition' ('the self-appointed leader of the republic of hell', in Malcolm Kelsall's witty gloss); it is in this legal role that he 'impeaches George III', wielding weapons not of moral judgement but 'forensic skill'.[18] The common vexation is the mob, swarming like 'a crowd / Of locusts' (459–60), as they clamour for audience.

In this culture of polite respect, the embarrassment is unembarrassable Southey. He joins the company in a preening lather, full of judgements 'conceited in [a] petty sphere' (700) with 'all the attitudes of self-applause' – this phrase completing a couplet rhyme with 'his own bad cause' (759–60), a wicked chime of self-stimulation with self-damnation. Southey's *Vision*, Byron reminds us, had tagged 'the Demon ... "multifaced"' (513); his *Vision* assigns the Laureate to the demon's party: 'multo-scribbling Southey' (514) is a 'pen of all work' (797). It may be that Southey's Tory turn (as he said in a retrospective headnote on *Wat Tyler*) concedes the errors of youthful Jacobinism. But another way to assess the growth of this poet's mind is by the measure of vision to commission. Here is his résumé:

> He had written praises of a regicide;
> He had written praises of all kings whatever;
> He had written for republics far and wide,
> And then against them bitterer than ever;
> For pantisocracy he once had cried
> Aloud, a scheme less moral than 'twas clever;
> Then he grew a hearty anti-jacobin –
> Had turn'd his coat – and would have turn'd his skin.
> (769–76)

From this damning string of equalizing anaphoras ('He had written'), Byron turns this Southeyan facility with 'turning' against Southey himself, 'Fed, paid, and pamper'd by the very men / By whom his muse and morals had been maul'd' (781–2), willing to revise his vision, as the market beckons:

> He had written Wesley's life: – here turning round
> To Sathan, 'Sir, I'm ready to write yours,
> In two octavo volumes, nicely bound,
> With notes and preface, all that most allures
> The pious purchaser; and there's no ground
> For fear, for I can choose my own reviewers:
> So let me have the proper documents,
> That I may add you to my other saints.' (785–92)

When Sathan shows enough vision of judgement to demur, the turncoat bard turns again:

> Well, if you,
> With amiable modesty, decline
> My offer, what says Michael? There are few
> Whose memoirs could be render'd more divine.
> (793–6)

In this pitch, 'divine' denotes no more than flourishes to feed a subject's vanity and market tastes. Southey's judgement is exposed as arbitrary manufacture, and the pretensions of his visionary poetics collapse utterly as Byron turns the Laureate's ungentle audience into a court of purely literary judgement. It is Horace's *Ars poetica* that Archangel Michael wields to silence this poet: 'Non Di, non homines' (728).[19] George III sustains this plea with a complaint about the famously bad previous Laureate: 'What! what! / *Pye* come again? No more – no more of that!' (735–6).

Byron stages the latest Laureate assault – 'you shall / Judge with my judgment! and by my decision / Be guided who shall enter heaven or fall! / I settle all these things' (803–6), his Southey trumpets – and then closes his *Vision* in a mock-heroic extravaganza of resilient failures and faux successes. Southey's *Vision* succeeds in getting George III through Heaven's gates not by any 'grand heroics' (817) of moral judgement but by means of its bad poetry. After just a few lines of spavined dactyls, there is a stampede for cover. By the 'fifth line', St Peter aborts the chaos by whacking the bard down with his keys, as Jove's thunderbolt punished the overreaching Phaëton (827–8). Unlike Phaëton, Southey survives to suffer the fate of his talents and character: 'He first sunk to the bottom – like his works, / But soon rose to the surface – like himself' (833–4), rising not to fame in heaven but to the infamy of self-exposure. With a summary judgement of Southey himself pre-empting his judgement, the king's eternal disposition plays as an anticlimactic postscript:

> . . . King George slipp'd into heaven for one;
> And when the tumult dwindled to a calm,
> I left him practising the hundredth psalm.
>
> (846–8)

The gate-crashing King never rises above the judgement of immortal inconsequence voiced by St Peter at his advent: 'And who *is* George the Third?' . . . / *What George? what Third*?' (138–9). In a draft, Byron makes George not even a canny opportunist: instead of 'slipp'd' (as if by shrewd skill), he 'squeezed' into heaven (as if in frantic hurry), just bright enough to know that his signature psalm had to be the one that carols 'enter into his gates with thanksgiving'.

Southey is de-authorized by a poetic disgrace and a king's accidental grace, but Heaven's gate hosts another author who commands Byron's serious, even canonizing, attention. He is one of the witnesses condemned by Southey: journalist Junius (Lucius Junius, the staunch republican of ancient Rome, Redivivus), known in Georgian times as 'The Shadow' (593) – an epithet derived from the title-page signature to his anti-monarchal pamphlets, *Stat Nominis Umbra* ('Stands for the Name a Shadow'). From 1769 to 1772, the Shadow published over sixty letters attacking the government of George III.

A pseudonymous critic, Junius shimmers as the ghost-father of Byron's pseudonymic satire. As his *Letter 35* was prosecuted for disrespect to the monarch, so Byron knew his *Vision* would be. Turncoat Southey is a foil for both writers of principle. Like the despised author 'Botherby' of *Beppo*, Southey is 'an author that is *all author*' (stanza 75), the sweaty careerist who shifts with opportunities and fashion. Yet the foil glints beyond this buffoon. Southey-double Botherby can also look like a repressed and alienated double for the market-conscious Byron, proposes Peter Manning. Jerome McGann sees something similar in *Don Juan*'s 'Southey': a figure of mobility's 'dark shadow' – yet ultimately 'un-Byronic' because of its immunity to pain, anxiety, or even minimal self-consciousness.[20]

If Byron's anxiety is a saving grace, Junius still remains as un-Byronic as he is un-Southeyan. All-author Southey is a promiscuous pen; by 1822, masked author Byron is legible in court satirists Quevedo Redivivus and Sathan. But Junius eludes 'author' altogether, casting only shadow-language: 'Quick in its motions, with an air of vigour, / But nought to mark its breeding or its birth' (595–6). Although this is descriptive of *Nominis Umbra*, the motions also apply to authorless writing; its features remain intractably those of the text alone. No one can

> distinguish whose the features were;
> The Devil himself seem'd puzzled even to guess;
> They varied like a dream – now here, now there
> (602–4)

This is not coterie Byronic mobilité, or Southey turncoatery. It is the epiphenomenon of writing where the principle, and agency, is of words rather than of offices, persons or personalities, where fame and name are not the issue, just a curiosity:

> The moment that you had pronounced him *one*,
> Presto! his face changed, and he was another
> (617–18)

> then you might deem
> That he was not even *one*; now many rays
> Were flashing round him. (627–9)

Because the shadow speaks a general voice of Whig opposition, Kelsall dismisses it as 'an amalgam of other people's words', a 'basic rhetoric' of 'sententious commonplaces' (139–40). But Junius is more than a figure of rhetoric. Writing by principle alone, he is the antithesis of the author of name: 'I loved my country, and I hated him', he says of the monarch, standing by his pen. 'What I have written, I have written' (664–5):

So spoke
Old 'Nominis Umbra'; and while speaking yet,
Away he melted in celestial smoke. (664–6)

Byron is remembering, probably echoing, the sigh that closed the Byron-signed *Childe Harold's Pilgrimage*:

what is writ, is writ, –
Would that it were worthier! but I am not now
That which I have been – (IV.1661–3)

In this self-dramatizing melting away, past being is anything but a show: it is the poem, hero, and author that made Byron's name, to say nothing of the rapid franchise into signature adjectives and nouns (Byronic, Byronism). Junius's 'I' reads out in the work of its verbs, love and hate ('he was a good hater', Byron wrote of him in 1813, when the name was still a guess).[21] What would it be like to be all language rather than 'all author'? Even with this speculation, Byron's visionary can not help self-advertisement:

I've an hypothesis – 'tis quite my own;
I never let it out till now, for fear
Of doing people harm about the throne,
And injuring some minister or peer,
On whom the stigma might perhaps be blown;
It is – my gentle public, lend thine ear!
'Tis, that what Junius we are wont to call
Was *really, truly*, nobody at all. (633–40)

To be really, truly nobody is no negation, but pure ethical potency. The authorial 'I' who plays to the public 'ear' and the Laureate 'Bard, glad to get an audience' (713), both really, truly proud of what is 'quite my own', meet a shaming antithesis in writing that puts the question 'if *there* be mouth or author' (647–8).

The Shadow is cast this way, moreover, by an author whose interventions in 1822 amounted, at best, to expatriate satire, however boldly Byronic. If this situation bears a nervous edge, Byron lets it stand as a critique not just of Southey, but also of the faux-pseudonymity of *The Vision of Judgment*. That the poem's first historical marker is 'the Gallic era "eighty-eight"' (5) pegs its production not only to the last year of the French *ancien régime*, nor only, on the British side, the year of George III's first regency crisis; 88 is also the year of Byron's birth. A consummate performance of Byronic style and Byronic politics, *The Vision* signifies the birth of Byronism – that is, authorial celebrity – out of these events. Byronism, however, is a circulation of absences, as well as presences. Byron was willing to suffer civil judgement for his *Vision*, telling Murray he would assure any publisher 'that if he gets into a scrape I will give up *my name* or person'.[22] When it was John Hunt who got prosecuted by the Constitutional Association for 'calumniating the late king, and wounding the feelings of his present majesty', Byron offered to stand trial in his place. Told he could not, he did pay legal expenses, even as he protested to a friend that the Hunts had acted rashly, ignoring his cautions.

In that promise to give up his name or person, Byron meant that he would stand by his word, but instead 'give up' played out in a series of surrenders to publishers and courts: 'I am also willing to be *both ostensible* and *responsible* for the poem – and to come home and face the consequences on the *Author*', he protested to his friend Kinnaird in October 1822, even though he added, 'I did *not* wish the publication of the V. and indeed particularly warned [John Hunt] to pause – or erase passages likely to be obnoxious'.[23] His syntax not only differentiates 'the *Author*' of the *Vision* from an 'I' of wishes and willingness, but also offers a publisher's will and the letter of the law (prosecutor, jury, and sentence) as co-authors of *The Vision* and its effects. This surrender continued even when Byron was only a name: shortly after his death, his estate paid a £100 fine for *lèse majesté*.

Yet having achieved a life of its own, Byron's *Vision* swept up Byron into its afterlife. A half decade on, the *Quarterly* was still deriding it on the eve of the first reform bill:

> The scandalous insults which Lord Byron offered to the late king were, of course, mainly designed, and excellently well calculated, to please certain *liberal* circles in those days, condemned as such circles then were to the blackest rancour of hopelessness. They excited, however proportional disgust, not only in the many that knew and appreciated the amiable qualities of George IV, but among the thousands and millions of right-hearted British subjects, of all orders and persuasions, whose notions of what was due to the constitutional dignity of the son of George III, happened to be independent of the accidents of *In* or *out*. Lord Byron had, in their view, degraded himself as a man, by lending his poetical talents to the purposes of a small exclusive knot of magnates, who, occasionally professing levelling principles on a wider scale – and perhaps well enough disposed to please the mob, if they could do so safely, at the expense of the people – have certainly shown unimpeachable consistency in their practical efforts to level that monarchy, which among its other claims to our respect is of such efficacy to hold aristocratic haughtiness in check.
>
> (XLIV (Jan. 1831), 197)

In 1866, however, the English poet Algernon Swinburne would take exactly the opposite measure of checks and levellings. *The Vision of Judgment* had levelled, even demoted, 'the funeral and fate of George III' to mere footnotes, while gaining a spectacular ascent in fame: 'it stands alone, not in Byron's work only, but in the work of the world' (380). Yet from that singular stance are cast the shades and shadows of multiple, conflicted, and sometimes self-damning visions of 'author' – a vision of judgement that is another name for Byronism.

NOTES

1. Quotations follow *A Vision of Judgement*, in *The Poetic Works of Robert Southey, Collected by Himself*, 10 vols. (London: Longman & c., 1838), x, 189–264.
2. *Ibid.*, x, 202–7.
3. *Ibid.*, 203.
4. *Ibid.*, 204.
5. *Ibid.*, 206.
6. *Ibid.*, 192–3.
7. The inspired alliteration is Frederick Beaty's, in *Byron the Satirist* (Dekalb, Ill.: Northern Illinois University Press, 1985), p. 180.
8. *BLJ*, VIII, 236, 229.
9. *CPW*, VI, 309–10.
10. Ernest J. Lovell, Jr (ed.), *His Very Self and Voice: Collected Conversations of Lord Byron* (New York: Macmillan, 1954), p. 148.
11. For the appendix to *The Two Foscari*, see *CPW*, VI, 223–5. For Medwin's report, see *Medwin's Conversations of Lord Byron*, ed. Ernest J. Lovell, Jr (Princeton University Press, 1966), p. 150.
12. 'Murray will have nothing to say to it just now, while the prosecution of "Cain" hangs over his head. It was offered to Longman; but he declined it on the plea of its injuring the sale of Southey's Hexameters, of which he is the publisher. Hunt shall have it' (*Medwin's Conversations*, ed. Lovell, p. 150). On this nexus of relations, see Peter J. Manning, 'The Nameless Broken Dandy and the Structure of Authorship', *Reading Romantics* (New York: Oxford University Press, 1990), p. 148.
13. See Malcolm Kelsall's view, *Byron's Politics* (Brighton: Harvester Press, 1987), p. 119.
14. *BLJ*, VIII, 240.
15. Southey, *Poetic Works*, x, 191.
16. Beaty, *Byron the Satirist*, p. 187.
17. *CPW*, VI, 345n.
18. Andrew Rutherford, *Byron: A Critical Study* (Edinburgh and London: Oliver and Boyd, 1962), pp. 229–30; Kelsall, *Byron's Politics*, p. 130.
19. 'Neither gods nor men' nor booksellers (says first-century BC Roman poet and satirist Horace) will abide mediocrity in poets. *Ars poetica* (The Art of Poetry) was an influential treatise on the rules for writing poetry.

20. Manning, 'The Nameless Broken Dandy'; Jerome McGann, *The Beauty of Inflections* (Oxford: Clarendon, 1985), p. 276.
21. *BLJ*, III, 215. Byron did not know, even in 1813, the identity of the Shadow, though by 1818 he accepted the claim of John Taylor's *The Identity of Junius with a Distinguished Living Character Established* (London: Taylor and Hessey, 1816; 2nd edition, 1818) that this was Sir Philip Francis (*BLJ*, VI, 18, 35).
22. *BLJ*, VIII, 232–3.
23. *BLJ*, X, 72.

11

ANDREW NICHOLSON

Byron's prose

Byron made a number of statements about prose as a medium of expression, and almost always in its relation to poetry. On 17 November 1813, he confided to his journal: 'I began a comedy and burnt it because the scene ran into *reality*; – a novel, for the same reason. In rhyme, I can keep more away from facts; but the thought always runs through, through . . . yes, yes, through' (*BLJ*, III, 209); six days later he added: 'I have burnt my *Roman* – as I did the first scenes and sketch of my comedy . . . I ran into *realities* more than ever; and some would have been recognized and others guessed at' (*BLJ*, III, 217). In *Beppo* on the other hand, he announces: 'I've half a mind to tumble down to prose, / But verse is more in fashion – so here goes!'; and in *Don Juan*: 'if ever I should condescend to prose, / I'll write poetical commandments' (*Beppo*, 52, and *Don Juan*, I, 204). Fashion? Inferiority? An unsatisfactory means of achieving and sustaining creative objectivity? As diverse as these reflections are, one thing they seem to tell us is that, unlike Wordsworth, Byron does perceive an 'essential difference' between poetry and prose, though not necessarily – and here he might agree with Wordsworth – between 'the *language* of prose and metrical composition';[1] a difference in kind, in creative discipline. I should like to take these as signposts and to begin with a few remarks about his prose in general before focusing a little more specifically on 'To the Editor of the *British Review*' (1819) and *Some Observations upon an Article in Blackwood's Edinburgh Magazine* (1820) (hereinafter referred to as 'To the Editor' and *Some Observations* respectively). The effort as a whole will attempt to suggest some answers to the questions: What is Byron's Prose, what characterizes it, what sort of subjects does it cover, how well does it work as a creative medium?

The full complement of Byron's prose in *The Complete Miscellaneous Prose* comprises Reviews, Parliamentary Speeches, various tales, anecdotes and recollections, his Armenian writings, the two replies to his reviewers which we shall be looking at, and his contributions to the Bowles–Pope controversy (that is, *Letter to John Murray* and *Observations upon Observations* supporting Pope against his detractors). These can be divided into those which are manifestly public utterances and were intended for publication – his formal prose, as I shall call it – the three Reviews, the three Speeches, his 'Preface to the Armenian Grammar' and 'Translations from the Armenian', 'To the Editor', *Some Observations*, and the *Letter to John Murray* and *Observations upon Observations* (though the latter was withdrawn before publication); and those which were neither offered nor intended for publication, and are of a fictional, anecdotal or note-like nature. The anomaly here would be 'Augustus Darvell: A Fragment of a Ghost Story', written in 1816 and published at the end of *Mazeppa* (1819); but the circumstances that prompted – nay, provoked – it into print tend rather to prove the rule: fictional items remained unpublished, fit at most for private consumption alone.

The formal prose pieces share certain readily observable characteristics. Briefly, each envisages a specific audience – literary or political – and, in the case of the Speeches, 'To the Editor' and the Bowles–Pope contributions, is actually addressed to particular individuals or auditors: 'My Lords', 'Dear Sir', 'My Dear Roberts'. Thus each posits itself within a precise discourse by which Byron's own discourse is governed: his Speeches by the formalities, decorum and reserve of parliamentary procedure; 'To the Editor', and the Bowles–Pope contributions, by the character and nature of the arguments already advanced. Furthermore each situates itself as a response to an imagined or perceived interlocutor, and is, to a certain degree, an interruption or intrusion into an already existing colloquy or debate: the Speeches are part of a processive discussion which began prior to their moment of delivery; the Bowles–Pope controversy had long been in motion already; even 'To the Editor' is conditioned by the initial charge – notwithstanding that Byron made it himself. This is not to suggest, however, that Byron did not flex the muscularity of his own voice or shape his own idiom. Indeed, far from feeling circumscribed or inhibited, the very restraint was paradoxically a release, a liberty: in all but the Speeches, the prescriptions enabled him to range freely within bounds. A fair example by way of a negative here is *Observations upon Observations* which he withdrew from publication because he felt he had not sufficiently observed the discursive formalities to which he had by implication willingly subscribed.

The fictional items, with which we shall remain a little longer, would include 'Bramblebear and Lady Penelope' (1813), 'The Tale of Calil' (1816), 'Augustus Darvell: A Fragment of a Ghost Story' (1816), 'Donna Josepha' (1817), 'Italy, or *not* Corinna' (1820), 'Some Account of the Life and Writings of the late George Russell of A – by Henry Ferguson' (1821), and 'An Italian Carnival' (1823). With the exception of 'The Tale of Calil' perhaps, what is noticeable about each of these writings is their brevity and their apparently unfinished state. But to call them 'fragments' would, I think, be a misnomer. They seem to have been written on the spur of the moment and at a single sitting, to have come to a suitable crisis or point of closure and then just stopped; as if Byron had said all he then had to say, put the piece aside, perhaps to resume it, but in the event never did. They possess a certain *ad hoc* character, an immediacy that engaged his attention at a particular time and for the duration of their composition only. 'Bramblebear and Lady Penelope: A Chapter of a Novel' is significantly only a contribution to, and part of, a larger enterprise understood and agreed upon to be continued 'jointly' with Dallas and in the event completed by him alone.[2] A helpful way of regarding such pieces, then, is to regard them all as chapters: complete in themselves, but with potential for further development. As such they argue persuasively for at least one of the reasons Byron gives for writing *poetry*: 'To withdraw *myself* from *myself* (oh that cursed selfishness!) has ever been my sole, my entire, my sincere motive in scribbling at all; and publishing is also the continuance of the same object, by the action it affords to the mind, which else recoils upon itself' (*BLJ*, III, 225). 'The Tale of Calil', written at the very height of the break-up of his marriage and Separation proceedings, and 'To the Editor', for that matter, written when Byron was alone in Bologna and desperately depressed in the absence of Teresa Guiccioli, bear ample testimony to the truth of this statement, and underscore the difference between the man who lives, eats, shaves, and so forth, and the mind which creates: the man who suffers, yet even out of his suffering creates something literally so 'diverting'. As he wrote to Moore in 1821: 'You seem to think that I could not have written the 'Vision', &c., under the influence of low spirits; but I think there you err. A man's poetry is a distinct faculty, or soul, and has no more to do with the every-day individual than the Inspiration with the Pythoness when removed from her tripod' (*BLJ*, IX, 64). The indications are, then, that the same impetus that drives Byron's poetry drives his fictional prose, but not with the same degree of success: in prose he is indeed all too apt to run into '*reality*'. 'The Tale of Calil' is evidently the most successful in this respect, not because it is the lengthiest of his fictional writings, but because he achieves that necessary self-abstracted distance – that withdrawal of self from self – securely enough to invest his creative 'self' in the 'other'.

To clarify this point just a little more by way of illustration: 'Bramblebear and Lady Penelope' and 'Donna Josepha' are both very obviously based on personal experiences in real life. The one draws on Byron's visit to the Wedderburn Websters at Aston Hall in October 1813; the other, on the Separation proceedings of 1816. The former finds its counterpart in the letters Byron wrote to Lady Melbourne during his stay at Aston Hall; the latter, its counterpart in *Don Juan*.[3] Here, then, we have the events of real life rehearsed, first, in two instances of prose, and second, in one of prose and one of poetry. The epistolary style of 'Bramblebear and Lady Penelope', its literary allusions, parenthetical asides and moral reflections, and even the spectatorial yet self-conscious participation of the narrator and his facetious, confidential – if not conspiratorial – tone, do nothing to distinguish it as a literary artefact from one of his letters to Lady Melbourne: indeed, substitute Webster and Lady Frances for Bramblebear and Lady Penelope and we have yet another letter to her. No clear distinction between the representations in either vehicle (the sole point at issue here) is observed or observable; the story neither transmutes nor translates what the letters evince. This is not intended as adverse criticism of what is, after all, a delightful vignette of a country-house gathering. But if it seems a little unjust to draw a comparison between private letters, to which we only now have access, and such a similar species of prose, consider the occasion of the shooting of the Commandant of Ravenna, which finds its way into several of Byron's letters at the time and, by contrast, into *Don Juan*.[4] In this instance, while there is no attempt at disguise – the event stated in the letters is rehearsed in the poem; the military commandant is the 'military commandant' (and it was a Friday, and it was at eight o'clock!) – the poetic rendition is so clustered about with literary contrivance and design, biblical associations and allusions, expediencies of verbal play and exigencies of rhyme, and the Commandant himself so distinctly and discretely dramatized, as to distinguish it very sharply from the representation of the incident in his letters. The letters aim functionally to 'show the state of this country better than I can' (*BLJ*, VII, 245); the poem prompts the metaphysical speculation 'Can this be death?' (*Don Juan*, V.36). The one dramatizes and philosophizes – transmutes and translates (to employ the same words as above) – what the other records and describes.

'Donna Josepha' and its corresponding passage in *Don Juan* provide an even more revealing example. From what we have of it, the story is so patently a barely concealed skit on the Separation, the names and places so evidently substitutes for their counterparts in real life (Don Jose for his father-in-law, Sir Ralph Milbanke, Donna Josepha for his wife, Annabella, Aragon for Kirkby Mallory, the Milbankes' place in Leicestershire), that, as with 'Bramblebear and Lady Penelope', no marked distinction is drawn between fiction and real life. In the poem, however, such transparent coincidence is avoided – as Byron knew very well and as his friends did not. The figures and events are masked not by merely altering the names, but by investing the characters with their own dramatic presences, recreating them, exaggerating their colours, playing with them as verbal constructs. Moreover the 'I', so prominent in 'Bramblebear and Lady Penelope' and 'Donna Josepha', is decentred and diversified, displaced onto the omniscient, participating narrator and disseminated amongst the other competing voices in the poem – the 'other' allowing Byron free passage to improvise, to caricature, to muddle fact and fiction and dance on the periphery of reality without slipping into its abyss.

What all this suggests is that Byron could indeed keep more away from the facts 'in rhyme' – not simply because it was literally in rhyme and therefore carried its own paradoxically liberating constraints which exercised his creative invention and enabled him to deface or distort a picture he was all too apt to frame in prose, but because poetry allowed him to version real life, distil the facts of '*reality*' and pare away the dross. Fictional prose, on the other hand, tended always to entrench him further in self, rendering him incapable of achieving and sustaining the necessary objectivity from the material upon which his recreative imagination worked.

With these same considerations in mind, I should like to say a word about Byron's own notes to his poetry. These often extend, counter or digress from the poetical text to which they are appended, acquiring thereby a didactic, illustrative, polemical or anecdotal independence of their own.[5] I shall take just two short examples: first, his note to 'Santa Croce's holy precincts' in *Childe Harold* IV, stanza 54. This has very little to do with Santa Croce itself, but everything to do with Madame de Staël; and we get from one to the other by a very interesting route. 'Corinna', being the name of both the novel and its eponymous heroine, and the metonymical name for its author (a crucial, if obvious, point to bear in mind), allows Byron to make a smooth transition from his own poetical description of Santa Croce to a fictional figure (Corinna) whose visit preceded his own and whose impressions he shares, and thence to the *real* author of that fiction whose description he echoes. And he does so in order not only to pay her (Madame de Staël) what is a remarkable tribute – at once her panegyric and obituary – but to associate himself with her in both her private and public capacities as another persecuted and egregious figure and writer in society. A similar procedure operates even more interestingly with 'Goats in their visage' (*Waltz*, 142), to which Byron appends a note on wearing whiskers. This opens with an allusion to Sterne's digressive chapter 'Upon Whiskers' in *Tristram Shandy*, continues with a list of real persons who, whether whiskered or not, have achieved 'valour in the field' (Scipio, Marlborough, Buonaparte), and closes with a reference to a work of fiction again, which thus underscores the ironic link between text and note (whiskered waltzers don't make gallants). In this case, matters are made all the more delightfully involved by the pseudonymous ("Horace Hornem"'s) 'To the Publisher' prefixed to the poem, in which Byron concocts a fictitious episode (which might have come from Swift, Pope, Goldsmith or Smollett), which itself mixes allusions to real and fictional persons and events: Wilhelmina in Goldsmith's *The Vicar of Wakefield*, for instance; Dr Busby and William Fitzgerald in real life (*CPW*, III, 22–3). In effect, then, we have to negotiate not only the variety of masks adopted by the poet, but the three different platforms from which he speaks to us ('To the Publisher', the poem, the notes), which themselves may or may not conspire with one another.

Such interweaving of fact and fiction – with little indication of there being any distinction between the two; the one prompting the other and together abiding in harmony – is extraordinarily revealing of the mind that creates it. For, unlike metaphor, simile or allegory, it suggests that what others have thought and created and written has exactly the same force and authority as what others have done (fact as fiction, fiction as fact): life *and* art, history *and* literature embody experiential truth. This in turn reflects on the status of the poem and the values it promotes: it too is claiming the same equality, the same truth. Such multiple ventriloquism – other considerations apart – breeds a sort of kindness: each platform, each voice, each mask tolerates the other, bound together by the poet himself who has distributed himself amongst them. By enshrining these disparate elements in a single work, the whole manoeuvre itself becomes an illustrative act of forbearance that looks forward to the polyphonic carnival of language in *Don Juan*. Byron seems to acknowledge this intuitively and prophetically in his Journal entry for 6 December 1813:

> This journal is a relief. When I am tired – as I generally am – out comes this, and down goes every thing. But I can't read it over; – and God knows what contradictions it may contain. If I am sincere with myself (but I fear one lies more to one's self than to any one else), every page should confute, refute, and utterly abjure its predecessor. (*BLJ*, III, 233)

Write it all down, but don't reread it; contradictory it may be, but keep it; it is the whole man. 'Do I contradict myself? / Very well then I contradict myself, / (I am large, I contain multitudes).'[6] Such is Byron in all his honesty: a container of contradictions, each of which is his very self at that given moment. There is nothing of hypocrisy here. As a gloss on 'mobilité' – that 'excessive susceptibility of immediate impressions – at the same time without *losing* the past' (*CPW*, V, 769, note to line 820) – it could hardly be bettered; and in this light it is extremely tempting to say more about the journals and the letters – which after all are prose too. For instance, the diversity of voices, stances and self-representations in his correspondence depends to a very large degree on the character and standing of the person to whom they are addressed and the nature of Byron's relationship with them. Indeed, as with his formal prose, his correspondent qualifies in a crucial and rudimentary way both what he writes and how he writes it – the subject raised, the choice of idiom: candid, literary, facetious, intimate, gossipy, cautious – all is relative, yet each again is the man himself at that moment of writing. However, I will resist taking this any further here and merely leave the reader with a comment of that other great man and copious letter-writer, Cicero. Writing to his friend Scribonius Curio in BC 53, he remarked:

> That there are many kinds of letters you are well aware . . . There remain two kinds of letters which have a great charm for me, the one intimate and humorous, the other austere and serious [unum familiare et iocosum, alterum severum et grave]. Which of the two it least beseems me to employ, I do not quite see. Am I to jest with you by letter? On my oath, I don't think there is a citizen in existence who can laugh in these days. Or am I to write something more serious? What is there that can possibly be written by Cicero to Curio, in the serious style, except on public affairs? Ah! but in this regard my case is just this, that I dare not write what I feel, and I am not inclined to write what I don't feel [quae sentio audeam, nec quae non sentio, velim scribere].[7]

Before moving on from this general view of the prose, I should like to mention briefly two peculiarities of Byron's which are particularly noticeable in his manuscripts, but which cannot always be reproduced in print: his use of the dash (—), and of the physical size of a manuscript page. In an undated letter of 1814 concerning *The Corsair*, Gifford remarked to Murray (using a dash for a full-stop!): 'Lord B. uses dashes for commas – this gives the work a very singular appearance, & in some places, mars the sense.'[8] A 'very singular appearance'? Certainly, and hurrah! But 'commas'? Is there really such consistency? It is true that Gifford is speaking in particular of the poetry, but even there dashes are not just substitutes for commas. Nor can it be said that Byron's use 'mars the sense': rather, it challenges interpretation. Many of his dashes are in fact hieroglyphs of verbal signification, gestures of meaning, nuancing his expression in ways that elude ordinary punctuation. To adapt Puff in Sheridan's *The Critic*, there is the dash impatient, the dash ironical, the dash comical, the dash furioso: there is the dash-and-be-damned-to-punctuation, the dash expletive, the dash imperative. But there is also the multiple dash which fills up the line to the edge of the manuscript, which might either quite literally just fill up the space between his written text and the margin of the page, or hint at a paragraph closure, or indicate exhaustion of thought (as if he were *saying*: 'I've said all I have to say on the subject', or 'So much for that', or 'and be damned to it'). Again, dashes often enshrine or capture Byron's accretive mode of thinking and writing. We think we have come to a full-stop or a rest, and then – with a dash (the dash connective, perhaps) – new material is added that rounds out the sentence, qualifies it, alters it entirely, raises or lowers it to a different pitch, or modulates it into a new key. I use the musical analogy deliberately; for this is precisely the quality his prose possesses.[9] It is full of musical effects to which the absence of conventional ('legitimate'?!) punctuation (the constricting laws of syntax *not* of grammar), and the use of dashes contribute. We change rhythm, move from the minor to the major with a seemingly casual enharmonic modulation; we have a developing variation here, a false cadence there; a passage of pure melisma followed by an outrageous emancipated dissonance and *coda ostinato*. The effect is extraordinarily symphonic, and the whole is orchestrated with more assured control than its dynamic may suggest. This seems to me one reason why the prose is so like the poetry: *aural*, performative, always energetic, digressive, parenthetical, yet never losing sight of the key issue. It is also one reason why it seems so modern. In a vital way his dashes reflect a passionate desire to gather the scattered impression and to communicate its immediacy; the race to get down in fixed form what is fleeting.

As for his use of the physical size of a manuscript page, this applies principally to his letters. Other writers in their letters frequently overcame the limitation of space by writing horizontally down the page as usual at first, and then writing vertically across and over what they had already written. The result is a criss-cross patchwork of ciphers, rather like a palimpsest (or one game of 'Noughts and Crosses' superimposed upon another), which in fact doubled the space, saved postage (especially from abroad) – and boggles the eyes of the unfortunate reader. This is very rare with Byron – though he does write notes, and additional lines or alternative stanzas, cross-wise in the *margins* of the manuscripts of his poetry. In letters, however, his tendency is to use the end of a manuscript page to conclude what he has to say – and to announce proudly that he is so doing. Thus we have: 'I have filled my paper' (*BLJ*, v, 122), 'My paper's out' (*BLJ*, v, 160), 'My paper is finished, and so must this letter' (*BLJ*, vii, 105) – all immediately followed by the closing signature. He even exploits this in the final stanza of *Beppo*: 'My pen is at the bottom of a page, / Which being finished, here the story ends' – which in the manuscript is precisely where it does end.[10] Now this might seem perfectly unremarkable; after all, do we not all do the same, and is there not always really another sheet of paper on which we could continue if we wished to do so: it is just a convenient excuse. But I do not think this is quite the answer. There is a bond, a tactile intimacy, between Byron and his writing materials, even a respect for them, even a fury with them. He treats the inanimate as if it were animate, almost human, and what he composes is to a certain extent conditioned thereby. Like 'rhyme', the paper is both a liberty and a restriction; it bounds, but it does not circumscribe. It is a space to be filled, but within whose limits he must accommodate himself; an area that disciplines, even as it is brought to life by, the Byron who elaborates himself upon it. This relationship seems to extend even to the choice of the paper he uses: the entire fair-copy of *The Prophecy of Dante*, for instance, is written on blue, gilt-edged, laid paper, and his handwriting is extraordinarily neat and clear. Such apparently minor details suggest much about his feelings towards what he has written and his own assessment of it – in this particular instance, 'the best thing I ever wrote if it be not *unintelligible*' (*BLJ*, VII, 59).

And here I think one essential difference emerges between Byron the poet and Byron the prose-writer: self-consciousness. In his letters, journals, and formal (non-fictional) prose, he is, or attempts to be, himself – however diverse that 'self' or those self-perceptions may be; in his poetry he is or attempts to be anything *other* than 'self' – to invest himself in the persona adopted or characters created. In his fictional prose he tries to follow the same procedure as in his poetry, but fails: the somewhat arbitrary partition between the two mentalities breaks down.

Enough of generalities. I should now like to turn to 'To the Editor' and *Some Observations* and to deal with them in individual ways and in a little more detail. In many respects these two items are opposite sides of the same coin: both are governed in some measure by the poem (*Don Juan*) which prompted the articles to which in turn they respond; both are replies. But while the first harks back to the lively and facetious 'To the Publisher' prefixed to *Waltz* (there had always been another 'Horace Hornem' in Byron longing to get out), the second looks forward to the more polemical *Letter to John Murray* (1821) and is somewhat severer.

Moreover, both are rooted in eighteenth-century literary discourse: 'To the Editor' devolving from the satirical, burlesque tradition of Swift, Pope, Fielding, and Johnson; *Some Observations* from the critical tradition of Pope and Johnson. Johnson apart, it is no accident that Pope should be the common denominator here; Byron's allegiance to that 'moral poet of all Civilization' (*CMP*, 150) whose poetry was 'the Book of Life' (*CMP*, 158) remained fixed and unshakeable throughout his life. This is evident enough in his poetry; but I should like to consider to what extent it might be so in his prose. This is not to say that both do not also partake of a contemporary idiom. Here again, 'To the Editor' shares much of the sprightly humour and pseudonymity and anonymity of Moore ('Thomas Little', 'Thomas Brown, the Younger'), and Scott (*Waverley*, 'The Author of Waverley') – the Celtic fringe to which Byron might be seen as belonging. *Some Observations*, on the other hand, takes issue with the critical discourse of reviewers and in particular, as I hope to show, of Southey.

'To the Editor'

I do not intend analysing 'To the Editor' (*CMP*, 78–85) minutely, 'for fear of seeming rather touched myself' either by the solemn inanity of Roberts, or the tedious pedantry of those commentators whom Pope in *The Dunciad* and other writers in their burlesque dramas mock in their annotations. Moreover, if it is difficult to speak about common things, it is even more so to speak about things which are, after all, funny, and kill the jest by examining it too closely. So I shall try to concentrate on how Byron manipulates his general theme and what qualities his prose seems to exhibit.

'To the Editor' was written in September 1819, in response to Roberts' response to the general charge of bribery Byron had made in the first canto of *Don Juan* (published anonymously with Canto II on 15 July 1819). Here is the initial charge in its full context:

> If, after all, there should be some so blind
> To their own good this warning to despise,
> Led by some tortuosity of mind,
> Not to believe my verse and their own eyes,
> And cry that they 'the moral cannot find,'
> I tell him, if a clergyman, he lies;
> Should captains the remark or critics make,
> They also lie too – under a mistake.
>
> The public approbation I expect,
> And beg they'll take my word about the moral,
> Which I with their amusement will connect,
> (So children cutting teeth receive a coral);
> Meantime, they'll doubtless please to recollect
> My epical pretensions to the laurel:
> For fear some prudish readers should grow skittish,
> I've bribed my grandmother's review – the British.
>
> I sent it in a letter to the editor,
> Who thank'd me duly by return of post –
> I'm for a handsome article his creditor;
> Yet if my gentle Muse he please to roast,
> And break a promise after having made it her,
> Denying the receipt of what it cost,
> And smear his page with gall instead of honey,
> All I can say is – that he had the money.
>
> (*Don Juan*, I.208–10)

I have taken stanza 208 as the point of departure because this is where the plot begins. Byron stakes his claim for the truth of his verse and singles out a 'clergyman' as a prospective unbeliever. Stanza 209 shifts from the reiteration of the claim – subtly personalized and less emphatically stated ('And *beg* they'll *take my word* about the moral'; emphasis added) – to the accusation itself in the final couplet (a fine cadence), which stanza 210 compounds with more precise (more 'convincing') particulars; by which time any person with an ounce of common sense would have seen the joke: the sheer extravagance of such a public avowal is a blatant signal of its fabrication.

Precisely the same tactics are deployed in 'To the Editor'. The opening address, 'My Dear Roberts', seems confidential and familiar at first, but its reiteration under various guises as we progress ('my dear Fellow', 'my dear good Roberts') soon betrays the mild mockery and touch of condescension that underlie it – importantly though Byron's laughter remains kindly and good-natured throughout. What seems to be complicity with the addressee gradually reveals itself as complicity with the very person who made the charge in the first place, viz. Byron himself as 'other' (the pseudonymous prose-writing Byron conspiring with the anonymous poet Byron), which also enables him to speak of himself as the public perceive him and to laugh at both himself and that image of himself – a perfect touch, relieving the humour of any malign intent. The conception – albeit a misconception – of Roberts as a clergyman adroitly picks up the reference to 'clergyman' in stanza 208 and allows Byron ingress into a whole moral apparatus only the most distantly connected with the issue in hand – at least, ostensibly. What on earth has a belief in the Church of England, or Roberts' subscribing to the thirty-nine articles (an irresistible pun) to do with the charge? Very little on the face of it. Well, what about simony, eh? How would that reflect on Roberts' character as a clergyman and even on the Church? Ah, not so good; yet there it is – were the charge to be believed, it might 'have damaged your reputation as a Clergyman and an Editor' (*CMP*, 78) – only lightly brushed, of course; even so, the connection between the editorial and clerical roles facilitates the smooth passage to questioning the credibility of all editors and reviewers, whose literary judgement is thus cast into doubt, and even the credibility of authorship and (later) sexual roles:

> An impeachment of this nature so seriously made there is but one way of refuting – and it is my firm persuasion – that whether you did or did not (and *I* believe that you did not) receive the said monies of which I wish that he had specified the sum, you are quite right in denying all knowledge of the transaction. – If charges of this nefarious description – are to go forth sanctioned by all the solemnity of circumstance – and guaranteed by the veracity of verse (as Counsellor Phillips would say) – what is to become of readers hitherto implicitly confident in the not less veracious prose of our critical journals?

> what is to become of the reviews? and if the reviews fail – what is to become of the Editors? (*CMP*, 79)

The humour works by taking Roberts' absurdity as earnestly as Roberts has taken the charge. The passage structures itself around belief ('veracity', 'veracious', and elsewhere 'credence', 'belief'), itself carried over from stanzas 208 and 209, and plays with the private knowledge of the falsity of the accusation. Byron ostensibly sympathizes with Roberts, employing the weighty vocabulary of his denial, but investing the text with references to other figures of fun with whom Roberts thus becomes associated, and then aggravating the initial charge under the guise of exonerating him from it:

> Shall I give you what I think a prudent opinion. – I don't mean to insinuate – God forbid – but if by any accident – there should have been such a correspondence between you and the unknown author whoever he may be – send him back his money, – I dare say he will be very happy to have it again – it can't be much considering the value of the article[.] (*CMP*, 83)

To have described this as 'Swiftian' (*CMP*, 348), I now think was a little hasty of me. In some respects Swift is obviously a pattern, as Byron tacitly acknowledges by alluding to the Bickerstaff–Partridge controversy (*CMP*, 84). In that controversy Swift too aggravates and compounds his initial prognostication, and disperses his voice amongst various persona (Bickerstaff, 'A Person of Quality', and an anonymous letter-writer), but his humour is darkly coloured, his irony edged with bitter even cruel acerbity. He is neither good-natured nor facetious; he embroils himself with the individual, and pursues him relentlessly through five publications. His is, and is intended to be, a *killing* 'jest'. It is true his attack was levelled against *all* false prophets, quack astrologers, and spurious almanac-makers ('the gross abuse of astrology' by 'gross impostors who set up to be the artists'),[11] and that he chose their own medium and echoed their own authoritative and hortatory tone to parody and confound them in the representative figure of Partridge; nonetheless, his performance is governed by personal animosity. Byron takes almost exactly the opposite course. He condenses the procedure (the personal 'I' of the poem, the third-party 'I' of the letter), inaugurating it in the poem with the general and unspecific ('If, after all, there should be *some* so blind'; 'my *grandmother's* review – the *British*'; emphases added), and once the bait is taken, rather than press his advantage, dangles his unfortunate victim at the end of the line and laughs at him before slipping him back into the water; shows him up and jollies him along, rather than knocks him down. Where Swift claims that his 'concern is not so much for my own reputation as that of the *republic of letters*, which Mr. Partridge hath endeavoured to wound through my sides',[12] Byron speaks as an individual and not in a representative capacity. Here is Swift in the fifth of his onslaughts, dismissing Partridge's refutation of his prediction:

> This he is pleased to contradict absolutely in the almanac he has published for the present year, and in that ungentlemanly manner (pardon the expression) as I have above related. In that work he very roundly asserts that he 'is not only now alive, but was likewise alive upon that very 29th of March when I had foretold *he* should die'. This is the subject of the present controversy between us, which I design to handle with all brevity, perspicuity, and calmness. In this dispute I am sensible the eyes not only of England, but of all Europe, will be upon us; and the *learned* in every country will, I doubt not, take part on that side where they find most appearance of reason and truth.[13]

Certainly there is humour and there is irony here, but both are overshadowed by the severity of tone and a chilling distance between the 'I' and the 'he'. Swift is principally concerned with the mode and impact of his discourse, its eloquence and conviction. He addresses an audience (England, Europe, 'the *learned* in every country'), to whom he appeals to decide the issue of the 'controversy'; his argument is founded on logic ('reason and truth'), and he refers to his rival in the third person. This is a debate or a case in law: judgement will be pronounced, a verdict given. Even the parenthetical '(pardon the expression)' is an apology to a jury for uncourtly expressions, which draws attention to the very word it excuses ('ungentlemanly') and reflects on the credentials of the parties concerned: the one who is a gentleman and will conduct his case accordingly ('with all brevity, perspicuity, and calmness'); the other who is not and whose case is therefore flawed from the start. This is rather far removed from Byron:

> I am sure, my dear Fellow – that you will take these observations of mine in good part – they are written in a spirit of friendship not less pure than your own editorial integrity – I have always admired you – and not knowing any shape which friendship and admiration can assume more agreeable and useful than that of good advice – I shall continue my lucubrations mixed with here & there a monitory hint as to what I conceive to be the line you should pursue in case you should ever again be assailed with bribes, – or accused of taking them. (*CMP*, 79–80)

Byron is revelling here in the play of language, how words perform and can be manipulated. The direct address preserves a sense of conversational geniality and goodwill, despite the 'spirit of friendship' being rendered suspect by its association with Roberts' 'editorial integrity' which was questioned at the very opening of the letter. The mixing of such verbal usages as the Latinate 'lucubrations', 'monitory', and elsewhere, 'asseverations', or, as in the earlier passage above, 'nefarious' and 'veracious' – which belong to the weighted discourse of argument and polemic and parody the gravity of Roberts' language – with colloquialisms such as 'Wag' and 'prank'; and the intermingling of such comedic figures and episodes as Sotheby and his tea-party, with its ludicrously inept parenthesis '(I wish by the bye Mrs. S. would make the tea a little stronger)', the somnolent 'sexagenary Aunt' and her broken spectacles, Counsellor Phillips, Liston, Incledon, and Puff, continually lighten the colour and tone of the text and collapse the boundaries between fact and fiction, truth and falsehood (hence reflecting the very subject of the matter in hand). This is the polyphony of *Don Juan*, the spirit of the poem played out in prose, at once familiar and facetious, jocular and social. Roberts has already made himself foolish; there is no need to argue the point, nor need his solemn utterances be answered in kind. Byron takes the foolishness itself and lets his words perform the masquerade, delighting in the carnival of language the occasion invites. In a way he is not really interested in Roberts at all; the laughter is less at him than at the language he uses. Words themselves do the laughing.

This is much closer to the spirit and tone of Pope. Here is a sample of his contribution to the *Guardian* 'On the Subject of Pastorals', in which he compares his own pastorals to those of Ambrose Philips, and to which Byron refers as 'that most admirable model of irony' in his *Letter to John Murray* (*CMP*, 144–5):

> Having now shown some parts, in which these two Writers may be compared, it is a justice I owe to Mr. *Philips*, to discover those in which *no man can compare with him*. First, That *beautiful Rusticity*, of which I shall only produce two Instances, out of a hundred not yet quoted.
>
> *O woful day! O day of Woe, quoth he,*
> *And woful I, who live the day to see!*
>
> The simplicity of Diction, the melancholy flowing of the Numbers, the solemnity of the Sound, and the easie turn of the Words, in this *Dirge*, (to make use of our Author's Expression) are extreamly elegant.
>
> In another of his Pastorals, a Shepherd utters a *Dirge* not much inferior to the former, in the following lines.
>
> *Ah me the while! ah me! the luckless day,*
> *Ah luckless Lad! the rather might I say;*
> *Ah silly I! more silly than my Sheep,*
> *Which on the flowry Plains I once did keep.*

> How he still charms the ear with these *artful Repetitions* of the Epithets; and how *significant* is the last verse! I defy the most common Reader to repeat them, without feeling some *motions of compassion*.[14]

Like Swift, Pope too pleads his cause before an audience, but his animus is not directed against Philips himself so much as his works. Nor does he attempt to persuade by reason and argument, but by illustration and ironical critical commentary – more in the nature of caricature; Philips' verses condemn themselves. Where Swift enjoys tormenting his enemy, Pope delights in using language to defeat language – exposing Philips' deficiency of wit, judgement and decorum by juxtaposing his verses with his own elegant prose. This is the *Essay on Criticism* put into practice; and this is the manner Byron follows.

Some Observations

The introduction of Pope brings us with reasonable dispatch, I hope, to *Some Observations*. As I suggested earlier, this is almost the exact obverse of 'To the Editor', and is neither anonymous nor pseudonymous, but written in Byron's own name and without the shelter of a persona. It was written in March 1820, again in response to an article on the first two cantos of *Don Juan* which had appeared in *Blackwood's Edinburgh Magazine* for August 1819 under the title of 'Remarks on Don Juan', and whose author Byron mistakenly believed to be John Wilson (but who was in fact John Gibson Lockhart).[15] As Byron says, while the poem itself 'receives an extraordinary portion of praise as a composition', the 'Greater part' of the article is 'neither more nor less than a personal attack upon the imputed author' (*CMP*, 89). Although not blind 'to its manifold beauties', Lockhart dwells at length and with 'indignation' on 'the morality of the poem', and on what he regarded as Byron's 'elaborate satire on the character and manners of his wife', which nonetheless she had the consolation of sharing with 'the lofty-minded and virtuous men [that is, Wordsworth, Southey and Coleridge] whom Lord Byron has debased himself by insulting' (*CMP*, 362–4). Uncharacteristically and for the first time in his life Byron rose to his own defence on both fronts – the personal and the poetic – and the result is quite unlike anything he had previously written. Against all appearances the piece is remarkably skilfully constructed, and might even be seen in terms of a thesis, antithesis, and synthesis; or, to resume the musical analogy suggested earlier, exposition, development, and recapitulation. Byron shifts from his opening self-defence, to an attack on the literary propensities of the day accompanied by his promotion of the cause of Pope, and thence finally to the conciliatory note on which he concludes (and by which time he has worked off his rage). The warfare motif is sounded at the very outset with the seemingly innocuous allusion, '"The Life of a writer" – has been said, by Pope I believe – to be "*a warfare upon earth*"' (*CMP*, 88), which subtly establishes Pope's presence (deflected for the present by the ingenuously casual 'I believe') and does not come into full prominence until the development section when Byron moves to his support of him proper. Their association is made even more explicit through their shared 'Ostracism' – Byron's exile from society; Pope's from the poetic community – which deftly links the exposition and the recapitulation sections. But the pivotal point in the piece occurs where Byron turns from defending himself to attack Wordsworth, Southey and, very marginally, Coleridge, against whom, of course, he had written his parody of the Ten Commandments in *Don Juan* (I, 1,633–50) (once more his prose engaging with and supplementing a specific injunction made in his poetry). And it is the attack on Southey – again anticipated at the start of the piece ('I shall have more to say on the subject of this person – not the devil but Mr. Southey – before I conclude' (*CMP*, 90)) – on which I should now like to focus.

Southey had not only commented adversely about *Manfred* and, as Byron once more mistakenly believed, circulated the story of incest about him, but he also, and alone of all other poets of the day, had recently published a personal defence of himself. Much to his embarrassment, early in 1817 his youthful jacobinical poem *Wat Tyler*, written in 1794, was piratically published. The preceding October, he had contributed an article to the *Quarterly Review* on Parliamentary Reform in which he expressed political sentiments diametrically opposed to those expressed in the poem. Unfortunately for him, the inconsistency was pounced upon by William Smith MP, who raised the matter in the House of Commons during a debate on the Seditious Meetings Bill in March 1817. After certain unsavoury deliberations, and having compared a passage from the poem with one from the article, Smith went on to ask 'why no proceedings had been instituted against the author', whose poem appeared to him to be 'the most seditious book that was ever written' (see *CMP*, 376–7). At this Southey leapt to his own defence in *A Letter to William Smith, Esq. M.P. from Robert Southey, Esq*. He claimed that Smith had no authority for ascribing to him an anonymous article in a review journal,[16] and went on to state:

> None of the innumerable attacks which have been made upon them [his writings] has ever called forth on my part a single word of reply, triumphantly as I might have exposed my assailants . . . It will not therefore be imputed to any habit of egotism, or any vain desire of interesting the public in my individual concerns, if I now come forward from that privacy in which both from judgement and disposition it would have been my choice to have remained.[17]

He did not deny his earlier republican sympathies, but attempted to exonerate them by saying that 'while I imbibed the republican opinions of the day, I escaped the atheism and the leprous immorality which generally accompanied them',[18] and wound up with the following spectacular peroration:

> How far the writings of Mr. Southey may be found to deserve a favourable acceptance from after ages, time will decide; but a name, which whether worthily or not, has been conspicuous in the literary history of its age, will certainly not perish. Some account of his life will always be prefixed to his works, and transferred to literary histories, and to the biographical dictionaries, not only of this, but of other countries. There it will be related, that he lived in the bosom of his family, in absolute retirement; that in all his writings there breathed the abhorrence of oppression and immorality . . . and that during the course of his literary life, often as he was assailed, the only occassion [*sic*] on which he ever condescended to reply, was, when a certain Mr. William Smith insulted him in Parliament with the appellation of Renegade. On that occasion, it will be said, that he vindicated himself, as it became him to do, and treated his calumniator with just and memorable severity.[19]

'It is ludicrous', wrote the reviewer of this *Letter* in the *Monthly Review*, 'while Mr. S. disclaims "the habit of egotism", to observe the numberless instances of inordinate vanity with which these forty-five pages are filled . . . The concluding passage, in which he writes a page in his own history, and proclaims the imperishable nature of his productions and his name, . . . forms a climax of self-conceit that has no parallel.'[20] That Southey should have been deeply offended and even hurt is perfectly understandable; but to show it with such arrogant self-righteousness and self-applause alienates the sympathy of the reader. He is oblivious of his own offensiveness in prescribing to his contemporaries and to posterity what they shall think of him.[21] His use of the third person to refer to himself – an unsuccessful attempt at assuming objectivity which in the event has something of the regal 'we' about it, dominating and irrefragable – and the reiterated assertion 'it will be said', emphasize his own sense of superiority, and throw the whole weight of the prospective biography on self, not on what another might be free to say about him. Indeed, he confuses biography with autobiography (with himself as judge in his own constituted tribunal), and claims by force what it is for others to grant. This is not a reply but a coldly calculated retort whose very pretension to unassailability provokes the answer it would seek to silence (and Hazlitt had a field day with it in the *Examiner*).[22] Moreover, Southey reveals nothing of the poet in himself – nor of the famed prose-writer for that matter: there is nothing for the imagination to grasp hold of or to attach itself to, no touch of the human or the social; the man dictates regardless of the susceptibilities of his audience. A particularly good instance here is the sentence, 'Some account of his life will always be prefixed to his works, and transferred to literary histories' – so far so good; a perfectly adequate sentence in itself, and a perfectly fair statement of *fact* (it is true, it is unavoidable, such is and will be the case); but when he adds, 'and to the biographical dictionaries, not only of this, but of other countries', we immediately feel uncomfortable: we are being bullied. The immodesty of a man who can boast of his enduring reputation all the world over, and whose posthumous fame already means more to him than the worth his living contemporaries may set upon him, is an affront; he makes us feel redundant.

Now hear Byron:

> How far my exile may have been 'polluted' – it is not for me to say – because the word is a wide one – and with some of it's branches may chance to overshadow the actions of most men; but that it has been '*selfish*' I deny. —— If to the extent of my means – and my power – and my information of their calamities – to have assisted many miserable beings, reduced by the decay of the place of their birth, and their consequent loss of Substance; – if to have never rejected an application which appeared founded on truth – if to have expended in this manner sums far out of proportion to my fortune – there and elsewhere, – be selfish then have I been selfish. —— To have done such things I do not deem much – but it is hard indeed to be compelled to recapitulate them in my own defence – by such accusations as that before me – like a pannel before a Jury calling testimonies to his Character – or a soldier recording his services to obtain his discharge. – . . .
>
> Had I been a selfish man – had I been a grasping man – had I been in the worldly sense of the word – even a *prudent* man – I should not be where I now am, – I should not have taken the step which was the first that led to the events which have sunk a Gulph between me and mine; but in this respect the truth will one day be made known – in the mean time as Durandarte says in the Cave of Montesinos 'Patience and shuffle the Cards.' ——————
>
> I bitterly feel the ostentation of this statement, the first of the kind I have ever made, – I feel the degradation of being compelled to make it; but I also feel it's *truth*, and I trust to feel it on my death-bed – should it be my lot to die there. ———— I am not less sensible of the Egotism of all this – but Alas! who have made me thus egoistical in my own defence? (*CMP*, 91–2)

What a contrast, reader, and a perfectly written piece of prose. The first two paragraphs are governed by the use of the conditional which does not operate to the same effect in both ('If' in the first paragraph, 'Had I been' in the second; and it is worth noticing here the superb cadential effect of the dashes in delaying the resolution of the conditional: indeed, replace the dashes with commas throughout the whole passage, or point it in any other way, and at once it becomes paralysed – the energy halting, the expression stiff). The first paragraph is carefully built up over a series of antecedents which at once reveals the injustice of the charge, and yet remains submissive to it depending on the consequent ('If . . . then have I been selfish'). The 'Had I been' of the second paragraph, however, develops the notion of selfishness itself through a variety of meretricious analogues which confutes (*not* 'refutes' which is not the same thing) the charge whilst granting that his failure to observe such selfishness has been to his own detriment ('Had I been . . . I should not'). Nowhere does Byron prejudge or prescribe for the reader. He does not blatantly repudiate the charge because it is not for him to do so; he leaves the testimony to others, and the 'truth' to time. He makes no claim to being a model of moral rectitude, he solicits no praise, he flaunts no merit. Unlike Southey, he does not embarrass us with a tasteless display of himself. Indeed, there is no 'Egotism' here: the modesty, the self-restraint, the self-effacement, even the self-deprecation ('To have done such things I do not deem much', and the whole of the second paragraph), bear witness to his evident disinclination to speak about himself and the ignominy of so doing in public. This is not just a matter of tact and self-respect, but poetic sensibility: the metaphors ('like a pannel . . . or a soldier'), the allusions (to the Bible, and to Cervantes – with a touch of humour here besides), and even the choice of adjectives ('grasping', 'worldly', '*prudent*'), and the dignified submergence of his own deep hurt, bespeak an imaginative awareness of the susceptibilities of others which renders his true feeling all the more poignant and palpable to the attentive reader (the pathos of 'Alas!', for instance).

I suggested earlier that *Some Observations* ends on a conciliatory note. This is an element that crept into Byron's poetry with increasing vigour during his years in Italy. It can be seen very clearly in the 'curse' of 'Forgiveness' passage in *Childe Harold* IV (stanzas 130–7), *The Prophecy of Dante*, and the important and atrociously neglected sonnet 'To the Prince Regent'. It can also be seen on a personal level in the stanzas addressed to Jeffrey in *Don Juan* X (stanzas 11–19), and even, one might say, in the mere dialoguing with the reader in *Beppo* and *Don Juan*, and in the mercy of *The Vision of Judgment*. In all these cases there is a profound effort to promote concord, unity, fellowship, and kindness amongst men – between sovereign and citizen, between factions and between individuals. Bearing this in mind – and the fact that the passage of Southey cited above is also from the conclusion of his *Letter* – I should like to end this review of the prose with the conclusion of *Some Observations*. And I would invite the reader to notice in particular how Byron has written himself back into a good humour, overcome his rage, and retrieved his kindliness towards his assailant; how he builds up to his climax without the least ostentation, and without the least stridency – returning to the very charge of parody raised against him, not in order to assail his critic withal, but to laugh with him socially over an innocence of which they are both 'guilty', and, even as he does so, not only names him, but in naming praises:

> I will now return to the writer of the Article which has drawn forth these remarks, whom I humbly take to be John Wilson, a man of great powers and acquirements, well known to the public as the author of the 'City of the Plague' 'Isle of Palms', and other productions . . . And in return for M^{r}. Wilson's invective I shall content myself with asking one question, did he never compose, recite, or sing, any parody or parodies upon the Psalms, (of what nature this deponent saith not) in certain jovial meetings of the youth of Edinburgh? —— It is not that I think any great harm if he did . . . But I wish to know if M^{r}. Wilson ever has done this, and *if* he *has* – *why he* should be so very very [*sic*] angry with similar portions of Don Juan? – . . .
>
> I will now conclude this long answer to a short article repenting of having said so much in my own defence, and so little on the 'crying left hand fallings off, and national defections' of the poetry of the present day. ——— Having said this, I can hardly be expected to defend Don Juan, or any other '*living*' poetry, and shall not make the attempt. —— And although I do not think that M^{r}. J^{no}. Wilson has in this instance treated me with candour or consideration, I trust that the tone I have used in speaking of him personally – will prove that I bear him as little malice as I really believe at the *bottom* of his *heart*, he bears towards me. —— But the duties of an Editor like those of a tax-gatherer are paramount and peremptory. ——— I have done. ——— (*CMP*, 118–19)

I do not know of any other writer who has had the generosity and great-heartedness to conclude a polemic of such a nature in so gracious and courteous a manner. If the example Byron sets us in his poetry is worth emulating, it is so in his prose. I have done.

NOTES

1. Preface to *Lyrical Ballads* (1800), emphasis added; see *Wordsworth and Coleridge: Lyrical Ballads*, ed. R. L. Brett and A. R. Jones (London: Methuen, 1965), p. 253.
2. For this understanding, see *CMP*, 315. I should point out, however, that the title, 'Bramblebear and Lady Penelope: A Chapter of a Novel', was supplied by myself.
3. See *CMP*, 315–16 and 346–8.
4. See his letters to Moore, Murray, Annabella, Augusta, and Kinnaird of December 1820 (*BLJ*, VII, 245–55), and *Don Juan*, V, 33–9. See also his Journal entry for 4 January 1821 (*BLJ*, VIII, 12).
5. Indeed, some have the status of self-contained essays – such as the various 'Papers referred to by Note' at the end of *Childe Harold* I and II, and the attack on Southey at the end of the Appendix to *The Two Foscari* (*CPW*, II, 199–212 and VI, 222–5, respectively).
6. Walt Whitman, *Song of Myself*, Part 51.

7. Cicero, *Epistulae ad Familiares*, II, iv, 1 (I have used the English translation by W. Glynn Williams in the Loeb Classical Library, Cicero, *Letters to His Friends*, 3 vols. (Cambridge, Mass. and London: Harvard University Press, 1927), I, 100–1).
8. Gifford to Murray, probably 3 April 1814. Byron himself was certainly aware of his deficiency in punctuating his poetry. Writing to Murray on 26 August 1813 concerning *The Giaour*, he asked: 'do you know anybody who can *stop* – I mean *point* – commas & so forth – for I am I fear a sad hand at your punctuation' (BLJ, III, 100; see also, IV, 94). I should like to express my thanks to John R. Murray for his kind permission to quote from material in the Murray Archives.
9. Since writing this I find that the use of the dash is also a characteristic of Jean Paul (Richter) whom Schumann imitates in his youthful prose writings. Drawing attention to this in his superb study of the composer, John Daverio suggests most aptly that 'the resultant paratactic style [is] a fitting emblem for a worldview that configures reality as a system of mysteriously related fragments' (John Daverio, *Robert Schumann: Herald of a 'New Poetic Age'* (New York: Oxford University Press, 1997), p. 42). Jean Paul himself not only uses dashes but comments on his very use of them (see, for example, *German Romance: Specimens of Its Chief Authors*, trans. Thomas Carlyle, 4 vols. (Edinburgh: William Tait, 1827), III, 41–2 and 159–60).
10. This can be seen in facsimile in *The Manuscripts of the Younger Romantics: Lord Byron: Vol. XII*, ed. Andrew Nicholson (New York and London: Garland Publishing, 1998), p. 286.
11. *The Oxford Authors: Jonathan Swift*, ed. Angus Ross and David Wooley (Oxford University Press, 1984), p. 193.
12. *Ibid.*, p. 212.
13. *Ibid.*, p. 214.
14. *Guardian*, No. 40, 27 April 1713. See *The Poems of Alexander Pope*, ed. John Butt (London and New York: Routledge, 1989), pp. 448–9.
15. For the text and commentary of *Some Observations*, see *CMP*, 88–119 and 358–99.
16. *A Letter to William Smith, Esq. M.P. from Robert Southey, Esq.* (London: John Murray, 1817), 3 (hereinafter referred to as *A Letter*). Cf Byron's similar disclaimer (*CMP*, 89).
17. *A Letter*, 10–11. Cf Byron's briefer and more modest, 'I have never shrunk from the responsibility of what I have written, and have more than once incurred obloquy by neglecting to disavow what was attributed to my pen without foundation' (*CMP*, 89).
18. *A Letter*, 19. Cf Byron's own repeated (not a misprint) reference to Southey's 'leprous leprous sense of his own degradation' (*CMP*, 101, line 26).
19. *A Letter*, 43–5. I apologize to readers for my misstatement concerning the word 'calumniator' in *CMP*, 377, note 65 (closing parenthesis).
20. *Monthly Review*, 83 (June 1817), 224.
21. See Chapter 10, p. 171.
22. Hazlitt reviewed *A Letter* with acid contempt in *The Examiner*, No. 488: Sunday, 4 May 1817 (284–7), No. 489: Sunday, 11 May 1817 (298–300), and No. 490: Sunday, 18 May 1817 (315–18). Hazlitt's identity is confirmed by Edmund Blunden, *Leigh Hunt's 'Examiner' Examined* (London: Cobden-Sanderson, 1928), p. 70.

3

LITERARY CONTEXTS

12

JEROME McGANN

Byron's lyric poetry

Byron's lyric writing needs to be understood in the context of Romantic lyricism in general. This move is particularly important in Byron's case because his writing develops a Romantic 'style' as distinctive and as influential as Wordsworth's, although historical circumstances have obscured this situation. With certain few exceptions, for example, nineteenth-century British poets followed a Wordsworthian line while Europeans were taking their lead from Byron. Not until the legacy of Baudelaire permeated the twentieth century would an access to Byron's lyric procedures open up for poets writing in English.

Romanticism is regularly and usefully characterized in terms lifted from a certain set of adjectives, such as: subjective, impassioned, personal, sincere, spontaneous, reflective, self-conscious. The terms point toward a body of work that, however diverse in other respects, shares the common feature signalled by those various descriptors. Here are several famous Romantic passages, more or less randomly chosen:

Sund'ring, dark'ning, thund'ring!
Rent away with a terrible crash,
Eternity rolled wide apart,
Wide asunder rolling,
Mountainous, all around
Departing, departing, departing.

(Blake, *The Book of Urizen*, 12–17)

My heart aches, and a drowsy numbness pains
My sense, as though of hemlock I had drunk

(Keats, 'Ode to a Nightingale', 1–2)

Behold her, single in the field,
Yon solitary highland lass!

Reaping and singing by herself –
Stop here, or gently pass!
(Wordsworth, 'The Solitary Reaper', 1–4)

Be thou, spirit fierce,
My spirit! Be thou me, impetuous one!
(Shelley, 'Ode to the West Wind', 61–2)

What do I say, 'A mirror of my heart'?
Are not thy waters sweeping, dark, and strong?
Such as my feelings were and are, thou art,
And such as thou art were my passions long
(Byron, 'To the Po. 2 June 1819', 9–12)

I am – yet what I am none cares or knows;
My friends forsake me like a memory lost: –
I am the self-consumer of my woes
(Clare, 'I Am', 1–3)

During the period of Romanticism's cultural dominance, Friedrich Schiller proposed a helpful formula for organizing these different kinds of text. He drew a (Romantic) distinction between what he called 'naïve' and 'sentimental' poetry. The formulation is dialectical and carries psychological as well as historical determinations. In an historical sense it sets 'modern', sophisticated poetry against earlier 'primitive' poetry, especially balladic verse. The former is reflective and self-conscious, the latter passionate and spontaneous.

In England, Wordsworth made much the same distinction in his 'Preface' to *Lyrical Ballads* when he sketched his theory of poetic process. Beginning 'naively' in what he calls a 'spontaneous overflow of powerful feelings', the process leads to a 'sentimental' phase of 'emotion recollected in tranquillity'. According to Wordsworth, the act of poetic 'composition generally begins' in this sentimental state (a view not shared by all romantics). The very title 'lyrical ballads' signals the sentimental/naive dichotomy.

In Romantic practice, both genres, lyric and ballad, could emphasize either a naive or a sentimental inflection. 'The Rime of the Ancient Mariner' and 'La Belle Dame Sans Merci' are both sophisticated, 'sentimental' ballads, whereas lyrical forms like Scott's 'Proud Maisie' cut a naive figure, as does Byron's 'I speak not – I trace not – I breathe not thy name' or Keats' late poems to Fanny Brawne. Coleridge titled several of his best early poems 'Effusions'.

Whether naive or sentimental, passionate or meditative, Romantic poetry characteristically marks itself with personal, subjective and local signs. Some of these marks are rhetorical, as when Coleridge in 'Frost at Midnight' writes as if there were no gap between the act of writing and the experiential event that is the poet's subject:

> The owlet's cry
> Came loud, – and hark, again! loud as before.
> ('Frost at Midnight', 2–3)

Others marks are, as it were, factive. Wordsworth specifies place and date in the title of 'Tintern Abbey', for example, a move that has many variations in Romantic poems. The title of Byron's last important lyric is very similar, but it goes somewhat further in making his poem an index of his personal involvement with events of world-historical import: 'Missolonghi 22 January 1824. On this day I complete my thirty-sixth year.' That title heads a birthday poem being written, we are asked to realize, in the eye of a current (Greek) revolutionary storm. Further, the title is slightly ominous: Byron does not *celebrate* his birthday, he gives it the sense of an ending. As it happened, he would be dead in less than three months' time, an historical fact that seems strangely forecast, even solicited, by this remarkable poem, which explicitly connects Byron's death with the rebirth of Greek freedom, as if the two events were joined by some historical fatality.

'The personal is the political.' That widely circulated current idea was never more fully realized than in the case of Byron. His Romantic subjectivity, whether reflexive or impassioned, regularly defines itself in spectacular terms. Studying and brooding upon themselves, Romantic poets produce cosmic theatricals from the dramas they write about their own lives, feelings, and experiences. In the lyrics of Wordsworth and much Romantic poetry, however, this 'poetry of experience', as it has been called, typically erases or sets aside its political and historical currencies. The poetic psychomachia focuses on the 'universal' import of personal experience. Byron's lyrical procedures are quite different in that they regularly draw upon a complex set of political, social, and world-historical mediations. Byron identifies himself with whole nations (Greece, Italy, England – with Europe at large) and with their national heroes (political as well as artistic). Those identifications produce in turn a series of further equations between Byron's personal life and the 'lives' of these nations and their leading figures. Byron's quasi-legendary stature is a function of such relationships, which he constructs with great imaginative deliberateness from a very early period in his life.

One wants to see this Byronic style of address very clearly for it helps to explain, on one hand, why certain readers have difficulty with his work – Wordsworth, for example, or Keats – while others – Pushkin, Heine, Poe,

Baudelaire – take it as their point of lyric departure. In one view Byron's poetry appears to lack intimacy, despite its flagrantly confessional character. 'Lord Byron cuts a figure but he is not figurative', Keats famously observed, meaning that Byron's subjectivity is entirely too theatrical. But for Baudelaire – and later, for poets like Auden or Merrill – that theatrical style defined Byron's greatness as a lyric poet.

Baudelaire's connection to Byron is most easily tracked in the history of dandyism. So far as poetry as such is concerned, dandyism is important as the ethos of a certain kind of rhetorical style. This aesthetic is announced in *Fleur du mal*'s famous opening poem 'Au lecteur', where key conventions of Romantic lyricism undergo an ironic meltdown. The sacred interiority of the Romantic *reveur* and his complicit partner, the sympathetic overhearing reader, is torn open and exposed. In the event, poet and reader are no longer permitted to imagine themselves saved by sympathetic imagination. On the contrary, that imagination is figured in the poem as hashish, source of illusion. The point of the poem is not at all to escape this illusion – to acquire aesthetic redemption through either more intense feeling or yet deeper understanding. Rather, the dandiacal poet offers the reader the flame from a cold lamp and the reflection from a pitiless mirror: 'Hypocrite lecteur, mon semblable, mon frère'.

To write in this way was to write under a Byronic sign, as Baudelaire told his mother immediately after the publication of his book. Not much later, in an (unpublished) review essay, Baudelaire supplied a paradoxical name for this verse style he wanted to cultivate: 'le poesie lyrique anonyme'. In the anonymous (Romantic) lyric, 'feeling' is a stylistic rather than a psychological function. As a result, a more impersonal standard than an individual's beliefs or preferences – whether poet's or reader's – comes to measure what will suffice for a poem. The move at once expands the range of what will be artistically possible precisely because the move is made in a Romantic context. Because Byron is a Romantic poet, because he inherits and deploys the style of Romantic self-expression, he becomes for Baudelaire a poet of masks and poses, a stage figure performing the drama of his subjectivity. Pain or pleasure, benevolence or cruelty, good and evil: the poem (as it were) will decide what to take up among this range of human things and in what point of view to consider the subject-poet and his overhearing reader. Theatricality replaces Sincerity as the measure of Romantic style.

Baudelaire's approach to Byron can be recovered by starting with the once celebrated 'Fare Thee Well!', the poem Byron addressed (in public) to his wife during the crisis of the break-up of his marriage. When the poem first appeared, Wordsworth read it and recoiled, pronouncing it mere 'doggerel'. Wordsworth read the poem as a failed and utterly debased effort at Romantic sincerity – a maudlin and factitious effusion in which Byron falsely poses himself as a confessed and repentant husband and sinner.

What Wordsworth could not see in this poem, however – what he probably could not have imagined for it – was its deliberate hypocrisy. Byron wears a mask of Romantic 'sincerity' in this poem in order to tell the deeper truth of his feelings of pain, anger, hatred, fear, and cruelty. Shrewd critical reader that he was, Baudelaire would thus see in such a poem a dramatic staging of the illusion resting at the heart of the Romantic lyric.

Byron's critique of Romanticism – for this is what his poetry is – argued that a style of art (Romanticism) was being transformed into an article of (bad) faith. Coleridge's famous definition of 'poetic faith' as the 'willing suspension of disbelief' is much to the point here. As in Coleridge's other technical discussions of poetry, this passage underscores the primacy of 'disbelief' so far as poetic artifice is concerned. Coleridge imagines highly self-conscious readers who are able to deliberately suspend their understanding that the poetry is a play of language. Problems will arise, however, if in suspending disbelief one should lose hold on the artifice involved – if a reader or poet should slip into a delusion and take the poetic expression for 'the truth' rather than a certain vantage on the matter.

As Byron observed the cultural development of Romantic ideas he saw a widespread capitulation to such delusions. *Don Juan*'s attack on 'the wrong revolutionary poetical system' of Romanticism is famous, but his earliest satire, *English Bards and Scotch Reviewers*, was already exploring the same issues. Its attack on Romanticism is especially interesting, and important, in one crucial respect: the poem climaxes as an exercise in self-criticism. In making that move the poem raises an important and troubling Romantic question: is the self-critique 'true' or is it a mere pose of art? In what sense should Byron's readers 'believe' Byron when he mordantly characterizes his own writing as 'the spoiler's art', as he does in *English Bards*?

Byron is a key figure for Romanticism because he is determined to force a confrontation with that question. To do so he placed himself at the centre of his work and made a Brechtian theatre of his self-expression and sincerity. In his poetry these Romantic conventions are deployed as if they were real. Byron's is not merely the poetry of his bleeding heart, it is the poetry that comes with bleeding heart labels. Whereas in (say) Wordsworth or Keats, the possibility of poetic truth remains a theoretical assumption, in Byron's work it is the central and explicit question of the writing.

The manifest sign of this fact about his work remains the biographical interest that dominates the readings and the criticism of the work. This focus represents a desire to have the textual scene validated by an extra-textual measure of truth – the emergence into critical or readerly view of 'the real Lord Byron'. That truth, famously, remains elusive – like most Romantic forms, 'something longed for, never seen'. The artifice of Byron's work thereby reinstalls a 'primary imagination' of disbelief into the scene of writing and reading. His is an art of seduction in which the seducer is as abandoned, in both senses of the word, as the object of seduction. Byron's poetry constructs an artifice of the living poet himself, 'Byron' *in propria persona*. Suspended thus between belief and disbelief, the poetry opens itself to the consequences that follow when a Romantic 'contract' between poet and reader is put into play. Unlike Wordsworth, Byron is not trying to draw up a new contract – to create the taste by which 'sincerity' and Romantic expression will be enjoyed. Byron's relation to his Romanticism is secondary and critical.

To do this, Byron had to construct artifices of himself in his work – illusory and theatrical selves who would summon their readerly brothers. Most famous of these is the suffering poet whose audience reciprocal is the sympathetic reader. (Poe, Heine, and Baudelaire represent the antithesis of that reader; all are 'Byronic' readers, cynical, playful, perverse.) Byron inherited the figure of the suffering poet from his Romantic forebears, in whose benevolent lyricism 'feeling comes in aid of feeling' (*The Prelude*, XII.269–70), as the suffering Wordsworth famously declared.

Byron's work comes to reimagine the import of that message. When feeling comes in aid of feeling in the Byronic/Baudelairean world the dynamic of sympathy breaks free of the horizon of benevolence. Theirs is no mere debunking move, however. Byron begins with the traditional Romantic assumption that the poet is a man like other men but endowed with more lively sensibilities and so forth. And he adopts the Romantic course of trusting his own vision, his own imaginative grasp of experience:

> 'Tis to create, and in creating, live
> A being more intense, that we endow
> With form our fancy, gaining as we give
> The life we image, even as I do now.
> (*CHP*, III.6.1–4)

The gods summoned by this 'being more intense' turn out Lucretian, however, not Christian, and they rule according to the mighty working of a primal duplicity. Aphrodite, Alma Venus Genetrix, Egeria: a 'shape and image . . . haunt[ing] the unquenched soul' (*CHP*, IV.121.8–9) in its eternal passage through an existence as radically contradicted as the paradoxes Byron fashions to explain it, like the famous 'unreach's Paradise of our despair':

Who loves, raves – 'tis youth's frenzy – but the cure
Is bitterer still, as charm by charm unwinds
Which robed our idols, and we see too sure
Not wealth nor beauty dwells from out the mind's
Ideal shape of such; yet still it binds,
The fatal spell, and still it draws us on,
Reaping the whirlwind from the oft-sown winds;
The stubborn heart, its alchemy begun,
Seems ever near the prize – wealthiest when most undone.

(*CHP*, IV.123)

If passages like this – they are all over Byron's work – appear demonic, they measure the cost of that 'being more intense' summoned by Byron. Indeed, they incarnate the presence of that being and hence draw our 'gaze of wonder' (line 201) like the Giaour.

What they do not draw, or even cultivate, is a reader's sympathy or empathetic response. What avenue for sympathy lies open for readers when the lyric voice clearly has no sympathy for himself? The verse is at once intense and indifferent, a poetry of self-expression in which the self has nothing to gain except further encounters, calculated and implacable, with its own folly and pain, blindness and insight. Such writing is exactly what Baudelaire called 'anonymous' – mannered and theatrical, the poetry of dandyism. The verse performs a kind of Faustian rite in which Byron agrees to use himself up – to *use* himself, treat himself like a thing to be coldly anatomized and observed. The reward? Simply increased self-awareness.

Byron cultivated this poetic style from his earliest days, as we can see in a juvenile poem like 'Damaetas', which involves a cool analysis of the figure of a wicked youth. Byron publishes the poem in his early book *Hours of Idleness* (1807) under a deceptive and cunning classical heading: the Theocritean name carries a sly homosexual overtone. But that obliquity is merely the sign of a deeper deceptiveness – which is also to say, in this masking poetic style, a deeper truth-telling. The original title of this poem was 'My Character'. The poem thus studies a slant truth about the writing poet, and in its act of slanting it tells a further and more revealing truth. The poem dramatizes an act of poetic hypocrisy. The fact that in this case Byron does not give the reader access to all he has done is important precisely because the public title does function as an oblique code available to the reader.

Byron will become master of this masking, 'anonymous' style, turning it loose upon all the forms of the European cultural inheritance. That technical breadth helps to explain the impact of his work on later writers. When he takes up the epigram – he wrote many – the same effect appears:

'Tis said – *Indifference* marks the present time,
Then hear the reason – though 'tis told in rhyme –
A King who *can't* – a Prince of Wales who *don't* –
Patriots who *shan't* – and Ministers who *won't* –
What matters who are *in* or *out* of place
The *Mad* – the *Bad* – the *Useless* – or the *Base*?

(*BLJ*, III, 117)

'Though 'tis told in rhyme': that conventional gesture of poetic modesty looks toward what the last line names directly. This poem is, in its own political terms and figures, a mad, bad, useless, and base piece of work, the moral equivalent of the world it attacks. It is a small but superb poem for that very reason, stripped of illusion, an affront and an offence – quite literally, a terrible truth.

In poems like these we have been examining, Byron does not repudiate his Romantic inheritance. Rather, he traces out a logic of Romanticism's internal contradictions. In simplest terms, Byron's poetry shows that 'sincerity' for the poet has to be a convention, an artifice of style. To write a Romantic lyric that will not fall victim to that artifice, suspending his disbelief in it, the poet must stand as it were anonymously before his own subjective presentations. 'Hypocrisy' (or contradiction) becomes a poetical issue – the subject for the poet and for the poem – as soon as the illusion of the convention of sincerity is exposed. Byron's lyric style is, in effect, a satire on itself and its cultural capital. As such it is equally a satire upon and critique of the moral and social orders carried in that capital. Byron's 'ideal self' is 'born for opposition' rather than for balance and reconciliation, which Byron marks down as a bourgeois illusion. Anticipating Baudelaire (and recalling Milton), Manfred will call that illusion of synthesis 'The last infirmity of evil' (*Manfred*, I.ii.29).

In a sense, of course, as readers have always known, all of Byron's poems are 'lyrical', self-expressive forms. He protested when his contemporaries identified him with Harold, the Giaour, the Corsair, Manfred, Sardanapalus but the protest is part of the masquerade. Because these figures are consciously manipulated masks, one has to read them – as Coleridge might have said – in terms of a 'sameness with difference'. The poetry lies exactly in the relation, the metaphor – the dialectical play between corresponding apparitional forms: on one side the spectacular poet, the man cut into a Keatsian 'figure', the person translated into what Byronic texts call 'a name'; on the other, the various fictional and historical selvings. In Byronic masquerade, we have difficulty distinguishing figure from ground because the presumptive ground, 'the real Lord Byron', has become a figural form in the verse.

Anonymous lyric depends upon this stylistic procedure, setting up a hypocritical contract with the Romantic reader. The texts deliver a merciless revelation of a uniform condition – a kind of 'Universal Darkness' but beyond the imagination of *The Dunciad* because Byron's revelatory text has itself been imagined as part of the darkness. This style of approach yields some amazing effects, as in the following passage from *The Prophecy of Dante.*

> I am not of this people, or this age,
> And yet my harpings will unfold a tale
> Which shall preserve these times when not a page
> Of their perturbed annals could attract
> An eye to gaze upon their civil rage
> Did not my verse embalm full many an act
> Worthless as they who wrought it; 'tis the doom
> Of spirits of my order to be wrack'd
> In life, to wear their hearts out, and consume
> Their days in endless strife, and die alone;
> Then future thousands crowd around their tomb,
> And pilgrims come from climes where they have known
> The name of him, who now is but a name.
> (*The Prophecy of Dante*, 1.143–55)

Is this text 'about' Byron or about Dante, about Renaissance Italy or Regency England and its European counterpart? Is Lord Byron recollecting the great Tuscan poet or are we to read it the other way round, with this textual Dante prophesying his future British avatar? A structure of convertibility turns everything into its opposite – it is the very emblem of a text 'born for opposition'. Byron/Dante declares 'I am not of this people or this age', a joking statement in several respects and not least because the verse 'embalms' the 'worthless' acts of the age. As the remarkable wordplay in 'harpings' suggests, a Mephisto comedy plays about this text. The word 'embalms' is especially volatile since it connects the verse with corpsed forms – as if he (Byron/Dante) were a literal figure of the nightmare life-in-death that he sees about him. To consult such a poet one must visit his tomb where, however, one encounters only his 'name'. The tombstone's engraved letters enter the text as a sign that even before death the poet lives a postmortem existence.

In his 'Preface' to the poem, Byron associates his prophecy with the vision of Cassandra, whose prophetic declarations would share the doom of Troy. Like Cassandra and Dante – like some utterly bleak democrat of Wordsworth's 'Preface' to the *Lyrical Ballads* – Byron is 'a man like any other men', but his endowment 'with more lively sensibilities' gives him a Cassandra view of things:

All that a citizen could be I was;
Raised by thy will, all thine in peace or war,
And for this hour thou hast warr'd with me, – 'tis done:
I may not overleap the eternal bar,
Built up between us, and will die alone,
Beholding, with the dark eye of a seer,
The evil days to gifted souls foreshown,
Foretelling them to those who will not hear
(*The Prophecy of Dante*, IV.144–51)

This is no self-celebrating text. Byron's citizenship – the social and cultural position he sought and found – establishes his special identity with his 'evil days'. Like the Napoleon of *Childe Harold* Canto III, the Byron of this poem – of all his poems – is 'the greatest [and] the worst' (*CHP*, III.36) of citizens, the literary Alcibiades of his country. The anonymous lyrical style delivers the famous poet over to his text, turning him into a cold symbolic form. The form is both beautiful and ineffectual – the very type of that dead knowledge that Manfred's Faustian quest revealed.

Byronic 'mobility', like Keatsian chameleonism, is therefore, as Byron declared, 'a most painful and unhappy attribute', at least if it is measured in functional terms. The Byronic text stands aloof from the dialectic of loss and gain, rewards and punishments, in which it is yet so deeply, so entirely involved. Its Satanism rests in that posture of aloofness, as if it stood indifferent to questions of judgement and valuation. Good and bad, better and worse, are deeply questioned, questionable, terms. Like Byron's Paolo and Francesca, the texts seek (and execute) something beyond our conceptual categories of judgement, whether moral or aesthetic:

The Land where I was born sits by the seas,
Upon that shore to which the Po descends
With all his followers in search of peace.
('Francesca of Rimini', V.1–3)

The speaker here is of course, originally, Francesca, but through the text's masquerade we translate that name into a Byronic equivalent – in this case, most immediately, Teresa Guiccioli. Francesca of Rimini, Teresa of Ravenna: the text applies to both. In his role as poet and as lover, Byron is then textually disposed as Dante and as Paolo. But exactly as in the case of Julia's farewell letter at the end of *Don Juan* Canto I, the Byron of this text seeks a gender translation as well, identifying himself as much with Francesca as he does with her poet and her lover.

As in the closely related text, Byron's 'To the Po', the river here is a figure of intense and ceaseless passion – Turgenev's 'torrents of spring'. All of the river's tributaries and 'followers' ride this river toward an extinguishing sea, where Lucretius' Aphrodite stands observing her universe.

> Love, which the gentle heart soon apprehends,
> Seized him for the fair person which was ta'en
> From me, and me even yet the mode offends.
> Love, who to none beloved to love again
> Remits, seized me with wish to please so strong
> That, as thou seest, yet, yet, it doth remain.
> ('Francesca of Rimini', v.4–9)

Damnation itself has not quenched this scene of passion, as the next two lines emphasize:

> Love to one death conducted us along:
> But Caina waits for him our life who ended.
> ('Francesca of Rimini', v.10–11)

Damned to hell herself, Francesca speaks her cold judgement on her murderer. The persistence of her passion, as of her love, is underscored in that curse, which is the emblem of her Byronic Satanism.

All such 'Souls' are, in Byron's nicely ambiguous translation, 'offended'. Dante/Byron has 'such a sympathy' in these offences that he pursues his inquiring translation, deepening his identification:

> We read one day for pastime, seated nigh,
> Of Lancelot, how love enchain'd him too;
> We were alone, quite unsuspiciously.
> But oft our eyes met, and our cheeks in hue
> All o'er discoloured by that reading were;
> But one point only wholly us o'erthrew.
> When we read the long-sighed-for smile of her
> To be thus kissed by such a fervent lover,
> He who from me can be divided ne'er
> Kiss'd my mouth, trembling in the act all over.
> Accursed was the book, and he who wrote.
> That day no further leaf we did uncover.
> ('Francesca of Rimini', v.31–42)

The force of that text comes through reading it as part of Byron's ventriloquist moves. The book of the tale of Lancelot, Dante's text, Byron's translation: all are 'Accursed' because all are committed, in Byron's view, to the immediate intensities of a Lucretian life. Paolo weeps as Francesca tells their accursed tale, Dante 'swooned as dying' in sympathy with their condition, and Byron replays the entire complex story in both his verse and his life.

In 1820, Byron finds himself in the same hell as Dante and the damned lovers. As Virgil – who will never achieve salvation – leads Dante through this hell, Byron internalizes the action as a whole. Becoming all these textual characters, Byron invents the myth of the *poete maudit*, whose work now falls under Francesca's curse of love. In Byron's text (unlike Dante's), the poet literally tells the tale of his own damnation, including the damnation of his poetry. What is worse (from any normative moral and aesthetic point of view), the poet does not ask his readers to transvalue the values by which it will be condemned. All is cursed. If a benevolent (and invisible) God watches over the events in Dante's text, and if this God reigns even in the love-hell of Paolo and Francesca, the children – the 'followers' – of Byron's text are children of a lesser god. Byron's anonymous and oneiric work takes possession of all its features. Here there is no God but god and his name is Byron. He is also called Dante, Francesca, Paolo, Virgil, Teresa, Gianciotto, and Satan. He is a god in name only.

Byron's translation of this famous passage in Dante is thus a key text for the clarity with which it lays out the terms of Byron's lyrical dialectic. The Byronic mode is to *take for its text* Lord Byron's personal life. Like the 'Sun of the Sleepless' – Byron's startling term for the Imagination in the stunning poem so titled – the lunar poem casts its cold, revelatory light upon its subjects. It is a light, however, 'That show'st the darkness thou canst not dispel' ('Sun of the Sleepless', line 3), a light 'Distinct, but distant – clear, but oh how cold' (line 8). This is a light that shines in the darkness but unlike John's salvific light, in comprehending the darkness it is equally comprehended by it. Byron's dark yet clarified knowledge emerges because Byron has agreed to collapse his 'personal life' and his 'poetical life' – because a final distinction cannot be drawn between the man who suffers and the poet who sees. Lord Byron's personal life is on one hand a fever of passionate intensities and on the other a cold set of representations: at once a life and a reflection, a self and a text. The work is engulfed in that dissolving, disillusioning ambiguity – an ambiguity which it also embraces.

Coda: Byron today

In our day Byron has emerged, has returned, as a figure of great consequence. We have had fifty years to look back with clarity and horror and an inevitably cynical wonderment at the spectacle of Western Civilization.

We have an Imperial view of this scene, we are – as Byron knew himself to be, as Wordsworth (for example) deliberately chose not to be – 'citizens of the world'. Byron's eyes have been here before, have seen all this. Most important of all, Byron saw himself as part of the scene: a player, a participant, 'doomed to inflict or bear'. Vietnam, Palestine, Northern Ireland – Bosnia, Kosovo, Cambodia, Chile, South Africa: these are not places we could any longer honestly set ourselves apart from, as spectators looking in.

How does one live in such a world and with such a disillusioned view of it, being in it? Byron's verse poses that question over and over again – it is one of his 'leading tendencies', to pose the question and to keep posing it. Here is one famous posing (from *Childe Harold*):

> Yet let us ponder boldly – 'tis a base
> Abandonment of reason to resign
> Our right of thought – our last and only place
> Of refuge; this, at least, shall still be mine:
> Though from our birth the faculty divine
> Is chain'd and tortured – cabin'd, cribb'd, confined,
> And bred in darkness, lest the truth should shine
> Too brightly on the unprepared mind,
> The beam pours in, for time and skill will couch the blind.
>
> (*CHP*, IV.127)

The truth of this text comes as the contradiction between its 'what' and 'how'. 'Reason' and a 'Right of Thought' are declared 'our last and only place of refuge', and the argument is that a persistence of disciplined inquiry will bring enlightenment. But even assuming this actual result, what then? To see thus clearly, this text grows to see, is to be astonished with a visible darkness stretching back across the forty-nine stanzas before this one and forward to forty-four that directly follow it, all linked to 'the electric chain of that despair' (*CHP*, IV.172.7) which is the Byronic byword. You shall know the truth and it will not set you free: that is the essential message being delivered.

It is not the whole of the message, however, for the text is imagining itself beyond its discursive form. The chain of despair is electric, forbidding rest or any but momentary comforts. To be Byronic is precisely not to be laid asleep in body to become a living soul. So beyond the dream of Reason and its Right of Thought is the driving verse, the famous passion emblemized by those astonishing enjambments that fractured for ever the purity of the Spenserian inheritance:

I know not why – but standing thus by thee
It seems as if I had thine inmate known,
Thou Tomb! And other days come back to me
With recollected music, though the tone
Is changed and solemn, like the cloudy groan
Of dying thunder on the distant wind;
Yet could I seat me by this ivied stone
Till I had bodied forth the heated mind,
Forms from the floating wreck which Ruin leaves behind;

And from the plank, far shatter'd o'er the rocks,
Build me a little bark of hope, once more
To battle with the ocean and the shocks
Of the loud breakers, and the ceaseless roar
Which rushes on the solitary shore
Where all lies foundered that was ever dear:
But could I gather from the wave-worn store
Enough for my rude boat, where should I steer?
There woos no home, no hope, nor life, save what is here . . .

There is the moral of all human tales;
'Tis but the same rehearsal of the past;
First Freedom, and then Glory – when that fails,
Wealth, vice, corruption-barbarism at last,
And History, with all her volumes vast,
Hath but one page, – 'tis better written here
Where gorgeous Tyranny hath thus amass'd
All treasures, all delights, that eye or ear,
Heart, soul, could seek, tongue ask – Away with words! draw near,

Admire, exult, despise, laugh, weep, – for here
There is such matter for all feeling: –
(*CHP*, IV.104–5; 108–9.2)

And so on, relentlessly. Brief quotation, it has been said, will not do for Byron's verse. These stanzas illustrate why (and how) that is true. This is a text observing its own passion of thought, the passion of its insistence, its determination to think and think again and again. The imagined 'refuge' – the dreams of home, hope, and life – are precisely 'here', in these moving lines that signal a decision never to cease this side of an absolute extinction. Nor is there any thought that the thinking will come out 'right', for this is thinking that lives in its expenditures. Unlike Wordsworth (once again), Byron's writing begins and thrives in disillusion. At its finest moments it is either ludic or it is failing. Like Beckett, however, the texts rise to unbuild themselves repeatedly. In the process they cast no shadows but a kind of invigorated negative textual space, 'darkness visible'. So here 'meaning' slips free of every conclusion, including the idea of conclusiveness, and fuses with its eventuality.

Byron's cultural re-emergence in the late twentieth century is thus an historical fate to be welcomed. Who else could so authoritatively redeem Romantic self-expression from its own illusions? Byron's lyric style is Romanticism's dark angel.

13

ANNE BARTON

Byron and Shakespeare

On the eleventh of August 1823, Byron took a brief holiday from Turkish naval blockades and the already exasperating factional squabbles of the Greeks. With several companions, he had himself rowed across from his temporary base in Cephalonia to the adjacent island of Ithaca. There, he insisted that he was interested neither in classical ruins nor in fiction, whether Homer's or his own. 'I detest antiquarian twaddle', Trelawny reported him as saying. To which he added, 'do people think I have no lucid intervals, that I came to Greece to scribble more nonsense? I will show them I can do something better.'[1] Offered a tour of supposed Homeric sites on the island, Byron resisted – only to wander off when the expedition nevertheless occurred, and seek out for himself, after a considerable climb, the cave in which Odysseus had reputedly secreted the treasures given him by the Phaeacians. Meeting with an old shepherd, he immediately identified him with Homer's loyal swineherd, Eumaeus, and invited him to share their picnic lunch. Byron liked Ithaca: 'If this isle were mine', Trelawny records him as exclaiming, 'I would break my staff and bury my book – What fools we all are!' (*HVSV*, p. 421) Trelawny's reports can never be entirely trusted. This, however, registers as a characteristically Byronic set of Shakespearean echoes and allusions, managing as it does to run together the cynical glee of Puck in *A Midsummer Night's Dream* ('Lord, what fools these mortals be!' (III.ii.115))[2] with *The Tempest*: Caliban's 'This island's mine' (I.ii.331), Gonzalo's 'Had I plantation of this isle' (II.i.144), and most explicitly, of course, Prospero's renunciation of his magic in Act V. But Byron has reinterpreted (as well as slightly misquoted) the last. Prospero was preparing for return to Milan and his dukedom. Byron, twisting Shakespeare's words, imagines for a moment that it might be possible to jettison both his military responsibilities and his poetry, not to mention Italy and England, and never leave Ithaca at all.

The contradictions running through all this were typical. Years before, Byron had habitually left his friend Hobhouse painstakingly to document the various classical sites they visited, while he rode up mountains on his mule, talked to the locals, or marked the flight of birds over Parnassus. Yet it had been important to him to stand (as he thought) upon the burial mounds of the heroes of the Trojan War, thus rescuing Homer from the suspicion that he wrote 'things *all fiction*' and so had 'but the talent of a liar' (*BLJ*, v, 203), to swim the Hellespont in order to demonstrate that the mythical Leander could have done so, and to authenticate for himself (after a hard scramble) Medea's clashing rocks, the Symplegades, at the entrance to the Black Sea. On Ithaca, it was almost certainly this same need to substantiate fiction that impelled him, despite all his disclaimers, up to the supposed grotto of Odysseus. Byron's Shakespearean allusions, however, during these few days, present a more complicated – though by no means unrelated – problem. He came up with several more. According to Thomas Smith, an Englishman who attached himself to the visitors from Cephalonia, Byron dispensed heady draughts of gin and water one day as they navigated around Ithaca, with the injunction to 'drink deep, or taste not the Pierian spring; it is the true poetic source. I'm a rogue if I have drunk today' (*HVSV*, p. 418). Here, one of the most familiar lines from Pope – England's *truly* great poet, as Byron liked to insist – nestles beside Falstaff's prose (*1 Henry IV*, II.iv.152) with blithe unconcern for their glaring incongruity. Most revealing of all was the episode (again reported by Smith) when Byron, on the evening they returned to Cephalonia, suddenly stretched himself out in an empty sarcophagus near a monastery on the hill of Samos, muttering indistinct 'English lines'. Somewhat guiltily, Smith bent over to listen, and discovered that they were disconnected fragments from the graveyard scene in *Hamlet*. His apprehensions were justified. Aware that he had been overheard, Byron sprang up, and immediately began as so often (especially in his later years) to denigrate Shakespeare: 'Hamlet, as a whole, is original; but I do not admire him to the extent of the common opinion' (*HVSV*, p. 423).

Smith's account is ambiguous. When speaking of 'him', was Byron referring to the character of Hamlet, or to Shakespeare in general? Either is possible. In an unsigned piece (probably by Thomas Medwin) printed after Byron's death in *The New Monthly Magazine* for 30 October 1830, Byron is initially represented – in dialogue with Shelley himself – as impatient with what he terms this 'most lame and impotent hero', a man 'without goodness or greatness'. His dissatisfaction with the prince, however, rapidly spreads to the play as a whole: the work of a dramatist 'of great genius but no art', episodic, full of unnecessary actions, 'wild rhapsodies', and superfluous figures (grave-diggers, players, and minor courtiers) surely introduced only to please 'the mob'. The Byron who began the discussion by declaring, 'who can read this wonderful play without the profoundest emotion?', rapidly demolishes his own position: first by asking 'And yet what is it but a colossal enigma?', then by moving on to isolate the various cruelties and inadequacies of Hamlet himself, as prelude to a more general attack. Although not specifically invoked, neoclassical criteria clearly underlie much of the diatribe – as does a stubborn adherence to essentially eighteenth-century ways of regarding Shakespeare's supposedly 'uncultivated genius', an attitude which most of Byron's contemporaries had long since abandoned. The dialogue (which turns out to be primarily a showpiece for Shelley as Shakespearean critic) cannot be authenticated. Nothing, however, that Byron is made to say in it is out of line with opinions expressed in his letters and journals, strictures incontrovertibly (at least during the particular moment in which he registered them) his own.

Yet, for a number of reasons, Byron cannot really be included in that curiously disparate group of notorious Shakespeare detractors, a line extending from Thomas Rymer in the late seventeenth century through Voltaire, Tolstoi, Wittgenstein, and George Bernard Shaw. In the first place, some of what he said was patently designed to shock – rather as it was when he led his credulous wife to believe that he had once committed a murder. In a climate of ever-increasing Bardolatry, especially among the English, contempt for Shakespeare could seem almost as reprehensible. On one occasion at Missolonghi, near the end of Byron's life, a gentleman apparently became so distressed by the poet's defence of the unities in drama, and concomitant attack upon Shakespeare, that he was obliged to rush out of the room to calm himself. When he returned, protesting, Byron delightedly redoubled his onslaught. Although occasions like these betray more than a trace of 'he only does it to annoy, because he knows it teases', that was by no means the only force at work. In most of his own plays, Byron did depend upon the unities to free him from the Shakespeare he once described in a letter to Murray as 'the worst of models, though the most extraordinary of writers' (*BLJ*, VIII, 152), with results that justified this strategy. His are arguably the only English tragedies of the period (with the possible exception of Shelley's *The Cenci*) that genuinely break new ground. It was also true that, for Byron, adulation of Shakespeare came to be associated with such contemporary worshippers at the shrine as Coleridge, Keats, Southey, and even Wordsworth, proponents of what he considered to be a wrong revolutionary poetic system, and also supporters of a political and religious conservatism of which he was increasingly intolerant. The Bowles controversy, during which Byron, in 1821, defended the worth of Alexander Pope against readers now elevating Shakespeare far above him and the other Augustans, added fuel to the fire. So, in Italian exile, did his gathering impatience with English insularity and pride, the tendency of his fellow-countrymen to run down foreign authors in favour of their own.

Over and over, those who encountered Byron after he left England in 1816 – Shelley, Mary Shelley, Stendhal, Thomas Moore, Lady Blessington, Medwin, Trelawny, Samuel Rogers, George Bancroft, Colonel Stanhope, Leigh Hunt, James Kennedy, not to mention his old friend Hobhouse – report quite independently how often, in conversation, he denigrated Shakespeare. Some of these listeners suspected that Byron was jealous of his great predecessor. Frequently, they remark on how difficult it was to reconcile Byron's depreciation with his extraordinarily detailed knowledge of Shakespeare's work, and quite a few of them suggest that his animosity was a pretence. ('Scherzo', Hobhouse noted laconically in his diary for 18 September 1822, after Byron had again 'declaimed' against Shakespeare.) When challenged on the subject, as he was by Lady Blessington, Byron had defences ready. His memory, he insisted, was extremely retentive: whatever he read stayed in his mind, whether he admired it or not. This excuse usually (and rightly) failed to convince. Few people doubted the formidable tenacity of Byron's memory. Still, that could not explain his continual recourse to Shakespearean characters, allusions, and quotations, drawn from what was virtually the entire canon, including the least popular and performed of the plays, and evidenced not only in conversation, but in his letters, journals, and poems.

Leigh Hunt remarked acidly how eager Byron was at Pisa and Albaro in 1822 to demonstrate that he had no copy of Shakespeare (or Milton) in his library. This, Byron assured him, was because he had so frequently been accused of borrowing from both. Plagiarism was always, for him, a sensitive subject. Revealingly, he seems to have complained to Medwin that Shakespeare after all may have been heavily indebted to authors whose plays are lost, although on this occasion he softened the indictment by conceding that he himself was 'not very scrupulous, I own, when I have a good idea, how I came into possession of it'.[3] As for his lack of any edition, it is true that none appeared among the books he had with him in Greece when these were sold in 1827, after his death. It is not, however, impossible that a copy, kept carefully concealed from Hunt, had already been disposed of in Genoa, before Byron embarked for Greece, a sale for which no catalogue exists. Certainly Bell's fourteen-volume acting edition – together with a representation of Kean as Richard III – formed part of the library he was obliged to auction off in London in 1816. On the other hand, given the evidence of Byron's own poetry and prose, his saturation in Shakespeare by the time he settled in Italy may have rendered a copy of the works almost unnecessary.

Unlike Coleridge, or Keats (who not only wrote a sonnet 'On Sitting Down to Read King Lear Once Again' but actually inscribed it in his facsimile of the 1623 Folio, opposite the opening of that play), Byron can almost never be caught actually perusing Shakespeare – not at least after his teens. In his edition of Byron's complete miscellaneous prose, Andrew Nicholson reproduces, from a notebook that the young Byron kept at Harrow, two pages featuring, respectively, a quotation from 2 *Henry VI* and one from *As You Like It*.[4] Byron clearly had an edition open before him when making these entries, because act, scene, and line numbers are scrupulously supplied. He seems to have looked up the passages – part of Queen Margaret's impassioned farewell to Suffolk, and Celia's description of herself and Rosalind as being like Juno's swans, coupled and inseparable – because they echoed his own feelings at having to leave Harrow and the intense schoolboy attachments he had formed there. When he went up to Trinity College, shortly afterwards, Byron must still have been enthusiastically reading Shakespeare. His early poem 'Thoughts Suggested by a College Examination' (1806) inveighs against a Cambridge curriculum concentrating upon classical history and literature, while leaving undergraduates ignorant of Agincourt and the Wars of the Roses, and 'Of Avon's bard rememb'ring scarce the name' (*CPW*, I, 92–3). He himself, by implication, was not that kind of undergraduate. The epigraph to another poem of the same period, 'Childish Recollections', published in *Hours of Idleness*, is taken from *Macbeth* – the first of a series of Shakespearean epigraphs that Byron was to attach to later and far more important poems: *English Bards and Scotch Reviewers*, *Manfred*, *Beppo*, *The Vision of Judgment*, and Cantos VI–VIII of *Don Juan*.

In chapter 34 of Jane Austen's *Mansfield Park* (1814), Henry Crawford, who has just been congratulated on his sensitive rendering of several speeches from *Henry VIII*, claims not to be able to remember if he ever saw the play acted, or merely heard of it from someone who did. 'But Shakespeare', he continues, 'one gets acquainted with without knowing how. It is a part of an Englishman's constitution. His thoughts and beauties are so spread abroad that one touches them everywhere; one is intimate with him by instinct.' Edmund Bertram concurs: 'His celebrated passages are quoted by everybody; they are in half the books we open, and we all talk Shakespeare, use his similes, and describe with his descriptions.' 'Everybody', of course, here means only the upper strata of English society (and by implication, the male sex). It was not wholly untrue. Byron, part of this narrowly defined 'everybody', must also to some extent have become acquainted with Shakespeare 'without knowing how'. But, although he certainly echoes Shakespeare at times 'by instinct', without being aware that he is doing so, he was not Henry Crawford.

From an early age, Byron was an indefatigable and wide-ranging reader. He had an extraordinary capacity, moreover, to remember what he read and he was given to mercurial and unexpected juxtapositions across space and time, fiction and fact. Taking into account both his poetry and prose, only *The Comedy of Errors* and *Venus and Adonis* seem to be missing from the long list of Shakespearean quotations and allusions, whether intentional or subconscious, that everywhere inform Byron's work. He had, moreover, an ability to draw on what at the time were marginal and unloved plays – not only all three parts of *Henry VI*, and *The Two Gentlemen of Verona*, but *Cymbeline*, *Timon of Athens*, and *King John*. At Mansfield Park, Henry Crawford, to whom it was as yet 'an untasted pleasure', dabbles (disastrously) in amateur theatricals, while not being sure if he ever saw a professional performance of *Henry VIII*. Byron's own involvement in private theatricals seems to have begun at Southwell in 1804. It extended through an apparently unrealized scheme to mobilize some of his Cambridge acquaintances to put on Edward Young's tragedy *Revenge* at Newstead in 1808 in a very Shakespearean form – without women, 'as I have some young friends who will make tolerable substitutes for females' (*BLJ*, I, 170) – a mysterious 'Epilogue to *The Merchant of Venice* Intended for a Private Theatrical', dated 26 January 1815, when he was at Seaham with Annabella's parents after the honeymoon, and the abortive *Othello* he planned in 1822, in which Mary Shelley was to have played Desdemona, Trelawny Othello, and Byron himself Iago (*HVSV*, p. 282). The audience, Byron envisaged, would be 'all Pisa'. Iago was one of Edmund Kean's most celebrated parts, and Byron had seen and admired him in it. An inveterate theatre-goer, he told Moore that 'I am acquainted with no immaterial sensuality so delightful as good acting' (*BLJ*, IV, 115), 'I could not resist the first night of anything' (*BLJ*, IV, 290). He was easily persuaded to join the subcommittee of Drury Lane in 1815, during which year the theatre put on seven Shakespeare plays, mostly tragedies. Once, he even appeared on stage himself, anonymously, during the performance of a Masquerade, in order to see what the view of a crowded house was like from there, and found it 'very grand' (*BLJ*, IX, 36–7).

Unlike Lamb or even (on occasion) Hazlitt, Byron was never moved to complain that in performance Shakespeare's greatest works must always fall short of the play when fully and imaginatively read. Such an opinion would have jarred both with his insistence that, whatever his contemporaries might think, Shakespeare belonged well this side of idolatry, and with his own attitude to the theatre. As soon, however, as his own (eventually eight) plays were involved, the situation became far less clear-cut. Apart from *Werner*, which he began during his period on the Drury Lane committee, partly out of despair at the dismal quality of the new scripts submitted, none was intended for performance. However much he admired Kean, Byron (unlike Keats) never thought of devising a starring vehicle for him. That was not the sort of play he wanted to write, nor could the theatre of his time possibly have realized and not travestied (as of course it was later to do) what he had in mind. Yet, with the exception of the biblical *Cain*, and *Heaven and Earth*, in both of which it vanishes almost entirely, the influence of Shakespeare on these firmly proclaimed closet dramas is everywhere apparent, as indeed it is in much of the rest of Byron's work. Far from being stifling, or resulting in pastiche, it is an influence that Byron proved more able than most of his English contemporaries to use creatively.

In the company of Samuel Rogers, Byron attended the lecture on Shakespeare that Coleridge delivered in the Great Room of the London Philosophical Society on 16 December 1811. He did not record his reactions. The lecture itself exists now only in the form of fairly extensive notes taken by John Payne Collier, backed up by an independent report in *The Morning Chronicle* on the following day.[5] Coleridge apparently began by attacking the neoclassical idea that 'nothing undignified must be brought into company with what is dignified', before moving on to assault the supposed Aristotelian unities. These, he insisted, narrowed the space of action, so that the great function of the dramatist, to be the mirror of life, 'is completely lost'. Reiterating his dissension from the old notion that Shakespeare was a 'Child of Nature', wanting art, or that he wrote for the mob ('no man of genius ever wrote for the mob'), Coleridge went on to assert that much of the greatness of Shakespeare consisted of:

> combinations of the highest & lowest, and of the gayest and the saddest. He was not droll in one scene and melancholy in the other but both the one & the other in the same scene: laughter is made to swell the tear of sorrow and to throw as it were a poetic light upon it, & the tear mixes a tenderness with the laughter that succeeds.

It is an oddly suggestive lecture for Byron to have heard. Then aged twenty-three, he would not only stubbornly support in later years that eighteenth-century idea of the artless Shakespeare that Coleridge was so determined to refute, but suggest that, like many of the old dramatists, he did indeed write for the 'mob' – something not at all to his advantage. On the other hand, Byron was to defend *Don Juan* in his famous reaction to Francis Cohen's criticism that 'we are never scorched and drenched at the same time' along lines remarkably similar to those articulated in Coleridge's description of Shakespeare's mixed mode: 'I will answer your friend', he told Murray, 'who objects to the quick succession of fun and gravity – as if in that case the gravity did not (in intention at least) heighten the fun . . . Blessings on his experience! – Ask him these questions about "scorching and drenching". – Did he never play at Cricket or walk a mile in hot weather?' (*BLJ*, v, 207). Byron's riposte then proceeds through a whole series of increasingly hilarious (and indecent) examples, from swimming in the noonday sun to gonorrhoea and Turkish baths. It ends, significantly, with a quotation (marked as such by Byron, though unattributed) from *1 Henry IV*: 'Oh for breath to utter' (II.iv.246). This is the voice of Falstaff, in Eastcheap, trying to extricate himself from the embarrassments of the Gadshill robbery, in a scene (and indeed a whole play) based upon quick successions of gravity and fun.

Scarcely the kind of treasure one would expect to find in one of those anthologies of the 'shining passages' or 'beauties of Shakespeare' so popular in the late eighteenth and early nineteenth centuries, 'Oh for breath to utter' says a good deal, in the context of Byron's letter, not only about his intimate and highly individual familiarity with the minutiae and byways of Shakespeare's texts, but just how profoundly (whatever his public protestations to the contrary) his own ways of thinking and writing had been influenced by the man from Stratford. Although he clearly knew the source of his quotation, Byron probably did not link it consciously, in a letter hastily dashed off to his publisher in London, with the scorchings and drenchings characteristic of Shakespeare's *1 Henry IV*. Almost certainly, if asked, he would have denied their resemblance to *Don Juan*. The connection nevertheless is there, and it matters. G. Wilson Knight's book *Byron and Shakespeare* (1966) may be eccentric in its programmatic insistence that in the course of his life the poet became the incarnation of various Shakespearean characters – Hamlet, Macbeth, Richard III, Falstaff, Timon, Prospero, and so on – but he was astute in isolating a ventriloquism generically different from mere allusion: Byron's habit of appropriating for himself, whether in earnest or in jest, the feelings of various figures in the plays. He did this irrespective of whether the fictional speakers were male or female, heroes, villains or clowns, and he selected them from across the canon.

The *locus classicus* here is those passages from the final pages of Byron's journal of 1814, dealing with Napoleon's abdication and retreat to Elba. In two brief entries, dated 9 and 19 April (*BLJ*, III, 256–7), he contrives to quote *Antony and Cleopatra* ('I see men's minds are but a parcel of their fortunes'), *Hamlet* twice ('excellent well', 'something too much of this'), *Macbeth* twice ('like the Thanes, fallen from him' and 'all our yesterdays have lighted fools / The way to dusty death'), *Romeo and Juliet* ('Hang up philosophy'), and *King Lear* ('O fool! I shall go mad'). The *Antony and Cleopatra* and the first of the two *Macbeth* quotations are inaccurate, but all the more interesting for what that suggests about a Byron writing passionately and fast, depending on his memory of Shakespeare without troubling to consult the text. In the first of these two journal entries, the Roman satirist Juvenal and the Restoration dramatist Otway figure briefly, but the presiding spirit throughout is Shakespeare's. Reading Napoleon's downfall through the lens of Shakespeare, Byron places himself initially in the position of wry commentator (Hamlet reducing Polonius to a fishmonger, Enobarbus reflecting on the disintegration of a 'pillar of the world') but subsequently in that of Hamlet, Macbeth, Romeo, and Lear as doomed protagonists: all of them, like Napoleon, finally outwitted by fate. He uses these characters' words to express his own shifting feelings as he writes, but lurking behind is something else – that complicated personal identification with Napoleon – later manifested in Byron's delight when, after his mother-in-law's death, he was legally obliged to sign himself 'Noel Byron'. This, as he liked to point out, gave him exactly the same initials as his 'poor little pagod'.

Only one journal entry intervenes between those of 9 and 19 April, when Byron tore out the remaining leaves of the volume in disgust at the restoration of the Bourbons. On 10 April, he recorded having boxed for one hour, consumed six biscuits and four bottles of soda water, read for a bit (he does not say what), advised a nameless friend about his troublesome mistress, and written 'an ode to Napoleon Buonaparte'. There are no Shakespearean allusions. These were reserved for the Ode itself.

'Weigh'd in the balance, hero dust / Is vile as vulgar clay' suggests that *Hamlet* (the noble dust of Alexander stopping a bung-hole, from the graveyard scene) was in Byron's mind, a suspicion strengthened by another line that he cancelled only in proof: 'who have not seen his like again' (*CPW*, III, 263–4). *Macbeth* was looming in Byron's imagination too as he contemplated the emperor's fall: 'crownless power . . . shakes her locks [head] at thee', another cancelled line deriving from the banquet scene ('Never shake thy gory locks at me' [III.iv.50]). That Byron cancelled both in proof suggests (as so often) an uncomfortable awareness that he was treading too closely upon Shakespeare's heels. But he could not bring himself to jettison 'And that last act, though not thy worst, / The very Fiend's arch-mock' in the final stanza of his poem. The result was Byron's admission, sent in a note to Murray on 12 April, that the reference (again slightly misquoted by him) was to *Othello*: 'The fiend's arch-mock / To lip a wanton and suppose her chaste'.

Appended notes of this kind, some intended only for Murray's eyes, others for the general reader, turn up intermittently, usually to justify some word or expression by appeal to its use in Shakespeare. Byron does this, for instance, with 'cold Obstruction's apathy' in *The Giaour*, where a note (*CPW*, III, 416) invokes Claudio's 'to lie in cold obstruction, and to rot' from *Measure For Measure* – most unusually supplying act, scene, and line numbers – again with 'had I not filed my mind' in Canto III of *Childe Harold*, where another note (*CPW*, II, 314) points to Macbeth's 'for Banquo's issue have I *filed* my mind', and with the form 'Ottomite' in Canto IV, for which he asserted in the proofs 'Shakespeare is my authority' (*CPW*, II, 321). Other notes explain or expand particular passages, as when Lord Elgin's desecration of the Parthenon prompts Byron in Canto II (*CPW*, II, 190) to invoke Isabella's lament in *Measure For Measure* ('Man, vain man, / Drest in a little brief authority'), or the phrase 'drapery misses' in *Don Juan* leads to an elaborate addendum (*CPW*, V, 749), including reference to *The Merry Wives of Windsor*'s Anne Page.

It is, however, in the poems themselves that Byron most often refers explicitly to Shakespeare, and to his characters, episodes and lines. (He had a particular predilection for Banquo in *Macbeth* perhaps because of his belief that he was descended from him on his mother's side.) In *Don Juan*, where the examples are widespread, they often come accompanied by a need to remind readers (and perhaps himself) that Shakespeare's supposedly towering genius is not something Byron takes seriously: 'I like so much to quote; / You must forgive this extract, 'tis where she, / The Queen of Denmark, for Ophelia brought / Flowers to the grave' (II.17.3–6). In Canto IX, he follows 'To be or not to be, that is the question' with 'Says Shakespeare, who just now is much in fashion' (IX.14.2) – a dismissal qualified by the fact that the three preceding stanzas, as McGann rightly points out in his Commentary, are heavily (and by no means jokingly) indebted to the graveyard scene in *Hamlet*. In Canto VII, savage reflections on the worth of posthumous military honour lead Byron to pretend to a vague memory that 'one Shakespeare puts the same thought in / The mouth of someone in his plays so doating, / Which many people pass for wits by quoting' (VII.21.6–8). (The 'some one' was, of course, Falstaff, as he knew perfectly well.) Similarly dubious is the assertion in Canto XIV that it was only 'in my extremity of rhyme's distress' that he was obliged to borrow 'There is a flower called "Love in Idleness"' from 'his British godship's' *A Midsummer Night's Dream*, this particular defence being undercut by the preceding stanza where – although of no service whatever to the rhyme, nor indicated by Byron as a quote – 'there lies the rub' (XIV.74.4) clearly echoes *Hamlet*.

In *Don Juan*, as elsewhere in Byron's work, pilferings from Shakespeare are sometimes signalled by inverted commas – and presumably meant to be recognized by readers – sometimes not. With some, but by no means all, of these unattributed lines, especially those where the allusion is very inaccurate or distant, it is difficult to determine whether Byron himself was aware of his source, or whether they are simply a product of that enveloping ambiance about which Henry Crawford and Edmund Bertram speak, whereby English people instinctively 'talk Shakespeare, use his similes and describe with his descriptions'. Once woven into his own verse, any line or phrase derived from Shakespeare tends to generate another, usually from a different play. So, in Canto VII, stanza 86, 'Hark! through the silence of the cold, dull night, / The hum of armies gathering rank on rank!' (where Byron is remembering the Chorus speech in *Henry V* on the eve of Agincourt) is followed by an echo of Lady Macbeth in 'The stars peep through the vapours dim and dark' (I.v.50).

Shakespearean allusions or quotations in *Don Juan* can be capriciously employed. When Keats, according to his travelling companion Joseph Severn, threw down the first two cantos of Byron's poem in disgust, during his last voyage to Italy, complaining of the 'paltry originality' of 'making gay things solemn and solemn things gay',[6] his reaction against the 'diabolical' comedy of the shipwreck scene must have embraced the way certain dark or tragic moments in the plays become springboards for the risible – as when Byron invokes Gertrude's 'sweets to the sweet' as a mock parallel to Juan's 'salt tears' for Julia dropping redundantly into 'the salt sea', or an echo of Macbeth's 'Canst thou not minister to a mind diseased?' (V.iii.40) bathetically introduces an attack of nausea (*CPW*, II, 17, 19). Instances such as these, however, are occasional in *Don Juan*. Far more often, Byron depends on Shakespeare to thicken and enrich the texture of his poem, and often where it is least laughable – as with the *Henry V* and *Macbeth* allusions in Canto VII, both of which work to heighten the horror of the siege of Ismail, and prefigure the carnage of the battle next day.

He can also draw upon Shakespeare in larger and more structural ways. *The Tempest* informs the entire idyll of Haidee's island in Cantos II-IV, where Byron re-casts the shipwrecked Ferdinand, the innocent Miranda, and her irascible father Prospero as Juan, Haidee, and Lambro, the tragic ending of his own tale becoming more poignant by contrast with its happier Shakespearean paradigm.[7] Never in thrall to his great predecessor, as so many of his contemporaries were, Byron can use him creatively – much as Shakespeare used his own source material. Here it conditions (even if only subliminally) the reader's response. *Marino Faliero*, again a tragedy seamed with allusions to no fewer than eighteen of Shakespeare's plays,[8] moves beyond all of them to engage in what is almost a dialogue with *Julius Caesar*, the political play against which Byron defines the nature of his own. Hazlitt complained that a fourteenth-century Doge ought not to sound as though he had read Shakespeare, but that was to miss the point. Faliero invokes Brutus and Cassius not because Byron is producing Shakespearean pastiche, but because Byron's whole play is a bold and original rethinking of Shakespeare's. *Sardanapalus*, as Richard Lansdown has argued, bears something of the same relation to *Antony and Cleopatra*.

In *The Frogs* (BC 405), Aristophanes imagines the necessity of choosing whether to redeem Euripides or Aeschylus from Hades – and selects Aeschylus. Byron, during the Bowles controversy, invented a not dissimilar fantasy. Were Great Britain, he speculates, to be swept away by some great natural disaster, leaving only its language and literature to be salvaged, an Englishman might wish for the preservation of Milton and Shakespeare, 'but the surviving World would snatch Pope from the Wreck – and let the rest sink with the People – He is the moral poet of all Civilization.'[9] Although Aristophanes was constantly poking fun at Euripides, his mockery is based on a suspiciously intimate knowledge of his victim's plays: plays which not infrequently are the starting point for his own. It cannot be taken at face value. Neither can Byron's disparagement of Shakespeare. In the English cantos of *Don Juan*, Byron tantalizingly brings Pope and Shakespeare face to face, in the form of Adeline Amundeville and Aurora Raby. Adeline, the narrator says ironically, 'Was weak enough to deem Pope a great poet, / And what was worse, was not ashamed to show it'. Aurora 'was more Shakespearian, if I do not err. / The worlds beyond this world's perplexing waste / Had more of her existence' (XVI.47–8). Not surprisingly, the two women do not get on. Adeline pointedly omits Aurora from her list of suitable matches for Juan. She is unsophisticated, a mere 'baby' (XV.49.7). Aurora, for her part, listens to Adeline being brilliantly satirical about her guests, at Norman Abbey, with silent distaste. Juan is drawn to them equally. Because the poem breaks off where it does, we are never told which one he chooses. Probably, however, the un-Aristophanic but very Byronic answer was – both.

NOTES

1. *HVSV*, p. 411.
2. Quotations from Shakespeare are taken from *The Riverside Shakespeare*, second edn ed. G. Blakemore Evans *et al.* (Boston: Houghton Mifflin, 1997).
3. *Medwin's Conversations of Lord Byron*, ed. Ernest J. Lovell, Jr (Princeton University Press, 1966), p. 140.
4. *CMP*, 203.
5. *Samuel Taylor Coleridge: Collected Works, Vol. V: Lectures 1808–1819*, ed. R. A. Foakes (Princeton University Press, 1987), pp. 344–68.
6. Quoted by Walter Jackson Bate in his *John Keats* (Oxford University Press, 1963), p. 665.
7. See my '*Don Juan* Reconsidered: The Haidee Episode', reprinted in *Byron* (Longman Critical Readers), ed. Jane Stabler (London: Longman, 1998), pp. 194–203.
8. See the Appendix, 'Shakespearean Allusions in *Marino Faliero*', in Richard Lansdown, *Byron's Historical Dramas* (Oxford: Clarendon Press, 1992).
9. *CMP*, 150.

14

BERNARD BEATTY

Byron and the eighteenth century

The Eighteenth Century was the first to be mythologised as a century. This happened almost as soon as it was over. Byron gives us the reason for this:

> Talk not of seventy years as age; in seven
> I have seen more changes, down from monarchs to
> The humblest individual under heaven,
> Than might suffice a moderate century through.
> (*Don Juan*, XI.82.1–4)

Byron means here that in seven years he has witnessed Napoleon's surrender, escape from Elba, defeat at Waterloo, and death on St Helena, together with the restoration of the old dynasties that ruled Europe before the French Revolution; but for him, as for us, these changes are all part of a larger single change. For virtually all Europeans, the bewildering events from the Fall of the Bastille in 1789, to the final defeat of Napoleon in 1815, shaped and symbolised a decisive break between eighteenth- and nineteenth-century history. When the cultural events initiated by or accompanying these socio-political changes came to be retrospectively characterised as a single phenomenon called 'The Romantic Movement', then it was natural that this 'movement' should be contrasted with 'The Eighteenth Century' which itself was seen as a single age.

Given this picture of the historical 'changes' that he refers to, Byron was always a problem and has remained so. On the one hand, he was the single most famous figure of the European Romantics but, on the other, he was often decisively out of step with what 'Romantics' ought to think and do. How could a 'Romantic' say that 'this is the Age of the Decline of English Poetry' and blame this degeneration on the 'absurd and systematic depreciation of Pope' (*CMP*, 104) when the received position by the middle of the nineteenth century was that the Romantics had restored the glories of pre-eighteenth-century literature? By some critics, Byron was labelled as an eighteenth-century poet surviving in Romantic circumstances. For others, he was essentially a Romantic poet with some eighteenth-century features that he could not shake off. It is because of these problems that there is, and should be, a chapter on 'Byron and the eighteenth century' in this book. We cannot understand him unless we understand this relation properly.

Our first problem is with the eighteenth century itself. We cannot take it for granted but have to disentangle various conceptions of it. The first conception was fashioned largely by those opposed to it and determined to contrast it, to its discredit, with later Romanticism or the preceding writings of Shakespeare, Spenser, and Milton. But what is it if we attend to it in its own right? We can distinguish between two main versions of its character.

The first and oldest version is directly in continuity with the account already given. We could call it the 'classicising' or 'enlightenment' account. It can be presented as a positive or negative reading. In either emphasis, 'the eighteenth century' is said to begin in the middle of the seventeenth century after the Thirty Years' War on the Continent and the Civil War in England. It means a French-dominated Classical taste, a suspicion of religious controversy, a corresponding sympathy with scepticism and with Deism, a preference for the universal rule over the divergent particular which is, in turn, linked to generalising preferences and norms in ethics, aesthetics, epistemology, and science. Finally, the age is thought to put a premium on social life and hierarchical kinds of social organisation so that decorum becomes a key feature of moral and aesthetic judgements. Primary references here are to Milton, Dryden, and Pope, as classic arbiters of taste and poetic register, to the tragedies of Corneille and Racine, the comedies of Molière and Congreve, neo-Horatian satire in French and English, to Newton's Laws, Locke's philosophy, Joshua Reynolds's aesthetics, to Continental sceptics such as Bayle, Voltaire, Diderot and D'Alembert, to Gibbon's ironic masterpiece *The Decline and Fall of the Roman Empire*, to enlightened Continental despots such as Frederick the Great and Joseph II, and to the Whig Ascendancy in British politics. Edinburgh's eighteenth-century New Town and the intellectual life associated with it would be a helpful single image of this 'eighteenth century'.

Byron certainly has relation to such an 'eighteenth century'. His poetic taste was formed by his childhood reading of Pope's translation of *The Iliad* and he bitterly resented the attacks made on this 'classic' version by Cowper and Wordsworth. He revered the great satirists Dryden, Pope, Swift, and Johnson, and wrote three satires in open homage to them. He was well read in the Continental sceptics. He wrote three self-consciously 'Classical' tragedies in the manner of Corneille and Alfieri and declared himself an admirer of Congreve. He professed his allegiance to writing based on 'precedent', detested many of the poetic experiments of his time, and loathed the diction of Keats's poetry since it constantly violated decorum. He genuinely admired the 'chaste' verse of his contemporary Samuel Rogers, by contrast, because it never did so. Byron shared, in many respects, the views of a typical Whig aristocrat. He was at home in Lady Holland's House with its links back to the last sixty years of Whig political life. There is enough here for the image of 'eighteenth-century Byron' to be plausible.

In Dickens's novel *Bleak House*, Mr Turveydrop keeps alive the dress, deportment, and manners of a Regency beau long after the age has ended. When Lady Blessington met Byron in Genoa towards the end of his life, she made a not dissimilar comment on his appearance. We could ask if there are Turveydrop elements in Byron's verse? I think that we could use the phrase 'Turveydrop poems' for Byron's three satires in heroic couplets (*English Bards and Scotch Reviewers*, 'Hints from Horace', and *The Age of Bronze*) because they try, half-successfully, to maintain an 'eighteenth-century' poetic stance and idiom in a world which less and less understands or sympathises with them. There is another connection too. One of Mr Turveydrop's favourite words is 'polish' by which he means an elaborate attention to the details of appearance. Byron often, though not always, continues to use this word approvingly about the civilising character of art at a time when, for instance, it was the primitive and unpolished character of the newly arrived Elgin marbles that was beginning to be admired by Keats and others. In general, however, Byron is no Turveydrop.

The second model of 'the eighteenth century' may help us since it complicates things. Indeed, it will be necessary to distinguish three phases or components within it. It presupposes the 'classicising' account which it critiques with varying degrees of emphasis. The simplest and earliest form of this does little more than call attention to all those eighteenth-century entities which are ignored by the 'classicist' version. There are many of these. What about the novel, not so much in the male adventure plots of writers such as Defoe and Fielding but in its more 'feminine' cult of feelings or exaggeration which we would associate with major and minor writers such as Rousseau, Richardson, Sterne, Fanny Burney, Horace Walpole, Beckford, Mackenzie, Mrs Radcliffe, John Moore? It is not only a matter of the new taste for the novel. There is a pronounced eighteenth-century cult of sensibility and sentiment which is there as early as Pope's 'Eloisa to Abelard' and is defended in the very influential writings of Shaftesbury. We find it later on in Gray's Eton College Ode, in Thomson, Collins, and Burns. The cult of sensibility links easily with the pronounced eighteenth-century taste for the exotic, the oriental, and the 'primitive'. This springs up in widespread interest in ruins, old ballads, or any usable non-Classical form – Norse, Welsh, 'Ossianic', or Chatterton's forgeries of 'mediaeval' style. Again, if 'the eighteenth century' privileged the heroic couplet satire which is always associated with it, yet it admired and, through Edmund Burke, articulated a complex and central sense of 'the Sublime'.

So we may suggest that where the old view of the eighteenth century emphasised Classical Reason and Order, the new one – usually more English than Continent-centred – tended to emphasise the unruly, discordant, subversive and popular elements of eighteenth-century life. The evidence adduced here would include the caricatures of Hogarth and others, Churchill's satires, the squabbles surrounding the exclusion of Wilkes from parliament, the turbulent energies which were beginning to found a world empire and world capital in the van of exploration and trade, and, more daringly, the sympathy of the major writers themselves for counter-images to decorous order. Here, Pope is presented as the champion of Homer's inventive fire rather than Virgil's 'polish' and even as imaginatively on the side of his Dunces whatever *The Dunciad* says officially to the contrary. In a similar way, Swift can be seen as a postmodern nihilist, and Johnson as, predominantly, the defender of the anarchic life of the 'wild' poet Richard Savage and a courageous champion of the necessary cul-de-sacs of human experiencing rather than as an Olympian sage.

These views, which have dominated the last two decades of criticism, cannot be wholly right as put, I think, but they do call attention to the exploratory pessimism and exuberant energies of some of the greatest eighteenth-century texts and to a host of minor writers who had been left out of the picture. It is certainly these energies and the strong sense of 'Life' as commanding our prior attention that Byron defends. He clearly thinks that he is far more in continuity with the previous century by doing so than his less robust contemporaries who prefer their 'Lakes' (i.e. the poets of the Lake District) to Byron's 'Ocean'. So this view helps us too. It does so especially when a distinction is drawn between the stance of the grand quartet of Dryden, Pope, Swift, and Johnson, and their contemporaries and successors. This has been argued most ably by Paul Fussell in the 1960s in his *The Rhetorical World of Augustan Humanism* and it gives us our final, and most helpful, version of the eighteenth century.

Fussell's argument picks up the obvious point that none of these four writers is in love with his own times and that is why they are primarily seen as satirists. What they are satirising is frequently the very things which other eighteenth-century writers and thinkers are increasingly valuing – opera, the novel, sensibility, science, self-reliance, trade, self-consciousness, England as a paradigm of inevitable human progress, idiosyncrasy and the accommodation of difference. Swift's *The Battle of the Books* (1697), for instance, enters the current argument as to whether Ancient Writings are superior to

Modern ones and sides with the former. He uses Dryden as an instance of the Moderns (in contrast with Virgil) but Dryden would have agreed with Swift's evaluation. So would Pope and Johnson. And so, of course, would Byron. He satirises his contemporary Moderns – Wordsworth, Coleridge, Southey, Keats, etc. – precisely because they disparage the Augustan 'Ancients', blow their own trumpets, and deliberately depart from Classical norms. These norms are partly a matter of style, partly a matter of range of reference, and partly a matter of ethics. The last of these governs the others and it is the most important. It is hard to explain this precisely because the 'Romantic' and 'Modern' reading of cultural history has prevailed and still governs our assumptions. To try to do so we need to make a distinction between 'Action' and 'Behaviour'.

Action is what we consciously do, it makes us what we are, and it is the proper subject of praise and blame, reward and punishment. Ethics is the delineation of right actions. Epic poetry and Pindaric Ode celebrate heroic action. Satire is the public and salutary ridiculing of bad actions and, consequently, of those who perform them. Language itself is a form of action and this is most obviously seen in the necessary public rhetoric of politics, law courts, sermons, drama, and traditional poetic forms. Action is properly represented in classically large-scale heroic images but human beings encounter their own inescapable limitation and littleness when placed in a heroic moral sphere for they are, as Pope says in *The Essay on Man*, only 'darkly wise and rudely great' or, as Byron more bitterly puts it in *Manfred*, they are 'half-dust' as well as 'half-deity'. Thus a sense of an inevitably recurring and chastening disappointment in the midst of a sense of human largeness is insisted upon by the great four Augustan writers who write, nevertheless, in the grand shadow of tragedy and of epic. Byron loved Johnson's version of Juvenal's Tenth Satire, *The Vanity of Human Wishes* (1749), precisely for this insistence. By and large, we must align Byron primarily with this emphasis on the interdependence of action, consequences, rhetoric, and ethics which was the basis for the synthesis of Classical and Christian values that largely governed European culture until the eighteenth century. He is a poet of action who always shows us the consequences of action. Byron continued to defend this idea of poetry and life when dominant opinion in his own time had swung decisively against such an understanding. Against the opinion of these new 'Moderns', Byron asserts the greatness of Pope specifically because Pope was manifestly concerned with ethics and, for Byron, the highest of all poetry is 'ethical poetry'. He understood exactly what was at stake but his voice was barely heard because the new regimen of poetry initiated by the Sensibility movement of the eighteenth century depended upon obliterating this view. But there was another, deeply paradoxical reason too why this could not be readily seen or acknowledged. Though Byron was clearly a man of action yet his behaviour was increasingly considered to be not 'nice' by the prim English world which, from the 1820s especially, reacted strongly against the manners of the Regency era. Later, in the Victorian age (and it is surprising how their 'shocked' attitude to Byron still persists) it becomes impossible for many to find a model of ethical poetry in the 'Satanic' Byron.

What then is the new idea of 'behaviour' which effects this shift from values based on action to a reading of human life which removes the centrality of responsibility and judgement? 'Behaviour' according to *The Spectator* (1711, No. 119) is concerned with Manners rather than with Morals. The word derives from the French *avoir* and thus implies having a mode of being rather than making one through how we choose to act. It comes to denote the general psychology and context which gives rise to action rather than action as such.

Hence it tends to blur human responsibility for actions and their consequences. Our attention is redirected to a complex of inner and outer pressures – social and psychological – which in turn make it difficult to disentangle reasoning from feeling, integrity from appearance. Public rhetoric, clear moral judgements, and actual political life, which are priorities in a Classical world and sit comfortably with Christian moral imperatives, will suddenly seem crudely external to new and vaguer models of a moral or social world founded on the affections, aspirations, or a universal potentiality for the good which emerge in the eighteenth century and still dominate modern thinking though they are increasingly subject to critique.

Pope is a particularly interesting case since he is on both sides of the fence and is an essential reference point for Byron and those who wish to understand him. Pope will provide us with a negative satirical version of behaviour based on blurring customary opposites in his famous portrait of Lord Hervey as an horrifically androgynous figure blurring basic sexual distinctions. Pope calls him 'one vile antithesis' in his 'Epistle to Dr Arbuthnot', but Pope gives us a much more positive version of such blurrings in his portrait of Eloisa in 'Eloisa to Abelard'. In the first case, readers are asked to exercise their judgement and thus 'act' for, etymologically, to criticise is to act and this is how it is seen in the Classical tradition. In the second case, they are asked primarily to sympathise and withhold judgement from Eloisa who magnificently oscillates between religious and erotic worlds and we do not seek to correct her.

Since there is no doubt that Byron bases Julia's letter in the first canto of *Don Juan* on elements in Eloisa's letter, we can enquire how Byron read his Pope. Are readers invited primarily to 'act' by passing a judgement on her actions and their consequences, or to sympathise with her behaviour as a given phenomenon which simply happens because she 'has' to act like that? What is so impressive about Byron is the delicate yet open way in which he provides the evidence for us to come to an opinion on this. Julia, we learn, is young, passionate, married not very happily to a jealous man who is twice her age. It is neither surprising nor especially culpable that she falls into an all-consuming relationship with the attractive sixteen-year-old Juan when she is continually placed, alone, in his company. The reader's sympathies are with her and remain so even when, changing tone, the poem presents her some months later, hiding Juan in her bed and there haranguing her husband for the injustice of his jealousy. When, however, found out, she is separated from her lover and forced to enter a convent, our persisting sympathy is tempered by our sense that she has erred in her actions and in her self-blinding to her own motives.

Byron says that the letter which Julia writes to Juan on this occasion (1.192–7) may better show her 'feelings' than anything else. It does so and we are moved by it, much as we are by Eloisa's, but we notice a curious commingling of a moral language ('I name my guilt') and a declaration of helplessness ('My breast has been all weakness') with a maintenance of exactly the same determination that led her to seduce Juan in the first place ('cannot cast aside / The passion'). Byron is at pains to make us notice that the letter, though presented as honest ('I struggle, but cannot collect my mind'), is carefully controlled as though from the outside. Julia is never wholly at the mercy of her real and strong passions whatever she says. Hence, though we do not pass a cold judgement on Julia, we cannot evade exactly estimating her responsibility for the actions which have led to this punishing consequence. We are close, surprisingly, both to Pope's sympathetic representation of Eloisa and to his vicious representation of Lord Hervey and we are reminded even more, perhaps, of Fielding's habit of giving his readers a fictional scene in full so that they can pass the kind of comprehensive and accurate judgement on it that Fielding might exercise when he was acting as a magistrate in a real human situation. If we contrast Byron's invitation to his readers to exercise both sympathy for and judgement on Julia with Keats's blocking out of any human sympathy with Porphyro and Madeline in his 'The Eve of St Agnes' and, even more, with the way that that poem makes any moral judgement on its characters' actions seem to be clumsily inappropriate, then we will understand the distinction between action and behaviour. We will understand too why Byron's poetry differs from that of virtually all his contemporaries except for Crabbe whom Byron saluted as 'the Augustan postscript'. Keats sets 'intensity' against fact and only values the former. Byron shares and partly shapes his age's interest, largely derived from some eighteenth-century strands, in 'intensity', but never separates this wholly from fact, action, consequence, and judgement. Fussell's distinction between 'action' and 'behaviour' in the eighteenth-century world helps us to see the sources of Byron's clarity and sure-footedness.

The argument here is quite easy to make and everyone agrees that *Don Juan*, together with *Beppo* and *The Vision of Judgment*, are indebted to and conscious advertisements for 'eighteenth-century' idiom and values – the judgements we pass on Laura, Wilkes, Southey, George III, Haidee, the Sultana, Suwarrow, English high society, and Lord and Lady Amundeville, are all as clear as that we pass on Julia – but what of Byron's most 'Byronic' poems? Certainly the reaction of Byron's contemporaries seems to support the opposite side of the argument. They objected not only to the immoral conduct of Byron's celebrated dark heroes such as Harold, Conrad, Lara, and Manfred but also to the author's apparently immoral complicity in presenting them to us as attractive. Is this then a case of Byron presenting 'behaviour' for our sympathetic attention rather than 'action' for our judgement? These heroes are certainly attractive, but Byron never shirks from showing us the destructive consequences of their actions and their own complicity in a self-blinding quite similar to that of Julia.

We can examine a typical case. Lara is the hero of one of Byron's most celebrated 'dark' tales. Byron calls him 'A thing of dark imaginings' (*Lara*, I.317). But we are told, in a phrase wholly typical of the poet's abiding concerns, that 'he at last confounded good and ill / And half mistook for fate the acts of will' (I.335–6). If we contrast this exact moral insight with Coleridge's 'The Ancient Mariner', which gives us all kinds of moral, religious, and psychological frameworks for the Mariner's crime but does not allow us to pursue any of them seriously apart from the game of interpretation, we are bound to think that Byron still takes action and its consequences seriously. Pope or Dr Johnson would understand this and would see Coleridge as dangerously directing us away from action and judgement altogether. Lara seduces the reader but we retain our customary hold on a moral universe of which Lara remains, though transgressing, a member. Lara is a hero whose extraordinary experience confirms our physical and moral limitation. Coleridge lavishly invokes Christian, ecological, and pantheist systems, but disallows any judgement on the Mariner at all, who remains exemplary and unlimited in some sphere beyond any morality which we might actually recognise or practise. Interest in behaviour and its intensities has displaced interest in action here by a kind of sleight of hand which sidelines ethics altogether by paying occasional noisy lip-service to it. Byron's poetry was the enemy of this for he used the new and potent imaginative resources of his age to represent enduring human dilemmas. It is indeed for this reason that he alone could adequately place the events and characters of his time in the company of Shakespeare's Richard III or Dryden's Charles II or Johnson's Charles XII. Byron's poetic portraits of Catherine the Great, of Suwarrow, of Rousseau, George III, and Napoleon, his judgement on the new kind of warfare at Waterloo, or his vivid delineation of different attitudes to love and marriage in Modern Europe, cannot be separated from his relentless concentration on the desires, excesses, grandeurs, horrors, tawdriness, and limitations of the human heart in his most 'Byronic' poems. It is possible but not finally helpful, then, to separate 'eighteenth-century' and 'Byronic' elements in his poetry.

Byron's contemporaries claimed to be reacting to his glamorising of evil. What upset them more thoroughly, I think, was that his dark poems did not allow them to bypass the old, but no longer correct, thought that there might be something inexplicably evil in the human will which engineers the very destructiveness which it repudiates. Many of Byron's contemporaries were nominally Christian but most were unused to taking the idea of 'sin' seriously. Byron's counterpart to what he calls this 'uneradicable taint of sin' (*CHP*, IV.126.3) is that conscious decision to withhold judgement that is forgiveness. Pope invites this relation to his Eloisa. Byron dramatises forgiveness in *The Vision of Judgment* and *Beppo* and it is the foundation of his comic understanding in *Don Juan*. He could not do so if he did not accept that connection between action and consequence which most of his contemporaries, fed by late eighteenth-century sentiment, were engaged in suppressing.

The relation of Byron to the eighteenth century is clearly not at all straightforward nor, indeed, is the notion of 'the eighteenth century' itself. We found Pope's writings, for instance, on both sides of the divide between action and behaviour and we might find Fielding straddling the same divide. But there are two dangers in simply staying here. In emphasising Byron's debt to the eighteenth century we seem to leave out of account that representative newness which was instantly recognised in him. Secondly, in stressing the diversity of opinions about, and strands in, the eighteenth century we seem to lose sense of it altogether and yet it was an actual particularised, relatively coherent, period of time which undoubtedly generated the forms available to Byron's initiatives. When we attend to something, we will never grasp it through its dispersed ingredients but only in the form of the whole. This time-worn Aristotelian insistence lies at the centre of Classical (rhetorical) and Romantic (organic form) aesthetics. Byron magisterially straddles both Classical and Romantic understanding of form. The most striking feature of Byron's thought and art is his grasp of the realisable coherence of an apparently chaotic or antithetical universe. He is the author of real tragedies and real comedies, of *Childe Harold's Pilgrimage* and of *Don Juan*. It is at least possible, then, that Byron reaches into the contrarieties of the eighteenth century in a manner that finds currents of connection between them.

I think that this is demonstrably so and that, by an intelligible paradox, it explains the peculiar force of Byron in his time. To argue this we will need to imagine the relation between Byron and the eighteenth century in a different way. Two analogies will help to make this new route clear. Edmund Burke, like Byron, was steeped in the traditions of the eighteenth-century Whig party. He never repudiated them. The philosophy of John Locke and the 1688 English Settlement, which are the essential reference points for Whig thinking, governed his explicit thinking about politics. He accepted, that is to say, a mixed constitution which preserved monarchy but handed practical powers of government to established property holders (aristocrats) and those elected by smaller-scale property-owners accomplished (in the long term) by the 1688 revolution. And he accepted that philosophical shift away from metaphysics and towards the philosophy of knowledge accomplished by Locke. Indeed when he had to come to terms, late in life, with the unprecedented events of the French Revolution and English reaction to them in his famous *Reflections*, he did so by entering even more thoroughly and consciously into the Whig tradition to which he related them. But Burke's most famous work, his *Reflections on the Revolution in France*, is not a Whig treatise at all for it articulates a view of the multiple bonds of a nation state as it actually develops in real history that belongs to a new time and a new way of thinking and without which, perhaps, those early nineteenth-century movements for Italian and Greek self-realisation which Byron supported would not have occurred as they did. Thus we have to locate Burke's originality precisely in his decision to base himself in mainstream eighteenth-century tradition. This is Byron's case exactly and this is the main thrust of this chapter. When Byron writes *Don Juan* in deliberate response to the revolutionary poetics of Wordsworth, Coleridge, Southey, and Keats, he digs back into the eighteenth century just as Burke did in response to revolutionary politics, but what both produce is what Shelley said of *Don Juan* – 'something wholly new yet relevant to the age'. Neither Burke nor Byron knew precisely what they were doing in this.

The first person to understand this paradox fully was Cardinal Newman and he provides us with our second analogy. Newman's attitude to the eighteenth century, as it happens, exactly fits the first version described above. For him, the eighteenth century was an arid, sceptical period from which the Romance imagination of Wordsworth, Coleridge, and Southey had rescued English culture, making it possible for there to be a revival of orthodox religious hope in his own time. Byron, so far as Newman was concerned, played no part in this because the poet still belonged intellectually in the earlier period. Newman does not help us here, he has nothing interesting to say on Byron, but his attitude to the Church of England helps us a great deal.

In his *Apologia pro Vita Sua* Newman replies to the charge brought against him by Charles Kingsley, namely that Newman's conversion to Catholicism in 1845 was based on a long-standing attraction to Rome which had motivated Newman throughout his adult life but which he had consistently kept secret. Newman's outraged reply to this charge was to demonstrate in minute detail every stage of the route to his conversion. It is as though he remembered or had record of every influence on him, every twist and turn of his subtlest processes of consciousness over a period of nearly fifty years. The important point is that he established beyond dispute that each step of his movement away from the Church of England was generated by his intense love of it which drove him ever deeper into the varied resources and forms which shaped that Church which, in turn, eventually forced him to find their embodiment wholly elsewhere in an older past and a different future.

Byron's case is even more like Newman's than it is like Burke's. In both cases it is the submission to the totality of an inherited and cherished dialectic that takes them into new, but also older, territory. This is why Byron's self-conscious but sincere defence of eighteenth-century writings is not really at odds with his profound debt to Shakespeare or with his modernity.

Hence, if we backtrack through our multiple classicist and anti-classicist versions of the eighteenth century and find Byron in all of them, this suggests that Byron touches so many of the diverse currents of life in the century that he embodies not only their diversity but also their unified capacity to generate something different of which they will yet be the acknowledged parent. To talk like this is to talk in metaphors but we are bound to do so. Byron is like Cardinal Newman and Burke (and Walter Scott) in this too, to think or to write is always to enter into the resources of a shaping history. Two examples will make this clearer and bring us to a conclusion.

It is easy to point to the eighteenth-century elements in *Childe Harold's Pilgrimage*. Its Spenserian verse form derives from ironic usage by such poets as Shenstone, Thomson and, less ironically, Beattie. Thomson's *The Seasons* and *Liberty* provide precedents for Byron's historical, political, and geographical panoramas. The eighteenth-century 'Graveyard school' of poetry underlies Harold's and Byron's propensity to meditate amidst ruins and tombs. The elegiac, Latinate, sententiousness of the poem comes from Johnson. Its sensibility comes from Gray, Rousseau, and the sometime tenderness of Pope together with motifs derived from the vogue for the Gothic. The buildings and sculptures and 'sublime' vistas celebrated in the poem are those of an eighteenth-century Grand Tour. The list seems endless and, in a way, that is the point. Byron's contemporaries were right in being wholly surprised by the poem. It is something new. What is new is not the ingredients but the capacity to unite so many diverse features as they had never been united before and, in so doing, generate and represent a new world. It seems that this is true of genetics too. It is the combination of the genes rather than their specification as such that individuates. Byron often appealed to 'life' as the source and authoriser of his poetry and genetics may point to an omnipresent but still mysterious model of synthesis and discrimination which fashions both art and life.

Childe Harold's Pilgrimage became almost instantly perhaps the single most influential and widely translated of all Romantic poems and established Byron as the epitome of a new age precisely because the contradictory changes of the period from the French Revolution until Byron's death concentrated the contradictions of the previous century which gave rise to them. Many European commentators understood that Byron's iconic status was granted to him because he manifested in a single striking figure all the contradictory energies of their pivotal time. My main argument is that this capacity derived from Byron's tentacular rootedness in the internal dialectic of eighteenth-century Europe between Catholics, Protestants, Deists and Sceptics, Whigs, Tories, and Radicals, libertines and moralists, sensibility and reason, action and behaviour, nature and art, general norms and historical particulars. The events of the French Revolution and its twenty-year aftermath of European conflict activate and cast into new shape this preceding dialectic much as they shape the creative personality of Byron who comes to embody them.

Byron's biblical drama, *Cain* (1821), shows us the same point in a different way and brings us to a conclusion. Again, we can point immediately to Byron's pervasive use of the sceptical notes on the main characters in Genesis and on God's justice in *Bayle's Dictionary* (1697–1702). Much of the sense of a domestic world in the drama comes from Gessner's mid-eighteenth-century *The Death of Abel*. The sense of empty cosmic space through which Cain and Lucifer move in Act II comes from Newton and eighteenth-century science. It is not surprising that *Cain* was read, and still often is, as though it demolishes the biblical story and any orthodox theodicy by bringing to them new reasoning and evidence which are incompatible with older beliefs. But this is to ignore the relation between the sceptical knowledge acquired by Cain from Lucifer (and by Europeans from French thinkers in the eighteenth century) with Cain's murderous act and his inability to put together his abstract reasoning and an actual dead body. Byron is primarily interested in this. Cain invokes the model of 'behaviour' to exonerate him from responsibility for his action – 'After the fall too soon was I begotten' (III.i.506) – but understands the insufficiency of this excuse. The play cannot possibly celebrate a

Knowledge which seems, here as in *Manfred*, to murder Life. The critique may seem similar to Keats's query in *Lamia*: 'Do not all charms fly / At the mere touch of cold philosophy?' (II.229–30), but Keats is an outsider to the question. *Cain* enters into a fully known and imagined eighteenth-century sense of space and reasoning but deconstructs it from the inside for Byron is as much the heir to the Christianity and suspicion of abstract sceptical systems found in Dryden, Pope, Swift, and Johnson, as he is the heir of those French encyclopedists who burrowed away in the eighteenth century to rid it of feudalism, superstition, and metaphysics and then produce a non-cohering map of all available knowledge held together by Enlightenment assumptions and the alphabetical letters of encyclopedia entries. They were consciously subversive and so was Byron but he is always misread, and could not be a convincing dramatist, if he is seen as simply subversive.

Cain is thus handed to the 1820s as an enigmatic text which could be the harbinger of the revival of interest in religion in the coming century (Chateaubriand, Lacordaire, Newman, Kierkegaard, Dostoyevsky) or of Nietzsche's and Feuerbach's nineteenth-century consolidation of eighteenth-century scepticism or of both. Byron's more intelligent readers – Goethe, Shelley, and Scott for instance – had some sense of his complexity and depth. A large part of that complexity and depth derives from his massive, creative investment in eighteenth-century culture.

15

PETER COCHRAN

Byron's European reception

It is not difficult to discover the huge impact which Byron, most Eurocentred of all the English 'Romantic' writers, had on Europe; but it may be difficult to credit it from the perspective of 2004, in which he is just one 'Romantic' name out of half-a-dozen. A document may help. Francesco Guerrazzi was a poet and historical novelist, who had met Byron at Pisa, and became famous later as a politician – he was made dictator of Tuscany on the flight of the Grand Duke in 1849. He records in his *Memorie* an apparition he experienced while studying law:

> At that time the rumour spread in Pisa that an extraordinary man had arrived there, of whom people told a hundred different tales, all contradictory and many absurd. They said that he was of royal blood, of very great wealth, of sanguine temperament, of fierce habits, masterly in knightly exercises, possessing an evil genius, but a more than human intellect. He was said to wander through the world like Job's Satan seeking a similar adventurer, or calumniator of God. It was George Byron . . . I had not seen Niagara Falls, nor the avalanches of the Alps, I did not know what a volcano was, but I had watched furious tempests, lightning had struck near me, and still nothing from amongst the sights which I had known produced anything like the bewilderment created in me by reading the works of this great soul.[1]

An 1817 review from Geneva helps us see Byron's reception in a more conservative perspective:

> The dominant feature of these works is a sombre grandeur and a delirious rapture. This poet seeks out places and scenes of horror; he takes delight in images of despair; he paints the torments of a soul prey to furious passions and to the memory of the evils they have produced, but always dragged towards them by destiny. The hero's character is the same in all the poems – he always possesses a courage more ferocious than intelligent; a mobile sensibility; an ardent, wayward imagination; a hostile pride directed against men, ungrateful and rebellious against nature and fate.[2]

Byron – or rather, European Byronism, for Byronism is often at odds with Byron as we now understand him – seems to have answered two needs: the need for what was perceived as a revolutionary voice, both literary and political, with which to identify, and the need for what was perceived as a similarly varied revolutionary voice from which to recoil in horror. His heroes, Harold, Selim, Conrad, and so on, who in truth pose no great threat to any political establishment, were read and recreated eagerly as if they did. *Manfred*, whose protagonist, in not relying on the Devil to destroy him, and in rejecting Christian solace to save himself, really did pose an ideological threat to the establishment, was read even more eagerly. Byron's life, as it was understood via international rumours such as those recorded by Guerrazzi, added the thrill of mysterious personal transgressions – even Goethe thought Byron to be a murderer.[3] *Don Juan*, in changing the world's perception of Byron's solemnity, did nothing to change its perception of his radicalism; and his sensational death in Greece capped all of the foregoing with an unanswerable martyrdom in one of the very causes he had been seen to propagate.

French translations, and French literature

It was not necessary to have English to 'know Byron': it was via the French translations of Amedée Pichot that his reputation spread. Pichot translated rapidly, and into prose: it was hard to see beyond his uniform tone and his occasional silent censorship (not all of Byron's lines could be published in France before 1830) and to intuit the variety in the original which his blandness disguised. Only Pushkin seems to have possessed the genius necessary to do this. European 'readers of Byron' were thus substantially divided between those who had English and those who had not. They were further divided between those who admired *Don Juan*, and those who did not.

Of *Don Juan*'s admirers, Stendhal may stand as an example. His early novel *Armance* is full of Byronic echoes. And his 1831 masterpiece *Le Rouge et le Noir* opens with comic scenes in which a married woman cannot face the fact that she is in love with the girlishly formed hero; he, in turn, goes off into the woods to meditate at moments of emotion; they declare their passion by touching hands on romantic evenings; he 'seduces' her by bursting into tears at her feet. Stendhal is playing witty games with *Don Juan*, as his epigraphs hint. The final chapter of the novel's first part (I, 30) in which Monsieur de Rênal searches the room in which Julien is hidden, Madame de Rênal hides Julien's hat (not his shoes) and Julien jumps naked into the garden, is an economical mixture of *Don Juan* and *The Marriage of Figaro*: in it, Stendhal happily advertises himself as a writer, at the very least, in the same tradition as Byron.

Of *Don Juan*'s detractors, Lamartine may stand as an example. Sharing with Byron an admiration for Pope, he is remarkable for having written a poem to Byron while Byron was yet living – he was fresh, when he wrote it, from a reading of *Manfred*, which he knew in the original,[4] even though his English was not good. The collection in which the poem appears, *Méditations Poétiques*, is generally considered the first real French 'Romantic' work:

> You, whom the world is still unable to name, mysterious spirit, mortal, angel or demon, whoever you are, Byron, good or bad spirit, I love the savage harmony of your music, as I love the way the thunderbolt and winds mix during the storm, together with the noise of the torrents![5]

Byron read this hyperbole, and was angered by it because Lamartine calls him at one point the 'Bard of Hell' ('chantre des enfers'). 'A pretty title to give a man for doubting if there be any such place!' (*BLJ*, VII, 127) he snarled, forgetting that 'Bard of Hell' (*CHP*, IV.40.3) was his own appellation for Dante in *Childe Harold* IV. However, Lamartine later described *Don Juan* as 'that revenge of a spirit, perverted by wounded pride, against those who lead an upright life'.[6]

Byron offered a variety of roles upon which a poet (indeed, a man) could model himself. Alfred de Musset adopted that of the Satanic dandy. One of his Byronic exercises, *Namouna*, was written at the publisher's request to fill up an extra sixty pages, but the style and nerve Musset displays are still remarkable. Its hero (named after Hassan, Byron's Islamic protagonist in *The Giaour*) gets out of his bath at the start of the first book, and by the end of the second book, nothing more has happened. The eponymous heroine is first referred to in the fourth stanza of the third book, and by the fourteenth stanza of the third book, she having tricked her way into the hero's bed, the poem is finished. For sheer *insouciance*, it out-*Beppo*s *Beppo* itself:

> I tell you this, Reader, so that you make some concessions in turn. I'm afraid my hero may appear strange to you – strangeness, truth to say, was his passion. 'When all's said, Madame, I'm no angel.' Which of us is, here below? – Tartuffe was right –[7]

Germany

German readers were granted one of the first European reviews of Byron's work, in 1816:

> The young Lord Byron competes, as poet, with Walter Scott. His poems are read greedily by the British public. Most have earned five, some even six editions. His Childe Harold is very popular; even more so is his Corsair; the same applause has greeted a sequel to the latter, Lara (in Two Tales, Lara et Jacqueline by Lord Byron and Mr Rogers). His Bride of Abydos and Giaour, etc., gain many admirers . . . Recently he has, at the suggestion of friends, written Hebrew Melodies, in which he versifies Psalms and other passages from the Old Testament, matching perfectly the tone of the Hebrew singer. These have received much public applause, and have been set to music by two famous Jewish musicians, Braham and Nathan.[8]

It is a much more informative account than the first French review, from Geneva, quoted above, and was read by, among others, Goethe, who rapidly became a devotee. His English was good – much better than Byron's German – and his reaction to *Manfred* is well known:

> The most marvellous event for me a day or two ago was Byron's Manfred, presented to me by a young American. This strange and witty poet has completely absorbed my Faust and sucked the most peculiar nourishment from it for his hypochondria. He has used all the motifs in his own way, so that none remains quite the same, and for that reason especially I cannot sufficiently admire his genius. The remodelling is so complete that very interesting lectures could be given about it, as well as about the similarity with the original and the dissimilarity from it; although I certainly do not deny that the sombre glow of an unlimited, abounding despair becomes tedious in the end. Yet the vexation one experiences on this account is always mixed with admiration and respect.[9]

Though denying the influence, Byron was aware of Goethe's admiration, and was proud of it. He tried to dedicate a number of works to the German poet, and finally succeeded on his third and briefest attempt – the dedication to *Werner*. Goethe's lasting counter-tribute came in *Faust* Part II, in which Byron figures as Euphorion, child of Faust and Helena, perhaps a pan-European combination of southern passion and northern control. Goethe is refashioning a passage which he had sketched in 1816; he published it separately, before the rest of Part II, in April 1827. Euphorion aspires to climb ever higher and higher, until he casts himself into the air and disappears in a blaze of light:

> EUPHORION: Yes! – and a pair of wings / See me unfold! / Thither! I must! – and thus! / Grant me the flight!
>
> *He casts himself into the air: the garments bear him a moment, his head is illuminated, and a streak of light follows.*

CHORUS: Icarus! Icarus! Sorrowful sight!
A beautiful Youth falls at the feet of the parents. We imagine that in the dead body we perceive a well-known form.[10]

The idea is at once glorious and patronising. But Goethe's admiration for *Don Juan* is well attested. Reviewing it in *Ueber Kunst und Altertum*, he wrote:

> The poet shows as little mercy to the characters as he does to the language, and as we look more closely we can clearly see that English poetry has a cultivated comic language which we Germans lack completely.[11]

Byron's death – in appearance so sensational, in reality so wretched – had a deep effect on Heinrich Heine, who wrote at the time:

> Since I started this I have heard that my cousin, Lord Byron, has died at Missolonghi. So that great heart has stopped beating! His was a mighty and singular heart – no tiny little ovary of emotions. Yes, he was a great man – from his pain he created new worlds, Prometheus-like he defied miserable man and his still more miserable gods . . . 'He was a man, take him for al in al [*sic*], we shall not look upon his like again' –[12]

The acknowledgement is moving in its under-punctuated spontaneity.

Theodor Adorno's essay on Heine is entitled *Heine the Wound*[13] and it's surprising that no one has ever said the same about Byron, whose major work constitutes one long, calculated affront to the English self-image. Heine's contemporaries saw the parallel. Metternich admired him, as he had Byron;[14] and Elise von Hohenhausen referred to *him* as 'the German Byron'; others as 'our little Byron'.[15]

Whether Heine's vein of romantic irony would have been the same without a reading of Byron to confirm and encourage it is unknowable. Like Byron, he was a man without a country. He expresses this most ironically in *Jetzt Wohin?* Asking the question 'Where next?' he goes through possible alternative homelands. In Germany he'd be shot, which he'd find disagreeable; England would be fine if it weren't for the English; America is rendered intolerable by tobacco-chewing and spittoons; and he'd not be able to bear the knout in Russia – not in winter, at any rate. His poem ends:

> I sadly gaze up into the sky, where many thousands of stars nod – but nowhere there can I see my own star. / Perhaps it has got lost in the golden labyrinth of the heavens, as I myself have got lost in the turmoil on earth'.
>
> (trans. Peter Branscombe)[16]

The idea of one's birth having occurred beneath a star condemned to wander is from *Manfred* (I.i.110–24) – though Heine treats the idea with an ironic wistfulness absent from Byron's play.

It was Heine who wrote, *à propos* of someone who had lamented the phenomenon of 'byronischer Zerissenheit' ('being Byronically torn apart'):

> Alas, dear reader! If you want to grieve over [Byron's soul] being torn asunder, grieve about the world being torn asunder. And as the heart of the poet is the centre of the world, it can't help being most pitifully torn these days.[17]

Italy

It was to Italian literature that the mature Byron owed most; but his reception in Italy was in inverse proportion to the debt. Leopardi disliked his early work, and, even if he had read *Don Juan* – he never refers to it – we may doubt whether he would have admired it. However, his aversion to his own partial version of Byron should not blind us to the spiritual similarity between the two poets, hard as it would be to reconcile the solemnity of the one with the defiant facetiousness of the other.

Although Byron had many Italian imitators, none were of stature. The pity of it was that his *ottava rima* satires, in which he owed most to Italian poets, were little known in nineteenth-century Italy. It seems Byron's English in them was too sophisticated, and their disillusion too lightly expressed, for the taste of the nation. Where Byron, an Englishman, could afford to be flippant, a nineteenth-century Italian poet could find little to be flippant about.

For it was as a political as much as a poetic figure that Byron was honoured in Italy. Giuseppe Mazzini published (in English) a comparative study of Byron and Goethe in 1839, having been himself imprisoned by the Austrians for nine years; in it, his final judgement is against the calm, Olympian Goethe and for the turbulent, revolutionary Byron (whose inconvenient if spasmodic anti-militarism he ignores). Of Byron's life in Italy Mazzini says, summing up:

> At Naples, in the Romagna, wherever he saw a spark of noble life stirring, he was ready for any exertion; or danger, to blow it into a flame. He stigmatised baseness, hypocrisy, and injustice, whencesoever they sprang . . . Never did the 'eternal spirit of the chainless mind' make a brighter apparition amongst us.[18]

But Mazzini could not publish his paper in Italy. In a country ruled by Ferdinand II of Naples, for example, to show any sort of Byronic influence was dangerous. 'My people,' proclaimed Ferdinand, 'have no need to think: I myself take care of their well-being and dignity.'[19] His prisons were full of potentially Byronic writers, for to write against him was to write Byronically in one way or another, and those whom he did not arrest remained silent. Obtaining any foreign books at all was difficult.

Russia

The influence of Byron got more powerful the more endangered freedom of action and expression became. In countries with assured national identities and complacent convictions about their past and future – in England pre-eminently – his power over poets waned rapidly, in so far as it ever existed. As Andrew Elfenbein writes, '*Don Juan* loomed as a road not to be taken.'[20] Where revolution was a feared and real possibility – in France and Germany, as in say Communist Czechoslovakia in the 1980s – he seems always to have found one writer, at least, who carried his torch. In countries where tyranny obstructed everything, such as Russia, the need for him was paramount, but dangerous to demonstrate.

Byron, who knew only a few Russian phrases, was not aware of Pushkin, and so could have had no knowledge at all of the genius over whom he exercised his greatest influence (though Pushkin took still more from Shakespeare). The influence of Byron on Pushkin is still not satisfactorily documented. Perhaps it is still hard for people to see how little important Russian poetry there was before Pushkin, and how great his need was to discover a sympathetic tradition. Pushkin's feelings about the English poet's death are displayed gloomily in some stanzas from *К Морю* (*K Moryu, To the Sea*):

> One cliff, the sepulchre of glory [St. Helena] . . . There majestic memories subsided into chill sleep: there Napoleon's flame died out. / There, midst torments, he fell into chill sleep. And following him, like the noise of the storm, another genius fled away from us [Byron], another ruler of our thoughts. / He disappeared, lamented by freedom, leaving his garland to the world. Resound and rage, stirred up by storm! O sea, he was your bard. / Your image was stamped upon him, he was created by your spirit: like you, he was powerful, deep and gloomy; like you, nothing could daunt him. (trans. John Fennell)[21]

Contrast Goethe's image of the dead Byron, in the overreaching Euphorion. For Pushkin – the younger writer, from a younger poetic tradition – Byron was not a child to be patronised: he was a force of nature to inspire awe. And the parallel with Napoleon shows how closely the two were linked in Pushkin's mind, and in those of many Russian intellectuals.

Pushkin's English seems not to have been enough to enable him to read Byron in the original.[22] He first became aware of Byron through the partial Genevan translations done by the *Bibliothèque universelle*, and at once started writing in a way which shows a strong Byronic influence. *A Prisoner in the Caucasus* and *The Fountain of Bakhchisarai* show a whole-hearted adoption of the early Byronic manner, amidst similar oriental matter.

To his brother Lev Pushkin wrote, early in 1824, *à propos* of Hippolyte's speech *D'un mensonge si noir justement irrité . . .* in Racine's *Phèdre* (IV.i):

> Read all that belauded tirade, and you will be convinced that Racine had no understanding of how to create a tragic character. Compare it with the speech of the lover in Byron's *Parisina*, and you will see the difference between minds.[23]

To Vyazemsky he wrote in the spring of 1825, comparing Byron's orientalism favourably with that of Moore:

> A European, even in the rapture of Oriental splendour, must preserve the taste and eye of a European. That is why Byron is so charming in *The Giaour*, in *The Bride of Abydos*, etc.[24]

Pushkin was too self-aware to allow himself to stay still for more than one poem at a time. The greater familiarity with the Turkish Tales which he derived from the first Russian translations may have instilled a measure of contempt, parallel to that which Byron was now showing towards his early style.

Just as Byron was distancing himself from his old manner, Pushkin distanced himself from his model. When Byron died, Pushkin resisted Vyazemsky's suggestion to write a Threnody, or to 'complete' *Childe Harold* (Lamartine did that): for he was engrossed in a greater tribute. In *Eugene Onegin*, he finally succeeded in mocking the Byron of *Childe Harold* and the Tales – but he did it in the satirical Byronic mode which he learned from *Don Juan* and Byron's *ottava rima* works, the qualities of which he seems to have deduced solely from Pichot.[25]

He worked at *Onegin* from 1823 to 1830. Its first chapter shows a number of parallels with *Don Juan*, and demonstrates how carefully he had studied Byron's epic. The most important things he took from the English poem were capaciousness and flexibility – *Onegin* is, like *Don Juan*, a rag-bag narrative, mixed with digressions on any topic, social, literary, or (within bounds) political, that strike the poet as he writes. Even through Pichot's French, however, he found in *Don Juan*'s style a freedom from cliché, and a confident approximation to spoken language, which encouraged him in his search for a way out of the jumble of jargons, Gallic or Slavonic, which bedevilled Russian poetry. He read Byron in defiance of the Russian censors, who regarded the Englishman with deep suspicion.

Pushkin's dissatisfaction with early Byron is shown in his portrayal of Tatyana's growing-up. Her bookish fantasies combine for her in Onegin, who has already (1.38) been described as modelling himself on Childe Harold, and the consequence for her is humiliation, when Onegin rejects the love she offers – very correctly, but without grasping what it is in him that she has fallen in love with. In Chapter Seven, she confronts the reality behind the dream, when she enters his deserted house and looks over his library. Her intuition tells her that she will find out something there about this man, who in theory ought not to be, but in reality is, indifferent to her. Sure enough, many of Onegin's books are by Byron, and a portrait of the poet hangs on the wall, over a statuette of Napoleon. Here is what then happens:

> And so, at last, feature by feature, / Tanya begins to understand / more thoroughly, thank God, the creature / for whom her passion has been planned / by fate's decree: this freakish stranger, / who walks with sorrow, and with danger, / whether from heaven or from hell, / this angel, this proud devil, tell, / what is he? Just an apparition, / a shadow, null and meaningless, / a Muscovite in Harold's dress, / a modish second-hand edition, / a glossary of smart argot . . . / a parodistic raree-show?[26]

Thus Tatyana's judgement of men, in both literature and life, starts to approximate that of her creator; and she develops the strength of character which will enable her, in the poem's last chapter, to repel Onegin when *he* belatedly falls in love with *her*. Pushkin can put his heroine at the forefront of the narrative in a way which Byron rarely seems to find interesting.

By this time Pushkin was getting seriously embarrassed by his earlier Byronic mode, and felt it necessary to apologise for it:

> Nikolai and Alexander Rayevsky and I had a good laugh at it [*The Prisoner of the Caucasus*] . . . *The Fountain of Bakhchisarai* is weaker than *The Prisoner* and, like it, reflects the reading of Byron, on whom I was mad at the time.[27]

But Pushkin still could not leave Byron behind. *Beppo* was to be the main influence behind his two further satirical tales, *Count Nulin* and *The Little House at Kolomna*. Part of his reaction against Byron may have been occasioned by the Russophobia of the middle cantos of *Don Juan*, which he obtained in December 1825. In 1830 he reversed the movement against Byron's influence which *Onegin* had signalled, and wrote his purest Byronic poem, *The Little House at Kolomna*. It is in *ottava rima*, and, like Musset's *Namouna*, is a direct imitation of the deceptively digressive *Beppo*. We know how much Pushkin admired *Beppo*: and in *Kolomna* he captures the Byronic mixture of profundity and facetiousness far more successfully than the Frenchman does. He was, in his letter to Pletnev of 9 December, even more coy about it than he had been about *Nulin*:

> in Boldino I wrote as I have not written for a long time. Here is what I have brought along: the two *last* chapters of *Onegin*, the eighth and ninth, completely ready for the press. A tale, written in ottava rima (of about 400 verses) which let's bring out *Anonyme*.[28]

Notice the simultaneity with which he completes the anti-Byronic *Onegin*, and the new *ottava rima* work. He had never written in *ottava rima*; his decision to do so now signals a further break with the passionate Byronism of works like *A Prisoner*, and an assertion, at the same time, of admiration for the older Byron – the result of further thought on his part, and further study of, especially, *Don Juan*. Here is how Pushkin 'marshals his vocabulary' near the start of *Kolomna*. A version might run:

> So, let's be having you! You make me ill,
> You 'orrible lot of endings, male or female!
> Fall in, chests out, eyes to the front! Keep still!
> In octave stanzas, 'ten . . . shun! Without fail!
> At ease, at ease; stand easy . . . By God's will,
> If you keep proper chime, all whole and hale,
> We'll very soon get used to one another,
> And you'll look on me as your loving Brother.
>
> It's quite a thrill to drill such tuneful Numbers,
> To see them all march past, their Heads held high –
> Not straggling out of line, with jolts and lumbers,
> Advancing against odds, all doomed to Die;
> Each syllable, each Foot, each line encumbers
> Its Neighbour not a jot; I tell no lie –
> The poet feels himself the Sword of Fate,
> Like Bonaparte, or Tamburlaine the Great.[29]

Kolomna is an exercise in that 'quiet facetiousness' which, Byron wrote (*BLJ*, VI, 67), was a principal motive behind the writing of *Don Juan*. *Kolomna* is, like *Don Juan* or *Beppo*, in part about its own writing; like them, it digresses without scruple, so that the digressions become as important as the narrative; like them, it advances so far into the depths of facetiousness as to form a sublime quintessentialisation of that quality. As *Beppo* does, it anchors itself with great precision in one city, using St Petersburg as Byron uses Venice, to the extent that the location becomes a kind of character in the story.

Last but by no means least, *Kolomna* is, like *Don Juan*, a comic hymn to the female sexual impulse – a phenomenon which Byron often found amusing. The idea of a woman smuggling a man in drag into her establishment for the pleasure of his person (as occurs in *Kolomna*) is familiar to anyone who knows *Don Juan* Cantos V and VI. It was not until *The Bronze Horseman*

(1833) that Pushkin found a non-Byronic narrative voice of his own – characterised by a sympathy for the nameless victims of history in a way which Byron's poetry rarely is.

A section of detail equal in density to the above could be written on Byron's influence on the verse and prose of Mikhail Lermontov.

Poland

Byron's influence on Poland, both poetically and politically, went as deep as it did elsewhere; perhaps deeper, as oppression increased, and poetry became a vital way of keeping the Polish sense of nationhood alive.

Unlike Byron, Adam Mickiewicz, Poland's greatest poet, managed to meet Goethe, although he seems to have been unmoved by the experience.[30] He was also friends with Pushkin – though their politics differed, especially after the suppression of the Polish insurrection of 1831 – which enraged Heine, but stirred Pushkin's Russian chauvinism. Mickiewicz kept at a safe distance from the insurrection – which caused him much subsequent guilt – and, like Byron, Heine, and Pushkin, he spent much of his life in exile – he never even visited Warsaw or Cracow. Unlike Byron, but like Pushkin, much of his exile was involuntary, and his detestation of tyranny was based on personal knowledge of what its effects were. As early as 1822 he wrote, 'It is only Byron that I read, and I throw away any book written in another spirit, because I detest lies.'[31] Byron's influence, both for good and bad, is seen throughout his work – though it seems uncharted in English.

The Byron poem with which Mickiewicz would have been most intimate is *The Giaour*, which he translated (with no help from Pichot). 'Wrote a version of' would be more accurate, for he changes the original, making it even more fragmented than it was on finally leaving Byron's hands – it is often printed as an original poem. A Catholic, Mickiewicz neutralises the poem's rejection of Christian solace, changes Byron's scepticism about Greece, and gives the protagonist the kind of conscience which might lead to that least Byronic of ends, redemption.

Mickiewicz's most-read poem, *Pan Tadeusz* (it is Poland's great national epic) was published in Paris in 1834 – the same year as his *Giaour* translation. It shows the clear influence of *Don Juan* and of *Eugene Onegin*, in its detailed depiction of rural Lithuanian society (Poland and Lithuania were one country between 1386 and 1772) and the social, hunting, wooing, dressing, wedding, and gastronomic rituals practised there a generation previously. Its authorial voice sometimes intrudes, but, unlike Byron's, bestows an Olympian calm on the narrative. Like *Onegin*, it is a novel in verse; like *Don Juan*, it takes recent history as its subject, and has as hero a Walter Scott-type innocent caught up in political and amatory escapades, the significance of which he cannot fully judge. The poem's title is his – 'Pan Tadeusz' means 'Master Thaddeus' – he is named after Tadeusz Kosciuzko, the freedom-fighter hymned by Byron in *Don Juan*, X.471.

Mickiewicz has a tighter chronology than either Pushkin or Byron: the first ten of his twelve books take up five days in 1811, the last two, a few happy but doomed hours in 1812 – as Napoleon's Polish auxiliaries prepare their fatal march on Moscow, the poem's hero and heroine are married, blissfully unaware of the horrors to come.

In Books X and XI we see a clear example of Mickiewicz reacting against Byron's nihilism. In them he seems to be offering a critique of the Giaour's confession, in the long speech of Jacek Soplica, and in its aftermath. It has been told in Book II how Soplica ('a mustachioed bully') father of Tadeusz, once shot the father of his beloved during a siege by the Russians, because his suit had been refused (his expertise with firearms is stressed). He has thereby gained the reputation of a murderer and a renegado. The unnatural tale is interpreted by one of its hearers almost as a western literary importation:

> Often have I heard and often do I read such traditions; in England and in Scotland every lord's castle, in Germany every count's mansion was the theatre of murders! In every ancient, powerful family there is a report of some bloody or treacherous deed, after which vengeance descends as an inheritance to the heirs: in Poland for the first time do I hear of such an incident.[32]

However, Soplica is present for most of the poem's early narrative, unrecognised, as a Bernadine monk called Father Robak: even his skill with firearms, shown in a bear-hunt in Book IV, does not betray his identity. He distinguishes himself for leadership in the poem's centrepiece – a battle between Russians and Poles in Book IX. He reveals himself publicly in Book X, and tells how he has tried to atone for his murder by becoming a real monk, leading a life of exemplary piety, unlike the Giaour with his malign and meaningless gestures. He has been flogged by Russians and imprisoned in the Spielberg by Austrians. Upon the completion of his confession he dies – just as news reaches him of the decree reuniting Lithuania and Poland. In Book XI it is further learned that he has fought the Allies in Napoleon's Polish legions. He is declared to have atoned for his sins. The Légion d'Honneur, awarded him by Bonaparte, arrives too late, but is hung on the cross over his grave as the congregation repeats the Angelus – a political and a religious benediction simultaneously.

Mickiewicz was unable to stop merely at translating *The Giaour*. Dismayed by its lack of any serious political content and by its protagonist's attitude to religion, he felt impelled in *Pan Tadeusz* to rewrite it in the context of the events of his own time, and to give his version of its protagonist, first an unambiguous sin, against morality and motherland, for which it was difficult to atone, and secondly a variety of ways – political, military, and religious – in which he could try to do so. And his own death in 1855 (from cholera, trying to establish a Polish Legion to fight the Russians) was in the tradition which Byron's had established. In 1837 he wrote:

> The epoch between 1815 and 1830 was a happy one for poets. After the great war, Europe, tired of battles and congresses, bulletins and protocols, seemed to become disgusted with the real, sad world, and lifted its eyes towards what it thought of as the ideal world. At that point Byron appeared. Rapidly, in the regions of the imagination, he took over the place which the Emperor had recently occupied in the regions of reality. Destiny, which had never ceased to furnish Napoleon with pretexts for continual warfare, favoured Byron with a long peace. During his poetic reign, no great event occurred to distract the attention of Europe, wholly taken up with its English reading.[33]

. . . which might stand as a head-note to this entire chapter.

NOTES

1. Francesco Domenico Guerrazzi, *Pagine Autobiografiche*, ed. Gaetano Ragonese, no provenance, 1969, pp. 155–6, trans. in part, Iris Origo, *The Last Attachment* (London: Jonathan Cape, 1949), p. 292.
2. *Bibliothèque universelle des sciences, belle-lettres et arts*, vol. v (Geneva, 1817), pp. 72–7.
3. *Ueber Kunst und Altertum* (repr. Berne, 1970) II.ii.186–92: reprinted at *BLJ*, v, 503–5.
4. Edmond Estève, *Byron et le romantisme français* (Paris: Librairie Hachette et Cie., 1907), 95, 325n and ff.
5. Alphonse de Lamartine, *L'Homme – à Lord Byron* from *Méditations Poétiques* (Paris: Au dépôt de la librairie grecque-latine-allemande, 3rd edn, 1820):

   Toi, dont le monde encore ignore le vrai nom,
   Esprit mystérieux, mortel, ange ou démon,
   Qui que tu sois, Byron, bon ou fatal génie,
   J'aime de tes concerts la sauvage harmonie
   Comme j'aime le bruit de la foudre et des vents
   Se mêlant dans l'orage à la voix des torrents!

6. Quoted Henri Guillemin, *Lamartine, Byron et Mme Guiccioli, Revue de Littérature Comparée*, 19 (1939), 377.
7. Alfred de Musset, *Namouna* I, XXV:

   Je vous dis cela, lecteur, pour qu'en échange
   Vous me fassiez aussi quelque concession.
   J'ai peur que mon héros ne vous paraisse étrange;
   Car l'étrange, à vrai dire, était sa passion.

<<Mais, madame, après tout, je ne suis pas un ange.>>
Et qui l'est ici-bas? – Tartuffe a bien raison.

8. *Intelligenzblatt der Jenaischen Allgemeinen Literatur-Zeitung*, 1816, pp. 4–5.
9. *Goethes Briefe*, ed. Bodo Morawe (Hamburg, 1965), III, 403.
10. Johann Wolfgang von Goethe, *Faust . . . Translated in the Original Metres*, trans. by Bayard Taylor, 2 vols. (London: Strahan & Co., 1871):

    EUPHORION: Doch! – und ein Flügelpaar
    Faltet sich los!
    Dorthin! Ich muß! ich muß!
    Gönnt mir den Flug!

    Er wirft sich in die Lüfte, die Gewande tragen ihn einen Augenblick, sein Haupt strahlt, ein Lichtschweif zieht nach.

    CHOR: Ikarus! Ikarus!
    Jammer genug!

    Ein schöner Jüngling stürzt zu den Eltern Füßen, man glaubt in dem Toten eine bekannte Gestalt zu erblicken. (Part II. 1897–2002)

11. *Ueber Kunst und Altertum*, III.i.81, trans. Victoria Brice.
12. Heinrich Heine, *Werke*, ed. F. H. Eisner, 27 vols. (Berlin: Akademie-Verlag, 1970–76), XX, p. 163.
13. Theodor Adorno, *Notes to Literature*, ed. Rolf Tiedemann, trans. Shierry Weber Nicholsen (New York: Columbia University Press, 1991), I, pp. 80–5.
14. Legend has it that Metternich knew *Childe Harold* IV by heart – in English.
15. Gerhart Hoffmeister, *Byron und der europäische Byronismus* (Darmstadt Wissenschaftliche Buchgesellschaft, 1983), 108.
16. Heinrich Heine, *Heine*, intro., ed. and trans. Peter Branscombe (Harmondsworth: Penguin Books, 1986).

    Traurig schau ich in die Höh,
    Wo viel tausend Sterne nicken –
    Aber meinen eignen Stern
    Kann ich nirgends dort erblicken.

    Hat im güldnen Labyrinth
    Sich vielleicht verirrt am Himmel,
    Wie ich selber mich verirrt
    In dem irdischen Getümmel. –

17. Heine, *Reisebilder* II, *Die Bäder von Lukka* IV, *Werke* 6, ed. Christa Stöcker, 83.
18. *Byron and Goethe*, in *Life and Writings of Joseph Mazzini* (1870), VI, 91–2.
19. Quoted in Antonio Porta, *Byronismo Italiano* (Milan, 1923), I, 250.
20. Andrew Elfenbein, *Byron and the Victorians* (Cambridge University Press, 1995), 46.
21. Pushkin, *К Морю*, 9–12:

    Одна скала, гробница славы . . .
    Там погружались в хладный сон
    Воспоминанья величавы:
    Там угасал Наполеон.

Там он почил среди мучений.
И вслед за ним, как бури шум,
Другой от нас умчался гений,
Другой властитель наших дум.

Изчез, оплаканный свободой,
Оставя миру свой венец.
Шуми, взволнуйся непогодой:
Он был, о море, твой певец.

Твой образ был на нем означен,
Он духом создан был твоим:
Как ты, могущ, глубок и мрачен,
Как ты, ничем неукротим.

22. *The Letters of Alexander Pushkin*, trans. J. Thomas Shaw (Bloomington, Ind: Indiana University Press; London: Oxford University Press, 1963), I, 263.
23. *Ibid.*, I, 150. The Byron speech is Hugo's to Azo, *Parisina* XIII.
24. *Ibid.*, I, 213.
25. Pushkin, *Eugene Onegin*, trans. and ed. Vladimir Nabokov (Princeton University Press, 1975), I, 156–163.
26. Pushkin, *Eugene Onegin*, trans. Charles Johnston (London: Penguin, 1977), Chapter VII, 24:

И начинает понемногу
Моя Татьяна понимать
Теперь яснее – слава богу –
Того, по ком она вздыхать
Осуждена судьбою властной:
Чудак печальный и опасный,
Созданье ада иль небес,
Сей ангел, сей надменный бес,
Что ж он? Ужели подражанье,
Ничтожный призрак, иль еще
Москвич в Гарольдовом плаще,
Чужих причуд истолкованье,
Слов модных полный лексикон? . . .
Уж не пародия ли он?

27. Tatyana Wolff (trans. and ed.), *Pushkin on Literature* (Stanford University Press, 1986), 252.
28. *Letters of Pushkin*, trans. Shaw, II, 446.
29. Pushkin, *Домик в Коломне*, 4–5. Text from *А.С.Пушкин, Собрание Сочиненнй*, III (Moscow, 1975), 224:

Ну, женские и мужеские слоги!
Благословясь, попробуем: слушай!
Равняйтеся, вытягивайте ноги
И по три в ряд в октаву заезжай!
Не бойтесь, мы не будем слишком строги;
Держисьвольней и только не плошай,
А там уже привыкнем, слава богу,
И выедем на ровную дорогу.

Как весело стихи свои вести
Под цифрами, в порядке, строй за строем,
Не позволять им в сторону брести,
Как войску, в пух рассыпанному боем!
Тут каждый слог замечен и в чести,
Тут каждый стих глядит себе героем,
А стихотворец . . . с кем же равен он?
Он Тамерлан иль сам Наполеон.

30. See Waclaw Lednicki, *Bits of Table Talk on Pushkin, Mickiewicz, Goethe, Turgenev and Sinckiewicz* (The Hague: M. Nijhoff, 1956), ix.
31. Letter to Franciszek Malewski, 22 November 1822: quoted by Stefan Treugutt, in C. E. Robinson, *Lord Byron and some of His Contemporaries: Essays from the Sixth International Byron Seminar* (New York: University of Delaware; London and Toronto: Associated University Press, 1982), 131, 143n.
32. Adam Mickiewicz, *Pan Tadeusz; or, the Last Foray in Lithuania*, Book II, trans. George Rapall Noyes (London and Toronto: J. M. Dent & Sons, 1917), p. 46.

Nieraz takie słyszałem i czytam podania;
W Angliji i w Szkocyi każdy zamek lordów,
W Niemczech każdy dwór grafów był teatrem mordów!
W każdej dawnej, szlachetnej, potężnej rodzinie
Jest wieść o jakimś krwawym lub zdradzieckim czynie,
Po którym zemsta spływa na dziedziców w spadku:
W Polsce pierwszy raz słyszę o takim wypadku.

Adam Mickiewicz, *Pan Tadeusz*, trans. Kenneth R. Mackenzie (New York, 1992) (parallel text), p. 79.

33. *Le Globe*, 25 May 1837, repr. Jerzy Swidzinski, *Puszkin i Ruch Literacki w Rosji* (1991), p. 9.

16

JANE STABLER

Byron, postmodernism and intertextuality

Something odd happens to the popular Turkish Tale in Byron's *Mazeppa*, a poem that is rarely discussed because the accident of its publication in June 1819 meant that it was almost completely overshadowed by the first cantos of *Don Juan*. Following the verse narratives of *The Giaour*, *The Bride of Abydos* and *The Siege of Corinth*, *Mazeppa*'s octosyllabic couplets, triplets and quatrains sweep its readers along in a pulsating adventure story.[1] In *Mazeppa*, however, the thrills and spills of another set of fugitive exploits are mockingly undercut by a narrative frame which draws attention to boredom in the audience. King Charles requests the tale but, as we discover at the end of the poem, he falls asleep almost as soon as it commences:

> And if ye marvel Charles forgot
> To thank his tale, *he* wonder'd not, –
> The king had been an hour asleep.
> (*Mazeppa*, 867–69)

Romantic egotism (Mazeppa's pride in being 'haunted . . . With the vain shadow of the past', 229–30) comes up against a more recalcitrant physical domain. King Charles demonstrates what Byron suspected of his own and all writing – that it was a literature of exhaustion.

Mazeppa offers a form of knowing hybridity akin to the parodic voice which cut through the 'lethargy of custom' in *Lyrical Ballads*.[2] Two decades after 1798, works which played between the borders of satire and sentiment still puzzled the reading public. *Mazeppa* provoked a wide range of responses from reviewers, from those who detected 'something new', to those who regarded *Mazeppa* as a continuation of Byron's restless identification with criminal types.[3] The poem was 'written in humour between grave and gay, neither tragic nor comic, a mule and mongrel between *Beppo* and the *Bride of Abydos*', claimed the *Literary Gazette*. It was a 'fragment' of 'cloudy narrative' for the *Theatre's* critic while *Blackwood's* praised the 'half serious, half sporting' narration of a 'wild story'.[4]

This lack of agreement about genre and the conflict between moral and aesthetic criteria for evaluation anticipate critical disputes about postmodernist art in our time. Postmodernism has been defined variously as a continuation of modernism or late modernism and also as a break with modernist abstraction. It has been categorised both as nostalgic and rootless: as an offshoot of cynical capitalism and as playing a part in the defence of minority cultures and communities; enervated, parasitic and playfully courageous. All these terms (including a suspicion that the writer and his publisher were exploiting the market) have been applied to literature produced long before the twenty-first century. Ihab Hassan observes that we now detect 'postmodern features in *Tristram Shandy* precisely because our eyes have learned to recognise postmodern features'.[5]

Following delightedly in the wake of Laurence Sterne's infamous 'oddity', Byron's work – especially *Don Juan*, the work he called his 'poetical T[ristram] Shandy' – supports the view that the postmodern is a genre coexistent with the rise of print culture as well as a late twentieth- and twenty-first-century epoch.[6] This chapter is concerned with generic features rather than political and economic contexts, but it is obvious that the technological developments which have mediated the reception of genre since the early nineteenth century are significant phenomena. In particular, developing journalistic coverage of daily – or hourly – events (as noted in Wordsworth's 1800 Preface) has contributed to an increasingly self-reflexive vein in literature. We need to take account of this shift as well as many other aspects of historical difference when we discuss Byron's (and Sterne's) literary forms of disruption as a proto-postmodernist.

Mazeppa's wry closing reflection on a capricious and thankless audience acknowledges the vagaries of reception which had always shaped Byron's career. The poem belongs to the period when Byron had ceased to be at the centre of fashionable London society, and was living in self-imposed exile in Italy. He began *Mazeppa* in April 1817 in Venice, abandoned it for a while (in the meantime starting and finishing *Beppo* and *Childe Harold's Pilgrimage* Canto IV), then returned to it in the summer of 1818 when he was again living in Venice, and finished it during a visit by the Shelleys. On this occasion Percy Shelley heard Byron read the first canto of *Don Juan*. Shelley greeted the *ottava rima* work enthusiastically, discerning a much-needed reform of Byron's philosophy. After the visit to Venice, Shelley wrote to Peacock:

> I entirely agree with what you say about Childe Harold. The spirit in which it is written is . . . a kind of obstinate and selfwilled folly, in which he hardens himself. I remonstrated with him in vain on the tone of mind from which such a view of things alone arises. For its real root is very different from its apparent

> one. Nothing can be less sublime than the true source of these expressions of contempt and desperation . . . He allows fathers and mothers to bargain with him for their daughters . . . He associates with wretches who seem almost to have lost the gait and physiognomy of man, and who do not scruple to avow practices which are not only not named, but I believe seldom even conceived in England. He says he disapproves, but he endures.[7]

Shelley's remonstrance takes a more generous form in *Julian and Maddalo*, but this letter recoils (somewhat squeamishly) from Byron's surrender to an 'orgasm of Buffoonery', a sort of negative sublime, as he submerged himself in the hectic carnality of Venice.[8] Byron's accommodation of what Shelley and others 'seldom even conceived' extended to art as well as life. Shelley, to take a revealing instance of their difference in taste, could not abide the Restoration comedies that Byron loved to quote. Byron's appreciation of artistic licentiousness grew out of a cosmopolitan Regency dandy pose, but by the time of *Mazeppa* it had matured into a more politically aware, ironic use of artifice.

Between 1817 and 1819 Byron's immersion in Venetian culture with its intricate social conventions (including Carnival and the male role of the *cavalier servente*) informed the conjunction of the homely and the exotic, the marginal and the sublime in his work. For many critics this matrix defines the conditions of postmodern writing. While T. S. Eliot's High Modernism flinched from the chaotic details of ordinary life and sought to transcend them with new artistic wholes, postmodern art accepts with Byron and Beckett that 'Existence may be borne' (*CHP*, IV.21.1). It builds on the foundations of modernism's 'unreal city', but emphasises an intermingling with (not distance from) quotidian particularity. If carnivalisation is one of the hallmarks of postmodernist writing, Byron is the Romantic poet most hospitable to the 'periodic Saturnalia' with all its 'laughing – flirting – tormenting – pleasant' plurality.[9] *Childe Harold's Pilgrimage* Canto IV dazzled its first readers by rapid shifts between different categories of existence: 'the transitions are so quickly performed . . . from Venice to Rome, from Rome to Greece . . . from Mr. Hobhouse to politics, and back again to Lord Byron; that our head is absolutely bewildered by the want of connexion', complained the *Literary Gazette*, anticipating the reading public's shock at the violent juxtapositions of *Don Juan*.[10]

Well before the first appearance of Byron's *ottava rima* verse, however, reviewers felt that Byron was misleading his readers about the genre of his poems. By the time they reached *Childe Harold's Pilgrimage* Canto IV, the progression implied by the word 'pilgrimage' had dissolved completely into an eclectic flux of 'fantastically tangled' (*CHP*, IV.17.1) Spenserian stanzas which came as close as any nineteenth-century poem had come to suggesting the simultaneity of modern life:

> still teems
> My mind with many a form which aptly seems
> Such as I sought for, and at moments found;
> Let these too go – for waking Reason deems
> Such over-weening phantasies unsound,
> And other voices speak, and other sights surround.
> (*CHP*, IV.7.4–9)

Whereas Shelley believed that 'poetry defeats the curse which binds us to be subjected to the accident of surrounding impressions', Byron's poetry draws attention to the mystery of an ever-shifting surface and involves the reader in the formation of that surface.[11] In the footsteps of Childe Harold on a journey through Italy, William Hazlitt viewed the waterfall at Terni and felt that this rather tame cascade ought to have been captured by the genial sparkle of a poet like Thomas Moore rather than the troubling force of Byronic textuality. The waterfall, he said:

> has nothing of the texture of Lord Byron's terzains, twisted, zigzag, pent up and struggling for a vent, broken off at the end of a line, or point of a rock, diving under ground, or out of the reader's comprehension, and pieced on to another stanza or shelving rock.[12]

This passage reveals the physicality of Hazlitt's (and other people's) reading experience of Byron's poetry. Byron's most subversive aesthetic technique was abrupt transition between different modes, a juxtaposition of types and qualities which was perceived first as Whiggish aristocratic caprice and later as more offensively radical disruption. Early readers of *Don Juan* were stunned by the callousness of a narrative which could veer between high sentiment and vomit, and yet, the reception of *Don Juan* was continuous with objections to the fragmentary form of *The Giaour*, the dangerous intermixture of satire in the notes to *Childe Harold* and the other Turkish Tales. Byron's sudden poetic breaks and gulfs were a form of sublimity, but they also violated the law of genre and the expectation that sublime poetic boundlessness would disturb its readers only within certain acceptable parameters. Above all, the sublime was supposed to sustain a mood of seriousness or reverence before God or Nature and Byron's infringement of this rule frequently took the form of casual, quotidian or comic interruptions to lyrical passages. His poetry allowed all that had been repressed by genre to return.

'The more enlightened our houses are, the more their walls ooze ghosts', Italo Calvino remarked as he contemplated the position of the writer in

1967.[13] Byron's texts comprehend an enlightened, unillusioned world in which 'spectres' and 'things familiar' jostle together as in Childe Harold's Venice. For Shelley the Lido offered 'The pleasure of believing what we see / Is boundless, as we wish our souls to be', whereas Byron's sinking and deserted city was endlessly 'peopled' by the texts of what the poet has read and done before in a place where 'Curiosity is always excited' (*Julian and Maddalo*, II.16–17).[14] Such inclusiveness lends his account of this Italian city an indeterminacy more unsettling than the melting loveliness of a Shelleyan sunset because it embraces not only idealised forms, but the multiple dislocated particulars (animal, vegetable and mineral) associated with 'Venice' as a place much over-written about by earlier artists, tourists and conquests: 'Shylock and the Moor, / And Pierre' (*CHP*, IV.4.6–7); 'The Bucentaur . . . rotting unrestored' (*CHP*, IV.11.3); 'blind old Dandolo' (*CHP*, IV.12.8); 'The "Planter of the Lion"' (*CHP*, IV.14.3); 'The camel . . . with the heaviest load' (*CHP*, IV.21.4). Both poets were wary (as Lacanian theory would be) of fantasies of wholeness, but while Shelleyan poetry reaches towards 'The One' which remains, Byron's verse follows 'the many' which 'change and pass', contemplating nostalgically or sardonically the prospect of ideal resolution.

Shelley and Byron's disagreement on the matter of ideal versus 'peopled' existence offers a way of conceptualising the contested ground between modernism and postmodernism. Like their conversations on poetry, this is a difference which can shade into reciprocity ('(I think with you / In some respects, you know)'[15] as Maddalo tells Julian). A vital point of comparison is their shared inheritance of earlier literature. Whereas Shelley believed with the High Modernists that the poet's work was to 'make it new', Byron was much happier to return to history, and he distrusted literary attempts to sever the past utterly. About the Pope–Bowles controversy, Shelley argued 'I certainly do not think Pope, or any writer, a fit model for any succeeding writer . . . it would all come to a question as to under what forms mediocrity should perpetually reproduce itself.[16] After helping the oriental verse-tale to become one of the most popular verse commodities of the day, Byron, on the other hand, urged his contemporaries to reinstate Pope's 'superartificiality'.[17] This discipline, he argued, would counter the egotistical experimentation of, for example, Cockney couplets. Byron was notoriously dismissive of Keats's early verse with its shibboleth of individual (adolescent) imagination. By contrast, Byron's imaginative play is more sporting in that it addresses itself to what is communal rather than what is 'mawkish'. Byron valued cosmopolitan polish above the self-indulgence of a sect – hence his impatience with the Lake School's insular organicism and Leigh Hunt's 'system'. Art that plays by only its own self-regarding conventions has no right to expect the audience to stay awake. Byron is clearly on the side of artistic frame breaking that has mastered traditional discipline first. His postmodernism is certainly not that which prides itself merely on the efficient vandalism of established forms.

Mary Shelley's report of Byron's and Shelley's debate on Hamlet neatly encapsulates the way Byron's performative scepticism affronts mystical system. After Shelley's eloquent discourse on the 'expressive unity' of *Hamlet*, we are told, he 'looked up, and found Lord Byron fast asleep'.[18] The physical presence of a dozing audience ironises the authority of the bard and comically deflates the transcendent potential of the lyric artist (as in Byron's aside on Keats's 'Sleep and Poetry': '(an ominous title)').[19] By displaying the artist at the mercy of the material, contingent world Byron unravelled the sealed, unified pretensions of the autonomous Romantic or High Modernist work of art. As well as fuelling a debate with Shelley, Byron's suspicion of self-contained poetry also shaped the peculiar dynamic of Romantic irony within his work which is, as Drummond Bone has observed,[20] distinct from both the disillusioned backlash of Irving Babbit's Romantic irony and the transcendental ascension of Friedrich Schlegel's Romantic irony. Byron's Romantic irony is a 'letting in' (or, perhaps, a 'letting be'), rather than an escape or a turning away from; its hospitality to contradiction is both Shakespearean and Negatively Capable as Anne Barton has pointed out.[21]

Entering into the uncertainty of postmodern experience, *Mazeppa* is strangely susceptible to accident. From the beginning, the realm of unpredictability is feminised as, for example, in the description of Mazeppa's adulterous liaison with the wife of Count Palatine which hinges on 'A restless dream or two, some glances' and 'the usual chances, / Those happy accidents which render / The coldest dames so very tender' (*Mazeppa*, 172; 174–6).

Reviewers objected to the easy imputation of sexual mutability in women, but *Mazeppa*, like many other of Byron's poems (especially *Don Juan*), allows feminine caprice a large say in the direction of the plot. Mazeppa's tolerance of adultery is mirrored in the poem's adulteration of form within loosely alternating tetrameter couplets and quatrains. To this extent Byron's embrace of previously outlawed detail and the openness of his works to 'mad, unconscious, improper, unclean, nonsensical, oriental, profane' existence anticipates feminist postmodern critiques of such late twentieth-century master narratives as 'Man, the Subject, History and Meaning', the philosophical priorities that are usually seen to expedite masculine authority over feminine volatility.[22] The consummation of Mazeppa and Theresa's passion follows the pattern of Dante's Paolo and Francesca but, significantly, Byron's couple meet over a game, not a book:

– There is a game,
A frivolous and foolish play,
Wherewith we while away the day;
It is – I have forgot the name –
And we to this, it seems, were set,
By some strange chance, which I forget:
I reck'd not if I won or lost,
It was enough for me to be
So near to hear, and oh! to see
The being whom I loved the most

...

Until I saw, and thus it was,
That she was pensive, nor perceived
Her occupation, nor was grieved
Nor glad to lose or gain; but still
Play'd on for hours, as if her will
Yet bound her to the place, though not
That hers might be the winning lot.

(*Mazeppa*, 252–61, 264–70)

The game without a name which both participants play to prolong the moment with no regard to the outcome presents an image of Byron's narrative game with his readers: 'in play, there are two pleasures for your choosing – / The one is winning, and the other losing' (*Don Juan*, XIV.12.7–8). The casual '– I have forgot the name –' above chimes with Mazeppa's negligence about the reason they were playing. For Byron's lovers and readers there needs to be no cause. The game, the kiss or the reading happens because we happen to be there. It is not simply that Byron makes unpredictability a theme in his poetry, but that his readers participate in unpredictability. Lapsing between rhymed couplets and alternating rhymes, the verse plays with our expectations of closure and containment. The narrative makes a shape out of history while acknowledging other versions of the same story:

My moments seem'd reduced to few;
And with one prayer to Mary Mother,
And, it may be, a saint or two,
As I resign'd me to my fate,
They led me to the castle gate:
Theresa's doom I never knew,
Our lot was henceforth separate. –

(*Mazeppa*, 335–41)

In these lines, the rhyme brilliantly enacts the parting of the ways between Theresa and Mazeppa. As Mazeppa's fate tightens around him like the cords which will fasten him to the wild horse, Theresa vanishes into history leaving only a ghostly trace in the web of narrative:

> Theresa's form –
> Methinks it glides before me now,
> Between me and yon chestnut's bough,
> The memory is so quick and warm;
> And yet I find no words to tell
> The shape of her I loved so well.
>
> (*Mazeppa*, 202–7)

In a few lines, she flickers into visibility for Mazeppa ('Methinks'; 'me now'; 'Between me'), but the imperfect rhyme of 'form' and 'warm' shadows her elusiveness which is the only thing Mazeppa can perfectly describe. It is a moment of poignancy, but crucially, Theresa's loss is survivable and is now part of the fabric of Mazeppa's story as opposed to the tragic conclusion of the earlier Turkish verse narratives. A cheerful acceptance that his art can be no more than 'telling old tales' (*Mazeppa*, 200) separates the Modernist appropriation of myth from postmodernist palimpsests and helps us to see a continuity between Byron's narrative techniques and those of Sterne, Joyce, Beckett and Nabokov. For them repetition is comically inescapable yet it yields the fraught possibility of finding a way onward. From Sterne's struggle to make headway with the history of his life we recognise Byron's '– the devil take it! / This story slips for ever through my fingers' (*Beppo*, 498), and Malone's frustrated efforts to write:

> The exercise book had fallen to the ground. I took a long time to find it. It was under the bed. How are such things possible? I took a long time to recover it. I had to harpoon it. It is not pierced through and through, but it is in a bad way. It is a thick exercise book. I hope it will see me out. From now on I shall write on both sides of the page.[23]

Malone's prosaic sense of time (and his tragicomical wish to extend it) are shared by Byron's narratives as well as the way physical obstructions, particularly bodily complications, interpose themselves between the tale and the telling. *Beppo* ends, we are told, because Byron has reached 'the bottom of a page' (689). Canto v of *Don Juan* ends because the muse needs 'a few short naps'. Postmodernist writers flag up the difficulty of telling a tale and take neither subject matter nor readers for granted. The materiality of the text is signalled by a variety of textual devices such as puns, parentheses and quotation of other texts. This is not the post-structuralist dream of everything dissolving into pure text, but an opening up of text to the impurities of life. The modernist text cannot bear very much reality, the postmodernist text talks about bearing the unbearable: 'I can't go on. I'll go on.'[24]

The relationship between historical and literary texts in *Mazeppa* was foregrounded when Byron included extracts from his source in Voltaire's *Histoire de Charles XII* in the advertisement. As *Blackwood's* remarked, the tale was 'well-known'. Like his contemporaries, Byron had to draw his poetic material from somewhere, but to a much greater extent, he fretted over historical accuracy. He was peculiarly concerned with the relationship between his poetry and 'fact': 'There should always be some foundation of fact for the most airy fabric, and pure invention is but the talent of a liar.'[25] Unlike most of his contemporaries, Byron's use of the word 'pure' here withdraws the word's accustomed ethical value. His insistence on the imperative of fact might seem to undercut postmodern *savoir faire* by suggesting a naive faith in the transparency of language. It is rather, I think, responsiveness to minute detail which answers accusations of nihilism levelled at postmodern modes.

Byron's quotations of earlier authorities and 'fact' are a good place to test contradictory views of postmodernist intertextuality. Does the citation of other works which is a familiar motif in postmodern art and architecture imply a recognition that there is nothing more to say or is something else going on? According to Rosalind Krauss, a critical difference between Modernism and postmodernism is that the former legitimates itself through a cult of originality upholding the 'singularity, authenticity, uniqueness' of art while the latter is more open to forms of repetition.[26] Byron's contemporaries believed in originality as the hallmark of genius and they expressed shock (like Sterne's readers) when Byron's literary borrowings were pointed out. 'They call me "Plagiary"', Byron remarked ruefully, 'I think I now, in my time, have been accused of *every* thing'.[27] Following Sterne's delighted apprehension of the way books become part of experience: 'many, I know, quote the book, who have not read it, – and many have read it who understand it not',[28] Byron's intertextuality diminishes the authority of the author by socialising with earlier texts and accepting the vagaries of readerly interpretation.

Although his Years of Fame (1812–15) made him the most famous poet of the day, Byron grew increasingly aware of the limits of authorial power. There were several reasons for this. First, Byron's aristocratic consciousness made him look down on 'inky-fingered' professional authorship. 'One hates an author that's *all author*', he wrote in *Beppo*, they are 'So very anxious, clever, fine, and jealous, / One don't know what to say to them, or think' (*Beppo*, 595). Secondly, for complex legal reasons, several of his works lost the protection of copyright and circulated freely in widely differing shapes and forms accompanied by spoofs and spin-offs pretending to be from the pen of Lord Byron. Byron exhorted Murray and Kinnaird to limit piracies, but the lack of control over all the various transmutations inevitably complicated his sense of the readership. Finally, geographical and political distance from Murray and John Hunt led to delays and mistakes in proof-correction for most of his poems after 1816.

Byron's rage about these accidents was gradually tempered by an acceptance of the haphazard element in authorship. Risk was enfolded within the verse as part of the dynamic of composition, co-existing with a commitment to the value of publication for which he admits, 'There are no rewards'. The question 'why publish?' in *Don Juan* is answered with a series of other questions, 'why do you play at cards? / Why drink? Why read?':

> Besides, my Muse by no means deals in fiction:
> She gathers a repertory of facts,
> Of course with some reserve and slight restriction,
> But mostly sings of human things and acts –
> And that's one cause she meets with contradiction;
> For too much truth, at first sight, ne'er attracts;
> And were her object only what's call'd glory,
> With more ease too she'd tell a different story.
>
> (*Don Juan*, XIV.13)

English *ennui* (which is discussed four stanzas later) is simultaneously courted and held at bay by the *ottava rima* verse. The boredom of the author meets that of his audience and confronts head-on the awkward question of how one continues when everything appears to have been seen and said before. 'One gets tired of everything, my angel', Byron was fond of (mis)quoting from *Les Liaisons Dangereuses*.[29] The last cantos of *Don Juan* present an image of English society as 'a brilliant masquerade' that 'palls'. They are also reminiscent of 'The truth in masquerade' which was Byron's earlier diagnosis of the condition of all art. 'True Truth' (*Don Juan*, XI.37.5) or Truth unmediated by language would lead to silence so appalling it is better to 'play out the play'. An inevitable side-effect of staying with the flotsam and jetsam of experience, however, is that nothing (including the poet) remains intact. By 1821 in *The Vision of Judgment* Byron could envisage an author who was 'really, truly, nobody at all' (*The Vision of Judgment*, 640).[30]

The radical post-structuralist view of authorship explored by Roland Barthes in the late 1960s was that it exists only as a 'function' of the text. Byron's furious outbursts against the 'cutting and slashing' of his work are notable instances of an author's belief in the integrity of his version of the printed page. Despite the commodification of 'Byron' in the nineteenth century, there was a George Gordon (Noel) Byron who set in motion the multiplicity of 'dialogue, parody, contestation' Barthes saw as making up a text.[31] Unexpectedly, perhaps, this author granted his readers considerable freedom in the production of meaning in his work especially after the move to Italy. When Mary Shelley made the fair copy of *Don Juan* Cantos VI and VII, Byron invited her to choose between different couplet endings for a number of stanzas. The published version of the second stanza of Canto VI ends: 'Men with their heads reflect on this and that – / But women with their hearts or heaven knows what!' In the manuscript, this couplet is followed by other variants:

> or
> Man with his head reflects – (as Spurzheim tells)
> But Women with the heart – or something else. –
> or
> Man's pensive part is (now & then) the head
> Woman's the heart – or any thing instead.

All three versions were left standing as equally valid ways of finishing the stanza and in this case Mary Shelley adopted the first one ('what comes uppermost') for her fair copy. As Peter Cochran remarks, Byron was either 'happy with her decisions' or 'fatalistically indifferent'.[32] His silent relinquishments of authorial control are a much more modest way of opening the work to readerly participation than the activities of later artists who display (and sell) the detritus of their studios, notebooks, beds, or those who, like George Oppen, literally build poems out of manuscript layers.[33]

Byron's ambivalent attitude to the power of the readership is evident in his reflexive and complex modes of intertextuality that are significantly different from the practices of his Romantic contemporaries. Writers like Charlotte Smith, William Wordsworth, Samuel Coleridge, John Keats and the Shelleys drew on a sentimental model of allusion in which the borrowed material harmonised with the affective design of the new poem. Byron could do this as well, but he also experimented with a more disruptive mixture of texts from eighteenth-century satire and stage parody, emphasising the plunder of incongruous material and readerly responsibility for the recognition of lost property. Stanza 158, which Murray left out of the first edition of *Don Juan* Canto V, begins 'Thus in the East they are extremely strict, / And *Wedlock* and a *Padlock* mean the same.' Murray may have been uneasy about the intimations of English marriage, especially about the strict Lady Byron. The italics also serve, however, to nudge the reader to Isaac Bickerstaffe's popular two-act farce, *The Padlock* which plays with the wedlock/padlock joke.[34] As well as italics, other marks of punctuation could signal allusions to classical literature or contemporary culture. One of Byron's early couplet parodies advertised the fact that the poem was 'Half stolen, with acknowledgements . . . Stolen parts marked with inverted commas of quotation'.[35] Byron later applied the omnivorous topicality of newspaper satire or performative parody to the more elevated fields of narrative and lyric poetry. Introduced at the beginning of the eighteenth century and popularised by Samuel Richardson's epistolary novels, quotation marks were a relatively new and showy typographic device. Thomas De Quincey disliked them because they tended to 'break the continuity of the passion by reminding the reader of a printed book'.[36] But Byron revelled in their potential for disruptiveness. The vast majority of quotation marks in his poems are present in the first draft and were not inserted (unlike other marks of syntax) in the editorial process. The effects he achieved through signalled quotation, parenthetical aside and direct address to the reader are remarkably close to the ones defined as 'paratextual conventions' by Linda Hutcheon in her discussion of the postmodern novel:

> What postmodern novels . . . do is to focus in a very self-reflexive way on the processes of both the production and the reception of paradoxically fictive historical writing. They raise the issue of how the intertexts of history, its documents or traces, get incorporated into such an avowedly fictional context, while somehow also retaining their historical documentary value.[37]

Many critics have pointed out that Byron's *ottava rima* poetry is, to some extent, 'novelised'. What is often not recognised is the extent to which historical material had been making repeated incursions across the generic boundary of lyric poetry from the beginning of Byron's career. Even in *Childe Harold* Canto III, obsessive self-exploration is interrupted by a digressive pull towards the curious circumstances of composition. Moments of Shelleyan–Wordsworthian vision are interrupted, literally and graphically on the page, as Byron's scribbled manuscript notes perform an historical dialogue with the lyric stanzas, emphasising the marginal, the haphazard and the contingent.

Immediately after the stanza on the ruined fortress of Ehrenbreitstein, Byron turns from the sublime 'height' of 'A tower of victory' to consider local anecdote:

> I was shown a window where [General Marceau] is said to have been standing – observing the progress of the siege by moonlight – when a ball struck immediately below it. – He was killed not long afterwards at Altenkirchen by a rifleman: it is rather singular – that these narrow escapes have in several instances been followed closely by death: – at Nuremberg shortly before the battle of Lutzen Gustavus Adolphus had his horse killed under him – Falconer

> but escaped one Shipwreck to perish by another more successful – The Prince of Orange died by the attempt of a *third* assassin – and Nelson rarely came out of action without a wound till the most fatal & glorious of all – which – instead of a scar – left him immortality.[38]

This note draws attention to the fictive contours of history. Bodily scars are a record of what happened and also a ghostly reminder of what might have happened. The allusions that run across Byron's narratives and lyrics have a similarly disconcerting effect. The possibility of different outcomes and the 'singularity' of the way things do turn out energise Byron's art of digression. Whereas the published version of *Childe Harold's Pilgrimage* relegated observations on local historical curiosity to a substantial section of end notes, the capacious *ottava rima* stanza form of *Don Juan* goes out of its way to include digressive trails of association in the text and notes. In Canto v just after Juan has been sold into slavery, Byron diverts to matters closer to home:

> The other evening ('twas on Friday last) –
> This is a fact and no poetic fable –
> Just as my great coat was about me cast,
> My hat and gloves still lying on the table,
> I heard a shot – 'twas eight o'clock scarce past –
> And running out as fast as I was able,
> I found the military commandant
> Stretch'd in the street, and able scarce to pant.
>
> (*Don Juan*, v.33)

The digression is one of several retellings of this incident for different audiences. The insistence on 'fact' (the time, the date, the particularity of being in the middle of dressing for the evening) is accompanied by an awareness of helpless human involvement in the stream of history:

> The scars of his old wounds were near his new,
> Those honourable scars which brought him fame;
> And horrid was the contrast to the view –
> But let me quit the theme; as such things claim
> Perhaps even more attention than is due
> From me: I gazed (as oft I have gazed the same)
> To try if I could wrench aught out of death
> Which should confirm, or shake, or make a faith.
>
> (*Don Juan*, v.38)

This stanza comprehends the sense of alternative endings: the old scars were survivable, the new wounds not and the contrast is 'horrid' (in its prickly sense) because it is random. The poet questions his own (or any) attempt to invest this randomness with meaning while the stanza gives it a form and wrenches a rhyme out of 'death'. This patterning supplants the orthodox Christian sense of death as a sure return, upholding instead a perilous transitory significance.

In Byron's texts, the ending often happens by accident: Manfred's 'Old man, 'tis not so difficult to die' (*Manfred*, III.iv.151) is a wry acknowledgement of this most arbitrary of processes. As in James Joyce's *Ulysses*, the finality of death in Byron's texts is dispersed by multiplicity. Throughout Dignam's funeral Bloom is distracted by recollections of food, *Hamlet* and *Julius Caesar*, the possibility of sex in graveyards, the different epitaphs on tombstones: 'Eulogy in a country churchyard it ought to be that poem of whose is it Wordsworth or Thomas Campbell'.[39] In the more experimentally fragmented 'Wandering Rocks' episode, larger-scale human tragedy (the *General Slocum* steamship disaster on New York City's East River in 1904) is enfolded in gossipy flow. Narrative drift passes over 'A thousand casualties. And heartrending scenes . . . Not a single lifeboat would float and the firehose all burst . . . And America they say is the land of the free.'[40]

Contemplating the commandant's untidy end in Ravenna, Byron rhymes his way through the same sort of bricolage: stomach; heart; liver; what is life or death; the parable of the centurion's daughter; the Napoleonic wars; butchery; 'But it was all a mystery.' There is no closure – only the continuation of narrative: 'No more; / But let us to the story as before' (*Don Juan*, V.39.7–8).

In this case, Byron interrupted his narrative with history, but *Don Juan* is also full of moments where history is interrupted with narrative. The Siege of Ismail cantos (VII and VIII) present readers with details from Castelnau's *Histoire de la Nouvelle Russie*. As Byron pointed out in his Preface, 'Some of the incidents attributed to Don Juan really occurred, particularly the circumstance of his saving the infant.' The oddity of this episode is that it materialises as a kind of fiction because 'to quote / Too much of one sort would be soporific' (*Don Juan*, VIII.89.5–6).

The rescue of Leila, therefore, becomes as much a sop to the audience as it was in Castelnau's *Histoire*. Byron highlights the literary tendency of historical narrative so that Leila is at once the child who was saved by the late Duc de Richelieu and a figure of our desire for such a rescue (counterbalancing, perhaps, the fate of Leila in *The Giaour*). Her doubleness is signalled in a number of ways. Juan finds her in 'a yet warm group / Of murdered women' (*Don Juan*, VIII.91.2–3), but she is 'chill as they' (*Don Juan*, VIII.95.1). As in the close encounters with death Byron recorded in *Childe Harold's Pilgrimage*, Leila is marked with an alternative history:

and on her face
A slender streak of blood announced how near
Her fate had been to that of all her race;
For the same blow which laid her Mother here,
Had scarred her brow, and left its crimson trace
As the last link with all she had held dear;
But else unhurt, she opened her large eyes,
And gazed on Juan with a wild surprise.
(*Don Juan*, VIII.95.1–8)

The scar 'announces' its significance and invites Byron's readers to revisit the scandalous turn in the plot of *The Corsair* where the 'light but guilty streak' (*The Corsair*, 1594) of blood on Gulnare's brow destroys her femininity and unmans the man she is rescuing. 'But else unhurt' simultaneously contracts and opens Leila's wound ('except for the sword stroke which had killed her mother before her eyes, she was unhurt'). The adverbial clause draws our attention to the way in which we can regard things as 'else' or apart from other things. By placing Leila in a particular grammatical frame she appears 'unhurt'; by selecting this contextual frame, we are able to move on. The last line of the stanza, with its haunting echo of Keats's 'wild surmise' from 'On First Looking into Chapman's Homer', is another hint that this episode is all about different ways of reading. Leila is a little narrative (in Jean-Francois Lyotard's positive sense) standing against the grand narrative of 'Epic poesy'. But Byron unsettles the narrative distance which would have permitted an untroubled consolatory interpretation. As readers we are cast adrift and, like Leila, have to come to terms with our refugee status. 'The episode of the little child . . . would have been extremely touching, had it not been bedevilled by that accursed mockery which the poet will indulge upon every event and every subject', fulminated the *Scots Magazine*. This reviewer's use of the conditional indicates the troubling co-existence of different narrative possibilities at the level of the reading experience.

There was, of course, a political point to the linguistic games of the Siege cantos. In his Preface to Cantos VI, VII and VIII, Byron attacked the way the Tory press had sentimentalised the suicide of Castlereagh:

> if a poor radical . . . had cut his throat, he would have been buried in a cross-road, with the usual appurtenances of the stake and mallet. But the Minister . . . merely cut the 'carotid artery' (blessings on their learning). and lo! the Pageant, and the Abbey! and the 'Syllables of Dolour yelled forth' by the Newspapers.[41]

The newspapers' scrupulously evasive pathology is interrogated by Byron's pincer-like inverted commas while Shakespearean allusion (with which newspapers were always keen to bolster patriotism) turns into an accusation of national perjury. The same newspapers had been less sentimental about the death of Shelley, nastily trying to impugn his atheism by suggesting that he had turned to God *in extremis*. Byron wrote back furiously to England, 'That * * * Galignani has about ten lies in one paragraph. It was not a Bible that was found in Shelley's pocket, but John Keats's poems.'[42] In the cantos Byron worked on 'to occupy [his] mind' in the weeks after Shelley's drowning, he indicts 'the joys of reading a Gazette' (VIII.125.1), flaunting 'Truths that you will not read in the Gazettes' (IX.10.3).[43] Readers have to co-produce the siege without the security of the Western discourses of Truth located in the established church and the national newspapers. The poem's zigzag turns disorientate us as the old Khan's suicide summons English truisms which jar (as soon as we recognise them) against a different cultural integrity:

> The soldiers, who beheld him drop his point,
>   Stopped as if once more willing to concede
> Quarter, in case he bade them not 'aroint!'
>   As he before had done. He did not heed
> Their pause nor signs: his heart was out of joint,
>   And shook (till now unshaken) like a reed,
> As he looked down upon his children gone,
> And felt – though done with life – he was alone.
>
> (*Don Juan*, VIII.117)

Through a defamiliarised literary texture, the *ottava rima* challenges us to relate this death to the canons of English tragedy. As the awkward Shakespearean 'aroint' fractures the line, the Khan's spirit breaks. He cannot read the Russian 'signs', as the soldiers struggle to read him through 'their blood-shot eyes, all red with strife' (*Don Juan*, VIII.119.7). *Macbeth*, *Lear* and *Hamlet* all jostle for attention as the poem juxtaposes different courses of action ('as if'; 'as he had done') and delicately renews the cliché 'to shake like a reed'. The poem does not attempt to turn a Muslim retrospectively into an English hero, but 'stops' before different set of values and insists, gently, that the reader should respect this distance. The ultimate moment of strangeness comes as the Khan fades out of the text taking a dim view of Keats: 'And throwing back a dim look on his sons, / In one wide wound poured forth his soul at once' (*Don Juan*, VIII.118.7–8). Readerly recognition of the 'Ode to a Nightingale' ('While thou art pouring forth thy soul') at this point would affirm a small endangered community of poets against the coarser crowd of military dispatch writers and newspaper hacks.

Here, I would argue, lies the difference between Byron's postmodernism and the mixture of trash and high art evident in other varieties of late twentieth- and twenty-first-century postmodern culture. Byron's world of things is inextricably bound up with the work of art and with questions of readerly and writerly responsibility towards those things. *Don Juan* dances along an ever-varying line, but it has its pools of commitment. Byron's fierce defence of Shelley is one and Juan's simple pledge to Leila is another – beautifully crystallised in the rhyme of fourteen syllables which brings Canto VIII to a close: 'And Juan wept, / And made a vow to shield her, which he kept' (*Don Juan*, VIII.141.7–8).

Byron's contemporary readers felt that by mingling sentiment and satire, his texts undermined the possibility of sincerity altogether. But the effect of his poetry is more complex than this as it invites its readers to invest imaginative energy in different and sometimes contradictory directions. In the letter of the Marquise de Merteuil which Byron knew from *Les Liaisons Dangereuses*, the potential of design is treated with disarming negligence:

> I have nothing more to say, but to tell you a trifling story; perhaps you will not have leisure to read it, or to give so much attention to it as to understand it properly? At worst, it will be only a tale thrown away.[44]

This sentiment is invoked in Byron's beguiling aside on the probable fate of what he 'meant to say' in *Don Juan* – 'Certes it would have been but thrown away' (*Don Juan*, IX.36.6). It epitomises the mixture of free-play and artfulness which characterises Byron's postmodernism. As Frank Kermode reminds us, 'without routine, without inherited structures, carnival loses its point; without social totalities there are no anti-social fragments'.[45] The patterns of English and Italian verse provide a structure which both energises and throws into relief the most sociable fragments in English Romanticism.

I have been arguing that Byron's intertextuality is inseparable from what we might call his postmodernism because it knowingly takes a risk on the reader to make or mar its effect. No one was more aware than Byron of the way that events could change the impact of a literary work and no one made a more conscious effort to inject biographical and historical detail into the realm of the aesthetic. Putting to one side his scepticism about the relationship between poet and reader, Byron went on writing poetry after his departure for Greece. There, he confided to Lady Blessington, he hoped that successful events would 'give a totally different reading to my thoughts, words, deeds'.[46] In his well-known 'On This Day I Complete My Thirty-Sixth Year', he returned to a favourite borrowing from *Macbeth* ('My days are in the yellow leaf', 5) and dallied for the last time with the image of a slumbering audience ('Awake! (*not* Greece – She *is* awake!'), 25). Irony at the expense of Romantic philhellenism did not, however, corrode the possibility of political commitment. In Byron's last known poem, usually called 'Last Words on Greece', he added to his wide range of poetic and dramatic allusions and the material he recuperated from newspapers a curious instance of self-quotation:

> What are to me those honours or renown
> Past or to come, a new-born people's cry
> Albeit for such I could despise a crown
> Of aught save Laurel, or for such could die;
> I am the fool of passion — and a frown
> Of thine to me is as an Adder's eye
> To the poor bird whose pinion fluttering down
> Wafts unto death the breast it bore so high ——
> Such is this maddening fascination grown –
> So strong thy Magic — or so weak am I.

The poem was addressed to the Greek boy, Loukas Chalandritsanos, who did not love Byron in return. In all the anguish of hopeless infatuation, Byron's poem keeps in mind the possibility of other readers 'Past or to come' and keeps an open mind about the ongoing political cause ('or for such could die'). The a b a b rhyme relentlessly exposes the unanswered nature of Byron's desire and the pathetic image of a bird helpless before a snake threatens a collapse into self-pity before the wry alternative perspective of the last line. Woeful lovers are archetypal stage characters and Byron holds this tendency to self-dramatisation at bay by turning to actual performance. Embedded in the heart of the verse is a quotation from Byron's late tragedy *Werner; or, the Inheritance* (1822).'I am the fool of passion' echoes a speech by Gabor, a blunt world-weary soldier, who rebukes himself for his faith in the treacherous young Ulric ('– you have vanquish'd me. / I was the fool of passion to conceive that I could cope with you' (II.i.304–6)).[47] The quotation of *Werner* is unsignalled and may be unconscious, but through a memory of this exchange, Byron rewrites his place in history as a marginal character in Loukas's eyes. With a simple shift of tense, Byron turns a dramatic *cri de coeur* into a self-deprecating summary of his new role. It is, however, consistent with his attitude to writing that a single disinterested reader has the power to sideline the most famous poet of the day. Like the Greek helmets Byron had made for his expedition, the allusion helps us to see the value of knowingly playing a role in a desperate situation. Byron was playing at being a soldier while striving to be one and his invocation of an earlier voice of experience reveals the quickening force of intertextual repetition which is not the 'blank' recycling of a spent art form, but an urgent encounter between poet and reader and what they might share in an increasingly alienating world.

NOTES

1. Bernard Beatty describes *Mazeppa* as a 'transition point' between the two halves of Byron's verse. See 'Continuities and Discontinuities of Language and Voice' in Andrew Rutherford (ed.), *Byron: Augustan and Romantic* (London: Macmillan in association with the British Council, 1990), pp. 117–35 (p. 131).
2. Samuel Taylor Coleridge, *Biographia Literaria*, ed. James Engell and W. Jackson Bate, 2 vols. (Princeton University Press, 1983), II, 7.
3. Donald H. Reiman (ed.), *The Romantics Reviewed: Contemporary Reviews of British Romantic Writers: Part B*, 5 vols. (New York and London: Garland, 1972), IV, 1797.
4. *Ibid.*, IV, 1403; I, 139.
5. Ihab Hassan, *The Postmodern Turn: Essays in Postmodern Theory and Culture* (Columbus: Ohio State University Press, 1987), p. xvi.
6. *BLJ*, x, 150.
7. P. B. Shelley, *The Complete Works*, ed. Roger Ingpen and Walter E. Peck, 10 vols. (London: Ernest Benn; New York: Gordian Press, 1965), x, 12.
8. 'An Italian Carnival', *CMP*, 191.
9. *CMP*, 192.
10. Reiman (ed.), *Romantics Reviewed*, *B*, v, 1399.
11. Shelley, *Complete Works*, VII, 37.
12. William Hazlitt, *The Complete Works*, ed. P. P. Howe, 21 vols. (London: J. M. Dent, 1930–4), x, 258.
13. Italo Calvino, 'Cybernetics and Ghosts', in Malcolm Bradbury (ed.), *The Novel Today: Contemporary Writers in Modern Fiction* (London: Fontana, 1977; repr. 1990), pp. 223–41; p. 235.
14. *CMP*, 192.
15. Shelley, *Julian and Maddalo: A Conversation*, III 240–1.
16. Shelley, *Complete Works*, x, 265–6.
17. *CMP*, 146–57.
18. Jonathan Bate, *The Romantics on Shakespeare* (Harmondsworth: Penguin, 1992), p. 349.
19. *CMP*, 117.
20. J. Drummond Bone, 'Romantic Irony Revisited' in *Byron: East and West*, ed. Martin Procházka (Prague: Charles University Press, 2000), pp. 237–47.
21. See Anne Barton, 'Byron and the Mythology of Fact', Nottingham Byron Foundation Lecture (University of Nottingham, 1968), p. 5.
22. See Alice Jardine, *Gynesis: Configurations of Woman and Modernity* (Ithaca and London: Cornell University Press, 1985), p. 73.
23. Samuel Beckett, *The Beckett Trilogy: Molloy, Malone Dies, The Unnamable* (London: Picador, 1979), p. 192.
24. *The Unnamable*, p. 382.
25. *BLJ*, v, 203 (to Murray 2 April 1817). See also Barton, 'Byron and the Mythology of Face', pp. 4–11.

26. Rosalind E. Krauss, *The Originality of the Avant-Garde and Other Modernist Myths* (Cambridge, MIT Press, 1985; repr. 1997), p. 161; discussed in M. Steven Connor, *Postmodernist Culture: An Introduction to Theories of the Contemporary*, 2nd edn (Oxford: Blackwell, 1997), pp. 101–2.
27. *BLJ*, VIII, 166.
28. Laurence Sterne, *The Life and Opinions of Tristram Shandy, Gentleman*, ed. Graham Petrie (Harmondsworth: Penguin, 1967; repr. 1986), p. 107.
29. *BLJ*, III, 220.
30. See Wolfson, '*The Vision of Judgment* and the Visions of "Author"', this volume, p. 171.
31. See Roland Barthes, 'The Death of the Author' in *Image. Music. Text*, trans. Stephen Heath (London: Fontana, 1977; repr.1990), pp. 142–8.
32. Peter Cochran, 'Mary Shelley's Fair Copying of *Don Juan*', *The Keats-Shelley Review*, 10 (1996), 221–41: 237.
33. See Michael Davidson, 'Palimtexts: Postmodern Poetry and the Material Text', in *Postmodern Genres*, ed. Marjorie Perloff (Norman: University of Oklahoma Press, 1988; repr. New York: Keats–Shelley Association of America, 1995), pp. 75–95.
34. *The Padlock* is included in Elizabeth Inchbald's (1808) *Collection of Farces and Afterpieces* which appears in the 1816 Sale Catalogue of Byron's Library.
35. *CPW*, III, 32.
36. Thomas De Quincey, *Recollections of the Lakes and the Lake Poets*, ed. David Wright (Harmondsworth: Penguin, 1970; repr.1985), p. 38.
37. Linda Hutcheon, *The Politics of Postmodernism* (London: Routledge, 1989; repr. 1993), p. 82.
38. [Byron], *Childe Harold's Pilgrimage Canto III. A Facsimile of the Autograph Fair Copy*, ed. T. A. J. Burnett (New York and London: Garland, 1988), pp. 106–11.
39. James Joyce, *Ulysses*, ed. Hans Walter Gabler, with Wolfhard Steppe and Claus Melchior (Harmondsworth: Penguin Books, in association with The Bodley Head, 1986), p. 93.
40. *Ibid.*, pp. 196–7.
41. *CPW*, V, 296.
42. *BLJ*, IX, 198.
43. *BLJ*, IX, 187.
44. Choderlos de Laclos, *Dangerous Connections; or, Letters Collected in a Society, and Published for the Instruction of other Societies*, by M. C***** de L***, 4 vols. (T. Hookham, 1784), IV, 101.
45. Frank Kermode, *History and Value* (Oxford: Clarendon Press, 1988), p. 143.
46. Lady Blessington's *Conversations of Lord Byron* (London, 1834), p. 227.
47. The phrase 'fool of passion' may have been drawn from the eighteenth-century tragedy, *Athelstan*, by John Brown. It was produced in 1766 and was almost certainly in the Drury Lane Theatre Library when Byron was involved in the theatre management subcommittee. Brown's earlier play *Barbarossa* (1765) was included in Elizabeth Inchbald's 1808 collection of *British Theatre* which appears in the 1816 Sale Catalogue of Byron's library.

SELECT BIBLIOGRAPHY

The following bibliography is a compilation of selected material referenced in the previous chapters. References that are relevant but not cited in the text may be found in Further Reading.

Adorno, Theodor, *Notes to Literature*. ed. Rolf Tiedemann, trans. Shierry Weber Nicholsen, 2 vols. (New York: Columbia University Press, 1991)

Barton, Anne, '"A Light to Lesson Ages": Byron's Political Plays', in *Byron: A Symposium*, ed. John D. Jump (London: Macmillan, 1975)

Barton, Anne, 'Byron and the Mythology of Fact', Notingham Byron Foundation Lecture, University of Nottingham, 1968

Bate, Jonathan, *The Romantics on Shakespeare* (Harmondsworth: Penguin, 1992)

Beaton, Roderick, 'Romanticism in Greece', in *Romanticism in National Context*, ed. Roy Porter and Mikulas Teich (Cambridge University Press, 1988)

Beatty, Bernard, 'Continuities and Discontinuities of Language and Voice', in *Byron: Augustan and Romantic*, ed. Andrew Rutherford (London: Macmillan in association with the British Council, 1990)

Beaty, Frederick, *Byron the Satirist* (DeKalb, Ill.: Northern Illinois University Press, 1985)

Beckett, Samuel, *The Beckett Trilogy: Molloy, Malone Dies, The Unnamable* (London: Picador, 1979)

Bernal, Martin, *Black Athena: The Afroasiatic Roots of Classical Civilisation*, 2 vols. (London: Free Association Books, 1987)

Blessington, Lady, *Conversations of Lord Byron with the Countess of Blessington* (London, 1834)

Bluemantle, Bridget (Elizabeth Thomas), *The Baron of Falconberg; or, Childe Harolde in Prose*, 3 vols. (London: A. K. Newman, 1815)

Bone, Drummond, *Byron* (Tavistock: Northcote House, 2000)

Bone, J. Drummond, 'Romantic Irony Revisited', in *Byron: East and West*, ed. Martin Procházka (Prague: Charles University Press, 2000)

Bostetter, Edward E., *The Romantic Ventriloquists: Wordsworth, Coleridge, Keats, Shelley, Byron* (Seattle: University of Washington Press, 1975)

Brisman, Leslie, *Romantic Origins* (Ithaca: Cornell University Press, 1978)

Broughton, Lord (John Cam Hobhouse), *A Journey Through Albania and Other Provinces of Turkey in Europe and Asia to Constantinople* (London: J. Cawthorn, 1813)

Buchwalter, Donald E., Letter to the Editor, *Star Tribune* (Sunday, 3 August 1997)

Burrough, Catherine B., *Closet Stages: Joanna Baillie and the Theater Theory of British Romantic Women Writers* (Philadelphia: University of Pennsylvania Press, 1997)

Butler, Marilyn, 'Byron and the Empire in the East', in *Byron: Augustan and Romantic*, ed. Andrew Rutherford (Basingstoke: Macmillan, 1990), 63–81

[Byron], *Childe Harold's Pilgrimage Canto III. A Facsimile of the Autograph Fair Copy*, ed. T. A. J. Burnett (New York and London: Garland, 1988)

Byron's Letters and Journals, ed. Leslie A. Marchand, 13 vols. (London: John Murray, 1973–94)

Calvino, Italo, 'Cybernetics and Ghosts', in *The Novel Today: Contemporary Writers in Modern Fiction*, ed. Malcolm Bradbury (London: Fontana, 1977; rpr. 1990)

Camus, Albert, *Carnets 1942–51*, trans. P. Thody, 2 vols. (London: Hamilton, 1966)

Carlson, Julie A., *In the Theatre of Romanticism: Coleridge, Nationalism, Women* (Cambridge University Press, 1994)

Christensen, Jerome, *Lord Byron's Strength: Romantic Writing and Commercial Society* (Baltimore and London: Johns Hopkins University Press, 1993)

Clarke, E. D., *Travels in Various Countries of Europe, Asia and Africa*, 4 vols. (1810–19; 2nd edn, 1811–23)

Clifford, James, 'On Ethnographic Allegory', in *Writing Culture: The Poetics and Politics of Ethnography*, ed. James Clifford and George E. Marcus (Berkeley, Los Angeles and London: University of California Press, 1986)

Cochran, Peter, 'Nature's Gentler Errors', *The Byron Journal*, 23 (1995), 22–35

Cochran, Peter, 'Mary Shelley's Fair Copying of Don Juan', *The Keats-Shelley Review*, 10 (1996), 221–41

Cochran, Peter, 'Byron in the Weird World of 1999', *The Byron Journal*, 28 (2000), 49–55

Coleridge, Samuel Taylor, *Biographia Literaria*, ed. James Engell and W. Jackson Bate, 2 vols. (Princeton University Press, 1983)

Colley, Linda, *Britons: Forging the Nation, 1707–1837* (New Haven, Conn.: Yale University Press, 1992)

Corbett, Martyn, *Byron and Tragedy* (Basingstoke: Macmillan, 1988)

Corbett, Martyn, 'Lugging Byron out of the Library', *Studies in Romanticism*, 31 (1992)

Crompton, Lewis, *Byron and Greek Love: Homophobia in 19th-Century England* (London: Faber & Faber, 1985; Berkeley: University of California Press, 1995)

Dakin, Douglas, *The Greek Struggle for Independence* (London: B. T. Batsford, 1973)

Dallas, R. C., *Recollections of the Life of Lord Byron, from the Year 1808 to the end of 1814* (London, 1824)

Davidoff, Leonore and Catherine Hall, *Family Fortunes: Men and Women of the English Middle Class, 1780–1850* (University of Chicago Press, 1987)

Davidson, Michael, 'Palimtexts: Postmodern Poetry and the Material Text', in *Postmodern Genres*, ed. Marjorie Perloff (Norman: University of Oklahoma Press, 1988; repr. 1995)

Dolan, Brian, *Exploring European Frontiers: British Travellers in the Age of Enlightenment* (London: Macmillan, 2000)

Eisler, Benita, *Byron: Child of Passion, Fool of Fame* (New York: Knopf, 1999)
Elam, Diane, *Romancing the Postmodern* (London: Routledge, 1992)
Elfenbein, Andrew, *Byron and the Victorians* (Cambridge University Press, 1995)
Elfenbein, Andrew, *Romantic Genius: The Prehistory of a Homosexual Role* (New York: Columbia University Press, 1999)
Elwin, Malcolm, *Lord Byron's Wife* (London: McDonald, 1962)
Erdman, David V., 'Byron's Stage Fright: The History of His Ambition and Fear of Writing for the Stage', *ELH*, 6 (1939), 219–43
Erickson, Carolly, *Our Tempestuous Day: A History of Regency England* (New York: William Morrow, 1986)
Estève, Edmond, *Byron et le Romantisme français* (Paris: Librairie Hachette et Cie, 1907)
Eton, William, *A Survey of the Turkish Empire, in which are considered 1. Its Government, 2. The State of the Provinces, 3. The Causes of the Decline of Turkey, 4. The British Commerce with Turkey and the Necessity of Abolishing the Levant Company* (London: Cadell & Davies, 1798)
Franklin, Caroline, *Byron's Heroines* (Oxford: Clarendon Press, 1992)
Franklin, Caroline, '"Some samples of the finest Orientalism": Byronic Philhellenism and Proto-Zionism at the Time of the Congress of Vienna', in *Romanticism and Colonialism: Writing and Empire, 1780–1830*, ed. Tim Fulford and Peter J. Kitson (Cambridge University Press, 1998), 221–42
Franklin, Caroline, 'Prelude: Byron's Gothic Inheritance', in *Byron: A Literary Life* (Basingstoke and New York: Macmillan and St Martin's Press, 2000)
Franklin, Caroline, *Byron: A Literary Life* (Basingstoke and New York: Macmillan and St Martin's Press, 2000)
Fussell, Paul, *The Rhetorical World of Augustan Humanism: Ethics and Imagery from Swift to Burke* (Oxford: Clarendon Press, 1965)
Galt, John, *The Life of Lord Byron* (London, 1830)
Gamba, Count Peter, *A Narrative of Lord Byron's Last Journey to Greece* (1825)
Gaull, Marilyn, *English Romanticism: The Human Context* (New York: Norton, 1988)
Goethes Briefe, ed. Bodo Morawe (Hamburg, 1965)
Goode, Jr, Clement Tyson, 'A Critical Review of Research', in *George Gordon, Lord Byron: A Comprehensive Bibliography of Secondary Materials in English, 1809–1979*, ed. Oscar Jose Santucho (Metuchen, N.J.: Scarecrow Press, 1977)
Graham, Peter W., *Lord Byron* (New York: Twayne; London: Prentice Hall, 1998)
Grimes, Kyle, 'William Hone, John Murray, and the Uses of Byron', in *Romanticism, Radicalism, and the Press*, ed. Stephen C. Behrendt (Detroit: Wayne State University Press, 1997)
Grosskurth, Phyllis, *Byron: The Flawed Angel* (Boston and New York: Houghton Mifflin, 1997)
Guiccioli, Countess Teresa, *My Recollections of Lord Byron and Those of Eye-Witnesses of His Life* (New York: Harper & Brothers, 1869)
Guillemin, Henri, *Lamartine, Byron et Mme Guiccioli, Revue de Littérature Comparée*, 19 (1939)
Hassan, Ihab, *The Postmodern Turn: Essays in Postmodern Theory and Culture* (Columbus: Ohio State University Press, 1987)

Hazlitt, William, *The Complete Works*, ed. P. P. Howe, 21 vols. (London: J. M. Dent, 1930–4)
Heine, Heinrich, *Werke*, ed. F. H. Eisner, 27 vols. (Berlin: Akademic-Verlag, 1970–76)
His Very Self and Voice: Collected Conversations of Lord Byron, ed. Ernest J. Lovell Jnr (New York: Macmillan, 1954)
Hobhouse, John Cam, *Byron's Bulldog: The Letters of John Cam Hobhouse to Lord Byron*, ed. Peter W. Graham (Columbus: Ohio State University, 1984)
Hobhouse, John Cam, *A Journey through Albania, and other Provinces of Turkey in Europe and Asia, to Constantinople, during the years 1809 and 1810* (2nd edn, London: James Cawthorn, 1813)
Hoffmeister, Gerhard, *Byron und der europäische Byronismus* (Darmstadt: Wissenschaftliche Buchgesellschaft, 1983)
Holmes, Richard, *Footsteps: Explorations of a Romantic Biographer* (New York: Pantheon, 2000)
Howell, Margaret, *Byron Tonight: A Poet's Plays on the Nineteenth Century Stage* (Windlesham: Springwood Books, 1982)
Hunt, Leigh, *Lord Byron and Some of His Contemporaries* (London, 1828)
Hutcheon, Linda, *The Politics of Postmodernism* (London: Routledge, 1989; repr. 1993)
Ingersoll, Earl, 'Byron's *Don Juan* and the Postmodern', *Forum for Modern Language Studies*, 33 (1997), 302–14
Jardine, Alice, *Gynesis: Configurations of Woman and Modernity*, quoted in Steven Connor, *Postmodernist Culture: An Introduction to Theories of the Contemporary*, 2nd edn (Oxford: Blackwell, 1997)
Kelsall, Malcolm, *Byron's Politics* (Brighton: Harvester Press, 1988)
Kermode, Frank, *The Sense of an Ending* (Oxford University Press, 1969)
Kermode, Frank, *History and Value* (Oxford: Clarendon Press, 1988)
Knight, G. Wilson, 'Lord Byron's Wife', *Times Literary Supplement* (1962)
Knight, G. Wilson, *Byron and Shakespeare* (London: Routledge; New York: Barnes & Noble, 1966)
Knox, Vicesimus, *Personal Nobility, Or, Letters to a Nobleman on the Conduct of his Studies, and the Dignity of the Peerage* (1793); Facsimile edn (New York: Garland, 1970)
Kosofsky Sedgwick, Eve, *Tendencies* (Durham, N. C.: Duke University Press, 1993)
Krauss, Rosalind E., *The Originality of the Avant-Garde and Other Modernist Myths* (Cambridge, Mass., MIT Press, 1985; repr. 1997)
Laclos, Choderlos de, *Dangerous Connections; or, Letters Collected in a Society, and Published for the Instruction of other Societies*, by M. C***** de L***, 4 vols. (T. Hookham, 1784)
Lamartine, Alphonse de, *L'Homme – à Lord Byron*, from *Méditations Poétiques* (Paris: Au dépôt de la librairie grecque-latine-allemande, 3rd edn, 1820)
Langford, Paul, 'Politics and Manners from Sir Robert Walpole to Sir Robert Peel', *Proceedings of the British Academy*, 94 (1996), 103–25
Langford, Paul, *Englishness Identified: Manners and Character, 1650–1850* (Oxford University Press, 2000)
Lednicki, Waclaw, *Bits of Table Talk on Pushkin, Mickiewicz, Goethe, Turgenev and Sinckiewicz* (The Hague: M. Nijhoff, 1956)

Lord Byron: The Complete Miscellaneous Prose, ed. Andrew Nicholson (Oxford: Clarendon Press, 1991)
Lord Byron: The Complete Poetical Works, ed. Jerome J. McGann, 7 vols. (Oxford: Clarendon Press, 1980–93)
Lovelace, Ralph, Earl of, *Astarte* (1905 – privately printed, rev. edn. 1921, ed. by his wife)
Luke, Hugh J., 'The Publishing of Byron's *Don Juan*', *PMLA*, 80 (1965)
MacCarthy, Fiona, *Byron: Life and Legend* (London: John Murray, 2002)
McGann, Jerome, *Fiery Dust: Byron's Poetic Development* (Chicago University Press, 1968)
McGann, Jerome J., *The Beauty of Inflections* (Oxford: Clarendon, 1985)
McGann, Jerome, 'Byron and Wordsworth', in *Byron and Romanticism*, ed. James Soderholm (Cambridge University Press, 2002), 173–204
Makdisi, Saree, *Romantic Imperialism: Universal Empire and the Culture of Modernity* (Cambridge University Press, 1998)
Manning, Peter J., 'The Nameless Broken Dandy and the Structure of Authorship', in *Reading Romantics* (New York: Oxford University Press, 1990)
Marchand, Leslie, *Byron: A Biography*, 3 vols. (New York: Knopf, 1957)
Martin, Philip W., *Byron: A Poet Before His Public* (Cambridge University Press, 1982)
Maurois, André, *Byron*, trans. Hamish Miles (New York: D. Appleton, 1930)
Mayne, Ethel Colburn, *Byron*, 2 vols. (New York: Scribner's Sons, 1912)
Mayne, Ethel Colburn, *The Life and Letters of Anne Isabella, Lady Byron* (New York: Scribner, 1929)
Medwin's Conversations of Lord Byron, ed. Ernest J. Lovell, Jr (Princeton University Press, 1966)
Medwin, Thomas, *Conversations of Lord Byron: Noted During a Residence with His Lordship at Pisa, in the Years 1821 and 1822* (London: Henry Colburn, 1824)
Mickiewicz, Adam, *Pan Tadeusz*, Book II, trans. George Rapall Noyes (London and Toronto: J. M. Dent & Sons, 1917)
Millingen, Julius, *Memoirs of the Affairs of Greece* (London: John Rodwell, 1831)
Mills, Raymond, 'The Last Illness of Lord Byron', *The Byron Journal*, 28 (2000)
Moody, Jane, *Illegitimate Theatre in London, 1770–1840* (Cambridge University Press, 2000)
Moore, Doris Langley, *The Late Lord Byron: Posthumous Dramas* (1961; Philadelphia and New York: J. B. Lippincott, 1977)
Moore, Thomas, *Letters and Journals of Lord Byron with Notices of His Life*, 2 vols. (London: John Murray, 1830; repr. 1932)
Moore, Thomas, *Life, Letters, and Journals of Lord Byron* (London: John Murray, 1892)
More, Hannah, *Coelebs in Search of a Wife Comprehending Observations on Domestic Habits, and Manners, Religion, and Morals*, 2 vols. (London: Cadell & Davies, 1809)
Morris, Edmund, *Dutch: A Memoir of Ronald Reagan* (New York: Random House, 1999)
Nathan, Isaac, *Fugitive Pieces and Reminiscences of Lord Byron: containing an entire new edition of the Hebrew Melodies, with the addition of several never before*

published . . . Also some original poetry, letters and recollections of Lady Caroline Lamb (London: Whittaker, Treacher & Co., 1829)

Newey, Vincent, 'Authoring the Self: *Childe Harold* III and IV', in *Centring the Self: Subjectivity, Society and Reading from Thomas Gray to Thomas Hardy* (Aldershot: Scholar, 1995), 178–210

O'Neill, Michael, '"A Being More Intense": Byron', in *Romanticism and the Self Conscious Poem* (Oxford: Clarendon Press, 1997), pp. 93–118

Origo, Iris, *The Last Attachment: The Story of Byron and Teresa Guiccioli as Told in Their Unpublished Letters and Other Family Papers* (London: Jonathan Cape, 1949)

Parry, William, *The Last Days of Lord Byron* (London, 1825)

Poovey, Mary, *Uneven Developments: The Ideological Work of Gender in Mid-Victorian England* (University of Chicago Press, 1988)

Porta, Antonio. *Byronismo Italiano* (Milan, 1923)

Protopsaltos, E. G., 'Byron and Greece', in *Byron's Political and Cultural Influence in Nineteenth-Century Europe: A Symposium*, ed. P. Graham Trueblood (London: Macmillan, 1981)

Pushkin, Alexander, *The Letters of Alexander Pushkin*, trans. J. Thomas Shaw (Bloomington: Indiana University Press; London: Oxford University Press, 1963)

Pushkin, Alexander, *Eugene Onegin*, trans. Charles Johnston (London, 1977)

Pushkin, Alexander, *Eugene Onegin*, trans. and ed. Vladimir Nabokov (Princeton University Press, 1975)

Quincey, Thomas De, *Recollections of the Lakes and the Lake Poets*, ed. David Wright (Harmondsworth: Penguin, 1970; repr. 1985)

Quinlan, Maurice J., *Victorian Prelude: A History of English Manners, 1700–1830* (1941; rpr. Hamden: Archon, 1965)

Reiman, Donald H. (ed.), *The Romantics Reviewed: Contemporary Reviews of British Romantic Writers: Part B*, 5 vols. (New York and London: Garland Publishing, 1972), pp. 2048–57

Richardson, Alan, *A Mental Theater: Poetic Drama and Consciousness in the Romantic Age* (University Park: Pennsylvania State University Press, 1988)

Robinson, C. E., *Lord Byron and Some of His Contemporaries* (University of Delaware Press, 1982)

Rutherford, Andrew (ed.), *Byron: The Critical Heritage* (London: Routledge, 1970; New York: Barnes and Noble, 1970)

Said, Edward, *Orientalism* (London: Routledge and Kegan Paul, 1978)

Shelley, P. B., *The Complete Works*, ed. Roger Ingpen and Walter E. Peck, 10 vols. (London: Ernest Benn, 1965)

Smiles, Samuel, *A Publisher and his Friends: Memoir and Correspondence of the Late John Murray, 1768–1843*, 2 vols. (London, 1891)

Soderholm, James, *Fantasy, Forgery, and the Byron Legend* (Lexington: University Press of Kentucky, 1996)

Southey, Robert, *The Poetic Works of Robert Southey, Collected by Himself*, 10 vols. (London: Longman & c., 1838)

Stabler, Jane, *Burke to Byron, Barbauld to Baillie, 1790–1830* (Basingstoke: Palgrave, 2002)

Stabler, Jane, *Byron, Poetics and History* (Cambridge and New York: Cambridge University Press, 2002)

St Clair, William, *That Greece Might Still Be Free: The Philhellenes in the War of Independence* (London, New York and Toronto: Oxford University Press, 1972)

St Clair, William, 'The Impact of Byron's Writings: An Evaluative Approach', in *Byron: Augustan and Romantic*, ed. Andrew Rutherford (London: Macmillan, 1990)

St Clair, William, *Lord Elgin and the Marbles: The Controversial History of the Parthenon Sculptures*, 3rd rev. edn (Oxford University Press, 1998)

Sterne, Laurence, *The Life and Opinions of Tristram Shandy, Gentleman*, ed. Graham Petrie (Harmondsworth: Penguin, 1967; repr. 1986)

Stowe, Harriet Beecher, *Lady Byron Vindicated* (1870)

Thornton, Thomas, *The Present State of Turkey; or a description of the political, civil, and religious, constitution, government and laws of the Ottoman Empire* (1807), 2 vols., 2nd edn, corrected with additions (London, 1809)

Thorslev, Peter L., *The Byronic Hero: Types and Prototypes* (Minneapolis: University of Minnesota Press, 1962)

Trelawney, Edward John, *Records of Shelley, Byron, and the Author* [First published in 1858 as *Recollections of Shelley and Byron*] (New York: New York Review of Books, 2000)

Watkins, Daniel, *A Materialist Critique of English Romantic Drama* (Gainesville: University Press of Florida, 1993)

Wolfson, Susan J., '"A Problem Few Dare Imitate": *Sardanapalus* and "Effeminate Character"', *ELH*, 58 (1991), 867–902

FURTHER READING

Material which is especially relevant to individual chapters is cited with chapter numbers in brackets.

Journals

The Byron Journal (London: The Byron Society, 1973–)
Keats-Shelley Journal (New York: Keats–Shelley Association of America, 1952–)
Romanticism (Edinburgh: Edinburgh University Press, 1995–)
Studies in Romanticism (Boston, Mass.: Boston University, 1961–)

Biography

Altick, Richard D., *Lives and Letters: A History of Literary Biography in England and America* (New York: Alfred A. Knopf, 1965) [Ch. 1]

Eisler, Benita, *Byron: Child of Passion, Fool of Fame* (London: Hamish Hamilton, 1999)

Grosskurth, Phyllis, *Byron: The Flawed Angel* (London: Hodder & Stoughton, 1997)

MacCarthy, Fiona, *Byron: Life and Legend* (London: John Murray, 2002)

Marchand, Leslie A., *Byron: A Biography*, 3 vols. (New York Belknap Press: Harvard UP, 1957)

Critical Studies

Almeida, Hermione de, *Byron and Joyce Through Homer:* Don Juan *and* Ulysses (London: Macmillan, 1981)

Barton, Anne, 'Byron and the Mythology of Fact', Nottingham Byron Foundation Lecture (University of Nottingham, 1968)

Barton, Anne, *Don Juan* (Cambridge University Press, 1992)

Beatty, Bernard, *Byron's Don Juan* (Totowa, N.J.: Barnes & Noble Books, 1985)

Beatty, Bernard and Vincent Newey (eds.), *Byron and the Limits of Fiction* (Liverpool University Press, 1988)

Beaty, Frederick, *Byron the Satirist* (DeKalb: Northern Illinois University Press, 1985)

Black, Jeremy, *The British Abroad: The Grand Tour in the 18th Century* (Gloucestershire: Sutton Publishing Ltd, 1992) [Ch. 6]

Bone, J. Drummond, 'A Sense of Endings: Some Romantic and Postmodern Comparisons', in *Romanticism and Postmodernism*, ed. Edward Larrissy (Cambridge University Press, 1999) [Ch. 16]

Bone, Drummond, *Byron* (Tavistock: Northcote House, 2000)

Borst, William A., *Lord Byron's First Pilgrimage* (New Haven, Conn.: Yale University Press, 1948)

Briscoe, Walter A., *Byron the Poet* (New York: Haskell House, 1967)

Bruhm, Steven, 'Reforming Byron's Narcissism', in *Lessons of Romanticism: A Critical Companion*, ed. Thomas Pfau and Robert F. Glecker (Durham, N.C.: Duke University Press, 1998) [Ch. 4]

Burwick, Frederick, *Aesthetic Illusion: Theoretical and Historical Approaches*, ed. with Walter Pape (Berlin: Walter de Gruyter, 1990) [Ch. 1]

Burwick, Frederick, *Illusion and the Drama: Critical Theory of the Enlightenment and Romantic Era* (University Park: Pennsylvania State University Press, 1991) [Ch. 1]

Burwick, Frederick, *Poetic Madness and the Romantic Imagination* (University Park: Pennsylvania State University Press, 1996) [Ch. 1]

Calder, Angus, *Byron* (Milton Keynes: Open University Press, 1987)

Cheeke, Stephen, 'Byron, History and the *Genius Loci*', *The Byron Journal*, 27 (1999), 38–50 [Ch. 5]

Chew, Samuel C., *The Dramas of Lord Byron* (Göttingen: Dandenhord and Ruprecht, 1915; New York: Russell & Russell Inc., 1964) [Ch. 8]

Christensen, Jerome, *Lord Byron's Strength* (Baltimore and London: Johns Hopkins University Press, 1993)

Connor, Steven, *Postmodernist Culture*, 2nd edn (Oxford: Basil Blackwell, 1997), [Ch. 16]

Cooke, Michael G., *The Blind Man Traces the Circle: On the Patterns and Philosophy of Byron's Poetry* (Princeton University Press, 1969)

Corbett, Martyn, *Byron and Tragedy* (Basingstoke: Macmillan, 1988)

Donelan, Charles, *Romanticism and Male Fantasy in Byron's* Don Juan*: A Marketable Vice* (Basingstoke: Macmillan; New York: St. Martin's, 2000) [Ch. 4]

Drinkwater, John, *The Pilgrim of Eternity* (London: Hodder and Stoughton Ltd, 1925) [Ch. 1]

Elfenbein, Andrew, *Byron and the Victorians* (Cambridge and New York: Cambridge University Press, 1995)

Elledge, W. Paul, *Byron and the Dynamics of Metaphor* (Nashville: Vanderbilt University Press, 1968)

Elledge, Paul, *Lord Byron at Harrow School: Speaking Out, Talking Back, Acting Up, Bowing Out* (Baltimore: Johns Hopkins University Press, 2000) [Ch. 1]

Elwin, Malcolm, 'The Lovelace Papers', *Times Literary Supplement* (1961), 753 [Ch. 1]

Fleming, Anne, *The Myth of the Bad Lord Byron* (West Sussex: Old Forge Press, 1999) [Ch. 1]

Foot, Michael, *The Politics of Paradise: A Vindication of Byron* (London: Collins, 1988)

Franklin, Caroline, *Byron: A Literary Life* (Basingstoke: Macmillan; New York: St Martin's Press, 2000)

Fulford, Tim, *Romanticism and Masculinity Gender Politics and Poetics in the Writings of Burke, Coleridge, Cobbett, Wordsworth, De Quincey, and Hazlitt* (New York: St Martin's, 1999) [Ch. 4]
Galperin, William, 'The Postmodernism of Childe Harold', in *The Return of the Visible in British Romanticism* (Baltimore and London: Johns Hopkins University Press, 1993) [Ch. 6]
Garber, Frederick, *Self, Text, and Romantic Irony: The Example of Byron* (Princeton University Press, 1988)
Garrett, Martin, *George Gordon, Lord Byron* (New York: Cambridge University Press, 2000) [Ch. 1]
Gleckner, Robert F., *Byron and the Ruins of Paradise* (Baltimore: Johns Hopkins Press, 1967)
Gleckner, Robert and Bernard Beatty (eds.), *The Plays of Lord Byron* (Liverpool University Press, 1997)
Graham, Peter W., *Don Juan and Regency England* (Charlottesville: University Press of Virginia, 1992)
Graham, Peter W., *Lord Byron* (New York: Twayne Publishers, 1998)
Gregson, Ian, *Contemporary Poetry and Postmodernism: Dialogue and Estrangement* (London: Macmillan, 1996) [Ch. 16]
Gross, Jonathan, '"One Half of What I Should Say": Byron's Gay Narrator in *Don Juan*', *European Romantic Review*, 9 (1998), 323–50 [Ch. 4]
Gross, Jonathan, *Byron: The Erotic Liberal* (Lanham, Md: Lexington Books, 2001) [Ch. 1]
Guest, Harriet, *Small Change: Women, Learning, Patriotism, 1750–1810* (University of Chicago Press, 2000) [Ch. 6]
Haggerty, George E., *Men in Love: Masculinity and Sexuality in the Eighteenth Century* (New York: Columbia University Press, 1999) [Ch. 4]
Haslett, Moyra, *Byron's* Don Juan *and the Don Juan Legend* (Oxford: Clarendon Press, 1997)
Hoagwood, Terence Allan, *Byron's Dialectic: Skepticism and the Critique of Culture* (Lewisburg: Bucknell University Press, 1993)
Huber, Werner, 'Dead Poets Society: Byron, Postmodernism, and the Biographical Mode', in *Lord Byron the European: Essays from the International Byron Society*, ed. Richard A. Cardwell (Lewiston: The Edwin Mellen Press, 1997) [Ch. 1]
Jamison, Kay Redfield, *Touched With Fire: Manic-Depressive Illness and the Artistic Temperament* (New York: Free Press, 1994) [Ch. 1]
Joseph, M. K., *Byron: The Poet* (London: Victor Gollancz Ltd, 1964)
Joyce, James, *Ulysses* (Harmondsworth: Penguin, 1986)
Jump, John, *Byron* (London and Boston, Mass.: Routledge & Kegan Paul, 1972)
Kelsall, Malcolm, *Byron's Politics* (Brighton: Harvester Press, 1987)
Kelsall, Malcolm, '"Once did she hold the gorgeous East in fee . . .": Byron's Venice and Oriental Empire', in *Romanticism and Colonialism, Writing and Empire, 1780–1830*, ed. Tim Fulford and Peter J. Kitson (Cambridge University Press, 1998) [Ch. 5]
Kermode, Frank, *The Sense of an Ending* (Oxford University Press, 1969)
Knight, G. Wilson, *Lord Byron: Christian Virtues* (London: Routledge & Kegan Paul, 1952)

Knight, G. Wilson, *Lord Byron's Marriage: The Evidence of Asterisks* (London: Routledge & Kegan Paul, 1957)
Knight, G. Wilson, 'Shakespeare and Byron's Plays', *Shakespeare Jahrbuch*, 95 (1959), 82–97 [Ch. 8]
Krueger, Christine L., *The Reader's Repentance: Women Preachers, Women Writers and Nineteenth-Century Social Discourse* (University of Chicago Press, 1992) [Ch. 4]
Lang, Cecil Y., 'Narcissus Jilted: Byron, Don Juan, and the Biographical Imperative', in *Historical Studies and Literary Criticism*, ed. Jerome McGann (Madison, Wis.: University of Wisconsin Press, 1985) [Ch. 6]
Lansdown, Richard, *Byron's Historical Dramas* (Oxford: Clarendon Press, 1992) [Chs. 8 and 13]
Leake, William Martin, *Researches in Greece* (London, 1814) [Ch. 6]
Leake, William Martin, *Travels in the Morea*, 3 vols. (London: John Murray, 1830) [Ch. 6]
Leask, Nigel, *British Romantic Writers and the East: Anxieties of Empire* (Cambridge University Press, 1992) [Ch. 6]
Longford, Elizabeth, *The Life of Lord Byron* (Boston: Little Brown, 1976) [Ch. 1]
Lynch, Deidre Shauna, *The Economy of Character: Novels, Market Culture, and the Business of Inner Meaning* (University of Chicago Press, 1998) [Ch. 4]
McGann, Jerome, *Fiery Dust* (Chicago and London: University of Chicago Press, 1968)
Manning, Peter J., *Byron and His Fictions* (Detroit: Wayne State University Press, 1978) [Ch. 5]
Marchand, Leslie A., *Byron's Poetry, A Critical Introduction* (Cambridge, Mass.: Harvard University Press, 1968)
Marchand, Leslie, 'Childe Harold's Monitor: The Strange Friendship of Byron and Francis Hodgson', in *The Evidence of the Imagination: Studies of Interactions between Life and Art in English Romantic Literature*, ed. Donald H. Reiman, Michael C. Jaye, Betty T. Bennett (New York University Press, 1978) [Ch. 6]
Marshall, William H., *The Structure of Byron's Major Poems* (Philadelphia: University of Pennsylvania Press, 1962)
Martin, Philip W., *Byron: A Poet Before his Public* (Cambridge University Press, 1982)
Metaxas, K. H., 'Byron's Intelligence Mission to Greece', *Byron Journal*, 10 (1982) [Ch. 6]
Minta, Stephen, *On a Voiceless Shore: Byron in Greece* (New York: Harold Holt, 1998) [Ch. 1]
Moore, Doris Langley, *The Late Lord Byron* (London: John Murray, 1961)
Moore, Doris Langley, *Lord Byron: Accounts Rendered* (London: John Murray, 1974) [Ch. 1]
Nicolson, Harold, *Byron: The Last Journey* (London: Constable, 1924) [Ch. 1]
Origo, Iris, *The Last Attachment: The Story of Byron and Teresa Guiccioli* (London and Glasgow: Fontana, 1962)
Page, Norman (ed.), *Byron: Interviews and Recollections* (London: Macmillan, 1985)
Paston, George and Peter Quennell, *'To Lord Byron': Feminine Profiles* (London: John Murray, 1939)
Quennell, Peter, *Byron: The Years of Fame* (London: Penguin, 1954) [Ch. 1]

Rawes, Alan, *Byron's Poetic Experimentation: Childe Harold, the Tales and the Quest for Comedy* (Aldershot: Ashgate, 2000)
Raizis, M. B. (ed.). *Byron: A Poet For All Seasons* (Missolonghi Byron Society, 2000)
Richardson, Alan, 'Astarté: Byron's *Manfred* and Montesquieu's *Lettres persanes*', *Keats-Shelley Journal*, 40 (Keats-Shelley Association of America, New York 1991) [Ch. 8]
Ridenour, George M., *The Style of Don Juan* (New Haven, Conn.: Yale University Press, 1960)
Ross, Marlon B., 'Scandalous Reading: The Political Uses of Scandal in and around Regency Britain', *Wordsworth Circle*, 27 (1996) [Ch. 4]
Rutherford, Andrew, *Byron: Augustan and Romantic* (London: Macmillan, 1990)
Rutherford, Andrew, *Byron: A Critical Study* (Edinburgh and London: Oliver and Boyd, 1962)
Schiffer, Reinhold, *Oriental Panorama: British Travellers in 19th Century Turkey* (Atlanta, Ga. and Amsterdam: Rodopi, 1999) [Ch. 6]
Stabler, Jane (ed.), *Byron* (Harlow: Longman, 1998)
Stabler, Jane, 'Byron's Digressive Journey', in *Romantic Geographies: Discourses on Travel 1775–1844*, ed. Amanda Gilroy (Manchester University Press, 2000) [Ch. 6]
Storey, Mark, *Byron and the Eye of Appetite* (Basingstoke: Macmillan, 1986)
Thornton, Thomas, *A Letter to the Rt Hon The Earl of D***, On the Political Relation of Russia, in Regard to Turkey, Greece, and France . . . with strictures on Mr Thornton's Present State of Turkey* (London 1807) [Ch. 6]
Tomaselli, Sylvana, 'The Enlightenment Debate about Women', *History Workshop Journal*, 20 (Autumn, 1985) [Ch. 6]
Wallace, Jennifer, '"We are all Greeks"?: National Identity and the Greek War of Independence', *The Byron Journal*, 23 (1995), 36–49 [Ch. 6]
Watkins, Daniel P., 'The Dramas of Lord Byron: *Manfred* and *Marino Faliero*', in *Byron*, ed. Jane Stabler (London: Longman, 1998) [Ch. 7]
Weiner, Harold, 'Byron and the East: Literary Sources of the "Turkish Tales"', in *Nineteenth-Century Studies Dedicated to C.S. Northup*, ed. Herbert Davis, William C. DeVane and R. C. Bald (New York, 1940) [Ch. 6]
West, Paul, *Byron and the Spoiler's Art* (London: Chatto & Windus, 1960)
Willson, David Harris, *King James VI & I* (New York: Oxford University Press, 1956) [Ch. 4]
Wilson, Frances (ed.), *Byronmania: Portraits of the Artist in Nineteenth- and Twentieth-Century Culture* (Basingstoke: Macmillan, 1999)
Wolfson, Susan, '"Their She-Condition": Cross-Dressing and the Politics of Gender in *Don Juan*', *ELH*, 54 (1987), 585–617 [Ch. 4]
Wood, Marcus, *Radical Satire and Print Culture 1790–1832* (Oxford, 1994)
Woodhouse, C. M., *The Philhellenes* (Worcester and London: Hodder & Stonghton, 1969) [Ch. 6]
Woodring, Carl, *Politics in English Romantic Poetry* (Cambridge, Mass.: Harvard University Press, 1970)

INDEX

CAMBRIDGE COMPANIONS TO LITERATURE

The Cambridge Companion to Greek Tragedy
edited by P. E. Easterling

The Cambridge Companion to Old English Literature
edited by Malcolm Godden and Michael Lapidge

The Cambridge Companion to Medieval Women's Writing
edited by Carolyn Dinshaw and David Wallace

The Cambridge Companion to Medieval Romance
edited by Roberta L. Krueger

The Cambridge Companion to Medieval English Theatre
edited by Richard Beadle

The Cambridge Companion to English Renaissance Drama, second edition
edited by A. R. Braunmuller and Michael Hattaway

The Cambridge Companion to Renaissance Humanism
edited by Jill Kraye

The Cambridge Companion to English Poetry, Donne to Marvell
edited by Thomas N. Corns

The Cambridge Companion to English Literature, 1500–1600
edited by Arthur F. Kinney

The Cambridge Companion to English Literature, 1650–1740
edited by Steven N. Zwicker

The Cambridge Companion to English Literature, 1740–1830
edited by Thomas Keymer and Jon Mee

The Cambridge Companion to Writing of the English Revolution
edited by N. H. Keeble

The Cambridge Companion to English Restoration Theatre
edited by Deborah C. Payne Fisk

The Cambridge Companion to British Romanticism
edited by Stuart Curran

The Cambridge Companion to Eighteenth-Century Poetry
edited by John Sitter

The Cambridge Companion to the Eighteenth-Century Novel
edited by John Richetti

The Cambridge Companion to the Gothic Fiction
edited by Jerrold E. Hogle

The Cambridge Companion to Victorian Poetry
edited by Joseph Bristow

The Cambridge Companion to the Victorian Novel
edited by Deirdre David

The Cambridge Companion to Crime Fiction
edited by Martin Priestman

The Cambridge Companion to Science Fiction
edited by Edward James and Farah Mendlesohn

The Cambridge Companion to Travel Writing
edited by Peter Hulme and Tim Youngs

The Cambridge Companion to American Realism and Naturalism
edited by Donald Pizer

The Cambridge Companion to Nineteenth-Century American Women's Writing
edited by Dale M. Bauer and Philip Gould

The Cambridge Companion to the Classic Russian Novel
edited by Malcolm V. Jones and Robin Feuer Miller

The Cambridge Companion to the French Novel: from 1800 to the Present
edited by Timothy Unwin

The Cambridge Companion to the Spanish Novel: from 1600 to the Present
edited by Harriet Turner and Adelaida López de Martínez

The Cambridge Companion to the Italian Novel
edited by Peter Bondanella and Andrea Ciccarelli

The Cambridge Companion to the Modern German Novel
edited by Graham Bartram

The Cambridge Companion to Jewish American Literature
edited by Hana Wirth-Nesher and Michael P. Kramer

The Cambridge Companion to the African American Novel
edited by Maryemma Graham

The Cambridge Companion to Contemporary Irish Poetry
edited by Matthew Campbell

The Cambridge Companion to Modernism
edited by Michael Levenson

The Cambridge Companion to Postmodernism
edited by Steven Connor

The Cambridge Companion to Postcolonial Literary Studies
edited by Neil Lazarus

The Cambridge Companion to Australian Literature
edited by Elizabeth Webby

The Cambridge Companion to American Women Playwrights
edited by Brenda Murphy

The Cambridge Companion to Modern British Women Playwrights
edited by Elaine Aston and Janelle Reinelt

The Cambridge Companion to Twentieth-Century Irish Drama
edited by Shaun Richards

The Cambridge Companion to Homer
edited by Robert Fowler

The Cambridge Companion to Virgil
edited by Charles Martindale

The Cambridge Companion to Ovid
edited by Philip Hardie

The Cambridge Companion to Dante
edited by Rachel Jacoff

The Cambridge Companion to Cervantes
edited by Anthony J. Cascardi

The Cambridge Companion to Goethe
edited by Lesley Sharpe

The Cambridge Companion to Dostoevskii
edited by W. J. Leatherbarrow

The Cambridge Companion to Tolstoy
edited by Donna Tussing Orwin

The Cambridge Companion to Chekhov
edited by Vera Gottlieb and Paul Allain

The Cambridge Companion to Ibsen
edited by James McFarlane

The Cambridge Companion to Proust
edited by Richard Bales

The Cambridge Companion to Thomas Mann
edited by Ritchie Robertson

The Cambridge Companion to Kafka
edited by Julian Preece

The Cambridge Companion to Brecht
edited by Peter Thomson and Glendyr Sacks

The Cambridge Companion to Walter Benjamin
edited by Davis S. Ferris

The Cambridge Companion to Lacan
edited by Jean-Michel Rabaté

The Cambridge Companion to Chaucer, second edition
edited by Piero Boitani and Jill Mann

The Cambridge Companion to Shakespeare
edited by Margareta de Grazia and Stanley Wells

The Cambridge Companion to Shakespeare on Film
edited by Russell Jackson

The Cambridge Companion to Shakespearean Comedy
edited by Alexander Leggatt

The Cambridge Companion to Shakespeare on Stage
edited by Stanley Wells and Sarah Stanton

The Cambridge Companion to Shakespeare's History Plays
edited by Michael Hattaway

The Cambridge Companion to Shakespearean Tragedy
edited by Claire McEachern

The Cambridge Companion to Christopher Marlowe
edited by Patrick Cheney

The Cambridge Companion to Spenser
edited by Andrew Hadfield

The Cambridge Companion to John Dryden
edited by Steven N. Zwicker

The Cambridge Companion to Ben Jonson
edited by Richard Harp and Stanley Stewart

The Cambridge Companion to Milton, second edition
edited by Dennis Danielson

The Cambridge Companion to Samuel Johnson
edited by Greg Clingham

The Cambridge Companion to Jonathan Swift
edited by Christopher Fox

The Cambridge Companion to Mary Wollstonecraft
edited by Claudia L. Johnson

The Cambridge Companion to William Blake
edited by Morris Eaves

The Cambridge Companion to Wordsworth
edited by Stephen Gill

The Cambridge Companion to Coleridge
edited by Lucy Newlyn

The Cambridge Companion to Keats
edited by Susan J. Wolfson

The Cambridge Companion to Mary Shelley
edited by Esther Schor

The Cambridge Companion to Jane Austen
edited by Edward Copeland and Juliet McMaster

The Cambridge Companion to the Brontës
edited by Heather Glen

The Cambridge Companion to Charles Dickens
edited by John O. Jordan

The Cambridge Companion to George Eliot
edited by George Levine

The Cambridge Companion to Thomas Hardy
edited by Dale Kramer

The Cambridge Companion to Oscar Wilde
edited by Peter Raby

The Cambridge Companion to George Bernard Shaw
edited by Christopher Innes

The Cambridge Companion to Joseph Conrad
edited by J. H. Stape

The Cambridge Companion to D. H. Lawrence
edited by Anne Fernihough

The Cambridge Companion to Virginia Woolf
edited by Sue Roe and Susan Sellers

The Cambridge Companion to James Joyce, second edition
edited by Derek Attridge

The Cambridge Companion to T. S. Eliot
edited by A. David Moody

The Cambridge Companion to Ezra Pound
edited by Ira B. Nadel

The Cambridge Companion to Beckett
edited by John Pilling

The Cambridge Companion to Harold Pinter
edited by Peter Raby

The Cambridge Companion to Tom Stoppard
edited by Katherine E. Kelly

The Cambridge Companion to David Mamet
edited by Christopher Bigsby

The Cambridge Companion to Herman Melville
edited by Robert S. Levine

The Cambridge Companion to Nathaniel Hawthorne
edited by Richard Millington

The Cambridge Companion to Harriet Beecher Stowe
edited by Cindy Weinstein

The Cambridge Companion to Theodore Dreiser
edited by Leonard Cassuto and Claire Virginia Eby

The Cambridge Companion to Edith Wharton
edited by Millicent Bell

The Cambridge Companion to Henry James
edited by Jonathan Freedman

The Cambridge Companion to Walt Whitman
edited by Ezra Greenspan

The Cambridge Companion to Ralph Waldo Emerson
edited by Joel Porte, Saundra Morris

The Cambridge Companion to Henry David Thoreau
edited by Joel Myerson

The Cambridge Companion to Mark Twain
edited by Forrest G. Robinson

The Cambridge Companion to Edgar Allan Poe
edited by Kevin J. Hayes

The Cambridge Companion to Emily Dickinson
edited by Wendy Martin

The Cambridge Companion to William Faulkner
edited by Philip M. Weinstein

The Cambridge Companion to Ernest Hemingway
edited by Scott Donaldson

The Cambridge Companion to F. Scott Fitzgerald
edited by Ruth Prigozy

The Cambridge Companion to Robert Frost
edited by Robert Faggen

The Cambridge Companion to Eugene O'Neill
edited by Michael Manheim

The Cambridge Companion to Tennessee Williams
edited by Matthew C. Roudané

The Cambridge Companion to Arthur Miller
edited by Christopher Bigsby

The Cambridge Companion to Sam Shepard
edited by Matthew C. Roudané

CAMBRIDGE COMPANIONS TO CULTURE

The Cambridge Companion to Modern German Culture
edited by Eva Kolinsky and Wilfried van der Will

The Cambridge Companion to Modern Russian Culture
edited by Nicholas Rzhevsky

The Cambridge Companion to Modern Spanish Culture
edited by David T. Gies

The Cambridge Companion to Modern Italian Culture
edited by Zygmunt G. Barański and Rebecca J. West

The Cambridge Companion to Modern French Culture
edited by Nicholas Hewitt

The Cambridge Companion to Modern Latin American Literature
edited by John King